ANTHROPOLOGICAL PAPERS

MUSEUM OF ANTHROPOLOGY, UNIVERSITY OF MICHIGAN
NO. 61

# FOR THE DIRECTOR:
# RESEARCH ESSAYS IN HONOR OF JAMES B. GRIFFIN

Edited by
CHARLES E. CLELAND

ANN ARBOR, MICHIGAN
1977

©1977 Regents of The University of Michigan
The Museum of Anthropology
All rights reserved

ISBN 978-1-949098-01-3 (paper)
ISBN 978-1-951519-10-0 (ebook)

# CONTENTS

Illustrations . . . . . . . . . . . . . . . . . . . . . . . . . . . . . . . . . . . . . . . . . . . . . . v

Tables . . . . . . . . . . . . . . . . . . . . . . . . . . . . . . . . . . . . . . . . . . . . . . . . . vii

Foreword
   *Moreau S. Maxwell* . . . . . . . . . . . . . . . . . . . . . . . . . . . . . . . . . . . . ix

Introduction
   *Charles E. Cleland* . . . . . . . . . . . . . . . . . . . . . . . . . . . . . . . . . . . . xv

## PART I. ADJUNCT DISCIPLINES

Ethnobotany as an Adjunct to Archaeology: Studies in the Aleutian Islands
   *Ted P. Bank II* . . . . . . . . . . . . . . . . . . . . . . . . . . . . . . . . . . . . . . . 3
Osteological Evidence for the Identification of Pre-Contact Karankawa
   *Richard G. Wilkinson* . . . . . . . . . . . . . . . . . . . . . . . . . . . . . . . . . 40
Microanalysis of *Chien* Temmoku Glazes
   *Frederick Bleicher* . . . . . . . . . . . . . . . . . . . . . . . . . . . . . . . . . . . . 55
Revision of the Two Rivers "Valders" Drift Border and the Age of Fluted Points in Michigan
   *William R. Farrand* . . . . . . . . . . . . . . . . . . . . . . . . . . . . . . . . . . . 74

## PART II. AMERICAN STUDIES

Fluted Points from the Parkhill, Ontario Site
   *William B. Roosa* . . . . . . . . . . . . . . . . . . . . . . . . . . . . . . . . . . . . 87
An Examination of Late Archaic Development in the Falls of the Ohio River Area
   *Donald E. Janzen* . . . . . . . . . . . . . . . . . . . . . . . . . . . . . . . . . . . 123
Some Observations on the Goodall Focus
   *Richard E. Flanders* . . . . . . . . . . . . . . . . . . . . . . . . . . . . . . . . . 144
Prehistoric Culture Areas and Culture Change on the Gulf Coastal Plain
   *William H. Sears* . . . . . . . . . . . . . . . . . . . . . . . . . . . . . . . . . . . 152
The Penetration of Northeast Arkansas by Mississippian Culture
   *Dan Franklin Morse* . . . . . . . . . . . . . . . . . . . . . . . . . . . . . . . . . 186

The Eighteenth-Century Overhill Cherokee
  *Alfred K. Guthe* .................................... 212
Women on the Lower Columbia River in the Early Nineteenth Century
  *George I. Quimby* .................................... 230

## PART III. FOREIGN STUDIES

The Ceramic Sequence at Kaminaljuyu
  *Ronald K. Wetherington* ............................. 245
The Edge-Trimmed Tool Tradition of Northwest South America
  *Wesley R. Hurt* ..................................... 268
Adaptations of the Early Neolithic Farmers in Central Europe
  *Sarunas Milisauskas* ................................ 295
Stylistic Behavior and Information Exchange
  *H. Martin Wobst* .................................... 317

## PART IV.

Published Works of James Bennett Griffin
  *Compiled by Richard I. Ford and Volney H. Jones* ............ 345

# ILLUSTRATIONS

## Part I

| | |
|---|---|
| The Aleutian Islands and Bering Sea region of western Alaska | 4 |
| Diagrammatic profile of an excavation at Eider Point, Unalaska Island | 6 |
| Prehistoric village (Waterfall Site) and adjacent plant habitats at Nazan Bay, Atka Island | 9 |
| Diagrammatic section of a typical small village site based on an actual site on Adak | 10 |
| Diagrammatic profile of prehistoric mound at Amaknak Island (Dutch Harbor) | 11 |
| Old village mound, Amaknak−D site | 12 |
| Diagrammatic profile of a small village site located in Amugul Bay, Unalaska Island | 13 |
| Diagram showing distribution of plants on a study strip across the former village, Nazan Bay, Atka Island | 14 |
| Prehistoric Aleut village at the western end of Attu Island as seen from the air in September 1949 | 17 |
| Soil-ash and midden profiles at Lash Bay, Tanaga Island | 19 |
| North Pacific Bering Sea Region | 27 |
| Texas Gulf Coast sites | 42 |
| Occipital views of three skulls from the Shell Point site | 45 |
| Representative *Chien* Temoku potsherds | 57 |
| Micrograph of calcium iron oxide crystals of the surface of *Chien* potsherd fragment | 59 |
| Optical micrograph of the glaze/body interface of a typical *Chien* sherd | 60 |
| Micrograph of *Chien* sherd, immersion etched | 61 |
| Micrograph of *Chien* sherd showing points at which x-ray fluorescence spectra were obtained | 62 |
| An SEM absorbed electron image of a polished *Chien* glazed sample | 64 |
| Set of microprobe photographs of a different area in the image of a polished *Chien* glaze sample | 65 |
| Micrograph of an area of a polished *Chien* glaze sample | 66 |
| Four stages in the deglaciation of the southern peninsula of Michigan | 75 |
| Distribution of fluted points in southern Michigan relative to late-glacial ice front positions | 80 |

## Part II

| | |
|---|---|
| Fluted Knives | 97 |
| Subtype II, and Groups A, F, G, Subtype III | 99 |
| Style Groups B-K Grid B | 102 |
| Major artifacts from three Mini Clusters | 104 |
| Miscellanous Artifacts Grids C, D, E, and elsewhere | 108 |

## Illustrations

Map of the area to be investigated by the Falls of the Ohio River Archaeological
  Project .................................................. 124
Physiographic Provinces in the Falls of the Ohio River area ............. 125
Archaic sites excavated by the Falls Project from 1969-1974 ............ 130
Radiocarbon dates from the Falls of the Ohio River area ................ 132
Period F-G .................................................. 154
Period E-F .................................................. 163
Periods C, D, E ............................................... 169
Chart of relative temporal relationships of complexes .................. 179
Mississippian culture, two spheres of household and pan-tribal artifacts and features  187
Map of northeast Arkansas and southeast Missouri (Zebree site) ........... 196
Barnes complex (Zebree site) ...................................... 199
Big Lake phase (Zebree site) ...................................... 202
Postmold Pattern of Circular Structure, Chota ....................... 216
Postmold Pattern of Chota Townhouses ............................ 218
White Spots Mark the Postmold Pattern of Log Cabin ................. 219
Overhill Plain Rim Sherd ........................................ 220
Overhill Complicated Stamped Sherds .............................. 221
Qualla Check Stamped Rim Sherd .................................. 222
Burial 5, Chota, with Brass Points at Shoulder ....................... 224
Projectile Points from Chota ..................................... 225
Stone and Pottery Pipes ......................................... 225

### Part III

Sample sizes and proportions, Kaminaljuyu ceramic analysis .............. 247
Frequencies of wares and selected types within ceramic phases .......... 250-251
Frequencies of selected vessel forms within ceramic phases ............ 250-251
General characteristics of the ceramic sequence at Kaminaljuyu .......... 252-253
Models of Core Artifacts, Miscellaneous and Chopper .................. 270
Flake Artifacts ................................................ 271
Stone Artifacts ................................................ 272
Distribution of Linear Culture Sites in Europe ....................... 296
Distribution of Linear Cluture Sites in Poland ....................... 297
Distribution of Linear Culture Sites in Central Germany ............... 299
Linear Culture Sites along the Szreniawa River near Szczepanowice, Miechow district, Southern Poland ........................................... 301
The Evidence for Trade Networks at the Müddersheim and Olszanica Sites ..... 310
Distribution of Mesolithic Sites in Southeastern Poland ................ 313
The target groups of stylistic messages ............................. 325

# TABLES

## Part I

Results of Pollen Analysis of Tanaga (Aleutians) Soil Samples . . . . . . . . . . . . . 22
Spectrographic and SEM X-ray Fluorescence Analysis of *Chien* Sherd Glaze Sample   63

## Part II

Radiocarbon dates from the Falls of the Ohio River area . . . . . . . . . . . . . . . 131
Proposed phases for western Michigan Woodland . . . . . . . . . . . . . . . . . . . 148

## Part III

Cultural chronology of Kaminaljuyu . . . . . . . . . . . . . . . . . . . . . . . . . . . . 249
Stratigraphic Units and Climate of the El Abra Rockshelters . . . . . . . . . . . . . . 273
Radiocarbon Dates from the El Abra Rockshelters and Bore Holes . . . . . . . . . . 275
Distribution of man-made flakes and flaked stone artifacts at El Abra . . . . . . . . 276
Distribution of Artifacts from El Abra Rockshelters . . . . . . . . . . . . . . . . . . 279
Sites on loess and various types of *czernozem*, sites not on loess . . . . . . . . . . . 300
Domesticated and wild plants found at Langweiler, Germany . . . . . . . . . . . . . 305
Frequency of animals based on the minimum number of individuals at Linear culture sites . . . . . . . . . . . . . . . . . . . . . . . . . . . . . . . . . . . . . . . . . 306
Message content in stylistic behavior . . . . . . . . . . . . . . . . . . . . . . . . . . . 324
Message distributions in Albanian folkdress exclusive of headdress . . . . . . . . . . 336
Romanian folkdress—message contents and stylistic forms . . . . . . . . . . . . . . 336

# FOREWORD

*Moreau S. Maxwell*
Michigan State University

Most intellectual disciplines have sudden periods of notable acceleration in their histories. Through some decades, ideas seem to simmer on back burners, or, to mix a metaphor, lie becalmed in the doldrums. Then, with a strange coalescence of thought and interstimulation of ideas, a critical intellectual mass is reached. Wind fills all the sails and the ship sails smartly on. In the seventh decade of this century the sails again are filling, but as yet the forward surge cannot be compared with that of the third decade.

The 1930s saw the virtual beginning of systematic North American archaeology. There had been isolated instances of careful investigation before, but the process by which archaeology was pulling itself up by the bootstraps was regionally uneven. By the thirties, there was a clear need for innovation in methods of collecting and synthesizing data. Suddenly North American archaeology became exciting as increasing information and a unique group of savants capable of organizing it coalesced. The Society for American Archaeology, founded to foster this interstimulation, embraced distinguished professors and interested amateurs. Even so, students of this then esoteric field barely filled one room at an annual meeting. In such an atmosphere teacher-student barriers easily disappeared in heated discussion.

Although partisans of other regions may disagree, I, like many others, would see the center of this intellectual foment in the Midwest. Admittedly it was a peculiarly bounded Midwest, including the Gulf States and Nebraska, New York and Arkansas, but focused at Chicago.

Illinois had been "Rediscovered." Its pre-contact cultural history was elucidated by excavation techniques insisting on precise spatial recording of recovered data. Vertical profiling of sites made stratigraphy observable and shifted emphasis from collecting relics to establishing their place in the passage of time. It was a beginning for processural archaeology. This "Chicago Method" may have occasionally been overdone. Few who saw the method in operation will forget halves of effigy bottles clinging to a twelve-foot, plumb-bobbed clay face in Pope County. Simultaneously, emerging classificatory schemes were reducing the chaos of too much data to manageable abstractions. Through syntheses like the Midwest Taxonomic System, a view of cultural contact across space could be coupled with our growing understanding of temporal change.

Throughout the decade, archaeology, along with other esoteric and non-profitable activities, swelled through government support of NYA, CCC, and WPA. Armies of diggers were producing such vastness of data that syntheses had constantly to undergo modification, and recovery techniques daily improved. As a colleague has suggested, it all could be reduced to the simple formula: Chicago Method plus WPA data plus Midwestern Taxonomic System equaled culture history.

Fortuitously, the archaeological problems of change through time and synchronous horizontal diffusion were being linked to broader anthropological issues, largely under the strong influence of Radcliffe-Brown, then at the University of Chicago, and of such protagonists as Linton and Sapir. The question was still being asked in universities: "Which are you interested in, pots or people?" but it was becoming more apparent that one way of studying people was through pots. In this atmosphere, archaeological discussion ended at night with exhaustion and began the next day when two or more discussants were awake. From this bubbling pot (what happened to the sailing ship metaphor?), James B. Griffin with his unique ability at marshalling facts and integrating them with ideas emerged as one of the strongest leaders in North American archaeology, if not, as many of us would maintain, *the* leader.

At this point it is appropriate to ask critically why and in what fashion he is seen as a leader. Intellectual leadership, particularly in the social sciences, is difficult to define. So-called leaders have generally been those who have enunciated innovative and seminal theories that succeeding scholars test, modify, elaborate, and controvert. In this 1976 year of papers, oral and written, in testament to the stimulation and guidance of Griffin, there have been many instances of his innovativeness cited. In many cases he was the first to see the relative usefulness to archaeology of such diverse activities as new techniques in nuclear physics and geomorphology. He has often been the one to start a new system of investigation, work out many of the bugs, and then turn it over to others for further pursuit. He is the virtual father of multidisciplinary research in archaeology. But, significantly, none of the papers in this volume speak of a "Griffin theory" as one might speak of the theories of Durkheim. Quite clearly Griffin's genius has been as a synthesizer rather than as a theoretician. With a remarkably retentive mind, back-stopped by voluminous cross-indexed files, he has been quick to pick up, reassemble, and make useful to students of prehistoric behavior a myriad of devices, techniques, and data gleaned from his eclectic contacts. The highly gregarious Griffin at a national meeting is more apt to be in deep conversation with an undergraduate with a new idea, or new way of doing something, than with a doctoral candidate trying to pick Jimmy's mind for the concluding pages of his thesis.

In this more technical age of non-human xerography and memory banks, even those of us living through it have difficulty remembering the nature of data storage, retrieval, and concomitant synthesis as it was up to and through the late fifties. Carbon paper was the copying device, limited to three copies and a faint fourth, and the use of marginal punch cards in the fifties constituted a marked breakthrough in the control of data. In general, one's ability to compare discrete variations in one's field data with those of another's, and to abstract from thousands of potsherds the significance of trends, depended on one's own memory storage and retrieval capabilities. In this Griffin continues to excel. From what was, in the thirties, a chaotic assemblage of discrete variables, particularly in the prehistoric treatments of clay, he was able to store vast numbers of these variables, from them to abstract the key ones, and to see their relationships to similar key variables over hundreds of miles of space. One of the favorite Griffin stories with the "Chicago crowd" occurred in the thirties when Central Basin, as a cultural manifestation, was seen as distinct from Hopewell. In heated discussion over a laboratory table littered with vessel fragments, Griffin ostensibly at random, picked two sherds from the welter, saying, "It is my contention that Central Basin and Hopewell go together like this . . .," and the two sherds did, indeed, fit. Later stories that Jimmy had sneaked into the lab the night before to break the sherd in two pieces are untrue—he didn't need to.

A colleague, as much an admirer of Griffin as I, once discussed this leadership of Griffin as one would discuss, for example, the leadership of Freud. There are followers of Freud, Neo-Freudians, Anti-Freudians, all based on the theories of the Master. While still recognizing the strong impact of Griffin on North American archaeology, how would we categorize a true follower of Griffin? We concluded that such a person could only be a replication of his unique abilities. I suppose this can be interpreted as a negative critical statement. So, also, could the following statement, that Griffin has always "done" archaeology as an art—at an exceptionally high level of talent. Lest I be thought to downgrade a justifiably internationally distinguished colleague as little more than a memory expert, I want to make it clear that I feel there will always be an important role in prehistoric interpretation for art as I am using the term here. The most explicative quantitative methods of analysis yet devised ultimately come down to a binary choice that is still largely subjective; there is yet a need and an important place for art in synthesis and abstraction.

An outstanding capability for integrating information, and for synthesizing a vast array of variables, then, is a strong reason for his leadership. Another element deals with information transfer. There are many technical reasons why information transfer is more rapid and more exact than in the olden golden days of the thirties. Jimmy was, and in many ways still is, our major medium of information transfer. Particularly in the WPA days he went everywhere, saw everything coming out of the ground, retained everything in his mind, and communicated it to everyone. Through him we collectively formed one information pool of American prehistory. In the early sixties I was talking with a colleague in another of the social sciences, referring to the unpublished works of three or four other archaeologists and the way in which each of us was building on the other's hypothesis. He was appalled. In his discipline such ideas would have been copyrighted before being discussed outside the immediate family. Thanks largely to Griffin, the field of archaeology has been a remarkably open one for the exchange of information prior to publication—a fact that unquestionably has facilitated its growth.

To these I would add, for Griffin, a role somewhere between "Keeper of the Flame" and policeman. Like so many of my colleagues, some of my most brilliant hunches about archaeology lie moldering in my basement, stifled a-borning by the facts in opposition that Griffin could marshal. I would contend that more than any other individual, Griffin, through four decades, has kept North American archaeology honest. His command of the factual evidence is simply too great to allow hypotheses based on empirical error to slip through unchallenged. The nomothetic approach, if insecurely founded, will have little chance against the factual evidence from ten sites that few others than Jimmy and the excavator will know about.

A critical way, I think, in which he has led a large number of people in the field is simply and directly a facet of his personality. In early boyhood he may perhaps have been ingratiating, but I sincerely doubt it. To my knowledge, no one has ever heard the phrase "Well done" from Jimmy. Once in forty years of close and affectionate acquaintance, he told me, "You almost sounded as if you knew what you were talking about." It is the highest praise I ever received from him, and I have been suspicious about what he may really have meant ever since! This ability to goad people beyond what they consider their maximum effort simply by withholding praise is in itself a high art, practiced only by the most skillful leaders. Not only University of Michigan students, but hundreds of the rest of us, tried harder in the vain hope of a Griffin accolade that we knew would never come. To be able, at the same time, to elicit the very warmest affection, as these papers demonstrate that he did, is indeed a blessing.

In retrospect, I am, of course, somewhat uneasy about what I have said here. There will be some who may be annoyed, thinking I have damned with faint praise. Others, less charitable toward Jimmy, will take comfort from what they may view incorrectly as my negative criticism. Some will think I have done less than intellectual honor to a man whose intellect I admire highly. Having read the papers that follow myself, however, I feel that no other reader can question the respect, admiration, and affection these scholars, and I, have for Jimmy Griffin.

# INTRODUCTION AND ACKNOWLEDGEMENTS

The retirement of James B. Griffin as Professor of Anthropology and Director of the Museum of Anthropology at The University of Michigan in July of 1975 brought an opportunity for his many students, friends, and colleagues to honor him and his remarkable career in American archaeology. This volume is appropriately published in the *Anthropological Papers* of the Museum of Anthropology, University of Michigan, an outstanding series of scholarly publications that owes its development to Griffin and of which he is justifiably proud. The papers collected here form a companion volume to *Cultural Change and Continuity: Essays in Honor of James Bennett Griffin* published by Academic Press. Both volumes are to be sold in support of the James B. Griffin Fellowship Fund that will provide financial assistance for worthy graduate students studying archaeology at The University of Michigan.

To honor Griffin's long and dynamic period of leadership at the Museum of Anthropology, this *festschrift* has been titled simply "For The Director." It is organized in four parts: Adjunct Studies, American Studies, and Foreign Studies, concluding with a list of Griffin's published works which is complete through 1976.

The first part, Adjunct Studies, points up the great contribution Griffin has made in developing an interdisciplinary approach to the study of prehistory. Contributions to our understanding of the prehistoric record are made by Banks in ethnobotany, Wilkenson in osteology, Bleicher in the study of ceramic glazes, and Farrand in geomorphology.

Part 2, American Studies, is a collection of papers that relate to the study of American archaeology. Griffin's influence in this area is clear to even the casual observer of archaeological knowledge. Here Roosa describes a Paleo-Indian site in Ontario; Janzen presents a new chronology for the Late Archaic at the Falls of the Ohio; and Flanders reevaluates the Middle Woodland Goodall focus. Sears, Morse, and Guthe discuss aspects of southeastern prehistory. The sequence of culture change on the Gulf coast is revised by Sears; Morse documents the spread of Mississippian influence in northeastern Arkansas; and Guthe describes the settlement of Historic

Overhill Cheorkee. Finally, Quimby offers his expert assessment of the role of women on the lower Columbia River during the fur-trade era.

The papers collected in Part 3, Foreign Studies, bring to our attention the fact that Griffin has long had an interest, and in fact considerable influence, in both Latin American and Old World archaeology. To a great degree, his interest has been manifested through the encouragement he offered to his students and colleagues working in these areas, and through the strong support for foreign studies he provided during his tenure as Director of the Museum of Anthropology. In the area of Latin America, Wetherington describes a large ceramic assemblage from Kaminaljuyu, and Hurt considers an early tool tradition from Columbia. Both Milisauskas and Wobst discuss European materials. Milisauskas provides an overview of early Neolithic settlement and, in a more theoretical vein, Wobst discusses information exchange in Eastern Europe.

The completion of this *festschrift* volume would not have been possible without the dedicated efforts of editors Alice Gibson, Mary Coombs, and Katherine Kelly at the Museum of Anthropology, University of Michigan, and Denise Fitch, editorial assistant at the Michigan State University Museum. Thanks is also due to Richard Ford, Director of the Museum of Anthropology and Editor of the *Anthropological Papers* for expediting the printing of this volume. Finally, I would like to thank Moreau S. Maxwell for his insightful summary of James Griffin's contributions to the field of archaeology that appear as the preface to this volume.

Charles E. Cleland<br>
East Lansing

# PART I

# Adjunct Disciplines

# ETHNOBOTANY AS AN ADJUNCT TO ARCHAEOLOGY: STUDIES IN THE ALEUTIAN ISLANDS[1]

*Ted P. Bank II*
Western Michigan University

The term "ethnobotany" was coined by Harshberger, who in 1895 used it narrowly in reference to aboriginal plant lore (Jones, 1941:219). In 1941 Volney Jones offered an ecological definition when he wrote that ethnobotany "deals not only with plant uses, but with the entire range of relations between primitive man[2] and plants" (Jones, ibid.). Today, ethnobotanical research often reflects this ecological perspective by focusing broadly on the interacton of the natural environment with human society and culture.

This article discusses several ethnobotanical studies which my colleagues and I have pursued as an adjunct to archaeology in the Aleutian Islands of southwestern Alaska, where a unique set of enviornmental factors have helped to mold flora, fauna and culture into patterns quite different from those on the Alaskan mainland.[3]

Most Americans had never heard of the Aleutians until they were bombed and occupied by the Japanese in 1942. In the years following the war, there has been increased interest in the area on the part of some scientists and commercial fishing operations. Yet the Aleutians remain one of the few bona fide frontiers on the North American continent. Our anthropological information about them comes from the field work of only a few individuals, and their studies have generally been limited to about a dozen of the more than eighty islands comprising the archipelago. Nevertheless, we are beginning to appreciate the Aleutians because of their varied topography and biota, and their geographic position. Lying as they do between America and Asia at the border of the subarctic and arctic climates, they are especially intriguing to anthropologists and bio-ecologists who are concerned with the biological and cultural affinities of Alaska and Siberia.

## Archaeological Reconnaissance

Archaeological reconnaissance in the Aleutians demonstrates the feasibility of identifying prehistoric village sites by the vegetational patterns peculiar to them. This was recognized by Dall (1877), Jochelson (1925) and Hrdlička (1937), who suggested that plants occurring on old villages might indicate the relative age of a site. My colleagues and I tested this idea during surface reconnaissance of forty-three islands in the Aleutian chain, from Attu to Unimak (Fig. 1) and two aerial surveys of the entire archipelago. We found that the abandoned villages are unique and easily discerned even from the air due to characteristic vegetational and topographic configurations which set them apart from other areas (Bank, 1953b). As a result, more than one hundred previously unreported archaeological sites are now plotted on charts (Bank et al, 1950; Bank, 1954, 1972b, 1975; McCartney, 1973).

This is not a new idea, of course; nor is the application confined to the Aleutians. Various writers have referred to the affinity of certain plants for archaeological sites (Drucker, 1943:114-115; Griffin, 1948:3-4; Heizer,

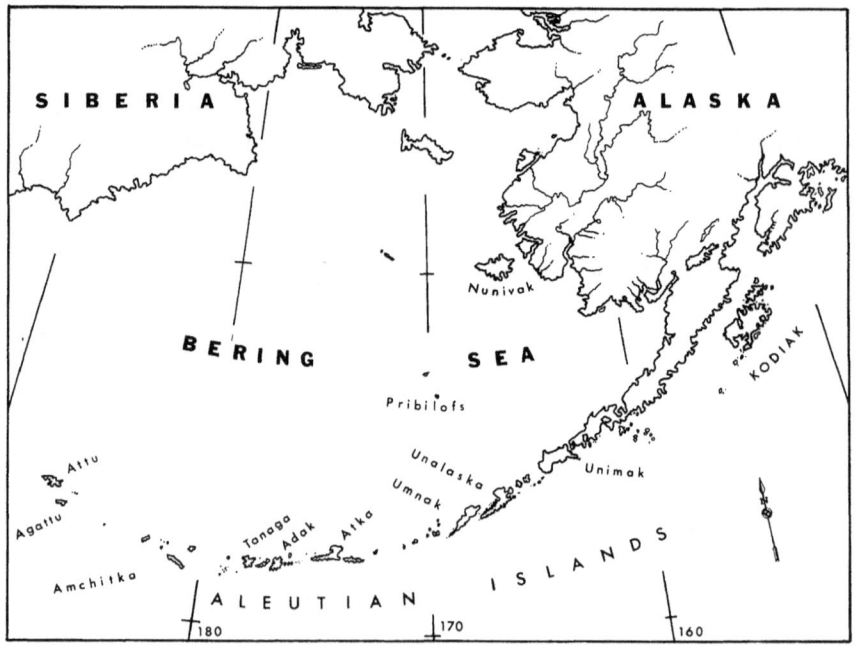

Figure 1. The Aleutian Islands and Bering Sea region of western Alaska.

1959:207-213; Yarnell, 1964, 1965), and aerial surveys have been used in archaeology, perhaps more frequently in Europe than in America, for example, by Fox (1923), Crawford (1923) and Hallam (1964). However, very few archaeological studies outside of Scandinavia have included an intensive inventory and interpretation of plant cover similar to that provided by Zeiner (1945) for the Angel Mound site and by our studies in the Aleutians.

*Aleutian Villages*

Practically every island in the Aleutians contains old village sites, which are found in bays, coves, inlets and bights—wherever there is some protection from the worst storms. Even the rockiest islands show village remains and small kitchen middens, which probably represent temporary fishing camps. Early Russian explorers estimated the population of the islands at more than 20,000 persons, although this may have been too high; a late nineteenth-century government census placed the number of surviving Aleuts at only 1,900 (Petrof, 1884:33). It is known, however, that the Aleut population dwindled rapidly through mass slaughter by early Russians, introduced diseases, and starvation. Today there are fewer than 1,200 Aleuts, and half of these reside outside their original homeland. Of the 100 to 150 villages that were probably inhabited in 1741, less than a dozen remain.

Prior to the arrival of the Russians, the choice of a village site seems to have been dependent upon finding a protected stretch of shore where there was sufficient accumulation of soil for constructing the Aleut style of semi-subterranean house (called a barabara by the Russians), and where there was access to fresh water (which is nearly always at hand in the Aleutians). According to Jochelson (1925:23) and Petrof (1884:146-514), most Aleut villages at the time of Russian discovery were located on points of land and narrow isthmuses, so that an escape route by water would be readily available in the event of an attack by enemies. Later, villages were moved to protected bays and river mouths where fishing was better and where the Russians had easier administrative control, since the inhabitants of several villages were now at a single location.

Recent surveys have encountered old villages that are as large as five acres, and the Russians describe some that were even larger, but the average village site covers approximately one acre. A single village might consist of five, twenty or more than fifty underground dwellings (barabaras). Prior to Russian contact, the entrance was through the sod-covered roof, but later the barabara was generally built above ground with a doorway in the side.

The earlier dwellings had earthen walls that were reinforced with driftwood, whale bones, and large slabs of stone. The driftwood and whalebone rafters were covered with woven grass matting, dried grass, and sod. Large communal barabaras were occasionally constructed with grass mats separating portions of the inside. The remains of one multi-family dwelling discovered at Kuliliak Bay, Unalaska Island, measured 50 x 90 feet.

Today, abandoned villages often remain as large mounds, some of them more than thirty feet high, whose archaeological deposits include both midden materials and structural remains of the underground houses. The latter collapsed following their abandonment, but supporting rafters and soil strata peculiar to them mark their positions in the earth. A sectional view of one such collapsed barabara uncovered at Unalaska is shown in Fig. 2.

Immediately below the old floor of the dwelling and to either side are

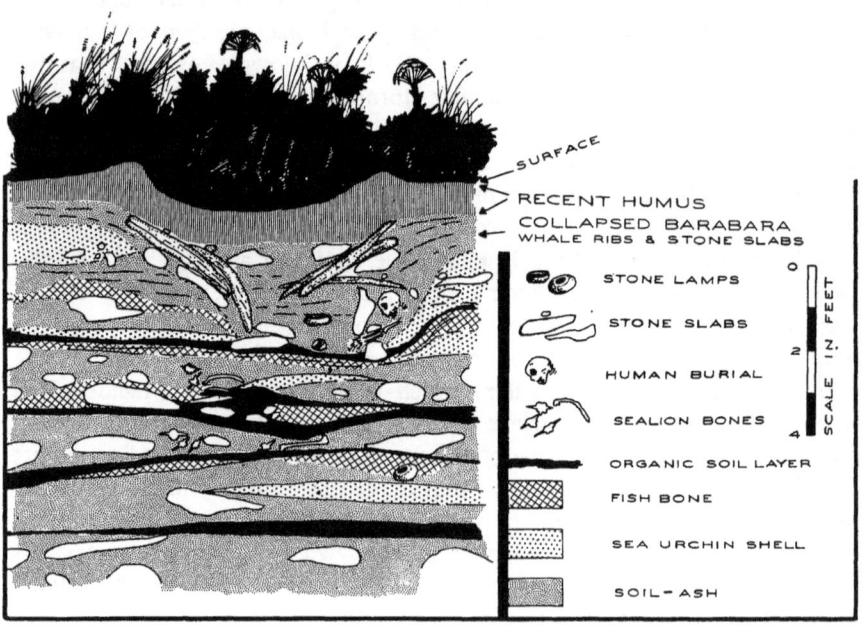

Figure 2. Diagrammatic profile of an excavation at Eider Point, Unalaska Island. A house pit (*barabara*: underground Aleut dwelling) and subsurface archaeological deposits are shown. Whale bones probably supported the sod roof. Typical plants found on such villages are listed in the text and in Figure 4. (Reprinted with permission from Ecology; copyright, Ecological Society of America.)

usually found layers of sea urchin shell, fish bone, clam shell, and intermingled bones of sea mammals, as well as cultural remains. Human burials are sometimes found in the earthen walls of the house, sealed up with stones and soil. Sometimes the cultural levels are interspersed with volcanic ash and humic layers, which suggests intermittent occupation of the site, but often the cultural deposits are uninterrupted throughout the midden, indicating continuous inhabitation. The middens contain thousands of individual trash piles, which show up in the profiles as corresponding lenses of sea urchin shell, compacted fish bones, clam shells, snail shells, sea-mammal bones and vegetable material, which no doubt represent seasonal accumulations.

*Procedure for Phyto-Ecological Study*

Detailed measurements are not always feasible at every site because of the insufficient time spent ashore at some locations. In these cases visual estimates, supplemented by plant collections, are used to determine the vegetational cover. In the majority of cases, however, the following procedure is employed.

Every site is measured by pacing or steel tape. Topographic features, generally elevation changes, were used initially to determine the borders of the village area, but it soon became evident that the vegetational patterns were much more reliable than any other surface indicator. One or more study transects, each ten feet wide, are arbitrarily laid out across the site so as to include at least one barabara pit, if discernible, and to extend into non-archaeological habitats adjacent to the village. In addition, control strips are established on the non-village areas. Numerical estimates of the plants occurring within each transect are supplemented by check counts, photographs and plant collections. Quadrats ten feet square are established at various intervals within the transects to provide data for the counts, which generally consist of a numerical count of all plants growing within the quadrat. We have occasionally checked our tabulations by determining the comparative dry weights of the plants, but this provides little additional information. Soil samples are collected from different areas and at varying depths by means of a peat borer or test trenches (which are used minimally to avoid disturbing cultural deposits), or from the exposed surface of the eroded margins found on the seaward side of most sites. We also conducted tests of soil pH with a La Motte indicator set in order to supplement other observations.

Generally, selection of sites for phyto-ecological study depends upon their accessibility and the amount of time that can be spent ashore. In the past, Aleut informants have provided us with the locations of some sites; others were discovered during the course of botanical investigations and coastal reconnaissance. The initial studies (1948-51) were carried out at sixteen abandoned villages located on ten islands (Attu, Agattu, Shemya, Tanaga, Kanaga, Adak, Atka, Umnak, Unalaska and Amaknak). In subsequent years, twenty additional sites were studied at Unalaska, Sedanka, Akutan, Akun and Tigalda islands, including five villages that were examined by several of my students to provide an independent check on previous results. For the purposes of this article, a few sites will serve as examples.

One of the prehistoric villages, known as the Waterfall Site, is located in the central Aleutians on the coast of Atka Island, approximately two miles southeast of the present Aleut village on Nazan Bay. Jochelson (1925: 30-45) and Hrdlička (1945:219, 319) each reported working here briefly. The situation of the site and the positions of our study strips are shown in Figure 3. Two additional villages are located in the eastern Aleutians at Eider Point (Unalaska Island) (Fig. 4) and on the southwestern shore of Amaknak Island (Dutch Harbor) in Unalaska Bay. Both are large village mounds. The one at Eider Point measures 170 X 280 feet. The Amaknak site, referred to as Amaknak-D (Quimby, 1946; Bank, 1953d, 1954, 1963) is 130 X 220 feet and is bisected by a military road constructed during World War II (Figs. 5, 6). According to Aleut informants, all three sites were abandoned as villages more than one hundred years ago.[4] However, portions of both Eider Point and Amaknak-D were stripped of their vegetation by recent military operations. It is noteworthy that in both instances the plant cover returned soon after the military abandoned the areas, and that the vegetational pattern is similar to the pattern found on old villages that have not been subjected to military use or other kinds of recent disturbance. The reinstated plant growth at Eider Point is particularly lush.

For purposes of this article, I shall merely summarize our findings at these representative sites, rather than repeat the detailed reports available elsewhere (Bank, 1953b, 1953c). Brief references will also be made to village studies at Krugloi Point on Agattu Island (investigated botanically by H. A. Miller in 1949), the Chaluka mound on Umnak, Konets Head on Unalaska Island, and Amugul Bay (Fig. 7), also on Unalaska Island (Bank et al., 1950; Bank, 1972b).

*Vegetation on Old Villages*

A distinctive vegetational pattern can be recognized on old villages. It is

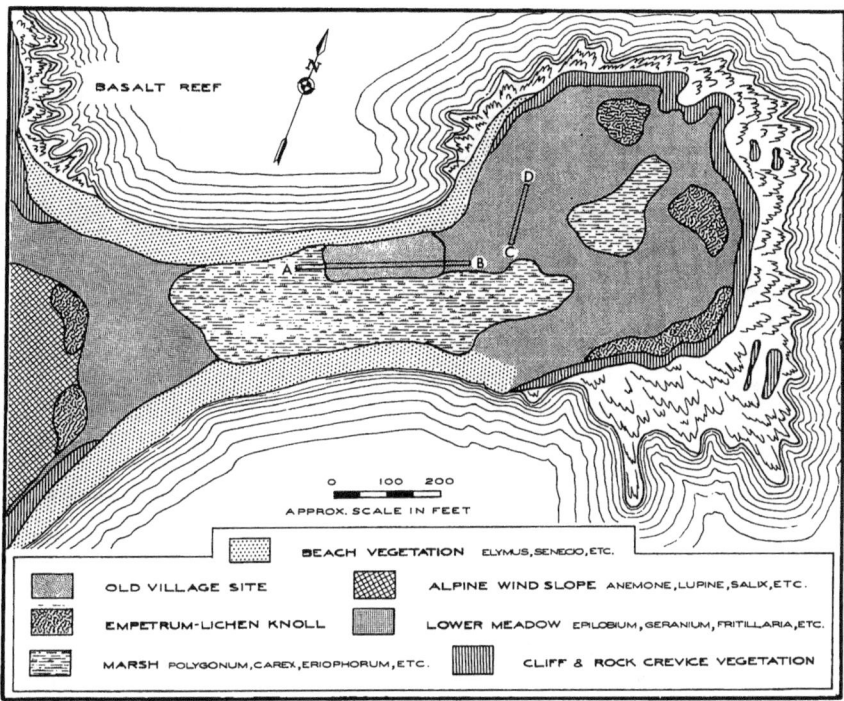

Figure 3. Prehistoric village (Waterfall Site) and adjacent plant habitats at Nazan Bay, Atka Island. Locations of the study transect (A-B) and the control strip (C-D) are shown. Both are ten feet wide. Plants occurring on the transects are shown in the text and in Figures 4, 5 and 8 (reprinted with permission from Ecology; copyright, Ecological Society of America).

not duplicated on adjacent habitats, and in fact is not found anywhere else in the Islands except on archaeological sites. The plants comprising this pattern normally occur somewhat separated in a variety of natural habitats, especially in the grass hummock zone near beaches, in wet ravines, and in the grass meadows of lowland valleys (Bank, 1952b). They appear together on abandoned villages, forming a particular kind of plant community which I have termed "an *association-segregate*," i.e., an association that has differentiated out of mixed associations of the lowland habitats; in this case not because of climatic influence but as a result of long-persisting edaphic changes brought about by man's occupation (Bank, 1953b:253).

The characteristic plants of this association-segregate include the wild rye grass *Elymus arenarius mollis, Achillaea borealis, Claytonia sibirica,* and

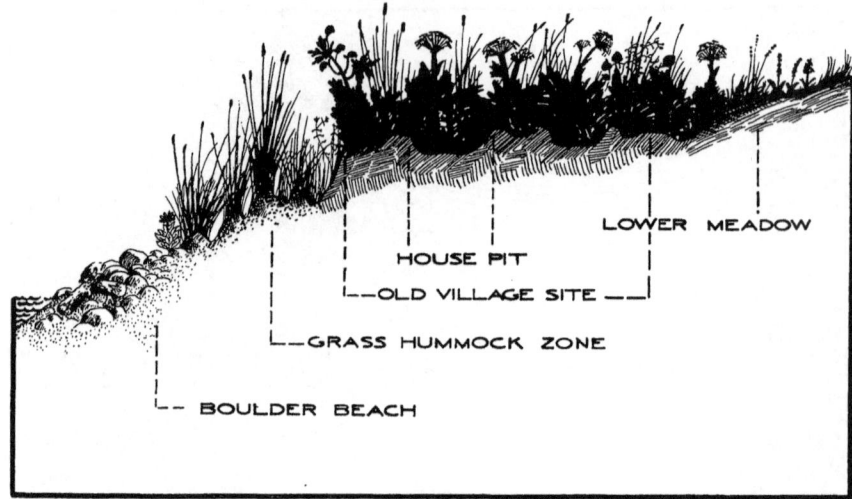

Figure 4. Diagrammatic section of typical small village site based on an actual site on Adak, showing barabara pits, lush vegetation usually occurring on old villages, and the characteristically narrow ecotones between the village plant community and adjacent communities. The most abundant plants on the village area are *Heracleum*, *Elymus* (tall wild rye), *Angelica*, *Conioselinum*, *Achillaea*, *Claytonia*, *Ligusticum* and *Aconitum*. (Reprinted with permission from Ecology; copyright, Ecological Society of America.)

the poisonous monkshood *Aconitum maximum*, together with various members of the family Umbelliferae (*Angelica lucida, Heracleum lanatun, Ligusticum scotium hultenii*, and *Conioselinum chinense*).[5] There are various companion plants, which have no pronounced affinity for this association but which nevertheless occur frequently on old village areas, including various ferns (usually *Athyrium* and *Dryopteris*), tall grasses such as *Calamagrostis, Festuca*, and *Deschampsia*, and a few other plants which usually frequent the meadows, namely *Anaphalis, Ranunculus, Epilobium* and *Cornus* (see Fig. 4). The relative abundance of the characteristic and companion plants may be given roughly as follows: constantly present (80-100%), *Achillaea, Elymus, Heracleum, Conioselinum* and *Aconitum* (the latter particularly in the western Aleutians); mostly present (60-80%), *Ligusticum, Angelica, Claytonia, Calamagrostis, Deschampsia* and other grasses; often present (40-60%), ferns, *Anaphalis*; occasionally present (20-40%), *Epilobium, Ranunculus, Cornus*. Rarely present (1-20%) are those plants recently introduced, such as clover and invaders from wet, boggy habitats, e.g., sphagnum.

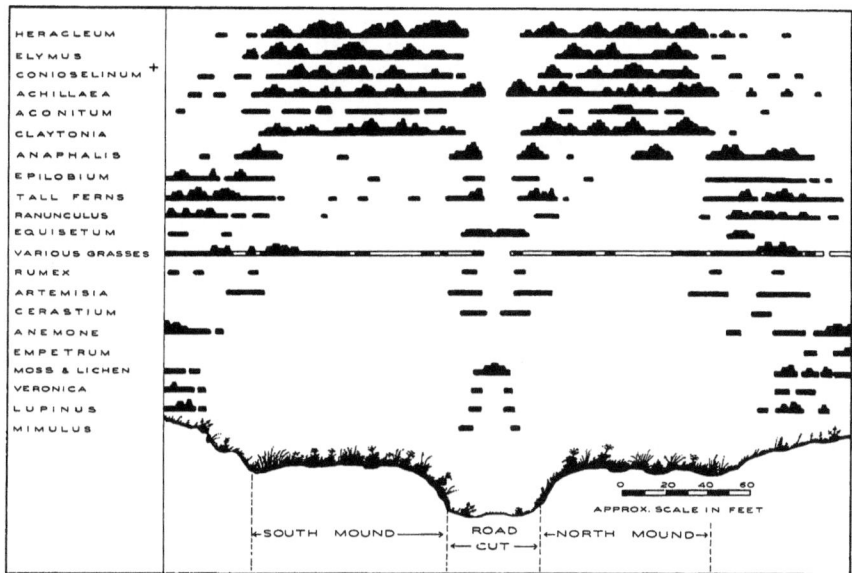

Figure 5. Diagrammatic profile of prehistoric mound at Amaknak Island (Dutch Harbor), the same shown in Figure 6. Distribution of the most abundant plants is indicated by horizontal bars; heavier bars indicate greater abundance; broken bars indicate scattered occurrence. + *Ligusticum scotium hultenii* and *Angelica lucida* also occur predominately on the mound with about the same pattern as shown for *Conioselinum*.

At Adak, Atka and several other locations, individual barabara pits were stripped of their surface vegetation to allow a close tally of the plant cover. We found that certain plants show a special sensitivity to topographic features of the site, i.e., they occur in greater abundance in some micro-habitats than in others. Data for *Heracleum, Aconitum, Elymus, Conioselinum* and *Polygonum* are graphically shown in Figure 8. Each dot represents a plant within the study transect. Barabara pits are indicated by patterns formed of plant species favoring them.

*Aconitum* exhibits no discernible preference for one part of the site over another, but *Heracleum* generally occurs most abundantly within house pits, although it also grows elsewhere on the sites (note: all barabara depressions do not show the same pattern). It is possible that the major factors affecting the distribution of *Heracleum* are soil pH and moisture accumulation (the soil is constantly damp within the pits). *Elymus* grows in dense stands along the slightly raised margins of the barabara pits and

Figure 6. Old village mound, Amaknak-D site, at Amaknak Island, Unalaska Bay, showing lush vegetation typical of old village areas. In places, the plant growth was more than six feet tall, particularly in the pit remains of former Aleut underground dwellings. A military road constructed during World War II bisects the site.

wherever there are slight elevations, e.g., on the hummocks that are found at the seaward margin of many village areas (Figs. 4, 7). This may be so because of a micro-difference in pH value from leaching of the soil, or because of the difference in drainage. The distribution of *Polygonum* is typical of that for several other plants which frequent habitats adjacent to old village sites but which show an intolerance for the sites themselves. Other plants, e.g., *Deschampsia* and *Calamagrostis*, as well as *Cornus*, *Ranunculus*, and *Epilobium*, appear to grow well, although in scattered condition, both on and off the village areas.

Similar studies were conducted in the western Aleutians at Attu, Agattu, and Shemya. Generally, the vegetational pattern and surface configurations of western archaeological sites are similar to those that occur elsewhere in

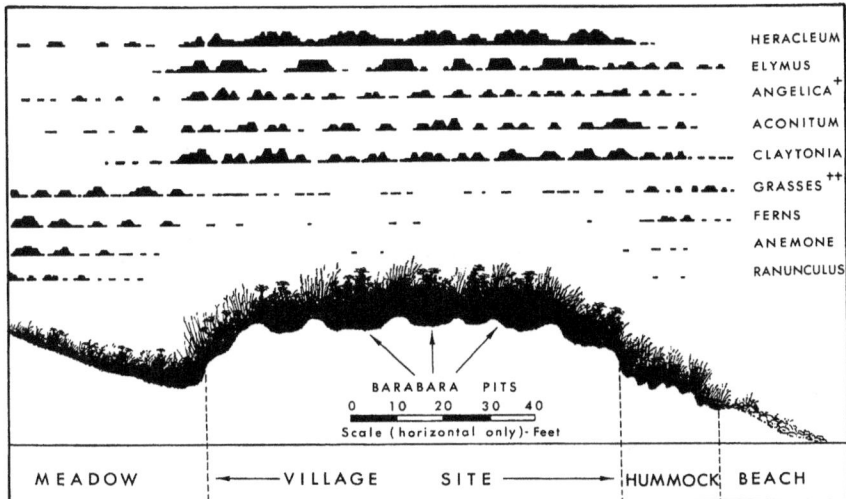

Figure 7. Diagrammatic profile of a small village site located in Amugul Bay, Unalaska Island. Distribution of the most abundant plants is indicated in the figure by horizontal bars; heavier bars indicate greater abundance. Only a few of the typical plants are listed. + *Ligusticum* and *Conioselinum* also occur predominantly on the village with about the same pattern as shown for *Angelica*. ++ The grasses that occur mainly on adjacent habitats include *Calamagrostis*, *Deschampsia*, *Agrostis*, and *Trisetum*. Although some of the typical village plants also occur in the adjacent habitats, their growth is not nearly so lush and abundant as on the village site.

the Aleutians. One interesting difference is that the poisonous plant *Aconitum* appears more frequently in the west than in the east.

There are village sites that do not exhibit the characteristic vegetational pattern. This is true, for example, at the large Chaluka mound and at most of the villages we examined on the western end of Umnak and Unalaska islands. But there is intensive sheep ranching in these areas, accompanied by constant grazing and trampling of the ground, which undoubtedly explains the differences noted. Some of the typical village plants do occur, but the characteristic lush growth is lacking. Other plants, not generally found on the sites, have succeeded in establishing themselves, e.g., *Trifolium* and *Galium*, which have been introduced from outside the Aleutian area.

*Soil Factors*

Generally speaking, the midden soils are very porous because of their

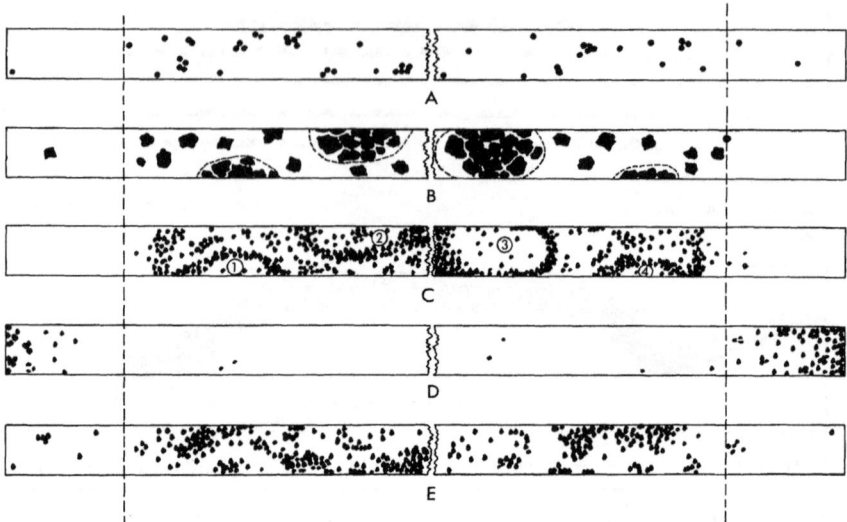

Figure 8. Diagrams showing distribution of plants on a study strip across the former village (Waterfall Site, Fig. 3), Nazan Bay, Atka Island. The strip is ten feet wide and about 330 feet long, but for convenience the middle segment is left out. The vertical broken lines indicate the margins of the village area. Each dot represents a plant; thus the diagrams present the distribution of: A) *Aconitum* B) *Heracleum* shows partiality to house pits; C) *Elymus* shows partiality to raised pit margins; D) *Polygonum viviparum* shows intolerance to village area; E) *Conioselinum*. Barabara (house) pits, 1-4, are indicated by the patterns of plants favoring them (reprinted with permission from Ecology; copyright, Ecological Society of America).

content of fish bone, shell, sea urchin spines and volcanic ash (Figs. 2, 10). Except in the barabara pits where the soil is somewhat more compacted, drainage is usually quite good on the sites. Despite this the midden deposits are frequently saturated with water, since there is almost constant precipitation in the Aleutians, and soil temperatures are quite low; thus there is probably a low rate of organic decomposition. This in turn results in the slow release of certain chemicals from the organic matter over an unusually long period of time. We surmise that midden soils contain considerably more calcium, phosphorus and nitrate than other Aleutian soils. Although we have not conducted the appropriate tests, it seems evident that there is a rich source of these chemicals in the abundant subsurface fertilizing deposits which make up the middens. Ordinarily, leaching of the soil removes nitrate fairly rapidly, but in the middens, nitrate removal would occur at a rate slower than elsewhere because of constant replenishment from the midden deposits. It is probably primarily the availability of calcium, phosphorus and nitrate that determines the growth characteristics of the plants comprising the village pattern. The poisonous *Aconitum* and members of the Umbelliferae, which grow in profusion on the sites, are perhaps the most reliable indicators of the increased presence of these chemicals.

*Aleut Plant Uses*

It is possible that there are other ecological factors, associated with Aleut plant uses, that are partly responsible for the occurrence of particular plants on abandoned villages. Aleut plant lore was formerly very extensive. More than seventy local plants were utilized for food, medicines, poison and in the manufacture of matting, baskets and so forth (Bank, 1953a, 1962b). The Aleuts never had to wander very far inland for useful plants; the majority of species sought by them are readily accessible in the stream valleys, marshes, lowland meadows, knolls and shoreline habitats near village locations. All of the characteristic plants today growing on prehistoric villages were at one time used by the Aleuts. *Heracleum, Angelica, Ligusticum, Conioselinum* and *Claytonia* were used for food, *Heracleum, Ligusticum, Aconitum* and *Achillaea* were medicines, *Elymus* was the main plant used in weaving, and *Aconitum* was used by some groups as a whale and fish poison.

Today these plants are found closely associated on archaeological sites, but are otherwise encountered more or less disassociated in widely differing and distinct habitats. This suggests that earlier Aleut economy may have been the primary historical determinant of the particular combination of plants on the sites. Undoubtedly, the Aleuts utilized the plants primarily at their villages, where the waste parts (such as seeds) accumulated in abundance, thus establishing a ruderal vegetation that persists today on the abandoned village areas.

*Use of Vegetation in Archaeological Reconnaissance*

Until now, one of the major difficulties attending archaeological work in the Aleutians had to do with the time, expense and physical exertion required to identify the most important sites. There was never a lack of old villages; the problem was one of selection. Archaeologists had only meager information concerning the relative size and probable importance even of the sites that were known. There were no complete surface surveys of any of the islands. Choice of a location for detailed study was usually determined by its accessibility, or by the fact that it was the only site known on a particular island. Once excavation was underway, additional villages might be discovered, too late to utilize the information.

Today, ecological studies at old villages provide an easy method of locating archaeological sites not only by surface exploration but also by aerial reconnaissance. Our expeditions have checked the accuracy of aerial surveys during two flights across the entire Aleutian archipelago, which were followed by surface reconnaissance along some of the same coastline. The procedure for locating sites from the air is summarized below in excerpts from a previous article (Bank, 1953b:262-264).

> When viewed from the air, old Aleut villages present a unique appearance, being seen as dark green areas against the lighter greens and yellows of the surrounding vegetation. This is explained by the greater abundance of tall dark-colored plants such as *Aconitum* and *Heracleum* on the sites as compared with the lower-growing plants which prevail on non-village areas. From the standpoint of lushness and greenness of vegetation, many valleys and stream margins show the same dark green coloration, although not as sharply defined and hence usually not mistaken for archaeological sites. The lateness of the season to which *Heracleum* and *Aconitum* retain their dark greenness gives to the margins of old villages an especially sharp delimitation in the early fall when the surrounding meadows and bogs have already taken on the yellow-orange coloration of winter. A strikingly distinctive feature of most village sites is the occurrence of depressed circular *barabara* (house) pits. These are likely to be choked with a heavy plant growth (as indicated in Figures 2, 7), as well as being sunken, so that they are easily discerned even from high altitudes (Figure 9).

Using this technique, it is now relatively easy to determine from the air not only the exact location of an abandoned village but also its approximate human population. This requires merely a search for the distinctive color patterns of the sites and a count of the barabara pits, which usually stand out quite clearly; it may even be done from photographs.[6]

Additional studies are needed to work out the finer correlations between surface vegetation and the time elapsed since abandonment of the village sites. As we have previously noted (Bank, ibid.):

> Such a correlation would seem to exist since the recently disturbed sites, such as Eider Point, present a denser vegetation than do villages abandoned longer, although it may prove too tenuous a relationship to be of practical value to the archaeologist. It may be a relatively temporary cultivation effect ... depth of leaching out of fertilizer constituents since abandonment might provide the reason for a correlation of vegetational differences with antiquity, if such differences can actually be discerned and measured.

Figure 9. Prehistoric Aleut village at the western end of Attu Island as seen from the air in September, 1949. Approximately 90 barabara pits can be counted, including several larger depressions, probably community dwellings. Old villages show up particularly well in the early fall, and better on color than on black and white photographs.

## Soil and Midden Deposits:
## Indices of Biological and Cultural Succession

Because of space limitations, this discussion will confine itself to only a few of the current methods used for obtaining data of correlative value from ancient plant remains in archaeological deposits. Suffice to say, such studies are becoming increasingly important in modern archaeology, as Deetz (1970:117) has observed:

> The most important thing to realize about archaeological material ... is that it reflects in its entirety the manner in which human behavior has made an impact upon the environment ... it is the explication of this relationship between behavior and environment which holds the greatest promise for sharpening archaeological studies.

A truly scientific explication of the relationship between behavior and environment, as reflected in archaeological remains, must consider all components of a site, including the buried plant debris, which in many cases will provide information equal in importance to that obtained from the recovered animal bones.

## Aleutian Soil and Midden Profiles

Aside from the porous and loosely packed midden deposits resulting from fish bone, shell, ash and other materials contained in them, there are also dense layers of wet compacted soil, rich in humus, occurring sporadically throughout most Aleutian middens. These strata may mark periods of time when the site was abandoned temporarily, possibly because of intertribal warfare or natural disasters such as tidal waves or volcanic eruptions. Violent volcanic activity of the past is frequently marked in archaeological profiles by well-defined strata of ash and pumice, and Aleut legends tell of entire villages that were destroyed.

Theoretically, the humic layers and ash strata can both be utilized for establishing relative chronology. Often, however, the ash deposits are not continuous across a village area and are intermixed with midden material because of trampling and other disturbances by later occupants of the site. Fossil pollen can be collected from the buried humus, but usually it is not preserved well enough for reliable pollen analysis. There is another method which provides much more reliable data for establishing relative chronology. This involves using non-archaeological soil-ash profiles along the margins of the archaeological site. One or several trenches are cut at the edge of the site in such a way as to expose the naturally formed soil-ash strata, and to extend a short distance into the village area. Soil and volcanic ash layers are well defined in non-archaeological profiles, and usually it is easy to trace them to the midden where they can be identified in the stratigraphy (Fig. 10).

Non-archaeological profiles show alternating layers of ash and humus, with some sand and occasional lenses of weathered till. A ferruginous band, possibly caused by leaching from above, shows up frequently in the middle soil zone and may prove to be a dependable point of departure for correlation (Anderson and Bank, 1952; Bank, 1952a). In addition, there are usually prominent bands of ash throughout the stratigraphy, which can be used in conjunction with humic strata and cultural horizons as index layers in the chronology. An analysis of particles comprising ash deposits at Tanaga, Atka and Unalaska indicates volcanic eruptions which began violently and gradually diminished to continuous, comparatively quiet eruptions of long duration. This appears in the profile as layers composed of coarse pumice overlaid by ash which becomes increasingly finer toward the top. Such ash falls undoubtedly exterminated the vegetation of a large area, and the plant cover probably needed considerable time to regenerate itself.

The western part of Unalaska Island was affected by this kind of heavy volcanic activity in the past, as shown by the thick deposits of ash and

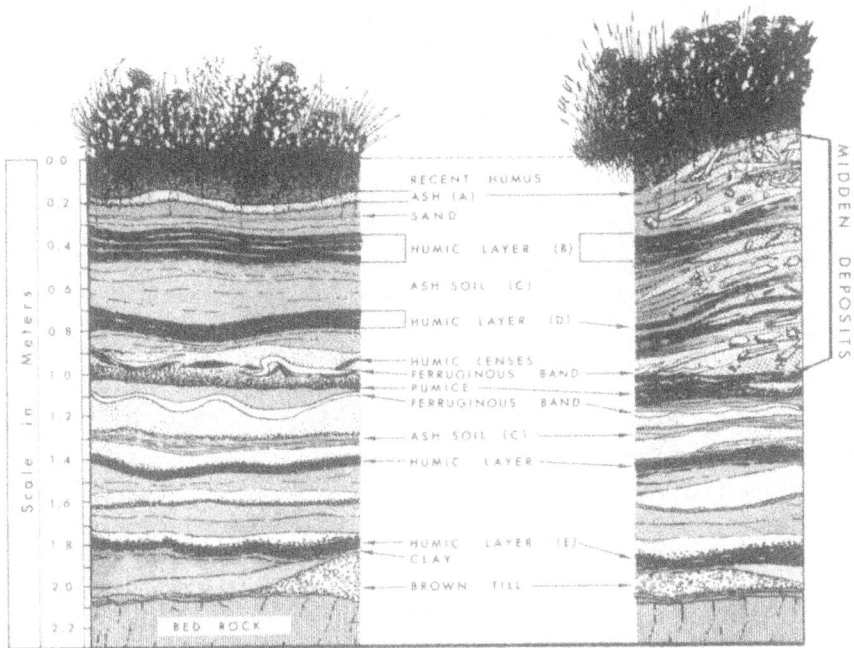

Figure 10. Soil-ash and midden profiles at Lash Bay, Tanaga Island. At left: non-archaeological soil-ash profile adjacent to a section (on the right) cut into the border of a small prehistoric village site. Strata of soil, ash, sand, and other deposits can be traced onto the village area. Ash (A) and the other ash layers are pumiceous, sometimes coarse, and are probably from Tanaga Volcano on the north side of the island. Humic layers (B, D, E and others) contain alternating bands of organic material and ash. Ash-soil deposits (C and others) consist mainly of weathered silty soil with fine ash. Humic layer (D), at 0.85 m depth, provided the sample T-18 for pollen analysis (Table I). Sample T-39 came from humic layer (E), at 1.83 m depth, which has a radiocarbon date of 4,900±400 years B.P. On the right, compacted fish bone, lenses of sea urchin and clam shell, sea mammal bones, whale bones, and other midden deposits are shown diagrammatically. Occupation of the village area began after a period of violent volcanic eruptions (indicated by the pumice layer between the two ferruginous bands.)

pumice intercalated between layers of humus and cultural remains which are found at Konets Head. The volcanics undoubtedly originated in the still active Okmok crater on nearby Umnak Island. The eruptions interfered with plant succession and also must have greatly affected the lives of the Aleuts. We have not yet excavated at Konets Head (except for a small test trench that was examined in 1970) but hope in the near future to be able to provide the intensive study which this large, and apparently very old, village site warrants.

*Pollen Analysis*

Several pollen studies were carried out to ascertain whether this method is applicable to Aleutian soils as well as to peats and mucks. Usually terrestrial ash-soil deposits do not contain much pollen, as the grains are ordinarily destroyed by oxidation. It was therefore somewhat surprising to find that these samples contained sufficient pollen for analysis (Anderson and Bank, 1952). This is probably because of the unusual Aleutian climate, which is marked by consistently high precipitation and fairly low soil temperatures. Saturation of the soils with water is undoubtedly the major reason why the pollen and spores are preserved.

Pollen samples were collected from humic layers in non-archaeological profiles located, whenever possible, adjacent to village areas. Pollen from the non-archaeological profile should represent the vegetation existing in the vicinity of the village at the times represented by equivalent humic layers in the midden.

The samples were collected at decimeter intervals from twenty soil-ash profiles at Tanaga, Adak, Atka, Unalaska and Amaknak islands. It was not always necessary to excavate; often a clean profile, suitable for our studies, could be obtained merely by cutting a fresh vertical face at an embankment that was already partially exposed due to wind erosion, water (stream cutting), or military operations. Several test borings were made at each site to ascertain the slope of the soil strata, and the macroscopic character of all the sections was recorded. Samples were placed in 2-oz. vials, treated with alcohol preservative, and later prepared for microscopic analysis as recommended by Faegri and Iverson (1950, 1965).

At Tanaga Island, two humus samples were collected for study from soil strata located at 0.92 meters depth (sample T-18) and 1.83 meters (sample T-39) in non-archaeological soil-ash deposits adjacent to an old village site at Lash Bay (Fig. 10). The soil layer at 1.83 meters was formed prior to human occupation of the nearby village. The site is at 75 meters elevation, located in a *Calamagrostis langsdorffii* meadow (described by Hultén, 1937; Bank, 1952b).

A comparison of the pollen in the lower soil stratum and that from the upper level indicates two entirely different plant communities (Table 1). The older pollen and spores provide high percentages of *Ericales* (55 percent), Gramineae (22), and *Lycopodium* (17). This mixture represents the *Empetrum* heath which today occurs primarily at higher altitudes. The younger sample shows high percentages of Gramineae (56), Cyperaceae (23), and Ranunculaceae (9.0), with some *Ericales* (3.7), *Dryopteris* (3.1), and Umbelliferae (2.2), thus indicating a vegetation quite similar to the grass meadow existing today at this locality.

Generally, the pollen samples suggest a change from an earlier *Lycopodium-Empetrum* heath to a *Calamagrostis*-Umbelliferae meadow. This can be interpreted as due to a change from a dry, continental-arctic climate to a moist, oceanic-subarctic climate. Usually it is hazardous to rely solely upon pollen shifts at a few isolated sites as an indication of widespread climatic changes. Volcanic ash falls, for example, can produce such radical alterations of the local habitat that the subsequent vegetation will be of a totally different character for edaphic reasons. Also, in the Aleutians, natural biotic groupings sometimes become modified by forces much less basic than climate (Bank, 1953c). However, results similar to those above were obtained with pollen samples from sites at Atka, Adak and Unalaska. Thus, there is an increased probability that climatic change was indeed responsible for the vegetational succession noted in the pollen series.

A radiocarbon date of 4,900 ± 400 years B.P. has been obtained from the lower soil sample (T-39) at Tanaga (Crane and Griffin, 1959a:1117). This data may mark, in the Aleutians, the beginning of amelioration of the climate in the postglacial development of the thermal maximum (postglacial optimum), which apparently began elsewhere in Alaska about 5,000 years ago (Heusser, 1952). Anangula Island, at the western end of Umnak, was occupied about 8,000 years ago (Laughlin, 1963a:90; Black and Laughlin, 1964), and early Aleuts began to inhabit the large Chaluka site on Umnak approximately 4,500 to 5,000 years later (Laughlin, 1963b; Laughlin and Reeder, 1962, 1966). It would appear, therefore, that early human migrants reached the eastern Aleutians when the climate was colder than today and that elaboration of Aleut culture, as reflected in the earliest levels at Chaluka, occurred during the latter phases of the postglacial climatic thermal maximum. However, further studies and radiocarbon dates are required to confirm this.

TABLE I

Results of Pollen Analysis of Tanaga (Aleutians) Soil Samples

| | Alnus* | Betula | Populus | Juniperus | Gramineae | Cyperaceae | Ericales | Ranunculaceae | Umbelliferae | Campanula | Unidentified pollen | Lycopodium | Dryopteris | Total pollen grains and spores |
|---|---|---|---|---|---|---|---|---|---|---|---|---|---|---|
| Tanaga-18 0.85 m depth | 0.3 | — | — | 0.3 | 56 | 23 | 3.7 | 9.0 | 2.2 | 0.8 | 0.6 | 0.8 | 3.1 | 356 |
| Tanaga-39** 1.83 m depth | 0.3 | 0.3 | 0.3 | — | 22 | 2.9 | 55 | 1.3 | 0.3 | — | 0.3 | 17 | 0.3 | 309 |

*Figures are percentages of the total of pollen and spores.
**From the same site as Tanaga-18 but deeper.
Data from S. T. Anderson and T. P. Bank II, 1952, Science; adapted with permission.

## Cultural Diffusion and Ethnobotany: Aleuts in Asia

The Aleuts have been known to scholars since the voyages of Vitus Bering and Alexei Chirikov in 1741, but their physical and cultural origins continue to puzzle anthropologists. They have variously been identified as Paleo-Asiatics, American Indians, Eskimos and wanderers from central Asia. Hrdlička, after three field seasons in the Aleutians, declared that there were two distinct populations: pre-Aleut and Aleut, and that the pre-Aleuts "... were definitely not Eskimo, nor even their very close relations; though the Eskimo may well have differentiated from the same far-back parental stock that gave also the less modified pre-Aleut people (Hrdlička, 1945: 579) ... their crania (pre-Aleut) show a close affinity with those of the continental Sioux Indians..." (p. 584).

Others see a definite close relationship between the Aleuts and Eskimos, physically, culturally and linguistically (Laughlin, 1951; Laughlin and Marsh, 1951; Bank, 1953d, 1958). The Aleuts may, in fact, be the oldest living remnant of ancient Eskimo migrations that fanned out from Bering Straits along Alaska's coast in early postglacial times. Once in the Aleutians, Aleut culture was influenced by the particular geographical features of the long island chain, which provided isolation and served as a kind of environmental filter where some early Eskimo traits survived long after they disappeared from other parts of the Bering Sea region.

Long-term intensive archaeological studies have been carried out by Laughlin and his associates, mainly at Umnak (Laughlin and Reeder, 1966). My own work, begun in 1948, has been concentrated primarily on the ecological factors that have affected cultural and biological succession, initially in the central Aleutians and more recently in the Unalaska area (Bank et al, 1950; Bank, 1972b, 1973, 1975). Hrdlička (1945) undertook the monumental task of trying to cover all of the Aleutians and the Commander Islands in only three summers. Dall's (1877) and Jochelson's (1925, 1933) investigations are especially useful for comparative studies. Others who have worked in the Aleutians include Weyer (1929, 1930), Turner (1970, 1972), Spaulding (1962) and McCartney (1973).

Fairly good inventories of Aleut culture exist, although there are gaps, e.g., in the areas of Aleut mortuary practices, regional cultural developments, beliefs about the supernatural, warfare, ethnobiology, and so forth. In summary, the Aleuts possessed such Eskimo traits as: open-sea hunting, both kayak-like and umiak-like skin boats, seal-oil lamps, semilunar pots, nets and weirs, communal houses, use of stone and whalebone in house construction, toggling and simple detachable harpoon heads made of bone, fish spears, pronged bird spears, stone knives with tang, bolas, both compound and simple fishhooks, stone ulus (chipped stone in the early phases of Aleut culture and ground slate later), labrets and tattooing, throwing boards, ivory needles with eyes, circle-and-dot design, elaborate tailored garments, covered flexed burials, cooperative hunting, sharing of food, and customs maintaining a dichotomy between land and sea mammals. Absent throughout most of the Aleut area (except in some instances where a trait has penetrated on the Alaska Peninsula) were such Eskimo traits as: pottery, sleds, dog domestication, equipment used for ice hunting, snow goggles, etc.

Recent exploration of small flat-topped islets lying offshore at Umnak and Unalaska have revealed polyhedral cores, burin spalls, lamellar flakes and blades which appear to antedate all previously known artifacts from the area (Laughlin and Marsh, 1954; Black and Laughlin, 1964; Hopkins, 1967; Bank, 1972a). Radiocarbon dates of 7,660 ± 300 years B.P. and 8,425 ± 175 years B.P. have been obtained from charcoal associated with the lamellar flake industry at Anangula Island (Black and Laughlin, ibid.). Muller-Beck (Hopkins, 1967:403) connects the Anangula assemblage with advanced Aurignacoid traditions of Eurasia. Laughlin and others, on the other hand, see an affinity with the later stages of pre-ceramic cultures of Hokkaido, Japan (*ca.* 13,000 years B.P.). There is some tenuous evidence directly linking the Anangula flake industry and the earliest cultural manifestations at nearby Umnak and Unalaska, which indicates that the Anangula people were proto-Aleuts (Laughlin 1975:515).

*Cultural Links With Asia*

One should not conclude that the Aleuts are derived unmixed from an Eskimo stock, or that they were cut off from influences originating outside the Eskimo area. There are important cultural and populational differences that separate Aleut from adjacent mainland Eskimo. The following elements of Aleut culture, for example, are lacking on the Bering Sea coast north of the Aleutians: dismembered burials, burial atop refuge island, trophy heads, wooden death masks, utilized human bone, underground houses with central entrance from the top, cave burials, nosepins, and many others. It is possible, of course, even probable, that some of these differences are a consequence of the isolation of the Aleutians, wherein a few very early, pre-Eskimo traits may have survived, which died out under the relative accessibility to outside influences of the Alaskan mainland. It is much more difficult to explain some of the similarities between cultural traits in the Aleutians and in the Sea of Okhotsk region north of Japan. They provide an intriguing archaeological puzzle, one which in the past has led a number of scholars, among them Collins (1937:280, 345, 373-378; 1940:577-583), de Laguna (1934:216-220), and Heizer (1943:452-453), to conclude that there must have been some direct, prehistoric cultural contact, via the Aleutians, between the Kamchatka-Kurile area and southwestern Alaska. Among the traits that were shared between the two areas are the following (Heizer, ibid.):

> ... roof entrance for the underground house; refuge island; notched and grooved stones; stone with hole; grinding stone and slab; oval stone lamp; hunter's lamp with ring; labret; large bone arrowhead with blade but no barbs; broken and cut human bones; and Japanese form of harpoon head, toggle type with closed socket and line hole in the same plane with the spur.

To which we can add a long list of traits that have a circum-Pacific distribution (Birket-Smith and de Laguna, 1938:519): raven myths, cremation, slavery, vegetable arrow (and harpoon) poison, open-water sea mammal hunting, twisted basketry, stone pecking technique, notched log ladder, and others. Birket-Smith and de Laguna concluded: "There can hardly be any doubt that the general direction of this circum-Pacific drift has been from Asia ... towards North America" (op. cit., p. 520). MacLeod (1925:143) contributes yet another trait, mummification, which he thinks reached southern Alaska and the Aleutians from northeast Asia.

On the other side, Japanese scholars have described an Okhotsk Sea Culture of late-Jomon or early post-Jomon age, between one and two thousand years old, which shows a remarkable affinity with eastern Aleutian-Kodiak Island cultures. Among the many shared traits are the following: circular pit house similar to the Aleut barabara, oval stone lamps and hunter's lamp with ring, grinding stones, stone and ivory labrets, large bone lance heads, toggle harpoon heads (similar to early Aleut and Dorset Eskimo), compound fishhooks, an assortment of chipped stone blades (including men's asymmetrical knife and ulu), points, drills and net sinkers, carved bone needle cases, a variety of bone implements similar to southern Alaska Eskimo-Aleut items, mortuary practices similar to the eastern Aleuts', and art styles with Eskimo patterns (including drawings etched on bone suggestive of kayaks and umiaks), as well as carved sea mammal penis bones (Baba, 1934, 1936, 1939; Chard, 1956b; Dikov, 1965; Kodama, 1948; Kodama and MacCord, 1954; Nakayama, 1933, 1934; Natori, 1948; Oba, 1950a, 1950b, 1955; Torii, 1919, Yonemura, 1950; Bank, 1956a, 1960, 1970). The physical anthropologist Kodama (1947) has described the

Okhotsk type skull as resembling Aleut crania from the upper levels of eastern Aleutian archaeological sites.

It is possible that there was a widespread early Eskimoid cultural base in the northern Bering Sea region, from which a variety of cultural traits flowed southward in both Asia and America. Thus, many of the cultural parallels noted above may derive not from direct contact between the two groups (Okhotsk Eskimoids and Aleut-Koniag peoples), but rather from a common early Eskimo or proto-Eskimo source far removed in time and space from both southern Alaskan and Okhotsk Sea cultures (Bank, 1956a, 1970:4). In any event, such problems raised by archaeologists open up intriguing avenues for research by ethnobotanists. The remainder of this article will describe one of these avenues, which entailed field work in the Aleutians and northern Japan.

*Aconite Poison Whaling and Aleut Plant Lore*

Despite a devastating impact on Aleut culture from Russian and U.S. intrusions, many older Aleuts remembered until recently much of the early native lore about plants and animals that have inhabited their environment. Their ethnobotanical knowledge was the most highly developed of any Eskimo group (Bank, 1953a, 1962b). The Aleutians are blessed with luxuriant vegetation, and the Aleuts used it for food, medicines, manufactures, and poison unknown among the northern Eskimos. Most of what the Aleuts needed was easily accessible in terrestrial habitats near their villages, in the intertidal zone, or on the sea which, in the Aleutians, remains free of ice throughout the winter. It is true there are no trees, but driftwood from both Asia and America is plentiful on the shore.

Of the plants available in their environment, including seaweed, more than 85 species were utilized by the Aleuts. Other Eskimo groups use plants, primarily in manufacturing and for medicine (Oswalt, 1957; Lantis, 1959), but none has the sophistication of the Aleuts in this regard. When a comparison is made between their plant uses and that of other western Alaskan Eskimos, there is correlation in less than 10 percent of the instances where the same plant genera are found in both areas. A study of Aleut and Ainu ethnobotanical lore shows a correlation of 55 percent (Bank, 1962b, 1962c). The body of practices and beliefs surrounding plants was more highly developed among the Ainu, but in some instances the similarity between Aleut and Ainu plant lore is remarkable: the most striking example is the custom of killing whales with aconite poison.

Aconite is a toxic alkaloid extracted from the roots of *Aconitum*, a plant of circumpolar distribution. It was formerly used as a powerful whale

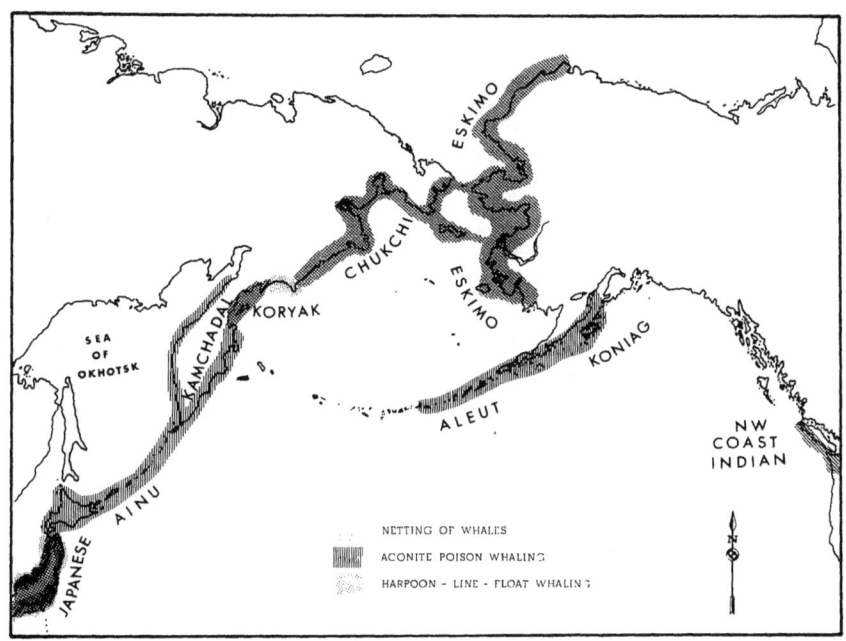

Figure 11. North Pacific-Bering Sea region. The distribution of prehistoric whaling methods is shown (following Heizer, 1943).

poison by the Ainu, Kamchadals, eastern Aleuts and the Koniags of southern Alaska (Fig. 11). North of Kamchatka and the Aleutian-Kodiak area, in contrast, whales were hunted by netting and the use of harpoon, line and float, a technique that depends upon the death of the whale through exhaustion (Heizer, 1943). In Asia, aconite was employed in war and for killing bears and sea lion, as well as in whaling. The Aleuts and Koniags used it almost exclusively in whale hunting. Juice obtained from the roots of *Aconitum* was mixed with animal fat, or frequently with fat from human corpses, and the concoction was smeared on the tip of the obsidian lance head used in whaling. Apparently the trait was not widespread in the Aleutians, because the Atkan and Attuan Aleuts did not know of it. Heizer believes that the poisoning of whales was never practiced among the Chukchi or in Eskimo territory north of the Aleutians (op. cit., p. 447). He writes: "... we cannot escape the conclusion that the presence of Aleutian Island-Kodiak poisoned lance whaling is attributable to introduction from the Kamchatka region, where it originated in connection with the use of aconite poison" (p. 450). And again: "... poison-lance whaling ... can be demonstrated to have entered the New World from Asia via the Aleutian Island chain" (p. 453). Chard (1956a, 1956b) disagrees but is unable to offer a convincing alternative explanation for the presence of poison-lance whaling in the new world.

There is, however, a possible botanical reason for the failure of aconite poison whaling to spread north in Alaska and Asia. Heizer considers it briefly, then puts it aside for lack of evidence. Nevertheless, botanists recognize that many plant genera, which are poisonous in southerly latitudes, lose their toxicity farther north. Thus, it is possible that not all species and races of *Aconitum* possess a sufficiently high alkaloid content, or even the right alkaloid, to be deadly. I once conducted a rough sort of test with specimens of *Aconitum* from different localities and was rewarded with some interesting (but inconclusive) results. In northern Japan, when a freshly cut root of *Aconitum* is applied lightly to the tip of the tongue, there is an immediate numbing sensation. The same experiment carried out in the eastern Aleutians produced similar results. Plants collected farther north on the Alaska mainland, however, produced no reaction at all.

There is yet another explanation, much better documented, for the particular distribution of aconite-poison whaling in the New World. It refers to extensive voyages known to have been undertaken in historical times by the Aleuts and Kodiak Islanders.

*Aleut-Koniag Voyages in Asia*

After 1741 Aleut hunters were forced to undertake long voyages to hunt fur seal and sea otter for their Russian overlords. They regularly paddled to the Pribilofs after the colony was established there, and on several occasions they accompanied Russian vessels as far south as California. Many of us are familiar with such exploits through reading accounts of the early history of Alaska. However, very little attention has been given to the large number of historical documents in Russia that tell of Aleut visits to Asia in the late eighteenth century, when the *Promishleniki* (Russian fur hunters) took hostages, including women and children, among the Aleuts and Koniags and transported them to the Kuriles. The purpose was to establish colonies of fur hunters. Later, when the practice of kidnapping became illegal, the Russian fur company "hired" Aleut and Koniag hunters of sea otters for long-term service in Asiatic waters.

There are other historical documents, mostly in Japanese, which refer to possible Aleut voyages to Asia prior to 1741. Japanese diaries written in the Edo Period, around 1605, contain scattered references to *"Kurumuse,"* or "strangers," who were supposed to live north of Yezo (Hokkaido) and who, unlike the Ainu, had skin boats and skin clothing, hunted sea otters and lived underground. However, the descriptions are based mostly on vague rumors (Baba, 1943; Matsumiya, 1631; Torii (1919). In 1623, Father Girolame de Angelis wrote of his trip to Yezo and of his conversation with the Japanese Duke of Matsumme, governor of Yezo, who spoke of the non-Ainu peoples to the north, saying,

> Yezo does not produce the sea otter; the Ainu natives go over to three islands (probably Kunashiri, Iturup and Urupp in the Kuriles) to buy skins. Inhabitants of these islands have no beard, and they speak quite a different language from that of the Ainu. Those who buy the skins are from eastern Yezo; the western Yezo Ainu do not know about the sea otter. (Kodama, 1941; Okamota, 1933.)

It is doubtful that the Kamchadals, with their relatively clumsy boats, could have made the long sea voyage to the southern Kuriles. Other references to the "Kurumuse" with skin boats and skin clothing (Arai, 1721) suggest an Eskimoid people. The Kurumuse may have been a remnant population, possibly of the Okhotsk Culture, derived from the early arctic Eskimoid substratum hypothesized previously, who survived until relatively recent times in the Kuriles. There is no concrete evidence that they were actually Aleuts.

There is no doubt, however, that the Russians were visiting Shumshir Island in the Kuriles as early as 1711 (Arai, 1721). Fur operations continued in the Okhotsk Sea region after the discovery of the Aleutians in 1741, and probably some of the Aleuts who were kidnapped for service in Kamchatka ultimately reached the Kuriles. The best evidence available from Japanese sources for the assumption that the Aleuts were already well settled in the islands by 1800 comes from Shigemori Kondo (1804) and others who visited the Kuriles (Kushihara, 1793; Matsumae, 1781). Kondo gives an interesting account of the non-Ainu inhabitants (Kurumuse) he observed on Urupp Island:

> This land is located east of Etrov ... the natives were inhabitants of Kurumuse ... all of them carry rings at their noses. One islander named Kimo-hei ... came to Urupp and made the canoe of his homeland. It was made of sea lion skin, like a bag in which he put wooden poles as ribs ... and he filled every space around the seat, rowing at right and left ... the natives call the canoe *'Tore-tó chipp'*, while the Russian name is *'Baidare'*. One day the Ainu chief of Kunashiri Island said he had seen the canoe of Kurumuse; they covered a small boat with skin and the rower sat in a seat. He put a stone in the bottom and closed the seat place tightly so the canoe with the rower could meet the big waves as if a bird.

In 1813 a Japanese fishing vessel was caught in a storm off southern Kyushu and was carried by ocean currents to the middle Kuriles where it went aground. Three of the crew survived. During their subsequent travels in the Islands, they saw and sketched various aspects of Kurilean native life, including women with tatoos on face and hands, natives wearing nose pins, and several skin boats. Their adventures and drawings appear in five published volumes by Chicanobu Kawakami (1815). There can be little doubt that the drawings depict people other than Ainu who were either Aleuts or had been in long contact with Aleuts.

The Russian-American Fur Company began extending its operations in Kurile waters in 1826—five years earlier than the date of official permission (Baba, 1943; Stejneger, 1899)—and shortly thereafter groups of eastern Aleuts and Koniags were settled at Urupp and Shumshir Islands. By 1871, according to Japanese governmental reports (1871-75), the two largest villages on the islands contained thirty-three and fifty-nine Aleuts, including women and children. Others were scattered in fewer numbers elsewhere. The government documents describe the immigrants as living in pit houses, wearing seal intestine clothing and boots (mukluks), using bone and iron harpoon heads, wearing lip tattoos and labrets, and in general following a life style only slightly modified from the one they had known in the Aleutians. After 1875, the Russians removed all Aleuts from Japanese territory, probably by taking them to Kamchatka and the Kommandorskis.

Apparently the Aleuts and Koniags traveled extensively in the Kuriles, especially at first, moving about in hunting brigades under the watchful eyes of the Russians. They frequently came into contact with the Ainu, who must have been impressed with the Aleuts' ability to paddle their skin boats great distances in all kinds of weather. On the other hand, we can assume the American natives were also impressed with some Ainu customs and observed them carefully. Undoubtedly, in time, groups of Aleuts and Koniags were allowed to return to their homeland aboard Russian vessels. Certainly they must have carried back information learned from the Ainu, particularly any hunting techniques and associated lore that would be useful to their own people. Some Ainu customs, such as those pertaining to edible, medicinal and poisonous plants, probably were adopted quickly by the subsistence-conscious Aleuts. Obviously, they would be much intrigued with the idea of using aconite poison to kill whales more efficiently.

Thus, it seems reasonable to believe that aconite-poison whaling is a recent cultural transfer from Asia to America in historical, not prehistoric, times. It is most likely that it was first introduced at Kodiak by sea otter hunters in the employ of Russain fur merchants. It is significant that the distribution of the practice in the New World is limited to an area extending from the eastern half of the Aleutian chain to Kodiak Island, since this is precisely where the Russians obtained the sea otter hunters who were taken to the Kuriles. The largest number came from Kodiak and presumably returned there after their service in Asia. This explains why the center of aconite-poison whaling in America, i.e., where it was practiced most intensively, was east of Unalaska. The easternmost Aleuts, but more particularly the Koniags, were already familiar with obsidian lance-head whaling which depended upon mortally wounding the whale and waiting for it to drift ashore. They would have been quick to see the advantages offered by the poison method, and probably the Russians encouraged its use as a means of extending the profitable whaling activities. In 1832, the Russian fur company hired Kodiak Islanders to teach whaling methods to the Andreanov Aleuts at Atka and Adak (Veniamenov, 1840), but it was too late for the practice to spread much farther. By 1850, modern whaling techniques were already beginning to supplant the native methods. Thus, there was no opportunity for the western Aleuts, Bering Sea Eskimos and southeastern Alaskan whalers to learn the Asiatic uses of aconite poison.

## Summary

The interaction of man with his environment is quite obviously a fundamental relationship. Nevertheless, in archaeology, as Butzer observes, "... the complex interactive relationships between culture and environment have not ever been explicitly formulated, let alone explored ... particularly ..,. regarding cultural adaptations to new or changing environments..." (1975: 108-109). J. Desmond Clark (1960:308) has added:

> ... it is essential that the environment and ecological setting of culture ... be established as accurately as possible, for without this knowledge, we can hardly begin to interpret the cultural evidence ... It is now fully apparent that unless there is teamwork with other disciplines, we cannot hope to extract more than a fraction of the evidence that in many instances our sites could yield.

Our ethnobotanical studies in the Aleutians are an attempt to provide the kinds of data that Butzer and Clark find lacking in archaeology. Specifically, we have shown that ethnobotanical findings are useful for identifying archaeological sites, establishing relative chronologies, and explaining some of the peculiarities of Aleut culture. In a broader perspective, they advance the understanding of the ecological factors that have affected both biological and cultural succession in the Aleutians. It is to be hoped that our studies will also provide ecological insights of use to archaeologists elsewhere.

## Footnotes

1. It is gratifying to note that these volumes, dedicated to James B. Griffin, contain articles dealing specifically with ethnobotany. Throughout his tenure as Director of Michigan's Anthropology Museum, Jimmy Griffin supported the Museum's Laboratory of Ethnobotany. He frequently urged his students in archaeology to become familiar with the unique facilities of the Laboratory and to learn ethnobotanical techniques. Those who came to him from botany were encouraged to pursue their cross-disciplinary interests by taking cognate studies in anthropology, so that they might engage themselves professionally in both fields.

2. This is a distinction aimed at separating ethnobotany from economic botany. In practice, ethnobotanical studies focus primarily on the interrelationships of plants and primitive man in the sense that "primitive" denotes a lack of a written language and therefore the preservation of traditions essentially by oral means, whereas economic botany is concerned with modern concepts of the science of plants and their uses. Obviously the boundary between the two is obscure, and there is much overlap.

3. Field work in the Aleutians was carried out under the auspices of the University of Michigan (1948-54), the American Institute for Exploration, and Western Michigan University (1969-74), with financial and logistical support from the U.S. Office of Naval Research, Michigan Memorial Phoenix Project, American Academy of Arts and Sciences, Wenner-Gren Foundation for Anthropological Research, Kalamazoo Civic Fund, Grand Rapids Museum Association, Society of the Sigma Xi, the Explorers Club, U.S. Coast Guard, and Standard Oil Company of California.

4. Portions of the Amaknak-D site were excavated by us in 1951, 1954 and 1971, and Fred Hadleigh-West studied part of the Eider Point mound in 1954. A radiocarbon date of $1880 \pm 200$ years B.P. comes from charcoal removed from a stratum several feet above the bottom of the Amaknak midden (specimen M-676, H. R. Crane and J. B. Griffin, 1959b:173).

5. Formerly designated *Conioselinum gmelini* and *Ligusticum hultenii*; terminology follows that of Hultén (1968).

6. We are currently experimenting with high altitude color photography via satellite through the cooperation of the Government's EROS Program. Preliminary results indicate that at least the larger village sites can be identified.

## References Cited

Anderson, S. T., and T. P. Bank II.
   1952    Pollen and radiocarbon studies of Aleutian soil profiles. Science 116:84-86.

Arai, H.
   1721    Yezo-shi (Description of Yezo): manuscript copy in the Hakodate Museum, Japan (in Japanese).

Baba, O.
   1934    Archaeological investigations in the Shimushu Islands. Journal Anthropological Society of Tokyo 49:39-62 (in Japanese).

   1936    A second archaeological investigation at Shimshir, an island in the Kuriles. Jour. Anthro. Soc., Tokyo 51:91-115 (in Japanese).

   1939    The northern Kuriles from the viewpoint of archaeology. Jinruigaku Senshigaku Koza, Tokyo 10, 11 (in Japanese).

   1943    The Aleuts in the Kuriles, I. Japanese Journal of Ethnology 1: 773-94 (in Japanese).

Bank, T. P. II.
1952a  A preliminary account of The University of Michigan Aleutian expedition, 1950. Asa Gray Bulletin, N.S. 1:211-18.
1952b  Botanical and ethnobotanical studies in the Aleutian Islands, I. Aleutian vegetation and Aleut culture. Papers of the Michigan Academy of Science Arts & Letters 37:3-30.
1953a  Botanical and ethnobotanical studies in the Aleutian Islands, II. Health and medical lore of the Aleuts. Papers of the Michigan Academy of Science Arts & Letters, 38:415-36.
1953b  Ecology of prehistoric Aleutian village sites. Ecology 34:342-64.
1953c  Biological succession in the Aleutians. Pacific Science, 4:493-503.
1953d  Cultural succession in the Aleutians. American Antiquity 19:40-49.
1954  Report of the archaeological expedition to Unalaska, 1954. Field Reports no. 3, Inst. Regional Exploration, Ann Arbor.
1956a  Prehistoric cultural exchanges between Asia and Alaska as viewed from northern Japan. Paper read at the Seventh Alaska Science Conference, Juneau (mimeographed distribution).
1956b  Aleut-Koniag voyages to Kamchatka and the Kuriles in historical times. Paper read at the Seventh Alaska Science Conference, Juneau (mimeographed distribution; published in Field Reports, no. 4, Amer. Inst. Exploration, Chicago, 1957, pp. 1-33).
1958  The Aleuts. Scientific American 199:112-20.
1960  Contemporary Ainu. Explorers Journal 38:12-24.
1962a  Recommendations. Report of the Subcommittee on Ethnobotany. Proceedings, 9th Pacific Sci. Cong., Bangkok, Thailand 4:21-23.
1962b  Medicinal plant lore of the Aleut. Proceedings, 9th Pacific Sci. Cong., Bangkok, Thailand 4:281-84 (abstract only).
1962c  Ethnobotany of northern peoples and the problem of cultural drift. Proceedings, 9th Pacific Sci. Cong., Bangkok, Thailand 4:279-80 (abstract only).
1963  Past ages of Unalaska. Explorers Journal 41:32-42.
1970  The Sea of Okhotsk Eskimoids. Reprint Series 4. American Institute for Exploration, Kalamazoo, Michigan.
1972a  Recent archaeological finds relating to paelo-human occupation of the Bering landbridge. Paper read at the Arctic and Mountain Environments Symposium, Glaciological and Arctic Sciences Institute. Mich. State Univ., East Lansing (published in Abstracts of the Symposium, pp. 10-11).
1972b  Results of archaeological reconnaissance at Unalaska, Akutan, Akun and Tigalda Islands in the Aleutians. Field Reports 12. American Institute for Exploration, Kalamazoo, Michigan.

1973 Aleutian-Bering Sea institutes and research program, II. Field Reports 13. American Institute for Exploration, Kalamazoo, Mich.

1975 Additional archaeological sites in the Aleutian Islands. Reports to the Bureau of Land Management and the Alaska Department of Natural Resources, Anchorage (mimeographed distribution).

Bank, T. P. II, A. C. Spaulding, H. A. Miller and Janet F. Bank.

1950 The University of Michigan Expedition to the Aleutian Islands, 1948-49. Report to the Office of Naval Research. Botanical Gardens, Univ. of Mich., Ann Arbor (mimeographed).

Bank, T. P. II and R. Williams.

1975 Urgently needed research on Aleut culture. International Committee on Urgent Anthropological and Ethnological Research, Bulletin 17: 11-30.

Bartlett, H. H.

1951 Radiocarbon datability of peat, marl, caliche, and archaeological materials. Science 114:55-56.

Birket-Smith, K. and F. de Laguna.

1938 The Eyak Indians of the Copper River Delta, Alaska. Hist. Filol. Medd. Udgivne, Dansk Vid. Sels., Copenhagen.

Black, R. F. and W. S. Laughlin.

1964 Anangula: a geologic interpretation of the oldest archaeological site in the Aleutians. Science 143:1321-22.

Butzer, K. W.

1975 The ecological approach to archaeology: are we really trying? American Antiquity 40:106-11.

Chard, C. S.

1956a Northwest Coast-Northeast Asiatic similarities: a new hypothesis. Paper read at the International Congress of Americanists, Philadelphia (manuscript).

1956b Chronology and culture succession in the northern Kuriles. American Antiquity 21:287-92.

Clark, J. D.

1960 Human ecology during the Pleistocene and later times in Africa south of the Sahara. Current Anthropology 1:307-24.

Collins, H. B.

1937 Archaeology of St. Lawrence Island, Alaska. Smithsonian Miscellaneous Collection 96:375-84.

1940 Outline of Eskimo prehistory. Smithsonian Miscellaneous Collection 100:533-92.

1964 The Arctic and Subartic. Item in: J.D. Jennings and E. Norbeck (eds.), Prehistoric man in the New World. Chicago: Univ. Chicago Press, pp. 84-114.

Coxe, W.
1803  Account of the Russian discoveries between Asia and America. London.
Crane, H. R. and J. B. Griffin.
1959a  University of Michigan radiocarbon dates, III. Science 128: 1117-23.
1959b  University of Michigan radiocarbon dates, IV. American Journal of Science Radiocarbon Supplement 1:173-98.
Crawford, O. G. S.
1923  Air survey and archaeology. Geographical Journal of the Royal Geographical Society, London.
Dall, W. H.
1877  On the succession of shell-heaps in the Aleutian Islands. Item *in:* Tribes of the extreme Northwest. Contributions to North American Ethnology 1:41-91. U.S. Geological Survey, Washington, D.C.
Deetz, J. F.
1970  Archaeology as a social science. Current Directions in Anthropology 3 (pt. 2):115-25.
Dikov, N. N.
1965  The stone age of Kamchatka and the Chukchi Peninsula in the light of new archaeological data. Arctic Anthropology 3:10-25.
Drucker, P.
1943  Archaeological survey of the northern Northwest Coast. Bureau American Ethnology, Bulletin 113:17-142.
Faegri, K. and J. Iversen.
1950  Textbook of modern pollen analysis. Copenhagen: E. Munksgaard (2nd ed. 1964).
1965  Field techniques (for collecting pollen bearing samples). Item *in*: B. Kummel and D. Raup (eds.), Handbook of paleontological techniques. San Francisco: W. H. Freeman, pp. 482-94.
Fox, C.
1923  Archaeology of the Cambridge region. Cambridge: Cambridge Univ. Press, (re-issued 1948).
Golder, F. A.
1922, 1925  Bering's voyages. 2 vols. New York: American Geographical Society.
Griffin, J. W.
1948  Green mound, a chronological yardstick. The Florida Naturalist 22:1-8.
Hallam, S. J.
1964  Villages in Roman Britain: some evidence. Antiquaries Journal 44:19-32.

Heizer, R. F.
 1943 Aconite poison whaling in Asia and America: an Aleutian transfer to the New World. Anthropological Papers 24. Bureau of American Ethnology, Bulletin 133:415-68.
 1959 The archaeologist at work: New York: Harper and Row.
 (ed.)

Heusser, C. J.
 1952 Pollen profiles from southeastern Alaska. Ecological Monographs 22:331-52.

Hopkins, D. M. (ed.)
 1967 The Bering landbridge. Palo Alto: Stanford Univ. Press.

Hrdlička, A.
 1937 Man and plants in Alaska. Science 86:559-60.
 1945 The Aleutian and Commander Islands and their inhabitants. Wistar Institute of Anatomy and Biology, Philadelphia.

Hultén, E.
 1937 Flora of the Aleutian Islands. Bokforlags Aktiebolaget Thule, Stockholm.
 1968 Flora of Alaska and neighboring territories. Palo Alto: Stanford Univ. Press.

Japanese Government
 1871- Documents relating to the exchange agreements between Japan
 1875 and Russia regarding the Kuriles and Saghalin Island. Copies in the Hakodate Museum, Japan (in Japanese).

Jochelson, W.
 1925 Archaeological investigations in the Aleutian Islands. Carnegie Institution of Washington Publication No. 367, Washington, D.C.
 1933 History, ethnology and anthropology of the Aleut. Carnegie Institution of Washington Publication No. 432, Washington, D.C.

Jones, V. H.
 1941 The nature and status of ethnobotany. Chronica Botanica 6: 219-21.

Kawakami, C.
 1815 Hokusai Kyoten (Story of wrecked ship in the North Sea). Manuscript copy in the Hakodate Museum, Japan (in Japanese).

Kodama, S.
 1941 On the "Relatione del Regno die Iezo" by de Angelis. Studies of the Research Institute for Northern Cultures, Sapporo, Japan 4:201-96 (in Japanese).
 1947 Peoples of the Moyoro shell heap. New Crinics, Sapporo, Japan 2:1-7 (in Japanese).

1948 Moyoro shell heap. Monograph of the Research Assoc. for Prehistoric Culture of Hokkaido, Sapporo, Japan (in Japanese).

Kodama, S. and H. A. MacCord.
1954 The Okhotsk Culture, a protohistoric culture of the northeastern Asiatic littoral. Paper read at the 19th annual meeting, Soc. Amer. Archae., New York (manuscript).

Kondo, S.
1804 Henyo Bunkai Suko (Illustration of Japan's frontier). Tokyo (in Japanese).

Kushihara, M.
1793 Stories and proverbs of Yezo. Manuscript copy in the Hakodate Museum, Japan (in Japanese).

Laguna, F. de
1934 The archaeology of Cook Inlet, Alaska. Philadelphia: Univ. Penn. Press.
1947 The prehistory of northern North America as seen from the Yukon. Memoirs of the Soc. Amer. Archae. 12.

Lantis, M.
1959 Folk medicine and hygiene: lower Kuskokwim and Nunivak–Nelson Island Areas. University of Alaska, Anthropological Papers 8:1-75.

Laughlin, W. S.
1951 The Alaska gateway viewed from the Aleutian Islands. Item *in:* W. S. Laughlin (ed.), The physical anthropology of the American Indian. New York: Viking Fund, pp. 98-126.
1963a The earliest Aleuts. University of Alaska, Anthropological Papers 10: 73-91.
1963b Eskimos and Aleuts: their origins and evolution. Science 142: 633-45.
1975 Aleuts: ecosystem, Holocene history and Siberian origin. Science 189:507-15.

Laughlin, W. S. and G. H. Marsh.
1951 A new view of the history of the Aleutian Islands. Arctic 4 75-88.
1954 The lamellar flake manufacturing site on Anangula Island in the Aleutians. American Antiquity 20:27-39.

Laughlin, W. S. and W. G. Reeder.
1962 Revision of Aleutian prehistory. Science 137:856-67.
1966 Studies in Aleutian-Kodiak prehistory, ecology and anthro-
(eds.) pology. Arctic Anthropology 3.

MacCleod, W. D.
1925 Certain mortuary aspects of Northwest Coast culture. American Anthropologist 27:122-48.

Matsumae, H.
  1781    Hakuzan-Hifu. Item *in:* Hokkaido-ski-shiry (materials on the history of Hokkaido). Tokyo (in Japanese).
Matsumae, T.
  1846    Yezo-to-kikan-hochu (notes on wonderful Yezo Island). Manuscript copy in the Hakodate Museum, Japan (in Japanese).
Matsumiya, K.
  1631    Yezo-danpitsuki (story of Yezo). Manuscript copy in the Hakodate Museum, Japan (in Japanese).
McCartney, A. P.
  1973    Archaeological sites in the Aleutians. Preliminary report, University of Arkansas (manuscript).
Nakayama, E.
  1933    Excavation of pit dwelling sites of Ust-Kamchatka on the eastern coast of the Kamchatka Peninsula. Journal of Anthropological Society of Tokyo, Japan 48:63-72 (in Japanese).
  1934    Neolithic remains from the western coast of the Kamchatka Peninsula. Journal of the Anthropological Society Tokyo, Japan 49:375-88 (in Japanese).
Natori, T.
  1948    Moyoro shell-mound and archaeology. Hopposhuppanshya, Sapporo (in Japanese).
Oba, T.
  1950a   The discovery of two cultural spheres in the Okhotsk Bay region. The Stone Age, Tokyo 2:46-54 (in Japanese).
  1950b   Concerning bone and horn objects found in the Moyoro kitchen midden. Kokoguku-zasshi, Sapporo 36:25-29 (in Japanese).
  1955    On the bone implements of the Moyoro shell mound at Abashiri. Studies of the Research Institute for Northern Cultures, Sapporo, Japan 10:173-249 (in Japanese).
Okamota, R.
  1933    The first Europeans who came to Yezo. Minjo-chiri, Tokyo (in Japanese).
Oswalt, W. H.
  1957    A western Eskimo ethnobotany. University of Alaska Anthropological Papers, 6:17-36.
Petrof, I.
  1884    Report on the population, industries and resources of Alaska. U.S. Census Office, Washington, D.C.
Quimby, G. I.
  1946    Toggle harpoon heads from the Aleutian Islands. Fieldiana: Anthropology 36, Chicago Nat. Hist. Museum, pp. 15-23.
Riley, D. N.
  1946    The technique of air archaeology. Archaeology Journal, London.

Spaulding, A. C.
1962 Archaeological investigations on Agattu, Aleutian Islands. University of Michigan, Museum of Anthropology, Anthropological Papers No. 18.

Steller, G. W.
1774 Beschreibung von dem lande Kamtschatka. Frankfort and Leipzig.

Stejneger, L.
1899 The Asiatic fur-seal islands and fur-seal industry. U.S. Govt. Print. Office, Washington, D.C.

Torii, R.
1919 Les Ainou des Isles Kouriles. Journal of the College of Science, Tokyo Imperial Univ., Tokyo 42 (1).

Turner, C. G. II.
1970 Archaeological reconnaissance of Amchitka Island, Alaska. Arctic Anthropology 7:118-28.
1972 Preliminary report on archaeological excavations at Akun Island. Tempe: Arizona State Univ. (mimeographed).

Veniamenov, I.
1840 Zapiski ob ostravakh Unalaškinskago Otděla (Notes on the islands of the Unalaska Division), 3 vols. St. Petersburg: Russia.

Waxell, S.
1952 The American expedition. Hodge; London. (reprinted ed.)

Weyer, E. M. Jr.
1929 An Aleutian burial. The American Museum of Natural History, Anthropological Papers 31 (pt. 3):219-38.
1930 Archaeological material from the village site at Hot Springs, Port Moller, Alaska. The American Museum of Natural History, Anthropological Papers 31 (pt. 4):239-79.

Yarnell, R. A.
1964 Aboriginal relationship between culture and plant life in the Upper Great Lakes region. University of Michigan, Museum of Anthropology, Anthropological Papers No. 23.
1965 Implications of distinctive flora on Pueblo ruins. American Anthropologist 67:662-74.

Yonemura, K.
1950 Moyoro shell-mound. Abashiri Municipal Museum, Hokkaido, Japan (in Japanese with English summary).

Zeiner, H. M.
1945 A botanical survey of Angel Mound site. American Journal of Botany 33:83-90.

# OSTEOLOGICAL EVIDENCE FOR THE IDENTIFICATION OF PRE-CONTACT KARANKAWA

*Richard G. Wilkinson*
State University of New York at Albany

One goal of skeletal analysis of prehistoric populations is the identification of populations ancestral to those encountered in later times. Such identification allows inferences on a number of time-related phenomena, notably adaptive change, both biological and cultural. The identification of prehistoric populations may also yield information on the origins of the descendent population and those related to it. Reasonable identification of such groups is usually difficult and often impossible because of such factors as lack of occupational continuity in a particular area and the extermination of the indigenous population prior to the collection of ethnographic, linguistic or biological data. The problems are often more serious from the biological standpoint, because osteological evidence is typically insufficient for statistically significant determinations, due to small sample sizes and morphological variability within populations. The validity of attempts to partition American Indian skeletal series into sub-racial varieties (Neumann, 1952) has been questioned from a statistical standpoint (Long, 1966; Wilkinson, 1971). These criticisms are based only on the metric features said to be characteristic of the varieties, and it must be noted that the varieties were established by Neumann on the basis of non-metric criteria as well. It therefore may well be the case that important populational criteria can be established, and meaningful subdivisions created, even if metric analysis fails to confirm the proposed varieties.

A good example of some of the problems encountered in skeletal studies is provided by Robbins and Neumann (1972) who have identified skeletal material from the Fort Ancient aspect as ancestral to the historic Shawnee in southern Ohio and northern Kentucky. The sample size of the Fort Ancient material is adequate, but the subsequent tribal identification is based on a very small Shawnee series, as well as inferences on the temporal and spatial continuity of the Shawnee. Information on temporal-spatial associations of pre-contact and supposedly related historic populations is perhaps the most valuable data in making pre-contact tribal identification. Data such as these have been used by Griffin (1937) to identify the Oneota aspect in Wisconsin and Iowa as Chiwere Sioux. Some of the difficulties encountered in dealing with early historic accounts of tribal designations was also well illustrated by Griffin in a paper dealing with the Tutelo and Mohetan (Griffin, 1942).

Keeping in mind the problems enumerated above, in this paper I will present evidence for the tribal identification of a number of pre- and post-contact skeletal series from the Texas coast. The problem of tribal identification is somewhat simpler in this region than others, because the number of historic tribes is small, and the time depth of the prehistoric material is not great. The impetus for this study was provided by an opportunity given me to analyze a small skeletal series recently excavated by an archaeological team from Rice University. The site, known as Shell Point (41BZ2), yielded skeletal material from a minimum of nine individuals (Hole and Wilkinson, 1973).

There are a number of sites in the same general area, the locations of which are indicated on the map (Fig. 1). Perhaps the best known of these sites is Oso, whose skeletal material has been discussed by several authors (Woodbury and Woodbury, 1935; Woodbury, 1937; Goldstein, 1957). This series was also used by Neumann (1952) as a type series for the establishment of his Otamid variety. The site is identified as a Karankawa settlement by both Woodbury and Neumann (ibid.). A second site, Caplen, is located north of Galveston (Woodbury, 1937; Campbell, 1947, 1957), and is identified as Atakapa by Woodbury (1937:9) on the basis of the material culture. The Jamaica Beach site, south of Galveston on Galveston Island (Aten, 1965; Aten et al., 1971) I believe to have seen Karankawa, for reasons discussed below. The Doering and Kobs sites (Newman, 1953) are located about sixteen miles west of Houston. Newman sees similarities between the skeletal material from the Doering site and that from the Caplen site, and he associates the Kobs site with the Oso site (ibid:265), suggesting the presence of Atakapa and Karankawa, respectively.

Since the Texas coast was occupied by the Karankawa and Atakapa, these two groups would be the most likely referent tribal populations. A third group, the Tonkawa, bordered the Karankawa to the west. The cultural affiliations of the Tonkawa are clearly with the Plains (Wolff, 1969), while both the Atakapa and Karankawa had adapted to coastal hunting and gathering (Schaedel, 1949; Swanton, 1946). Hasskarl (1962) prefers a more marginal Plains affiliation for the Tonkawa than Wolff,

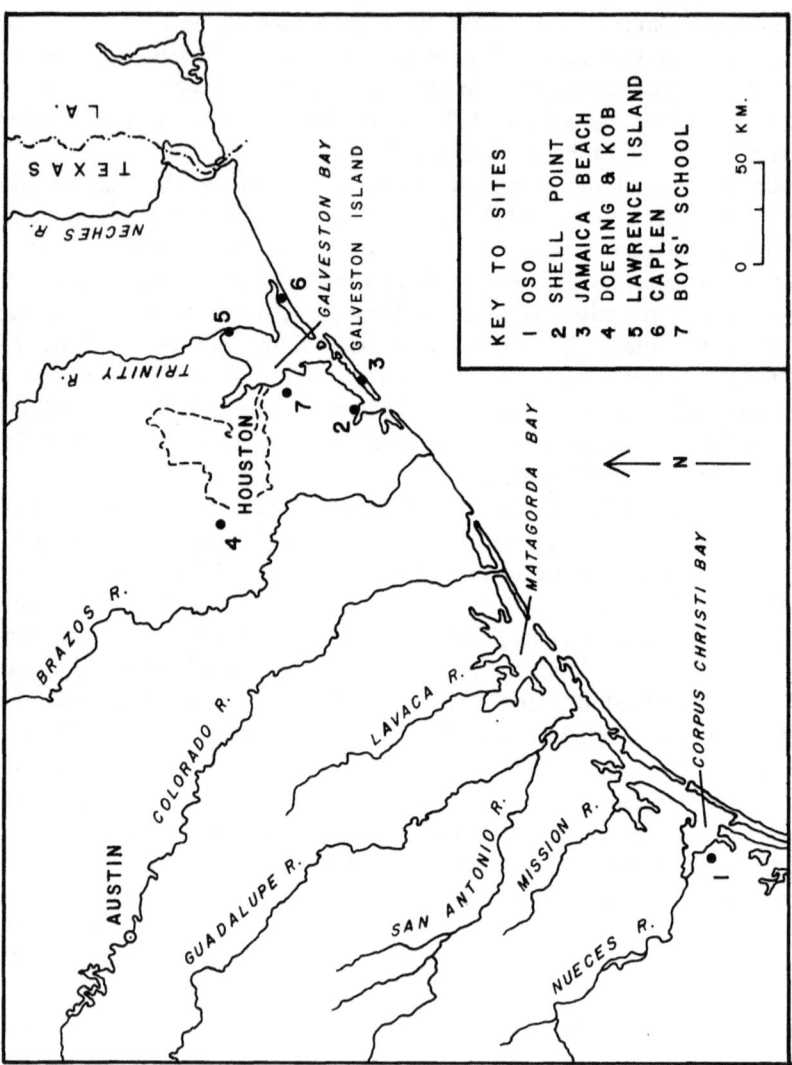

Figure 1. Texas Gulf Coast sites discussed in text.

noting characteristics linking them to foraging groups of southern Texas. The Tonkawa and Karankawa came together briefly in the mid-nineteenth century (Gatchet, 1891:101), presumably as a result of internal tribal disruption. The association of the Tonkawa with the Plains is largely irrelevant to our problem, however, since we are concerned with pre-contact groups. The pre-Plains activities of the Tonkawa are not well known, although we do know that they were not a coastally adapted group.

The main Karankawa center was in the Matagorda Bay area, while the Atakapa were further north, extending into the Louisiana coast area. A region of territorial overlap between the Karankawa and Atakapa occurred in the vicinity of Galveston. As late as 1824 Karankawa were within fifteen miles of the Shell Point site, and fifteen of them were killed on the banks of Jones Creek in that year (Gatchet, 1891:95). As a result of this overlap, the proto-historic and early historic skeletal material from the Galveston-Houston area cannot be readily assigned to one of these two groups. Fortunately, sufficient archaeological and ethnohistorical evidence exists to make tribal designations possible with an acceptable degree of certainty.

The skeletal material from the Shell Point site consists of nine individuals, including four males, two females and three children, one of whom appears to be a male. Five of the skeletons were found buried together and may represent a food foraging party caught in a winter storm (Hole and Wilkinson, 1973). Of special interest for the purposes of tribal identification is the overall morphology of the skeletal material. The skeletal series is homogeneous in its morphology, and three aspects are especially pertinent to the present study. First, the Shell Point series shows very strong sexual dimorphism. The impact of the dimorphism is somewhat limited, however, because of the small female sample. The two females were both in the over-forty age category at death, and are quite gracile. The males, on the other hand, are all robust, with the usual sex-determining characteristics being very marked. The extent of sexual dimorphism can be indicated by expressing the female measurements as a percentage of the male measurements. This comparison results in a range in dimorphism of 2.7 to 31.7 percent in the cranio-facial skeleton, and 20.7 to 47.1 percent in the post-cranial skeleton. These values are obviously tentative because of the small sample size, but the fact remains that this small group exhibits very marked sexual dimorphism. The dimorphism is primarily a factor of male robusticity. This is of some importance, because the early descriptions of living Karankawa stress the physiques of the males.

The overall morphology of the skulls of these few individuals is very distinctive, and the same general shape is seen in both sexes, despite differences in robusticity. The marked homogeneity alluded to above is perhaps most evident in the area of skull shape, and allows a description of the "typical" Shell Point skull. The skulls are long, narrow and high, and are further characterized by marked parietal bossing and supramastoid constriction, giving the skulls a pinched-in, vaulted appearance when viewed from the rear (Fig. 2). The male mandibles show a large, bilateral chin, thick bodies with marked lateral swelling at the level of the second molars, and broad, nearly vertical ascending rami. The female mandibles are much smaller, with pointed chins and less vertical rami. The dimorphism in the mandibles was so marked that the sex of an eleven-year-old was determined with considerable certainty, for the jaw was identical to those of the adult males, except for the size differential.

A third morphological feature of this skeletal series is the estimated stature. Stature estimates were based on the formulae of Trotter and Gleser (1958), using femoral and tibial measurements. The results indicate that the measureable males ranged in stature from 5'5" to 5'11", with a mean of 5'9". This is tall for American Indians, easily surpassing the values of six Middle and Late Woodland (A.D. 0-1200) series from the Midwest, which had stature estimates ranging from 5'4½" to 5'6½" (Wilkinson, 1971). The Shell Point males are also taller than northern groups such as the Arikara (Bass, Evans and Jantz, 1971) and a Middle Woodland group from Kansas (Phenice, 1969). Hrdlicka (1938) describes some isolated skeletons from northern Texas and notes the tall stature; the values, using the same formulae as in the present study, range from 5'7" to 5'10", with a mean of just under 5'9". The Shell Point series thus appears to have been as tall as some of the Plains Indians studied by Hrdlicka and considerably taller than many groups of the Eastern Woodlands.

The total morphological pattern which emerges from the Shell Point skeletal material suggests a group with long-headed, tall, muscular men and rather small women. The males are also characterized by their large, square chins. In order to make a tribal identification, we must turn to early descriptions of the living populations in this same general area and also to the skeletal material from other sites in the area.

Considering first the comparative skeletal material, it is clear that the morphology of the Shell Point individuals is not unique, neither is it the only morphological pattern present. The Oso site, to the south on Corpus Christi Bay, is identified as Karankawa. The Oso skulls are described as having well-developed chins and "perpendicular sides" when viewed from the rear (Woodbury and Woodbury, 1935). Neumann's description of his

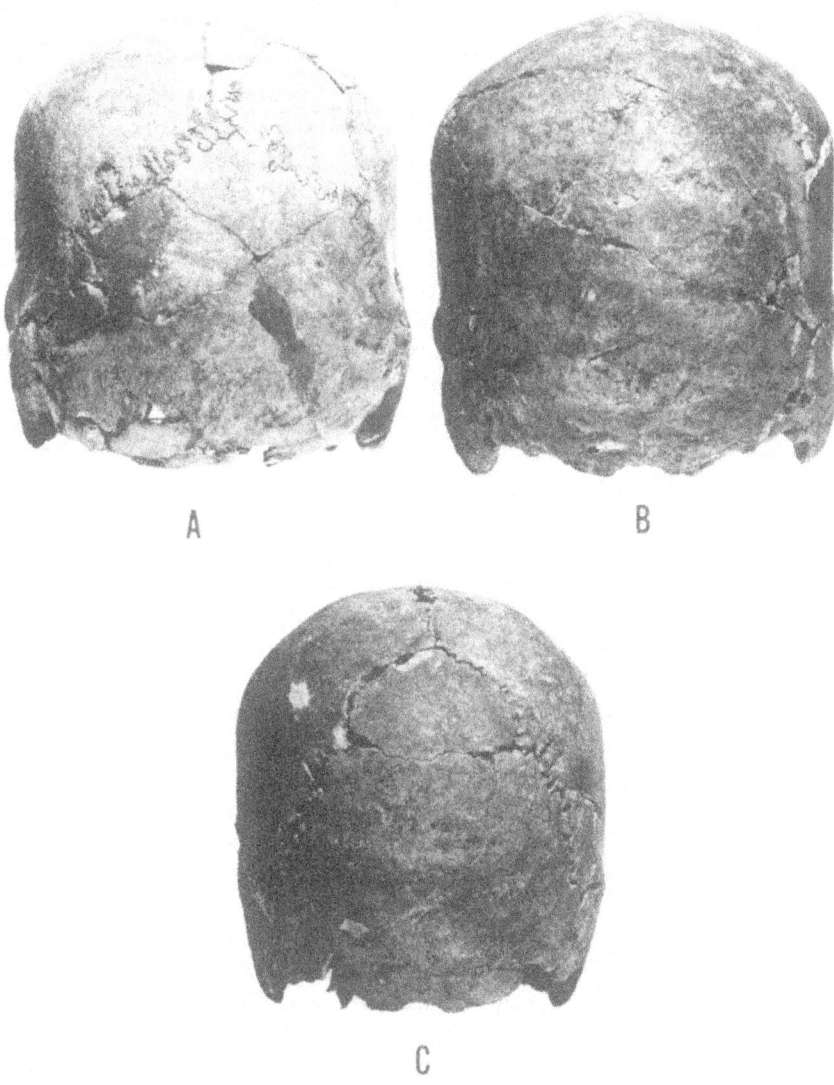

Figure 2. Occipital views of three skulls from the Shell Point site. A and B are males, C is a female.

Otamid variety also includes reference to the dolichocranial, high skulls, the pronounced muscle relief and the massive mandibles with bilateral chins (Neumann, 1952:16).

The cultural material from the Caplen site is said to be very different from that found at the Oso site (Woodbury, 1937), and the site is alleged to be Atakapan. It contains European beads and pottery and is located in the area of the historic Atakapa (Campbell, 1947:283). Woodbury (1937) notes a difference in the cranial indices of the Caplen crania and those from the Oso site. The Caplen crania are considerably more brachycranial than those from Oso; the mean Caplen index is 77.3, and the Oso index is 70.1. The male indices from Shell Point are 72.0, 72.2 and 73.3.

The Jamaica Beach site, located on Galveston Island, yielded the skeletal remains of nineteen individuals (Aten, 1965; Aten et al., 1971). In the earlier report, Aten discusses five of the skulls, and notes the long, narrow, high vaults. I was given an opportunity to examine some of the Jamaica Beach skulls in the collection of the Houston Museum of Natural Science, and with one exception the skulls were long, narrow and high, closely resembling those from the Shell Point site, and presumably those from the Oso site as well. The single exception may be significant. This skull is referred to as Burial D (Aten et al., 1971), and was the only skeleton oriented toward the east. It is also the only brachycranial skull from either the Jamaica Beach or Shell Point sites. Burial D is a female, and I would suggest that she was brought into the group from the outside. The broad skull points to affinities with a population related to the Caplen group, and we may thus have evidence of female exchange between two populations, presumably Karankawa and Atakapa. This single skull could obviously be an extension of the normal variation within the Jamaica Beach population, but the peculiar burial orientation suggests that this individual was considered different by those interring her.

Seven skeletons were recovered from the Doering and Kobs sites, located near the Addicks Reservoir just west of Houston (Newman, 1953). Two males and two females were found at the Doering site, and the Kobs site yielded two females and a male. All seven individuals were adults. Three of the four Doering skulls are described as long-headed, as are all three of the Kobs skulls. The fourth skull from the Doering site has a cranial index of 81.5, which is considerably broader than the Shell Point or Oso material. Newman (ibid:265) associates the Doering skeletal material with that from the Caplen site, and Kobs with Oso, indicating a possible combination of Atakapan and Karankawan elements. The two Doering males have estimated statures of 5'5" and 5'7". These values are less than those of the Shell Point and Oso males and would offer some support for an Atakapan identification of the Doering material. The single Kobs site male has an estimated stature of slightly over 5'9", equal to the Shell Point mean.

A site on Lawrence Island, near the mouth of the Trinity River in Galveston Bay, yielded the remains of five individuals. The skeletal material was examined by Georg Neumann, who noted that "the physical type is not the same as at the Caplen site" (Campbell, 1947:287). Unfortunately, we do not know what these skeletons were similar to, but it is most likely that they were of the Shell Point–Oso–Jamaica Beach variety, since there seem to have been only two distinguishable skull "types" along the Texas coast.

These considerations of gross skeletal morphology suggest that a minimum of two morphologically different populations were located in the Galveston-Houston area of the Texas coast. Since this area was a buffer zone between the historic Karankawa and Atakapa, the protohistoric and historic skeletal material may be assigned to these two groups with reasonable certainty. The question now becomes one of connecting particular sites with tribal groups. Here we must turn to ethnohistoric sources for early descriptions of the physiques of the Texas coast natives.

The first description of Texas coast Indians is that of Alvar Nuñez Cabeza de Vaca, whose incredible seven-year odyssey is described in his journal, first published in 1542 (Hodge, 1907; Nuñez Cabeza de vaca, 1905; 1972). Cabeza de Vaca and three of his men were all that remained of a shipload of Spaniards who traveled the Gulf Coast from Florida to Texas in 1528 and were shipwrecked, probably on Galveston Island, in November of that year. In the next seven years Cabeza de Vaca wandered over much of the Southwest and northern Mexico. His journal provides some descriptions of the Indians he encountered. The island on which Cabeza de Vaca landed was inhabited by two Indian groups; he called one *Han*, the other *Capoques* (Hodge, 1907:54; Nuñez Cabeza de Vaca, 1972:60). The *Capoques* were most likely to have been the Cocos, a northern branch of the Karankawa; Gatchet (1891:98) identifies the *Han* as Atakapa. *Han* may be a synonym for *añ*, the Akokisas word for house, according to Swanton (1946, cited by Newcomb, 1961:317). The Akokisas were the southwestern-most division of the Atakapan-speaking tribes, and they were therefore probably the group in contact with the Cocos. Cabeza de Vaca's first description of the inhabitants of the island was clearly clouded by his psychological state: "Our fright was such that, whether tall or little, it made them appear giants to us" (Nuñez Cabeza de

Vaca, 1972:45). After determining that the Indians were friendly (and in fact they had saved the Spaniards' lives), Cabeza de Vaca simply stated that the natives were "tall and well-formed" (ibid.:53). Indians on the mainland, called *Iguaces* by Cabeza de Vaca, are described as "archers and well built, although not as tall as those we had left behind us, and they have the nipple and lip perforated" (ibid.: 73). The lip and nipple perforation was also noted among the island groups. After noting the presence of two different groups on the island (on the basis of perceived linguistic differences), Cabeza de Vaca does not explain which one of these he lived with. Despite the probable linguistic difference, the two groups were apparently living peacefully together and practicing a common subsistence pattern. A peaceful relationship was also seen among the *"Cocos* and *Mayeye"* by Fray Juan Augustin Morfi in the eighteenth century, and he explained that these groups were "two distinct nations that now live together and whose members have intermarried" (Morfi, 1935:81). The groups described by Morfi were living on the Texas coast between the Colorado and Brazos rivers at the time.

The Karankawa have been extinct for well over a century, and more than 80 years ago Gatchet lamented this fact:

> The appearance of the Karankawa men and women can now only be described from the impression it made on persons who lived in their country, as we have no accurate anthropologic data of measurements to determine it scientifically (Gatchet, 1891:120).

Gatchet's source of information about the Karankawa was Mrs. Alice W. Oliver, who had lived on the Texas coast in the 1840s. Of the physical appearance of the Karankawa people. Mrs. Oliver remembered that "the men were very tall, magnificently formed, with very slender hands and feet . . . the women . . . were generally plain, short of stature, stout and usually disagreeable looking" (ibid.: 80). The difference in stature between the males and females is interesting in view of the dimorphism noted in the Shell Point material. Mrs. Oliver specified that the stature of the males was about 5'10" (ibid.: 120), very close to the Shell Point estimate.

Gatchet also notes that Mrs. Oliver's Karankawa practiced cràdle-board deformation, which resulted in the flattening of the frontal bone (ibid.: 122). No deformation was noted in the Shell Point series, nor is it mentioned as being present in the other Texas coast series. The degree of deformation seen by Mrs. Oliver is unknown, and Gatchet merely says that it was "perceptible" in adults (ibid.:126). Given the lack of evidence for artificial deformation in the extant skeletal series, it would appear that the practice was begun at a relatively late date, that it was a very localized practice, that the skeletal material is not representative of later groups, or that Mrs. Oliver was mistaken. An astute observer of the Indians of Texas, Jean Louis Berlandier, noted in the journal of his travels in Eastern Texas in 1828-29 that "Nowhere among these people have I seen the disfigured head forms so common among the roaming herds of south America" (Berlandier, 1969:51).

Other early settlers and travelers in the Texas coast region were also impressed with the size of the Karankawa males. Gatchet (1891:95) cites an 1854 publication by W. B. Dewees, who stated that the Karankawa were "tall men of a stout magnificent exterior." Newcomb (1961) cites several "old Texans' " reactions to the Karankawa. The "old Texans" were settlers who arrived in east Texas in the 1820s, under the leadership of Stephen F. Austin. Austin's colony occupied the coastal and riverine areas from the Trinity to the Guadalupe rivers, stretching inland past Washington, Texas, on the Brazos River. Later colonies expanded towards the present city of Austin. Noah Smithwick, a Texas Ranger, blacksmith and Indian trader, noted that the Karankawa "were the most savage looking human beings I ever saw. Many of the bucks were six feet in height, with bows and arrows in proportion" (Newcomb, 1961:64). The use of the long bow was also noted by Gatchet (1891:76): "The bows of red cedar conformed to a certain rule of length according to stature, reaching from the foot to the chin or eye." A more interesting version is provided by J. H. Kuykendall, one of Austin's settlers who wrote his reminiscences in 1857:

> In stature they were scarcely surpassed by the Patagonians, the average height of the men being fully six feet, and every warrior's bow when strung, was precisely as long as his person and as useless in the hands of a man of ordinary strength as was the bow of Ulysses in the hands of the suitors (Kuykendall, 1903:324).

Jean Louis Berlandier was a biologist on a scientific and mapping expedition from Mexico City to Texas in 1828 and 1829. He made an extensive study of the Comanche from his headquarters in San Fernando de Bexar (San Antonio) and visited Austin's colony on the Brazos and the Aransas Bay area, where he observed the Karankawa (Berlandier, 1969). Berlandier's journal is noted for its objectivity, and in the introduction, John C. Ewers argues that Berlandier was "one of the most enlightened and most objective amateur ethnographers of the American West during the frontier period" (Berlandier, 1969:22). Berlandier said "the *Carancahueses* are a big people, with robust, well-formed athletic bodies" (ibid.:149) and further noted that the males were very tall, equivalent to 5'10" to 6'1½", although he did not measure them (ibid.:32). Lino Sanchez y Tapia, an artist on the expedition, provided what is reputed to be the only extant illustration of a Karankawa; the watercolor shows a tall, ruggedly muscular male with a long bow (Berlandier, 1969: Plate 15).

John Holland Jenkins came to Texas in 1829 as a boy, and was a member of Austin's "Third Colony," which settled on the Colorado, thirty miles below the present city of Austin (Jenkins, 1958). Jenkins recounted his boyhood in a series of newspaper articles beginning in 1884 and claimed familiarity with three Indian tribes, the Lipan, Tonkawa and Karankawa. The Karankawa made quite an impression on Jenkins: "They might have been giants, for they were most magnificent men in size and strength, seldom below six feet in height" (ibid.:158). Knowing several Indian tribes, Jenkins had some basis for comparison, and noted that the Lipan "were second only to the Karankawa in physical size and strength" (ibid.:161). The early descriptions of the Karankawa are uniform in the area of stature and muscularity, and these descriptions fit the skeletal material very well; unfortunately, head forms were not described.

The Karankawa were driven south along the coast in the mid-1800s by the settlers, and were eventually pushed into Mexico. The last of the Karankawa were exterminated in the 1850s (Gatchet, 1891:115), less than forty years after the arrival of the settlers. Some of the seemingly overzealous descriptions of the Karankawa physique may be due to the settlers' attempts to justify their behavior toward the natives, but it is nevertheless true that the skeletal material indicates very robust, tall males. Also, Berlandier was presumably free of this bias yet his descriptions echo those of the settlers (Berlandier, 1969).

Although descriptions of the physiques of native groups adjacent to the Karankawa are rare, several that do exist suggest that the neighboring peoples were considerably smaller in stature than the Karankawa. As noted above, Berlandier (1969) was impressed with the Karankawa physique, although he had observed many other Indian groups in Texas, and the settler Jenkins (1958) also saw the Karankawa as the largest Indians of the several tribes he encountered. The Atakapans are ignored in the early accounts, and we have only a few vague clues concerning their appearance. Newcomb cites a "word-of-mouth" ethnography of the Lake Charles Atakapa, written by a J. O. Dyer in 1917: "their bodies stout, stature short, and heads of large size placed between their shoulders" (Newcomb, 1961:320). This reference to large heads may refer to broad heads, and if so it would represent some evidence for the Atakapan identification of the

Texas coast sites containing brachycranial skulls. Another early visitor to the Texas coast was Simars de Bellisle, a French officer who was stranded on Galveston Bay in 1719 (Folmer, 1940). He lived with a group of Indians identified as Akokisas, but did not provide a description of their physical characteristics.

## Summary

A combination of biological, archaeological and ethnohistorical data suggests that a number of proto-historical and early historical sites along the Texas Coast can be associated with the historic Karankawa and Atakapa tribes. The Galveston Bay area was occupied by both groups, who apparently were freely intermating by the eighteenth century. The distribution of the sites and their tribal designations suggests that Galveston Bay and the rivers entering it may well have marked the Atakapa-Karankawa boundary in proto-historic times (Fig. 1). By the late 1700s this area of interface had shifted to the south or disappeared altogether as both groups were reportedly located between the Colorado and Brazos rivers at that time (Morfi, 1935:81).

The sites I would associate with the Karankawa on the basis of morphological and archaeological data are Oso, Jamaica Beach, Shell Point, Lawrence Island (?) and the two Addicks Reservoir sites, Doering and Kob. The latter two sites and the Jamaica Beach site contain skeletal material which differs from the rather uniform morphology of the Karankawa, indicating the probable presence of a second group. The Atakapa would seem the most likely choice for this second group, based on their presence in the area in early historic times and on their coastal hunting-gathering adaptation. The combination of physical "types" at the sites mentioned above may be an indication of the early mingling of the two groups. The Caplen site contains skeletal material morphologically distinct from that seen in the sites identified above as Karankawa. Caplen would be an early historic site which represents the southward intrusion of Atakapan speakers into the Texas coast from their Louisiana homeland. As Gatchet points out, "only a small part of Texas, east of Houston city and [the] Neches River could have harbored Indians of the same nation which spoke the dialect once heard upon the Bayou Teche, the Mermentá-u, Calcasieu and Sabine rivers of Louisiana" (Gatchet, 1891:103).

The unusually impressive physique of the males from the several sites mentioned above would identify them as Karankawa, especially because of the tall stature and muscularity, the latter determined by the rugosity of the bones. The stature and strength of the Karankawa males are alluded to by nearly all early explorers and settlers who knew them, and such descriptions are recurrent and consistent enough to give the tribal designation of the skeletal material a reasonably strong foundation.

The association of prehistoric skeletal and cultural material with known historic tribes obviously would be strengthened with the addition of more information. Our assumptions are based on admittedly small skeletal samples, on temporal and spatial inferences about the historic tribes, and on early accounts which have any number of biases. Yet we must deal with the information available, and in so doing construct hypotheses that may be tested as additional data become available. With such *caveats* in mind, then, it does appear that the various archaeological sites dealt with here can be assigned to the historic Karankawa and, with less certainty, to the Atakapa.

## References Cited

Aten, L. E.
    1965    Five crania from the Jamaica Beach site (41GV5), Galveston County, Texas. Bulletin of the Texas Archaeological Society 36:153-62.
Aten, L. E., C. K. Chandler, A. B. Wesolosky and R. M. Malina
    1971    Archaeological investigations at the Harris County Boys School cemetery. MS., Texas Antiquarian Committee.
Bass, W. M., D. R. Evans and R. L. Jantz
    1971    The Leavenworth site cemetery; archaeology and physical anthropology. University of Kansas Publications in Anthropology, No. 2.
Berlandier, J. L.
    1969    The Indians of Texas in 1830. Washington, Smithsonian Institution Press.
Campbell, T. N.
    1947    The archaeology of the Texas Coast and its relation to that of Mexico and the lower Mississippi Valley. Ph.D. Dissertation, Harvard University.
Campbell, T. N.
    1957    Archaeological investigations at the Caplen site, Galveston County, Texas. Texas Journal of Science 9:448-71.
Dyer, J. O.
    1917    The Lake Charles Atakapas cannibals. Period of 1817-1820. Galveston (cited in Newcomb, 1961).
Folmer, H.
    1940    De Bellisle on the Texas coast. Southwestern Historical Quarterly 44:204-31.

Gatchet, A. S.
   1891   The Karankawa Indians, the Coast People of Texas. Archaeological and Ethnological Papers, Peabody Museum of American Archaeology and Ethnology, IV (14).

Goldstein, M. S.
   1957   Skeletal pathology of early Indians in Texas. American Journal of Physical Anthropology 15:299-311.

Griffin, J. B.
   1937   The archaeological remains of the Chiwere Sioux. American Antiquity 2:180-81.

Griffin, J. B.
   1942   On the historic location of the Tutelo and the Mohetan in the Ohio Valley. American Anthropologist 44:275-80.

Hasskarl, R.
   1962   The culture and history of the Tonkawa Indians. Plains Anthropologist 7:217-31.

Hodge, F. W. (ed.)
   1907   Spanish explorers in the southern United States, 1528-1543. New York: C. Scribner's Sons.

Hole, F. and R. G. Wilkinson
   1973   Shell Point: a coastal camp and burial site in Brazoria County. Bulletin of the Texas Archaeological Society 44:5-50.

Hrdlicka, A.
   1938   Skeletal remains from northern Texas. Texas Archaeological and Paleontological Society Bulletin, 10:169-92.

Jenkins, J. H. (ed.)
   1958   Recollections of early Texas. The Memoirs of John Holland Jenkins. Austin, University of Texas Press.

Kuykendall, J. H.
   1903   Reminiscences of early Texas. Southwestern Historical Quarterly 6:236-53; 311-30.

Long, J. K.
   1966   A test of multiple-discriminant analysis as a means of determining evolutionary changes and inter-group relations in physical anthropology. American Anthropologist 68:444-64.

Morfi, Fr. J. A.
   1935   History of Texas, 1673-1779. C. E. Castenada, translator. Quivira Society Publications VI, Albuquerque: The Quivira Society.

Neumann, G. K.
   1952   Archaeology and race in the American Indian. Item *in:* J. B. Griffin (ed.), The archaeology of the eastern United States, pp. 13-34. Chicago: University of Chicago Press.

Newcomb, W. W.
   1961   The Indians of Texas, from prehistoric to modern times. Austin: University of Texas Press.

Newman, M. T.
   1953   Indian skeletal remains from the Doering and Kobs sites, Addicks Reservoir, Texas. River Basin Survey Papers 4 (pt II), Bureau of American Ethnology, Bulletin 154:253-66.

Nuñez Cabeza de Vaca, A.
   1905   The journey of Alvar Nuñez Cabeza de Vaca and his companions from Florida to the Pacific, 1528-1536. A. F. Bandelier, ed., New York: A. S. Barnes and Co.

Nuñez Cabeza de Vaca, A.
   1972   The narrative of Alvar Nuñez Cabeza de Vaca. Barre: Massachusetts, The Imprint Society.

Phenice, T. W.
   1969   An analysis of the human skeletal material from burial mounds in north central Kansas. University of Kansas Publications in Anthropology, No. 1.

Robbins, L. M. and G. K. Neumann
   1972   The prehistoric people of the Fort Ancient culture of the central Ohio Valley. The University of Michigan, Museum of Anthropology, Anthropological Papers, No. 47.

Schaedel, R. P.
   1949   The Karankawa of the Texas Gulf Coast. Southwestern Journal of Anthropology 5:117-37.

Swanton, J. R.
   1946   The Indians of the southeastern United States. Bureau of American Ethnology, Bulletin 137.

Trotter, M. and G. C. Gleser
   1958   A re-evaluation of estimation of stature based on measurements of stature taken during life and of long bones after death. American Journal of Physical Anthropology 16:79-123.

Wilkinson, R. G.
   1971   Prehistoric biological relationships in the Great Lakes Region. University of Michigan, Museum of Anthropology, Anthropological Papers, No. 43.

Wolff, T.
   1969   The Karankawa Indians: their conflict with the white man in Texas. Ethnohistory 16:1-32.

Woodbury, G.
   1937   Notes on some skeletal remains from Texas. University of Texas Publications, Anthropological Papers 1:9-16.

Woodbury, G. and E. Woodbury
   1935   Prehistoric skeletal remains from the Texas coast. The Medallion Papers, No. 18.

# MICROANALYSIS OF CHIEN TEMMOKU GLAZES

*Frederick Bleicher*
The University of Michigan

Temmoku glazes were first used by Chinese potters on heavy stoneware during the Sung dynasty (960-1280 A.D.). A major production center for this ware was in the district of Chien-an, Fukien, in southen China (Plumer, 1935) and (Bushell, 1899:163).

Products of these kilns are known by the Chinese term *Wu-ni-yao* ("Black-clay ware") but are more commonly called *Chien-yao* ("abbreviation for Fukien"-"ware"). The widely used Japanese name, *Temmoku*, is often applied to all manner of pottery with a brown-black glaze but particularly to Sung ware, similar to *Chien-yao* in appearance. Sung temmoku was produced at kiln sites throughout China, often by means of different glazing techniques. Temmoku pottery is covered by a thick, rich, dark, reddish-brown to black glaze which exhibits a range of characteristic patterns of color variations that are described by such imaginal terms as "hare's fur," "oil spot," "partridge feather" and "lizard skin." The variation of shape and texture of the spots and streaks within or on the surface of the rich black matrix of glass is due to the formation of several different crystalline phases (perhaps ten or more) within the alkaline feldspathic formulation, containing 8 to 15 percent iron oxide. Geometric patterns and designs incorporating leaves or insects were also made in glazes of similar formulation and are known as "tortoise shell" among other names.

The enigmatic history of temmoku pottery remains an open question. Writers since Sung have disagreed as to its importance and status. The degree of control of the firing operation remains in doubt. Various attempts by early potters and modern ceramists to achieve the temmoku effects have been moderately successful but have often lacked reliable reproducibility. Many scholars maintain that *Chien-yao* was simply humble peasant ware (Plumer, 1937). Indeed, many of the surviving examples are rough and crude. A case is made for the most prized examples being simply a product of the *Chien* potters' serendipity (Harder, 1955). However, the presence of an inscription *Kung-yü* meaning "gift for the Emperor," found on a few *Chien* bowls and fragments (Plumer, 1972:76-78) and of a single example of the impressed characters *Chin-tsan*, meaning "to present a *tsan*"[1] (Sung, 1955), implies that the artisans who made these marks in the leather-hard pottery had some idea that these particular bowls would be of highest quality after firing. Whether the control exercised by Sung potters was simply a matter of kiln placement (Plumer, 1972; and Leach, 1971), application of iron oxide to the glaze surface prior to firing (Sundius, 1963:406), to controlled additions to the glaze formulation, or to careful manipulations of the firing cycle is the question (as yet unanswered) which gave rise to this research in progress.

The research program consists of two closely interrelated parts, the first of which involves a systematic study of the composition and microstructure of temmoku potsherds, which will be carefully selected to include several representative specimens showing each of the characteristic patterns. Specimens for this work have been obtained from the J. M. Plumer collection of temmoku artifacts which is in the University of Michigan Museum of Anthropology. Examples of these potsherds are shown in Figure 1. The collection was excavated by Professor Plummer at the *Chien* sites of the Sung dynasty kilns which he discovered near Shui-chi in Fukien province in 1935. This is perhaps the largest single collection of temmoku sherds in the western world, and it constitutes an unusually rich resource for this investigation. Specimens obtained from other collections as available, will also be examined for comparative purposes.

The second part of the research program will involve an attempt to reproduce the temmoku glaze effects and to determine the controlling process conditions needed to achieve these effects with reasonable reliability.

## Previous Investigations

Sir Herbert Jackson made important contributions to the understanding of temmoku and other Chinese glazes by studying samples with an optical microscope and by performing certain glaze experiments. A. L. Hetherington's description of this work, *Chinese Ceramic Glazes*, remains the classic in its field, although since its first publication in 1937 some of the material has been supplanted by more recent investigations.

Microscopic examination of a "hare's fur" example (Hetherington, 1923, 1941) showed that the main part of the glaze consisted of a blackish-brown glass. At the surface, and penetrating slightly below the

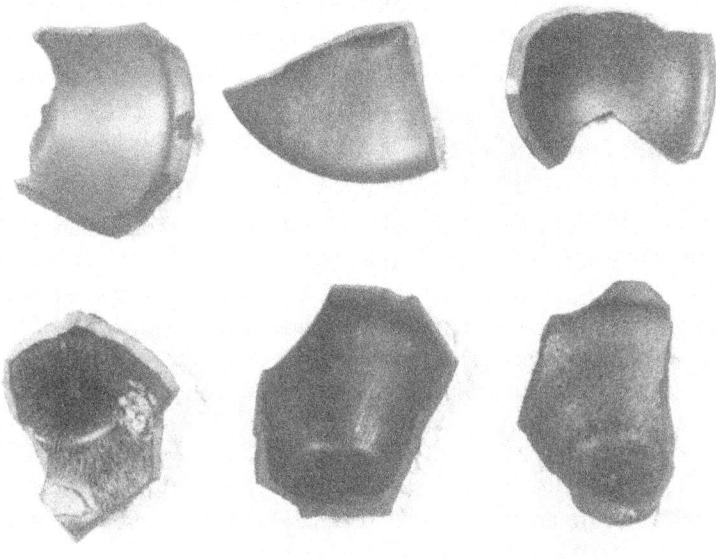

Figure 1. Representative *Chien* Temmoku potsherds from the University of Michigan Museum of Anthropology collection.

surface at the "hare's fur" markings, opaque brown particles or finely divided, but closely aggregated, minute spheres were observed. Where the particles were smallest and sparsely distributed, light scattering from them had a bluish tinge. At the mouth rim, where the glaze was thinnest, the dry-appearing rough surface showed a network of interlacing crystals, giving no evidence of fine particles. The brown particles and crystals were identified as ferric oxide, and the "hare's fur" effect and variations were explained by its precipitation from the glaze during cooling. Earhart (1941) in a later examination of a similar sherd gathered by Plummer found no crystal formations within the glaze itself and concluded that the "hare's fur" effect was not due to divitrification (or crystallization) of the glaze as claimed by Hetherington. Sundius (1963:405), noting a layered structure within the glaze, described variations and coloration effects in terms of multiple glazes rather than of the variation of the glaze's alkalinity during firing resulting in a variation of iron oxide solubility, as concluded by

Hetherington among others. Mullite (Chu, 1966) and anorthite (Sundius, 1961, 1963) are the only crystalline phases that have been previously identified within *Chien* glazes; others have only been described (Hetherington, 1941; Yamasaki and Koyama, 1967).

## Experimental Procedure

Slices were cut from selected sherds with a dental engine using a diamond abrasive cutting wheel. For identification of crystalline phases present in the glaze, x-ray diffraction and analysis of the dust collected during cutting was performed, using a Guinier-type powder camera. The dust will also be used to determine the elemental composition of the glaze by means of emission spectroscopy or neutron activation analysis.

The fragments cut from the sherds were mounted metallographically or prepared as petrographic thin sections for optical microscopic examination, using bright-field and dark-field reflected light and transmitted polarized light. The mounted test specimens were then subjected to electron microprobe analysis with an ARL model EMX-SM microprobe, equipped with three crystal spectrometers and a Kevex energy dispersive detector with multi-channel analyzer.

Certain sherd fragments and mounted samples, some of which were immersion etched with an HF/KF solution, were examined using a JSM-U3 scanning electron microscope, equipped with a Kevex retractable energy dispersive detector. X-ray maps, semi-quantitative point analysis, absorbed electron (sample current) images and secondary electron images were obtained from both microprobe and SEM analysis.

Transmission electron microscopy using a JEM-6A instrument has been limited to obtaining electron diffraction patterns from small samples of glaze-cutting dust on carbon support films. Analysis of thin films prepared from sherd samples awaits completion and debugging of an ion-thinning device.

## Experimental Results

The X-ray diffraction patterns produced from glaze samples confirmed the presence of mullite ($3Al_2O_3 \cdot 2SiO_2$) and of anorthite ($CaO \cdot Al_2O_3 \cdot 2SiO_2$) in several cases. Many other lines were also present in the diffraction patterns. However, due to extensive possibilities of overlapping and the weakness of some of the lines, other crystalline phases have not been confirmed with x-ray diffraction.

Crystals forming "hare's fur" streaks on the surface of one sample have been conclusively identified by electron diffraction as CaO · FeO · $Fe_2O_3$. A distinctive d-spacing of 6.32 angstroms in the diffraction pattern and microprobe x-ray maps showing the crystals to be both calcium and iron-rich rule out other possibilities. Optical microscopy shows that crystals of similar microstructure are present in other samples exhibiting "hare's fur" streaks. Figure 2 is a scanning electron micrograph showing these crystals on the surface of a sherd fragment.

Figure 3 is a dark-field, reflected-light optical micrograph of a typical *Chien* sherd. A cluster of anorthite crystals (A), surrounded by clouds of a number of other phases is seen suspended in the black glassy matrix of the glaze. The apparent smearing and foggy areas are actually dispersions of fine particles (small fractions of a micron in size) beneath the surface of the sample; they are shown progressively out of focus the deeper they become. Mullite needles (M) are seen growing from the body/glaze inter-

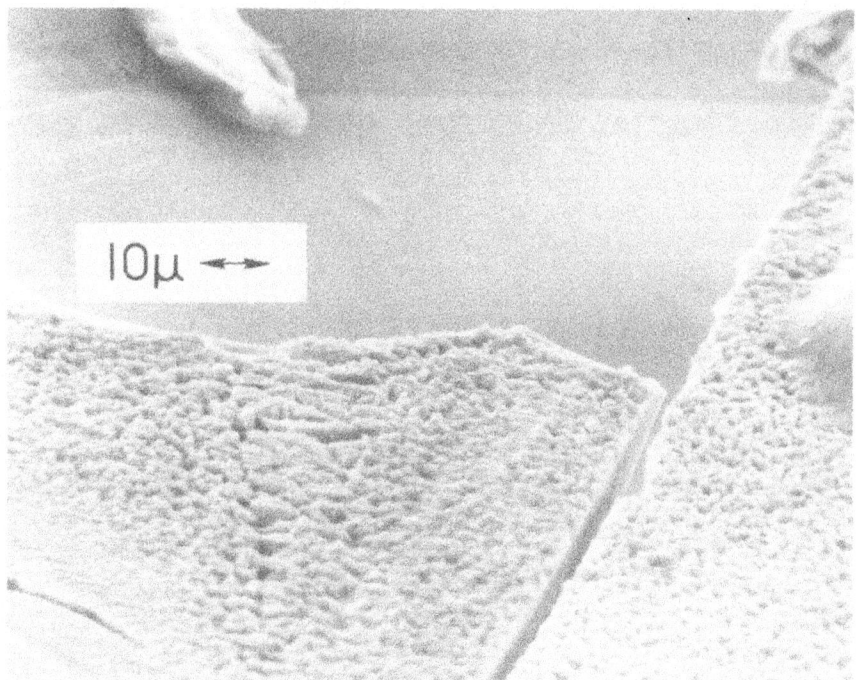

Figure 2. Scanning electron micrograph of calcium iron oxide (CaO · FeO · $Fe_2O_3$) crystals of the surface of *Chien* potsherd fragment with "hare's fur" streaks.

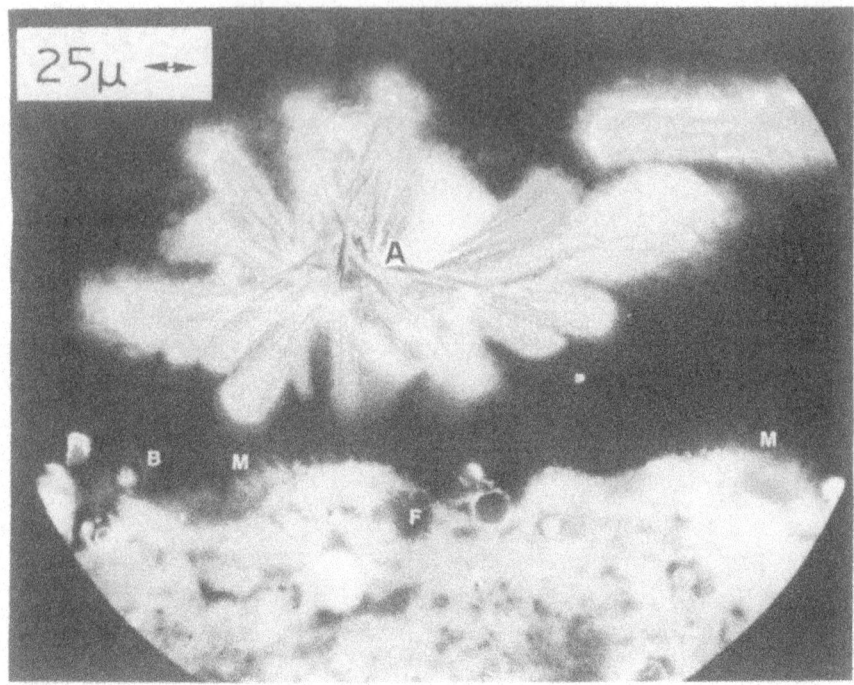

Figure 3. Dark-field reflected-light optical micrograph of the glaze/body interface of a typical *Chien* sherd. Note the mullite needles (M), the cluster of anorthite crystals (A) surrounded by clouds of other phases, the entrapped gas bubbles in both the glaze and the body, and particle of magnetite (F).

face. A particle of magnetite (F) is also visible in the body near the interface. Bubbles of entrapped gas (B) are present in both the glaze and the body. This image is much more spectacular when the subtle shades of reds, browns, and blacks can be viewed in color. A three-dimensional effect can also be obtained by focusing the microscope on areas beneath the sample surface.

Figures 4 and 5 are scanning electron micrographs of a similar sample that has been lightly etched with an HF/KF solution. The same microstructures present in Figure 3 are this time shown in relief. The undissolved quartz sand grain (Q) shown in Figure 5 is outlined by areas of heavy etching. This artifact is probably due to accelerated etchant attack on regions of high residual stress caused by difference in thermal contraction during cooling of the quartz and the glassy matrix, rather than to major chemical com-

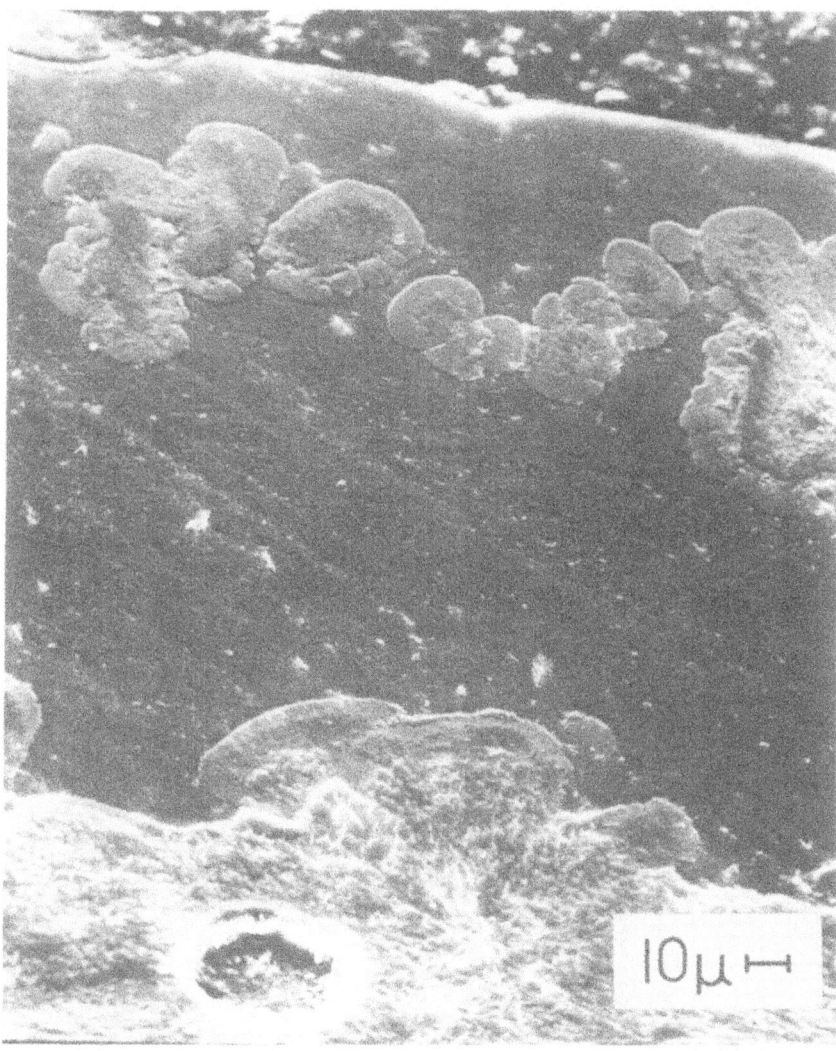

Figure 4. Scanning electron micrograph of sherd similar to that shown in Fig. 3. Specimen has been immersion etched with an HF/KF solution to show the microstructure in slight relief.

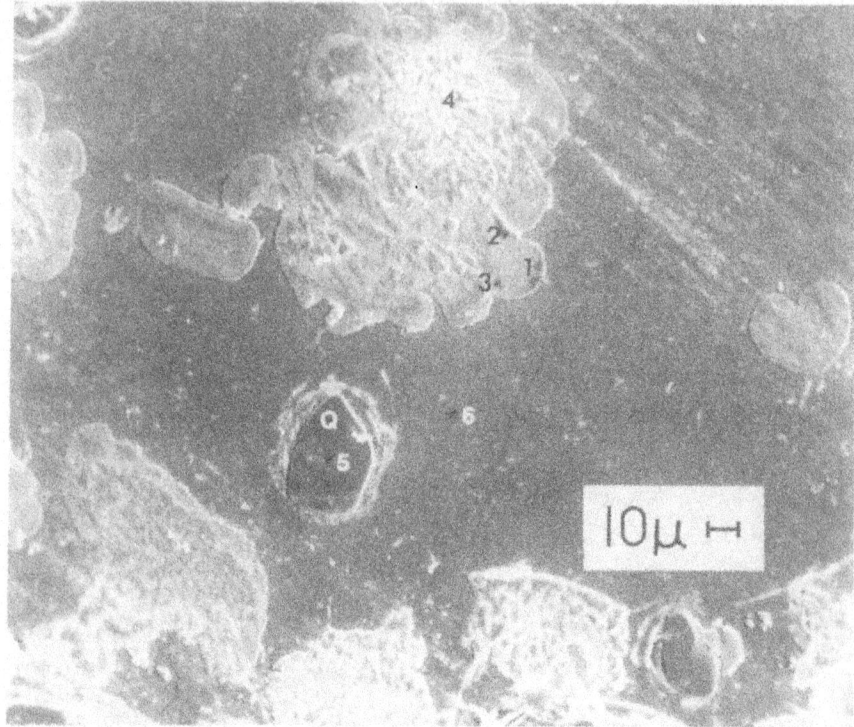

Figure 5. Scanning electron micrograph of same specimen shown in Fig. 4. Locations are indicated for points at which x-ray flourescence spectra were obtained. Note the undissolved quartz grain (Q).

positional differences. However, the glass surrounding the sand grain would certainly be somewhat enriched in silica. Figure 5 also shows the location of various analysis points for which x-ray flourescence spectra were obtained on the SEM.

Table 1 lists the results of spectrographic analysis of an overall glaze sample from a representative specimen and raw x-ray data from analysis points shown in Figure 5. For a variety of reasons[2] the point analysis data is good for little more than order of magnitude interpretation and as a qualitative aid to other methods of identification. However, limited conclusions can be drawn. Points 1 and 3 are located in apparently similar regions of slightly higher silica concentration than other crystalline phases. Point 2 shows low Al and enriched K. Point 4, located in a nest of

TABLE I

Spectrographic and SEM X-ray Fluorescence
Analysis of *Chien* Sherd Glaze Sample

| Element | Overall Spectrographic Analysis (Wt. %) | X-ray Fluorescence Analysis (Ref. Fig. 5) (Peak counts/500 sec.) Points: | | | | | |
|---|---|---|---|---|---|---|---|
| | | 1 | 2 | 3 | 4 | 5 | 6 |
| Si | 27.9 | 7344 | 5165 | 7173 | 4505 | 12000 | 7284 |
| Al | 5.4 | 2563 | 1588 | 2447 | 2611 | 847 | 2408 |
| Ca | 5.0 | 1021 | 703 | 988 | 1533 | 210 | 883 |
| Mg | 1.3 | 526 | 465 | 493 | 422 | 337 | 492 |
| K | 1.3 | 734 | 3722 | 763 | 2951 | 443 | 799 |
| Na$^b$ | .3 | – | – | – | – | – | – |
| Fe | 2.2 | 383 | 333 | 338 | 729 | 175 | 369 |
| Mn | .02 | 145 | 167 | 159 | – | – | 149 |
| Ti | .4 | 207 | 204 | 200 | – | – | 204 |
| S$^a$ | .2 | – | – | – | – | – | – |
| O$^{b,c}$ | 56.0 | – | – | – | – | – | – |
| Au$^d$ | – | 1312 | 973 | 1293 | 1120 | 1255 | 1286 |

$^a$Sulphur not detected above background with SEM.

$^b$Sodium and Oxygen not measurable with SEM detector.

$^c$Oxygen determined by difference for spectrographic analysis.

$^d$Gold present in the SEM analysis due to a glow discharge coating applied to make the sample surface electrically conductive. Uniformity of counts from one analysis to another is an indication of uniformity of the coating or of instrumental stability of the SEM.

anorthite crystals, shows high Fe concentration in addition to the expected Si, Al, and Ca. The sand grain, point 5, indeed shows high silica; however, the presence of the other x-ray peaks indicates the presence of a marked matrix effect in this and all other points, rather than significant impurities in the quartz. The glaze matrix, point 6, shows all elements, present in the overall composition, to be in solution glass.

Figure 6 is an SEM absorbed electron (sample current) image of a sample that was successively polished through Linde B abrasive, unetched, and coated with an evaporated layer of carbon. Image contrast in such a photograph is chiefly a function of differences in average atomic number from point to point. The range of intensities and the variety of morphologies present in this picture suggest the presence of perhaps as many as ten crystalline phases. However, their small size and close proximity to one another indicate that the only conclusive way in which to sort out their identification will be transmitted electron diffraction. Such analysis awaits

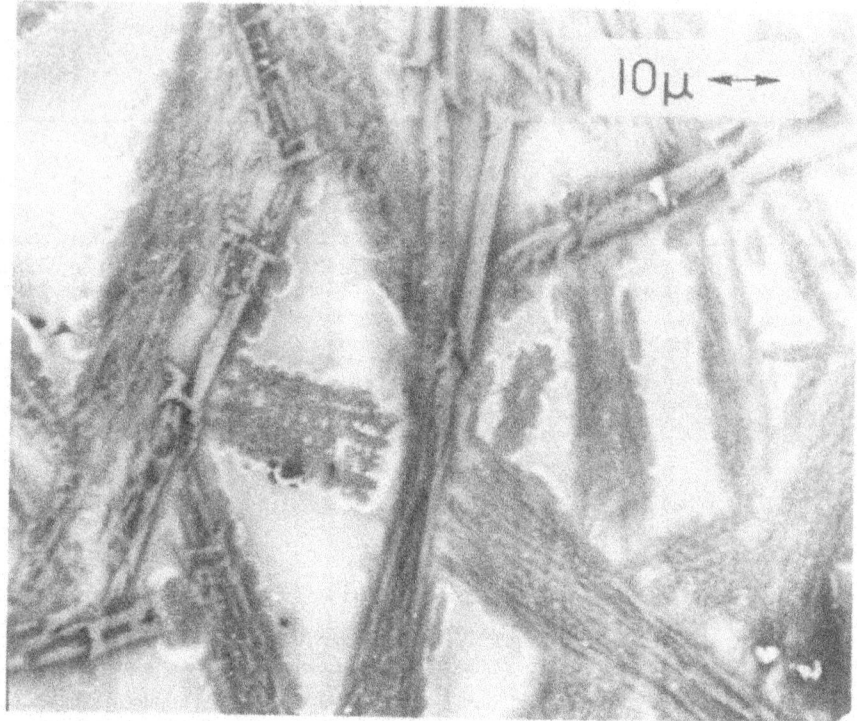

Figure 6. An SEM absorbed electron (Sample Current) image of a polished *Chien* glaze sample. Image contrast is primarily a function of differences in average atomic number from point to point. The range of intensities and the variety of morphologies present suggest the existence of perhaps as many as ten crystalline phases.

completion and debugging of an ion-thinning device for the preparation of thin films from sherd samples.

Figure 7 is a set of microprobe photographs of a different area in the same sample shown in Figure 6. The absorbed electron image (Fig. 7a) is of much poorer quality than Figure 6 due to electronic noise introduced by the extremely high amplifier gain required to obtain the image. Both Figures 6 and 7a also show charging effects due to the presence of magnetic phases in the body of the sherd sample. The accompanying x-ray intensity maps (Figs. 7b through 7f) show the elongated anorthite crystals to be richer in Ca and Al than the surrounding phases and depleted in Fe, Mg, and K. A similar map of Si (not presented here) showed high silica throughout the

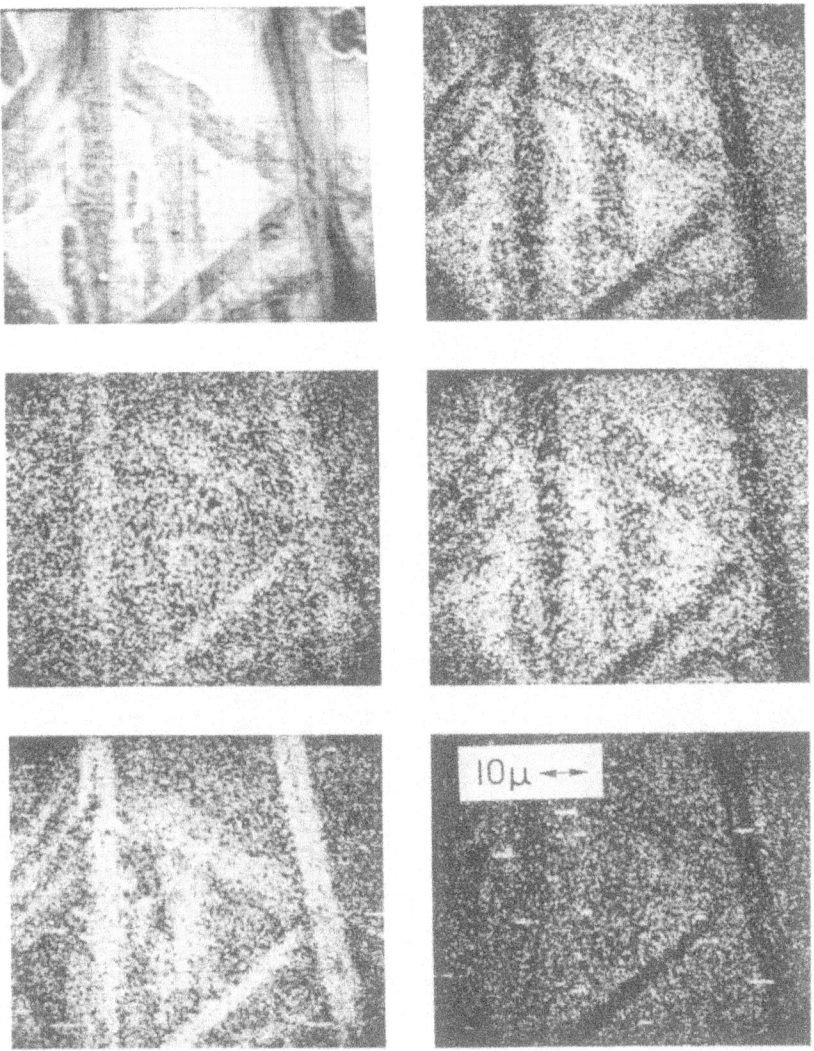

Figure 7. Set of microprobe photographs of a different area in the same sample shown in Fig. 6.
7a Absorbed electron image.
7b Iron x-ray intensity image.
7c Aluminum x-ray intensity image.
7d Magnesium x-ray intensity image.
7e Calcium x-ray intensity image.
7f Potassium x-ray intensity image.

entire area. The halo areas in Figure 7a, which appear as nubbins attached to the anorthite in Figures 3 and 6 can be seen from Figure 7b to be rich in iron.

Figure 8 is a dark-field reflected light optical micrograph of an area similar to that shown in Figure 6 (note that the image is essentially reversed; comparable light regions in Fig. 8 appearing dark in Fig. 6). The region on the left edge of the photograph is also illuminated to some extent from the side by reflection from the internal surface of a large bubble underneath the surface. The "nubbins" mentioned in the previous paragraph appear in this photograph to be either bubbles or droplets of a second immiscible glass phase. In either case very fine suspended particles appear to have been concentrated at the interface with the glaze matrix.

## Glaze Reactions

A great many things "happened" to temmoku glaze during firing.

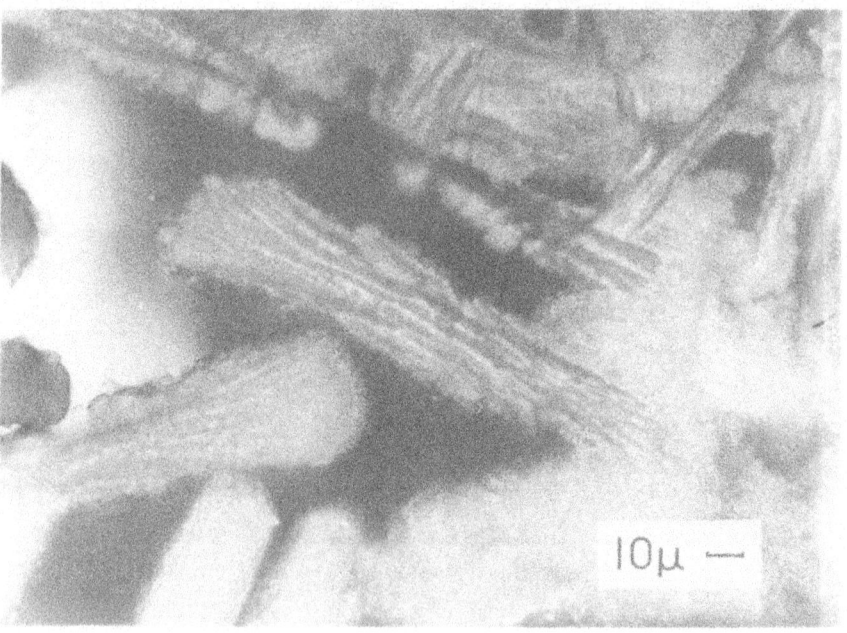

Figure 8. Dark-field reflected-light optical micrograph of an area similar to that shown in Fig. 6. Note the bubbles or droplets of a second immiscible glass phase attached to the anorthite crystals at the left edge of the photograph.

Nevertheless, some order can be brought to this chaotic situation if events are considered in the time sequence in which they occur. Norton's short chapter entitled "Life History of the Glaze" (1970:281-92) is an excellent summary of the reactions that occur within a glaze during firing.

Although a thorough understanding may be lacking, a generalized explanation of temmoku glaze reactions and production methods can be given. Temmoku-type glazes are made primarily from slip clays, containing typically 6-10 percent of all sorts of mineral impurities and organic matter. Having some knowledge of Sung kilns and firing procedure and of the general behavior of slip clays, one can conclude that, especially for volume production runs, kiln firing would not produce the same results from the same material in all parts of the kiln. The kilns used were large, capable of accommodating several hundred bowls, stacked in saggers, for a single firing. Control of the firing schedule, which lasted several days, was a formidable task indeed.

*Melting Reactions*

Temmoku-type glazes are applied on the body in a heavy layer from a slurry of fine particles, primarily clays. Along with quartz, calcite, and feldspars, certain ferrugineous minerals might be expected (Orton, 1903), including: 1) Ferric oxide, anhydrous, or in various stages of hydration; 2) Ferrous carbonate; 3) Ferric sulfide or pyrite; 4) Ferrous silicate minerals, such as biotite, hornblend and others; 5) Ferric sand minerals, like magnetite, menaccanite, chromite, etc.

Upon first heating, hydroscopic water is driven off. As the temperature is increased to between 400 and 600°C, combustion of organic matter takes place. Distillation of sulfur from any pyrite present to form FeS would occur at approximately the same temperatures. Between 550 and 650°C, dehydroxylation of the clays, ferric hydroxide, and other hydrous minerals occurs. As the temperature is further increased, calcination of carbonate minerals such as calcite, dolomite, and siderite begins (Orton, 1903). At this point the glaze structure has opened up to probably 40-50 percent porosity, and the original constitutents have changed sufficiently to have lost their identity (Koenig and Lyons, 1955a, 1955b; Brindley and Ougland, 1962). Now, only by study of phase-equilibrium relationships (Schairer, 1957) can this information be inferred.

Decomposition of the carbonate minerals produces basic oxides, important during vitrification because of their reaction with the silicates of the clays. Occurring concurrently with decarbonization there are oxidation reactions due mainly to action of the fuel-combustion gases on solid reducing agents in the clay (Orton, 1903). Interaction of the gases produces a complicated set of circumstances that persist well into the vitrification period.

Initial glass formation in temmoku glazes can be expected before a temperature of 1100°C is reached. Gaseous reactions are apparently most vigorous at about cone 10 (Harder, 1955; ~1285°c [Orton Foundation, 1965], but perhaps much lower in the slowly heated Sung kilns) and fairly complete by cone 12 (~1300°C, same comment) when glaze maturity is reached.

A number of studies of the behavior of bubbles in a variety of ceramic glazes have been performed. A summary of their conclusions that may apply to temmoku-type glazes is listed below.

The surface of the body is a persistent source of bubbles (Williamson, 1960). The gas reactions described above are important during initial stages of melting. Bubbles travel to the glaze surface because of their buoyancy only if this surface faces upward. Downward movement of bubbles, through the glaze on the underside of a *Chien* bowl, would have been possible only if gas issued as jets from pores within the body.

The expansion or movement of bubbles can concentrate particles suspended in the glaze and can also orient them dimensionally. Thus vesicular striations, filled by clearer glaze, may mark paths along which bubbles traveled. Sulfates are said to cause this phenomenon in high-iron glazes (Orton, 1903). Suspended particles that collect around expanding bubbles will remain around the craters left when they burst and the subsequent flattening of such craters leaves spots of concentrated particles (Williamson, 1960). Bubbles remaining at the glaze/body interface may cause accentuated attack. Hollows in quartz grains, etched to conform to the peripheries of associated bubbles, have been observed.

Due to reduced glaze viscosity at the maturing temperature, most bubbles are drawn to the surface and escape by the time it is reached. In general, the thicker the glaze layer the slower bubble removal occurs; the lower the glaze viscosity the faster it occurs (Orton, 1903).

Compositional layering in glazes, parallel to their surfaces, can be caused by interaction with the body or the kiln atmosphere, or by volatization. It results from diffusion that occurred after the melt had become relatively still (Scholze, 1970).

Important glaze/body reactions also occur during the heating of the glaze. Molten glaze dissolves portions of the body. The surface of the body is dissolved differentially by the glaze, leaving silica grains protruding from it (Williamson, 1960). Differential attack may be especially obvious where the contact with the glaze is approximately perpendicular to the plane in which the flatter particles in the body tend to lie.

*Cooling Reactions*

The surface of molten glaze at its maturing temperature is almost perfectly smooth. During cooling, however, the gas in the bubbles that remain just below the surface contracts, causing shallow dimples (Norton, 1970) that have been shown to cause loss of glaze reflectivity. Thus this property can be related to maturing temperature, time at temperature, and heating and cooling rates, as these factors affect size and rate of bubble formation.

At the glaze/body interface the glaze is often supersaturated with silica and alumina, which crystalize out as mullite needles during cooling. Anorthite, wollastonite (Ruddleson and Airey, 1967; Rogers and Williamson, 1969), and diopside have been found in lime glazes by petrographic methods. Crystallization can also occur at the glaze surface and through the glaze. Although some crystals develop during the heating and maturing period, most crystallization occurs during cooling (Norton, 1970). The crystals in matt or related glazes are not collected or oriented by bubbles, and thus they originate during cooling.

The effect of iron oxides on crystallization in glasses of the system (Klemantaski and Kerrison, 1966) $CaO-MgO-Al_2O_3-SiO_2$ has become of recent interest to the glass and steel industries. These four constituents are major components of temmoku glazes, iron oxides being the other. Thus a close look at the published data is warranted.

Small additions of iron oxides to the glass have a marked effect upon the rates of crystallization or anorthite, wollastonite, and diopside in the glass (Rogers and Williamson, 1969). The crystal growth rates were found to be proportional to the square of the ferrous in concentration. The activation energy for crystallization was found to vary from 30 to 150 kcal/mole depending on the ferrous/ferric ratio of the glass (Williamson, Tipple, and Rogers, 1968). At high ferrous/ferric ratios, this energy approached the activation energy for viscous flow in glasses of the same composition. These results are discussed in terms of the glaze structure in the next section.

*Glaze Structure*

Any consideration of the crystal structure of the glassy state begins with a review of the work of Zachariasen (1932). Bloor discusses the application of glass structural theory to glazes (1956). General material of this nature will not be reviewed here. Consideration will be given only to the structural state of iron in glasses of composition similar to that of temmoku glazes.

It has been proposed that $Fe^{3+}$ ions can act as nucleating agents for a spinel phase in the system $CaO-MgO-Al_2O_3-SiO_2$. Diopside and melitite crystals have been observed to grow on the spinel nuclei (Klemantaski and Kerrison, 1966).

The coordination state of $Al^{3+}$ ions in silicate glasses has been the subject of considerable debate. Strong evidence is reported for both four-fold and six-fold co-ordinated $Al^{3+}$ ions in alkali silicate glasses (Yoldas, 1969) and (Douglas, 1970). Another study (Kurkjian and Sigety, 1968) concluded that ferric ions were all present in tetrahedral co-ordination in silicate glasses. It is proposed that additions of $Fe^{3+}$ ions to tetrahedral sites in the $CaO-MgO-Al_2O_3-SiO_2$ glasses may upset the balance of four-fold and six-fold co-ordination $Al^{3+}$ ions from that present in the iron-free glass. In the normal spinel structure all the $Al^{3+}$ ions are in six-fold coordination. Addition of $Fe^{3+}$ to the glass would favor the formation of six-fold coordinated $Al^{3+}$, thus producing a glass in which the aluminum ions were in more favorable positions for the production of spinel nuclei.

$Fe^{2+}$ ions, too large for tetrahedral sites, probably act in a similar way to $Mg^{2+}$ and $Ca^{2+}$, modifying the glass structure and breaking the Si-O-Si bonds. As mentioned in the previous section, the effect is to lower the viscosity of the glass. It is concluded that an increasing ferrous/ferric ratio and subsequent change in anion size distribution in the glass is responsible both for increased rates of crystallization and for changes in apparent activation energies of crystallization.

## Conclusion

It is probable that if sophisticated process control was available to the *Chien* potter it was employed, since the Chinese pottery industry was developed to its height during Sung times. As to whether or not such control was possible, the answer is that one need not understand the complex glaze reactions but has simply to demonstrate empirically that it can be done. Indeed some modern Japanese potters appear to have different varieties of temmoku glaze effects under control. However, the temmoku glaze reactions are of interest to modern technologists in applications never dreamed of by the Chinese potter. It would be rewarding if some of the contemporary applications were to prove as enduring as a *Chien-yao* tea bowl.

## Footnotes

1. *Tsan* is the word for one shape for a cup that is usually made of jade. The implication is clearly that a bowl bearing such an inscription must be of high quality.
2. For a specific gravity of approximately 2.2 (that of a *Chien* glaze) and an accelerating potential of 15 KV (that used to obtain the spectra) the predicted penetration of the electron beam is 2.7 microns (Anderson, 1967). Even reduction to a 10 KV accelerating potential would reduce the penetration only to about 1.5 microns. Thus the excited x-rays are coming from a volume substantially larger than that occupied by the phases being analyzed. In addition corrections for back scatter and absorption for samples of these compositions can result in a very large overall correction factor. For instance, in a sample containing from 1 to 10 wt. % iron, for operation over the range of 7 to 30 KV, the overall correction factor for sodium varies between 2.5 and 9.0.

## Acknowledgments

The kindness of Dr. James Griffin in allowing access to the Plumer sherds and the encouragement and advice of Dr. W. C. Bigelow during the course of this research is gratefully acknowledged. Also the help of Dr. W. C. Hu in translating Chinese source materials, of Dr. Anne Rowe in assistance in preparation of electron diffraction patterns, and of Larry Allard in obtaining SEM sample current images was invaluable.

## References Cited

Anderson, C. A.
    1967  An introduction to the electron probe micro-analyzer and its application to biochemistry. *In:* Methods of Bio-chemical Analysis, Vol. 15, edited by David Glick. New York: Wiley.

Bloor, E. C.
    1956  Glaze composition, glass structural theory and its application to glazes. Transactions of the British (English) Ceramic Society 55:631.

Brindley, G. W. and Ronald M. Ougland
    1962  Quantitative studies of high-temperature reactions of Quartz-Kaolinite-Feldspar Mixture. Transactions of the British (English) Ceramic Society 61:599-614.

Bushell, S. W.
    1899  Oriental ceramic art: collections of W. T. Walters. New York: Appleton.

Chu, Gordon P. K.
    1966  Microstructure of complex ceramic. *In:* Ceramic microstructures, edited by Richard Fulrath and Joseph Rask. New York: Wiley.

Douglas, R. W.
    1970  Colored glasses. Journal of the British Ceramic Society 7:28.

Earhart, W. H.
   1941    Examination of a Chinese Temmoku glaze and body. Bulletin of the American Ceramic Society 20:121-22.

Harder, Charles M.
   1955    A letter from the Temmoku glaze. Far Eastern Ceramic Bulletin 7:19-25.

Hetherington, A. L.
   1923    The chemistry of Temmoku glazes. Transactions of the Oriental Ceramic Society 1923-24.
   1941    Chinese ceramic glazes. Los Angeles: Commonwealth Press.

Hsü, Chih-heng.
   1915    Yin-liu-chai shuo-tz'u. Ch'ao-chi shu-she, Shanghai.

Klemantaski, S. and B. Kerrison.
   1966    A material produced by devitrification of a glass made from a metallurgical slag. Chemical Industry 1747-1753.

Koenig, John H. and S. C. Lyons.
   1955    Some ceramic mechanisms and new materials. Ceramic Age 4:26-36, 53-57.

Koenig, John H. and S. C. Lyons
   1955    Correlation of kaolinite crystal shape with particle size and some effects on ceramic behavior. Ceramic Age 7:8-14.

Kurkjian, C. R. and E. A. Sigety.
   1968    Co-ordination of $Fe^{3+}$ in glass. Physics and Chemistry of Glass 43:359T-403T.

Leach, Bernard.
   1971    Discussion of methods of glaze control. Personal communication.

Norton, F. H.
   1970    Fine ceramics, technology and applications. New York: McGraw-Hill.

Orton, Edward.
   1903    On the role played by iron in the burning of clays. Transactions of the American Ceramic Society 5:377-430.

Orton Ceramic Foundation.
   1965    The properties and uses of pyrometric cones. Ohio.

Plumer, James M.
   1935    The place of origin of the world-famous Chien ware discovered. London Illustrated News October 26, 1935.

Plumer, James M.
   1937    Humble ware of Chien. Magazine of Art: March.

Plumer, James M.
   1972    Temmoku: a study of the ware of Chien. Idemitsu, Tokyo.

Rogers, P. S. and J. Williamson.
   1969    The nucleation of crystalline phases in silicate glasses containing iron oxide. Glass Technology 10:128-33.

Ruddleson and Airey.
 1967 Potentialities of the instrument. Transactions of the British (English) Ceramic Society 66:587-98, pt. 2 66:599-606, pt. 3 66: 607-29.

Schairer, J. F.
 1957 Melting relations of the common rock-forming oxides. Journal of the American Ceramic Society 40:215-35.

Scholze, H. V.
 1970 Formation of an interlayer between the glaze composition during the firing of porcelain. Berichte der Deutschen Keramik Gesellschaft 47:45.

Sundius, Nils.
 1961 Some aspects of the technical development in the manufacture of the Chinese pottery of Re-Ming age. Bulletin of the Museum of Far Eastern Antiquities 33:103-24.

Sundius, Nils and Walter Slezer.
 1963 The constitution and manufacture of Chinese ceramics from Sung and earlier times. *In:* Sung sherds by Nils Palmgren. Stockholm: Almquist and Wiksell.

Sung, Po-yin.
 1955 Chien yao t'iao-ch'a chi. Wen Wu 2:50-60.

Williamson, W. O.
 1960 Bubbles and associated structures in fired glazes: hypothesis and microscopical observations. Transactions of the British (English) Ceramic Society 59:455-78.

Williamson, W. O., A. J. Tipple, P. S. Rogers.
 1968 Influence of Iron oxides on kinetics of crystal growth in $CaO\text{-}MgO\text{-}Al_2O_3\text{-}SiO_2$ glasses. Journal of the Iron and Steel Institute 9:898-903.

Yamasaki, Kazuo and Fujio Koyama.
 1967 The Yohen Temmoku bowls. Oriental Art. New Series 29:17-18.

Yoldas, B. E.
 1969 The nature of the coexistence of four- and six-coordinated $al^{3+}$ in glass. Owens Illinois Research seminars 1969.

Zachariasen, W. H.
 1942 The atomic arrangement in glass. Journal of the American Ceramic Society 54:3841.

# REVISION OF THE
# TWO RIVERS ("VALDERS") DRIFT BORDER
# AND THE AGE OF FLUTED POINTS IN MICHIGAN

*William R. Farrand*
Quaternary Research Laboratory, University of Michigan

## Introduction

About ten years ago J. B. Griffin reviewed the state of knowledge of prehistoric archaeology in the northeastern United States, covering thoroughly the available data on Paleo-Indians in Michigan. He noted, however, that "the Pleistocene geology of this area has been intensively studied, but the complexity of the problems involved is such that an adequate interpretation of the Pleistocene history is still many years in the future." Moreover, "... the constant revisions make it difficult for the archaeologist to keep pace with new interpretations ... of the geologic features" (Griffin, 1965:655).

The interpretation of Pleistocene stratigraphy in Michigan is still in flux, and this paper will present some of the most recent revisions of importance to archaeologists. A recent review by Farrand and Eschman (1974), treating glaciation, deglaciation and glacial lakes of southern Michigan, may serve as general background for the reader. Here, however, I wish to concentrate on the latest ice advances into the state, those that were contemporary with the occupation of the southern part of the state by prehistoric men, namely the Port Huron and the Two Rivers (formerly "Valders") readvances.

## Chronology of Ice Movements

*Ice Borders in Southern Michigan.*

The deglaciation of the southern peninsula of Michigan occurred in three phases. First, the extreme south-central part of the state (St. Joseph and Branch counties) was definitively deglaciated more than 15,000 years ago. All the southern third of the lower peninsula was probably ice free at that time (during the Erie Interstade of Mörner and Dreimanis, 1973), but a subsequent major and apparently very rapid advance brought the ice front

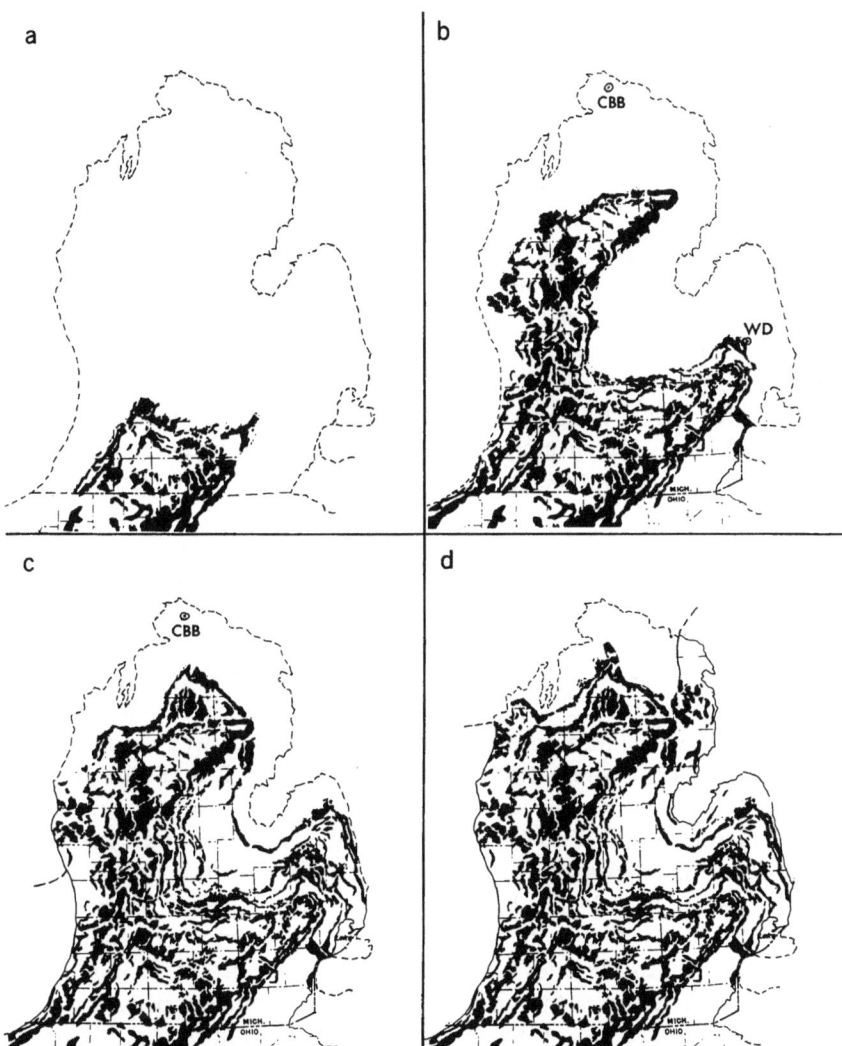

Figure 1. Four stages in the deglaciation of the southern peninsula of Michigan. Black areas are end moraines formed at or prior to the time represented by the map. *a:* at the time of the Kalamazoo and Mississinewa moraines, about 14,800 years ago; *b:* at the time of the Lake Border, West Branch, Ionia and Birmingham moraines, about 1000 years later than *a*; WD = Weaver Drain radiocarbon locality, 13,770 years; CBB = Cheboygan Bryophyte Bed locality, 13,300 years; *c:* at the time of the outer Port Huron Moraine, about 12,500 years ago; *d:* at the time of the Two Rivers readvance, about 11,800 years ago. (After Farrand and Eschman, 1974.)

to the line of the Mississinewa and Kalamazoo moraines about 14,800 years ago (Fig. 1a). The second phase comprised a rather regular retreat of the ice front, with the Saginaw lobe retreating relatively more rapidly than the more massive Lake Michigan and Erie lobes (Fig. 1b). This retreat carried the ice front beyond the present shores of southern Michigan, with the possible exception of the Straits of Mackinac area. We know, for example, that the Cheboygan County Bryophyte locality, only a few miles south of Mackinaw City, was definitely ice free at this time, which is known as the Cary/Port Huron, or Lake Arkona, Interstade dated around 13,000 years ago (Farrand et al., 1969).

Phase three, occurring about 12,500 years ago, brought the ice front back onto the southern peninsula. The ice covered about one-fourth of its surface and filled the Saginaw and Grand Traverse embayments along the line of the Port Huron moraine. The Port Huron moraine constitutes one of the clearest morphologic boundaries in the state of Michigan, being readily traceable from its type-area near Port Huron northwestward to Gaylord in Otsego County and thence southwestward into the area between Manistee and Cadillac. Farther to the southwest the Port Huron moraine has not yet been clearly sorted out from the scrappy morainic segments in Mason and Oceana counties, but, as we shall see, its southern terminus is now definitely placed at the Whitehall moraine in Muskegon County. Phase three also includes a subsequent pulsation of the ice front, which has been called the Valders readvance. The Valders readvance was defined on the basis of the red till overlying the Two Creeks Forest Bed in Wisconsin, that forest bed being correctly taken as evidence of an ice retreat prior to the Valders advance. The Two Creeks retreat must have been sufficient to open a low-level drainageway in or near the Straits of Mackinac area in order to lower the lake level in the Lake Michigan basin at least to its present-day level. The limit of the Valders advance in southern Michigan had been suggested by both Thwaites and Bretz, and was mapped by Melhorn (1954) who followed it across the northern part of the southern peninsula on the basis of the red color of Valders till, which contrasted with the grayish brown color of the older Port Huron till. Bretz (1951) had previously suggested that the red till bordering Lake Michigan from the Whitehall moraine northward to the Manistee moraine must also be Valders on the basis of its color. The Whitehall-to-Manistee portion has subsequently been shown to be older than Valders; otherwise the Valders border of Melhorn is as shown in Figure 1d.

A stratigraphic marker equivalent to the Two Creeks Forest Bed has not yet been found in Michigan. In fact, data from the Cheboygan County

Bryophyte locality strongly suggest that the ice front did not free the Straits of Mackinac during Two Creeks time. An alternative drainageway through the Indian River lowland (from Petoskey to Cheboygan) was ice free and adequate in size to accommodate the eastward outflow of Lake Michigan water during the Two Creeks Interstade.

At the height of the Valders advance, shortly after 11,850 years ago, the ice sheet was fronted by two separate proglacial lakes, the Toleston in the Lake Michigan basin and an early phase of Glacial Lake Algonquin in the Lake Huron basin. As the ice retreated and the Indian River lowland was once more freed of ice, the two lakes merged into the Main Algonquin level, which expanded progressively as the ice retreated northward.

*Revisions of the Port Huron and Valders Ice Borders.*

The history outlined above is in general well known to archaeologists, ecologists, and others interested in the prehistoric evolution of Michigan. However, there have been several recent revisions to this story. First of all, the identification of Valders till on the basis of its red color alone is no longer valid. Pre-Valders red tills, already known in northern Wisconsin and northeastern Minnesota, have recently been shown to exist in Michigan as well. Four different occurrences will illustrate this point. First, the Cheboygan Bryophyte Bed (Farrand et al., 1969) is sandwiched between lithologically identical red clayey tills. On the basis of the age of the Bryophyte Bed, the overlying till must be Port Huron in age and the underlying till pre-Port Huron; thus, there are two tills in the midst of the Valders drift area of Michigan that are red and clayey, but not Valders. To the southwest (in Wexford County) the outer Port Huron moraine near Petersen Bridge is composed of red till, for example. Still farther to the southwest, the Whitehall moraine, now considered Port Huron in age, is made of red clayey till. Finally, the Port Huron till of the Lake Huron lobe (in Oscoda County, for example) has been reported to be definitely reddish brown by W. A. Burgis (unpublished). Clearly, not all red tills in Michigan are Valders.

The second revision concerns the age of the red tills from Whitehall to Manistee, and this has been touched on above. Bretz (1951) thought these red tills were Valders, because of their color and the similarity of their position to the red till in the Milwaukee area that had been correlated with the till at Valders, Wisconsin. However, on the inside (Lake Michigan side) of the Whitehall moraine first Farrand (1970) and then Evenson (1973) documented the presence of Glenwood and Calumet shorelines, which could not by any interpretation be post-Valders in age. The same situation was amply demonstrated as far north as the south side of the city of Manistee. North of Manistee, on the other hand, only Algonquin shorelines are found on the red till. From these observations it was concluded that the line of red till moraines between Whitehall and Manistee must be older than the Valders readvance, probably being Port Huron in age, and that the Valders advance came only as far south as Manistee. Evenson (1973) clearly demonstrated that the same conditions obtained on the Wisconsin side of Lake Michigan, showing that the southern limit of the Valders advance was at Two Rivers, Wisconsin.

The third revision stemmed from the second. In his research, Evenson (1973) observed that the red till at Two Rivers is continuous with the red till overlying the Two Creeks Forest Bed, only eleven miles to the north, but that this red till does *not* extend westward across the Twin Rivers lowland (which lies between Two Rivers and Manitowoc, Wisconsin) to the Valders type-locality, about twelve miles west of Manitowoc. (One often loses sight of the fact that the Valders type-locality is in the Green Bay ice lobe, whereas Two Creeks is in the Lake Michigan lobe, and that the two are separated by the Kettle Interlobate Moraine.) The Twin Rivers lowland is covered by deposits of the Glenwood stage of Glacial Lake Chicago. These deposits have not been overrun by the ice that laid down the red till at Two Rivers and at Two Creeks, but the Glenwood sediments are underlain by another red till, which appears to be the same as the red till that *underlies* the Two Creeks Forest Bed. (The till below the forest bed was originally reported to be gray, but that appears to have been only a local deviation from its generally red color.) Therefore, Evenson (1973) suggested—and this seems to be borne out by a drilling program by Mickelson and Evenson (1975)—that the lower till at Two Creeks (Port Huron in age?) is continuous with the red till at Valders. This leads, of course, to the awkward conclusion that the type-Valders till is itself Port Huron in age. This is by no means the first time that geological stratigraphers have faced a similar problem of nomenclature. Evenson wisely offered a new name, "Two Rivers Till," for the red till overlying Glenwood sediments at Two Rivers and for the (same) red till overlying the forest bed at Two Creeks. This step is in accord with the rule of the American Code of Stratigraphic Nomenclature that a name with age implications not be applied to a lithologic (till) unit.

It appears at the present time, therefore, that the red till at Valders, Wisconsin, and that extending southward from Manitowoc to Milwaukee across Lake Michigan to Whitehall and thence north to Manistee should all be assigned to the Port Huron moraine. A proper age-term for the time represented by the Port Huron moraine and its equivalents has not yet been proposed. It apparently includes the type-Valders till, but cannot be regarded as part of the Valderan Substage of Willman and Frye (1970) because that substage has been (unsatisfactorily) defined on the basis of the till *overlying* the Two Creeks Forest Bed. This nomenclatural problem is discussed in detail by Farrand (1976) and Evenson et al. (in press).

The corollary of this revision is that the Two Rivers Till in Wisconsin is now seen as the logical correlative of the red till north of Manistee, which was formerly—even in the first part of this paper—called "Valders." Therefore, to be consistent, the red till mapped by Melhorn (1954) as Valders north and east of Manistee should now be called "Two Rivers Till" instead. A band of till mapped across the floor of Lake Michigan (Lineback et al., 1974) between Manitowoc-Two Rivers and Manistee appears to provide the necessary physical link between the Michigan and Wisconsin shores of Lake Michigan.

*Implications for Michigan Prehistory.*

Chronologically the period of the deglaciation of southern Michigan coincides with the Paleo-Indian Period, which is characterized by the presence of fluted-point cultures (Griffin, 1965:655). Fluted points in Michigan have unfortunately come only from surficial collections without stratigraphic depth. Nevertheless, numerous fluted points have been found, and distributional analysis of them has led to certain limiting conclusions concerning their age (Mason, 1958; Quimby, 1958, 1963). A modified version of Mason's (1958) map presented here (Fig. 2) includes the Port Huron and Two Rivers till borders as now conceived for the southern peninsula of Michigan as well as the shoreline of Glacial Lake Algonquin. Certainly it seems more logical at the present time to select the Port Huron border, rather than the Two Rivers, as a limiting boundary to the distribution of fluted points in Michigan. Extensive areas between those two ice borders along both the Lake Michigan and Lake Huron shorelines (especially in Muskegon, Oceana, Mason, Manistee, Alcona, Iosco, Arenac, Huron and Sanilac counties) were available for habitation at the time of the Two Rivers advance, but no fluted points have been found there. It seems highly unlikely that finds have not been made in these areas either because of chance or lack of investigation. On the other hand, only two finds of fluted points are known from the area inside the Port Huron moraine—in Bay County (Mason, 1958)—but they are well beyond the Two Rivers ice front position. Therefore, of the two ice border positions, the Port Huron seems a more logical natural barrier to the penetration of the Fluted Point Hunters into the northern portion of Michigan.

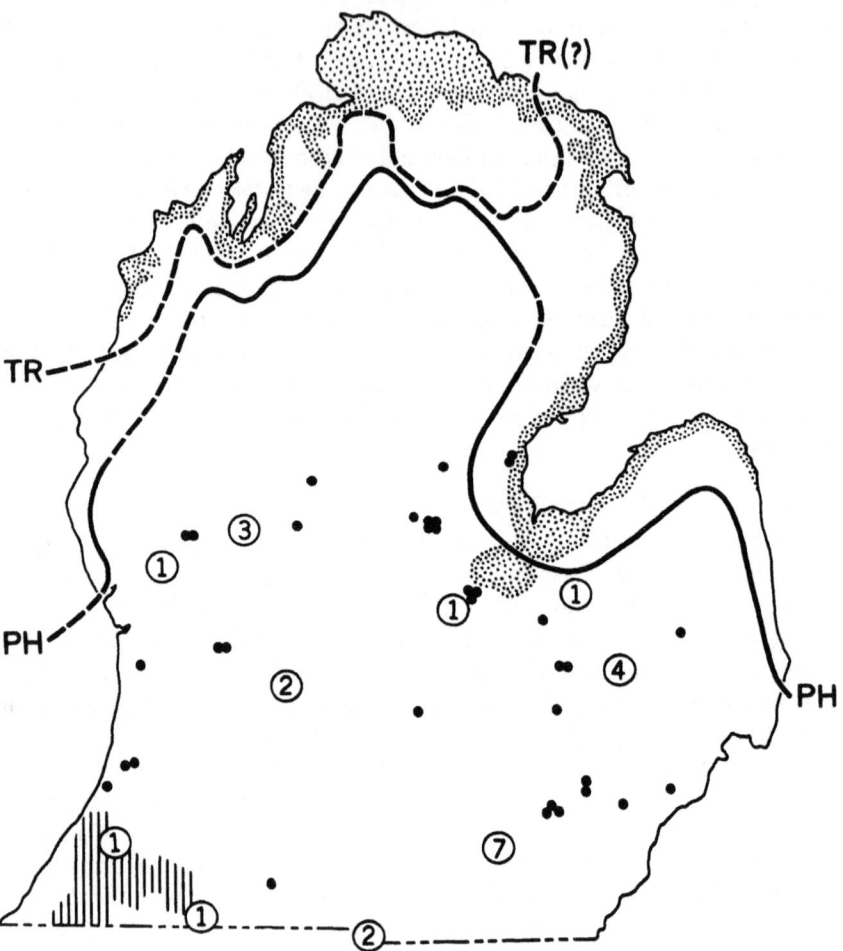

Figure 2. Distribution of fluted points in southern Michigan relative to late-glacial ice front positions. Black points locate specific finds of fluted points, and the vertically lined area in the southwest indicates an area of abundant finds. Circled numbers are additional fluted points that cannot be located more precisely than the county in which they were found. (Adapted from Mason, 1958.) P.H. = Port Huron ice border. T.R. = Two Rivers ice border. Stippled area = area inundated by the main stage of Glacial Lake Algonquin.

In addition, a few fluted-point sites are located on geological features that provide other sorts of limiting dates. The Barnes Site in Midland County sits on a Warren II beach, and it is probable that the site was utilized at the time of the Warren II lake level, or shortly after, because significantly later, at times such as those of the Two Creeks low level or of Lake Algonquin, the site would have been unfavorably isolated in the midst of swampy terrain (Wright and Roosa, 1966). The Warren lakes occurred after the Port Huron ice maximum but before the Two Creeks low lake, and long before the Two Rivers maximum.

On the Lake Michigan side of the state two other sites provide similar data. First, two fluted points were recovered from the surface of a high outwash terrace along the Muskegon River in Newaygo County (Prahl, 1966). That terrace, at 660 to 680 feet above sea level, must have been graded to the Glenwood stage of Glacial Lake Chicago. Although, of course, the points could have been dropped on that terrace at any time after the Glenwood stage, they could also be contemporary with that high lake, which existed until just after the Port Huron maximum. Similarly, the Yaggie fluted point find in Ottawa County (Quimby, 1958) appears to be associated with the Calumet beach of Glacial Lake Chicago, and the Calumet stage, which followed the Glenwood, must be placed between the Port Huron maximum and the Two Creeks minimum. All three sites are directly or indirectly associated with glacial lake levels that are correlated closely in time with the Port Huron readvance, but are separated by a relatively long interval of time from the Two Rivers maximum.

At the other end of the time scale, no fluted points have yet been found on the floor of Glacial Lake Algonquin, while Early Archaic industries are "consistently associated" with Lake Algonquin and post-Algonquin shorelines (Griffin, 1965). The two fluted point finds in Bay County and the one in Grand Traverse County (Fig. 2) are apparently associated with, or just above, the Algonquin beach, and several finds in Saginaw County may bear some relation to the shoreline of an embayment of Glacial Lake Algonquin just distal to the Port Huron moraine in that area (Mason, 1958). In fairness it must be admitted that the shoreline of Glacial Lake Algonquin so closely approximates the present shoreline south of Manistee and of the tip of the Thumb that distributional analysis is probably not very useful in those areas. These portions of the Algonquin shoreline, furthermore, either have been subsequently eroded or are covered with younger dune sand. The Skegemog Point in Grand Traverse County occurs inside the Two Rivers moraine (Dekin, 1966) and remains problematic. It is clearly separate from all other known occurrences and additionally is unusual because of its extremly small size (only 39 mm long). It was found "probably in association with the highest" Lake Algonquin beach in the area, but more clarification is needed.

Nevertheless, it is consistent with the present data to conclude, as Griffin (1965) did, that the fluted point industry had disappeared from Michigan prior to the major stand of Glacial Lake Algonquin. Since Lake Algonquin was the proglacial lake fronting the Two Rivers ice, its shoreline in the areas of the state that concern us must be dated close to 11,800 years ago on the basis of the Two Creeks site chronology. Radiocarbon dates from the Kutsch and Mielock Road sites in the Saginaw Bay area confirm this dating (Crane and Griffin, 1966:258, 259). Thus Griffin's (1965) interpretation which assumes that fluted points in the northeastern United States, or at least in Michigan, are more than 11,000 years old (9,000 B.C.) still is eminently valid.

## Conclusion

The purpose of this paper has been to present some recent, important revisions in the glacial stratigraphy of Michigan and to re-evaluate the chronological position of Paleo-Indian artifacts within the state. The two main revisions are (a) the assignment of the red till along the Lake Michigan shoreline from Whitehall to Manistee to the Port Huron morainic system, rather than to the Valders, and (b) re-naming the "Valders" drift of the northern part of the southern peninsula the "Two Rivers Till." Studies of Evenson (1973) pointed out the uncertainties, to say the least, in the correlation of the type-Valders till at Valders, Wisconsin, with the tills at Two Creeks and in Michigan. Moreover, it has been indicated here that the Two Rivers (formerly Valders) is by no means the only red till in the southern peninsula of Michigan.

The distribution of fluted points in Michigan is logically consistent with a limiting ice border at the Port Huron moraine, rather than with the Two Rivers ("Valders") ice border as previously suggested (Mason, 1958; Quimby, 1963). The possible association of fluted points with Warren and Calumet beaches and with outwash graded to the Glenwood level suggests that the Fluted Point Hunters were in Michigan just after, during and most likely before the Port Huron maximum around 12,500 years ago. Most of the fluted points in Michigan occur in areas that have been ice free for only about 14,800 years (Fig. 1b and Fig. 2). On the other hand, fluted points do not occur on the floor of Glacial Lake Algonquin, and this suggests a limiting date of about 11,800 years ago for the youngest fluted points in the state. The 3,000-year interval from 14,800 to 11,800 years ago thus appears to encompass the greatest part of the Fluted Point Hunter occupation in Michigan.

## References Cited

Bretz, J. H.
    1951    The stage of Lake Chicago: their causes and correlations. American Journal of Science 249:401-29.

Crane, H. R. and Griffin, J. B.
    1966    University of Michigan radiocarbon dates XI. Radiocarbon Supplement 8:256-85.

Dekin, A. A. Jr.
    1966    A fluted point from Grand Traverse County. Michigan Archaeologist 12:35-36.

Evenson, E. B.
    1973    Late Pleistocene shorelines and stratigraphic relations in the Lake Michigan basin. Geological Society of America, Bulletin 84: 2281-98.

Evenson, E. B., Farrand, W. R., Mickelson, D. M., Eschman, D. F. and Maher, L. J.
    1976    Great Lakes Substage: a replacement for Valderan in the Lake Michigan basin. Quaternary Research 6:411-24.

Farrand, W. R.
    1970.    Revision of the Valders drift border of the Lake Michigan lobe. Geological Society of America, Abstracts with Programs 2 (6): 387.
    1976    Was there really a Valders? Michigan Academician 8:477-86.

Farrand, W. R. and Eschman, D. F.
    1974    Glaciation of the southern peninsula of Michigan: A review. Michigan Academician 7:31-56.

Farrand, W. R., Zahner, R. and Benninghoff, W. S.
    1969    Cary-Port Huron interstade: evidence from a buried bryophyte bed, Cheboygan County, Michigan. Geological Society of America, Special Paper 123:249-62.

Griffin, J. B.
    1965    Late Quaternary prehistory in the northeastern woodlands. Item *in:* Wright, H. E. Jr. and Frey, D. G., The Quaternary of the United States, Princeton: Princeton Univ. Press, pp. 655-67.

Lineback, J. A., Gross, D. L. and Meyer, R. P.
    1974    Glacial tills under Lake Michigan. Illinois Geological Survey. Environmental Geology Notes 69. 48 p.

Mason, R. J.
    1958    Late-Pleistocene geochronology and the Paleo-Indian penetration into the lower Michigan peninsula. University of Michigan Museum of Anthropology, Anthropological Papers No. 11.

Melhorn, W. N.
   1954   Valders glaciation of the southern peninsula of Michigan. Unpublished Ph.D. dissertation, University of Michigan, Ann Arbor.
Mickelson, D. M. and Evenson, E. B.
   1975   Pre-Twocreekan age of the type Valders till, Wisconsin. Geology 3: 587-90.
Mörner, N. A. and Dreimanis, A.
   1973   The Erie Interstade. Geological Society of America, Memoir 136: 107-34.
Prahl, E. J.
   1966   The Muskegon River survey: 1965 and 1966. Michigan Archaeologist 12:183-209.
Quimby, G. I.
   1958   Fluted points and the geochronology of the Lake Michigan basin. American Antiquity 23:247-54.
Quimby, G. I.
   1963   A new look at geochronology in the Upper Great Lakes region. American Antiquity 28:558-59.
Willman, H. B. and Frye, J. C.
   1970   Pleistocene stratigraphy of Illinois. Illinois State Geological Survey, Bulletin 94.
Wright, H. T. and Roosa, W. B.
   1966   The Barnes sites: a fluted point assemblage from the Great Lakes region. American Antiquity 31:850-60.

# PART II

# American Studies

# FLUTED POINTS FROM THE PARKHILL, ONTARIO SITE

*William B. Roosa*
University of Waterloo

## Fluting Techniques as Clues to Antiquity and Cultural Affinity

Some years ago (Roosa, 1965) I suggested the use of fluting techniques as an aid in recognizing fluted point types. I still consider this to be very useful, although it has not been widely understood or much used by others. Non-Folsom fluting techniques include the Clovis and Enterline techniques. In many cases it is not necessary to be able to distinguish the various non-Folsom techniques from each other; all that is needed is the ability to recognize the Folsom technique. In effect this identifies two classes of fluting techniques, Folsom and non-Folsom.

What is needed is a simple rule for recognizing the Folsom technique, one that will work in a significant majority of cases. I suggest the following rule of thumb for identifying Folsom type fluting: well-centered single fluting that is 30 to 40 mm long or longer, at least 8 to 10 mm wide—often 12-15 mm wide, and relatively parallel sided or expanding (as opposed to contracting at least to the widest part of the point) is probably Folsom fluting. It is usually neatly hinged out if terminated short of the point tip or feathered out the tip if fully fluted.

In eastern North America the base of the wide single Folsom type flute may be overriden by one or two fairly large (probably direct percussion) finishing flakes. These finishing flakes serve to widen the base of the flute scar, but do not contribute materially to the length or width of the flute. In contrast, on double or triple fluted points the lateral flutes make a real contribution to the width and length of the combined flute scar and are quite basic to the technique.

This rule of thumb can be applied in two different ways. First, the mean length of fluting may be computed for all the reasonably whole points in an assemblage. If this figure exceeds 30 mm the assemblage probably utilized Folsom type fluting. If it exceeds 40 mm this is almost a certainty. A sample of thirty-six Clovis points from the Clovis, Dent, Miami, Naco and Lehner sites gives a range of fluting length of from 10 to 46 mm with a mean of 25.11 mm. A sample of Enterline points from the Shoop site—measured from photos supplied by John Witthoft—gives a figure of 16 to 26 mm for the range and 21.7 mm for the mean length of fluting.

The other method, obviously more subjective, requires the making of a value judgment on each relatively whole point in an assemblage as to whether or not it has Folsom type fluting. In a few cases it is impossible to be certain which type of fluting is involved. These data can then be used to compute an Index of Folsom Fluting, which is the percentage or ratio of Folsom fluting present on the points in a given assemblage. This should be very high for a Folsom assemblage, and very low for a Clovis or Enterline assemblage. It would be fairly high for a Barnes point assemblage but not so high as that for a Folsom assemblage because two fluting techniques occur on Barnes points. Some Barnes points have a double fluting technique distinct from but clearly related to the Folsom technique.

## Fluted Point Hafting and Possible Weapons Systems, Clovis, Folsom, Barnes

Art Jelinek and I suggested about fifteen years ago that Clovis fluted points were probably hafted on stabbing spears and were designed to slide out of the haft and remain in the animal. Minor stylistic differences in Clovis points could thus have served to identify the hunter who made the kill. Differences in material could serve the same purpose.

A small amount of pitch may have been placed in the slot in the haft to prevent the points from being lost. A light binding of sinew or grass would have served the same purpose, but the use of pitch would have permitted more rapid replacement of spear points under the stress of making a kill.

The presence of grinding on the lateral basal edges of fluted points has often been interpreted as indicating that the points were bound in place with sinew; however, this may not have been its function. The grinding and the fishtails often found on Great Lakes (and Southeastern) fluted points may have functioned to prevent the point from pulling out of the wound when the spear was withdrawn from the animal. They may also have helped the hunter to grip the point while inserting it in the haft or when removing an old broken base that might have become wedged in the haft.

Whatever system of hafting was used on Clovis points it apparently functioned so that the points were left in the mammoths. This could also have been accomplished by hafting the points on detachable foreshafts. If these were bone we might logically expect to find a few still in place. To the best of my knowledge only the Clovis points are found in the beasts, never bone foreshafts, although bones of small diameter such as ribs, are preserved.

Clovis points could have been hafted in detachable wooden foreshafts which have since decayed. This negates the idea that fluting had some special functional significance beyond that of hafting, and fluting may simply be the oldest known method of hafting in the New World. As such it probably developed from the practice of thinning the butts of Mousterian and other Middle and late Paleolithic points.

I do not agree with Lahren and Bonnichsen's recent (1974) reconstruction of the Clovis hafting system. The beveled bone "foreshafts" from their Clovis burial could have been used to hold Clovis preforms while they were being fluted. What they interpret as a point hafting kit may be a point *making* kit, complete with lanceolate Clovis preforms.

Judge gives the basal width (BW) of his sample of 26 Clovis points as ranging from 19.1 to 29.2 mm, with a mean of 23.92 mm (Judge, 1973: 249, Table 15). The BW of his sample of 33 Folsom points ranges from 17.2 to 22 mm, with a mean of 19.42 mm (1973:165, Table 6). The BW of Barnes points from the Parkhill site ranges from 12.4 mm (for an atypical fluted knife) to 20 mm. Precise measurements of BW are impossible on many because they lack part of one or both ears, but in some cases accurate estimates of the BW were possible. The mean BW of a sample of 34 Parkhill site Barnes points (with some estimated) is 16.625 mm.

Given a small sample after the 1973 dig it appeared that there might be a tendency for a bimodal distribution of BW for Parkhill site Barnes points with a cluster at 15 mm and another at ca. 17 to 19 mm. Judging from the larger 1974 sample, this is not so.

Barnes points are obviously narrower than Folsom points, which in turn are narrower than Clovis points. It should be noted that the variability of the BW of the Barnes points is high with a standard deviation of 2.019 and Coefficient of Variation of 12.12; compared with the Folsom sample's standard deviation of only 1.125 and a Coefficient of Variation of 5.79. The standard deviation for the Clovis sample is higher at 2.565, while the Coefficient of Variation is also high at 10.06.

For what it is worth the range of BW for Judge's 23 Cody points is from 15 to 19 mm with a mean of 17.31, a standard deviation of 1.185, and a Coefficient of Variation of 6.84, (Judge, 1973:236, Table 14). The Cody range and mean thus roughly approximate that of the Barnes points.

The above differences in mean BW suggests that Clovis, Folsom and Barnes points were hafted on shafts or foreshafts of different diameters, and this may indicate hafting on different kinds of weapons. I suggest heavy stabbing spears (lances) for Clovis points; lighter smaller diameter spears (javelins) better adapted to throwing for Folsom points; and still lighter smaller diameter spears for Barnes points. All three could have been hafted on detachable foreshafts. The smaller the BW, the greater the probability is that the points were on detachable foreshafts or on atlatl darts.

Barnes points could have been used on atlatl darts. However, I have contended for years that the shift from Paleo-Indian with fluted points to Archaic with stemmed and side notched points coincided with a major shift in weapons—probably from spear to atlatl.

## The Parkhill Site

The Parkhill site is located on the Lake Algonquin shore several miles west of Parkhill, Ontario. The Algonquin shoreline makes a major right-angle bend about half a mile south of the site. The area was probably excellent for caribou hunting, which would account for the location of the site (B. Deller, personal communication).

*In situ* Paleo-Indian artifacts are in a sandy loam that may represent old sand dunes. This loam overlies a lake (probably Lake Warren) clay which in turn overlies laminated waterlaid sand at grid B. The clay has been subjected to intense loading action in places, apparently well before the occupation (A. Cooper, Al Morgan: personal communication).

A similar thin laminated waterlaid sand overlies the clay at grid C. The few *in situ* artifacts from C are in the sandy loam which overlies the waterlaid sand and may have been derived from it.

A pollen sample from just below a Paleo-Indian feature (Feature 9 grid B) contains a predominance of pine over spruce. Dr. J. McAndrews of the Royal Ontario Museum has suggested that this represents pollen zone 2 which has been dated elsewhere at between 9,750 and 10,750 years BP (McAndrews: letter of January 28, 1975).

A backhoe strat. cut in a small swamp on the site just west of grid D shows a gray till (probably Port Huron) at the bottom of the cut. A reddish lake clay (probably Lake Warren) overlies the till. This lake clay has been eroded away in places. A peaty deposit containing a variety of plant material overlies the lake clay. Field identification of some of the material includes oak and hemlock, suggesting that it is of Nipissing or post-Nipissing age. Deposits of Paleo-Indian age (i.e., Lake Algonquin age) have apparently been eroded away in this immediate area (A. Cooper, J. McAndrews, and Al Morgan: personal communications in the field).

Some of the Paleo-Indian material at grids B and C is *in situ* in the subsoil in and near probable Paleo-Indian features. Many artifacts were in the plowzone. The provenience of plowzone artifacts was plotted as carefully as possible. There is good clustering of plowzone finds and of plowzone material with subsoil Paleo-Indian artifacts and features, especially at grid B. A fluted point base with hard dark red ochre adhering to one face came from the plowzone about three feet from a small subsoil hearth (Fea. 21) with an area of hard cemented dark red ochre at one edge. Elsewhere on B three pieces of another fluted point were found in three adjacent five-foot squares. Two pieces were in the subsoil, the third was in the plowzone. A recurring pattern of small clusters of artifacts occurs at least 7 times on grid B. Each of these clusters contains 2 discarded fluted artifacts (usually point bases), 3 or 4 channel flakes and usually one scraper or used flake. It appears that the effect of the plow has been to blur or slightly enlarge the clusters. Material in the plowzone taken in conjunction with the *in situ* material provides us with a slightly distorted shadow image or ghost image of the site layout at grids B and C. In contrast, subsoil Paleo-Indian material at grid D, which is on a low hill, appears to have washed in from its original locus higher on the hill.

*Fluting Techniques; Barnes Points; Parkhill Site*

Judging from the Parkhill site sample of over 80 fluted points (or major portions thereof) there are three fluting techniques present. They are designated as types 1a, 1b, and 2. There is also a basal thinning or basal finishing technique designated as type 3.

Type 1 fluting (1a and 1b) is essentially Folsom type fluting. It involves a well-centered, relatively long wide flute. It was probably done by indirect percussion and may have utilized heat treated preforms. It was often partly overridden by one or two large pressure or percussion basal thinning flakes, i.e., the Barnes finishing technique. These finishing or basal thinning flakes destroy the base of the main flute and the remains of the carefully prepared, chipped and ground Folsom type striking platform (basal nipple) (see Fig. 2).

Type 1a Fluting: Folsom Type Fluting

This is essentially full-length fluting, often exceeding 50 mm in length. On finished points it usually appears to feather out or go out the tip. Preform tips from Folsom sites (Judge, 1970) and the Parkhill site indicate that the flute was sometimes hinged out near the tip of the preform which was then snapped off and a new tip chipped on the point.

Type 1b Fluting: Short Folsom Type Fluting

This usually runs about 50 percent of the point length, often in the 30-40 mm range. It appears to have been deliberately hinged out, probably by holding the wrapped preform at about the midpoint. It differs from type 1a fluting mainly in length. What appears to be very short 1b fluting, i.e., 15-20 mm long, also appears on a few points.

Type 2 Fluting: Double Fluting

The double fluting technique found on Barnes points probably utilized a simple convex beveled base. It apparently did not use the well-centered Folsom striking platform. The first flute is relatively narrow and off center but relatively parallel to the long axis of the point. The second flute, usually a little shorter, is offset slightly toward the other edge of the point. Both usually terminate in hinge fractures. They combine to produce a wide flute scar. The length of fluting approaches that of short Folsom type fluting. It may have used indirect percussion and heat treated preforms. This double fluting is often found on only one face of the artifact.

Type 3: Basal Thinning and Basal Finishing

If this occurs alone it is called basal thinning. This involves one or two large pressure or percussion flakes very similar to the basal finishing flakes noted above. These are short wide flakes seldom more than 10 or 15 mm long. If it is over prior fluting it is called basal finishing. If carefully centered, a single basal finishing flake blends well with the main flute and may be very difficult to distinguish from it visually. The transition from the basal thinning flake scar to the main flute scar can often be felt by running a fingernail along the flute up from the base toward the tip. Basal thinning or finishing flakes were often removed from only one face; however, occasionally they were removed from both.

If only one basal thinning or finishing flake was removed from a face it usually feathered out or hinged out very slightly. If two finishing flakes are present on one face, they may run up along one or both edges of the main flute for 15 or 20 mm. Type 3 thinning may have been done by direct percussion using a piece of bone or antler.

Combinations of Fluting Techniques

Both faces of a point may have the same fluting technique, usually type 1. Combinations are not uncommon; 1a and 1b may occur together (usually on opposite faces). Either 1a or 1b may occur opposite type 2 or 3, and type 2 occurs with 3 (on opposite faces). One point from the site has 2-2 fluting (type 2 on each face) and another has type 3-3. The latter is by definition unfluted. Some type 3 basal thinning is as good as some Clovis fluting and may involve the same technique.

On bases (some 60 percent of the sample) that have broken off near or below the midpoint it is often impossible to distinguish type 1a from 1b fluting. On such bases, it is occasionally difficult to differentiate between type 1 fluting, where the basal finishing flake runs to one edge of the main flute, and type 2 fluting. On very short bases (ca. 10 to 15 mm) it is difficult to distinguish between fluting types.

Type 1 is the most common fluting technique on Parkhill points. Type 1a is more common than 1b on points where it is possible to tell them apart. Type 2 occurs on all the perfect or nearly perfect points from the site, and on some of the others, usually unifacially with type 1 fluting or type 3 basal thinning on the other face.

*Material*

Most of the Paleo-Indian artifacts from the site are made of Amabel chert which occurs in the Niagara Escarpment south of Georgian Bay (Peter Storck, personal communication). It varies in color from solid white to creamy yellow and occasionally pinkish orange. It often has gray, pink, orange, yellow or brown bands. Much of it has tiny black dots that show up as pits under 20X magnification. Texture varies from chalky to slick and glassy when seen with the unaided eye. Under the 20X lens it all appears to be very glassy. Some of the differences in texture and color appear to be the result of intentional or accidental heat treatment. Some of the bands in the chert resemble chalcedony. Nine points are chalcedony. This translucent chalcedony occurs in almost the same range of colors and color combinations as the opaque chert. Some of it is banded, and some has the tiny black dots. What I am designating as chalcedony and chert are probably variations of the same thing from the same source.

Ten points are from a dark brown chalky chert, which probably falls into the Amabel category. Four others are made from a smooth chocolate brown chert—not to be confused with four more which are made of a dark gray to black chert. Material in these eight points may not be from the same source as that of the majority of the Paleo-Indian artifacts from the site.

*Discussion of the Terms "Type," "Subtype," "Style Group"*

The terms "type," "subtype," and "style group" refer to classes of artifacts and are based primarily on macro-morphological formal attributes. "Type" is the largest most inclusive class of the three with considerable internal variability. "Style group" is the smallest, most exclusive class with little internal variability.

The term "style group" is used here to designate the smallest typological grouping of artifacts (i.e., fluted points in this case). A style group includes artifacts that are stylistically identical, thus there is no significant stylistic variation between the points in a style group. Inherent in the concept is the idea that it probably represents artifacts made by a single individual, at about the same time, and from similar or identical material. A super-splitter might call them "sub-subtypes"; however, I see them as representing individual styles in point making, hence, my term "style groups."

The term "subtype" as used here refers to a larger class than a style group. Thus a subtype may include many style groups, i.e., a wide range of stylistic variation. The three simple subtypes used herein are based primarily on fluting techniques and on whether the points are unifacially or bifacially fluted. Points of the three subtypes occur together in clusters around features on the site. They also have many other attributes in common. This would seem to indicate that all are the products of the same cultural group. The three subtypes may also have some functional significance without their functions appearing to be mutually exclusive.

I could have designated these subtypes as types, but I chose to use the term type to designate all the fluted points and fluted knives from the fluted point component of the site. Presumably they were made by the men of one band. By extension the type also includes similar artifacts from other sites occupied by the same group at about the same time, as well as sites occupied by other closely related bands who shared the same culture, that is, the same technology as it pertains to the making and using of fluted points.

As defined here, the Barnes point type thus includes three subtypes with possible functional significance. Each Barnes subtype in turn includes style groups that apparently reflect individual styles in pointmaking. The Barnes point type and the three Barnes point subtypes are diagnostic artifacts of the Parkhill complex. The style groups are probably diagnostic of various individuals.

*Subtypes*

These are based on gross morphology, including fluting techniques. Most of the points fit into these three subtypes. Subtype I consists of unifacially fluted knives with type 2 fluting on one face, and short type 3 thinning on the other. This includes four nearly perfect "points" which appear to have been used as knives. The fact that all four are virtually perfect may indicate that they were never used as points—i.e., that they were intended for use as knives.

Subtype II is also essentially unifacially fluted with type 1a fluting overridden by short 1b fluting or type 3 basal finishing on one face and very short type 1b fluting or type 3 basal thinning on the other face. There are no whole points in this subtype.

Subtype III includes all the bifacially fluted points from the site. Although it is difficult to be certain about some of the shorter subtype III bases, most of them appear to have type 1 fluting.

*Style Groups*

In many cases the lateral edges and the tips of more or less whole points, tips, and midsections show wear patterns. This sort of evidence of use does not usually occur on the basal edges. Thus functional classification is not possible with most point bases.

However, certain clusters of minor attributes present on the bases of some of the points apparently have non-functional (stylistic) significance. Stylistic variation occurs within all three subtypes. Some stylistic variation may have originally been present on the blades or tips of the points, but this has been obscured by resharpening, use, etc. My style groups are limited to those specimens that have more or less intact bases and depend almost exclusively on basal attributes.

The three subtypes are subdivided into style groups. Each style group exhibits a cluster of minor attributes that contrast with those of other style groups. The idea originated in Haury's comments on Naco site Clovis points to the effect that points of the same (exotic) material were probably made by the same person (Haury, 1953). An examination of the Naco points (from the photos) indicated that there are minor stylistic similarities between points of the same material and minor stylistic differences between those of different materials. Some of these similarities and differences are probably due to similarities and differences in material, while others, *especially minor differences in basal shape*, probably are not functions of material.

This suggested the possibility of estimating the number of hunters—that is, the number of point makers at a given Paleo-Indian kill or armament site. I dealt with this briefly in reference to the Naco & Lehner sites in my dissertation (Roosa, 1967). Now with an adequate sample of points from one site at my disposal, I decided to apply the idea again. We also used a computer, with some success, to test these style groups.

## Grid B Fluted Points, Parkhill Site

*General*

The site was divided into a series of grids for testing and excavation. Early surface finds from grid B, the second to be tested, include two fluted points, Field Catalog numbers (FC) 47, 48 and two channel flake fragments. These find locations were marked with stakes and a grid was laid off in the area from the north-south baseline. More than eighty five-foot squares were subsequently excavated in the area (980 N – 1040 N, 40 – 75 E).

Grid B yielded about two-thirds of the fluted points from the site. Many of the style groups are also found in grid B. The grid B sample includes three almost perfect Subtype I points; four bases, three tips, and two fluted point blades—representing seven Subtype II points; plus 29 bases, four fluted point blades—one (in two pieces) is part of the same point as a base, three tips, and two midsections of Subtype III fluted points. This is a total of 50 major portions of fluted points, representing 46 or 47 points.

The grid B sample also includes three basal halves, 14 ears, and nine miscellaneous fluted point fragments. None of these fit each other or the above points. A total of 26 more fluted points is represented by these bits and pieces. The grid B sample thus represents some 73 fluted points. It also includes 140 channel flakes, none of which match the grid B points. However, at least two grid B channel flakes match grid D points. One grid B channel flake matches the only fluted preform base from B.

In addition, there are three snapped tips of fluted point preforms and one base of a fluted preform. Thousands of flakes of bifacial retouch and pressure retouch flakes were also recovered from grid B. Scrapers are rare with only ten examples, and two scraper retouch flakes. The artifact concentration on grid B is just north of and just below the crest of a very low east-west ridge with an overview of a small swampy area about eight hundred feet south which could have been a kill site. Preliminary analysis indicates that grid B was a point-making area similar to Judge's armament areas (Judge & Dawson, 1972; Judge 1973). Several possible Paleo-Indian features were found in this area.

*Subtype I*

This subtype apparently constitutes a functionally distinct artifact category with primary use as fluted knives.

This group, which includes three grid B artifacts FC 76 (Fig. 1), and 85 (Fig. 5), is unique in several ways. All three are perfect (or nearly so), and

Figure 1. Fluted Knives (on 5 mm grid).
Top Row L to R: 3 Subtype 1 Fluted Knives Type 2 Fluting—FC 92, FC 76 Grid B, FC 204; Fluted Point Blade Type 1b Fluting—FC 208 Grid B.
Bottom Row: Fluted Point Blades used as Heavy Duty Knives: FC 374 Grid B, FC 24 Grid E, both have short 1b fluting over 1a fluting Subtype II; FC 2 Grid D, FC 207 Grid B, both have type 1a fluting. FC 92 was in Feature 5, FC 374 was in Feature 17.

they have type 2 fluting on one face and type 3 basal thinning or no basal modification on the other. Basal lateral edge grinding is very light. These three and FC 204, a surface find with the same kind of fluting from an area east of B, are the only perfect points on the site. While it is not unusual to find perfect points on kill sites, there is nothing in grid B or the FC 204 find area to indicate that they were kill areas. These three grid B artifacts are the only reasonably whole fluted points in a point making area. This suggests that they represent a special class of artifacts not used in the same way as the other 44 fluted points from grid B or as most of those from elsewhere on the site.

FC 92, the biggest whole point from the site (77 mm long), is worthy of note. There is no basal edge grinding; both lateral edges are very sharp and sinuous. There is little if any pressure retouch on the lateral edges. One edge shows possible use as a knife.

Basal shape of FC 76 and 92 is sufficiently different to suggest that they belong in two style groups and probably were made by two different men. FC 85 is too much reworked to be comparable.

FC 204 (Fig. 1) from outside grid B has a slight fishtail, a tiny bit of one ear is missing. Lateral basal edges are very lightly ground, and the basal concavity is very regular. The edges of the blades are very sharp and were apparently resharpened with a fine intermittant unifacial pressure retouch, giving the effect of a fine tooth saw. Heavy demi-quina (step) wear on one edge of the tip suggests that it has been subjected to heavy use as a knife. It belongs in another style group.

The fluted knives in subtype I share certain attributes, including fluting techniques and material, and occur in the same clusters around features with fluted points in subtypes II and III. They are all probably products of the same culture.

These artifacts, especially FC 76 and 92, have a resemblance to Holcombe points (Fitting et al., 1966). However, I would not identify them as such because the fluting is better than that found on most Holcombe points.

*Subtype II*

Grid B artifacts in this subtype include two bases and two tips, probably from the same two points, two fluted point blades, a probable tip, a possible tip fragment, and two other bases (See Figs. 1 and 2).

The subtype is characterized by unifacial type 1a fluting overridden by a 1b flute or type 3 basal thinning. (The type 1a flute runs off to the left on two bases and three tips.) The other face has very short 1b fluting or type

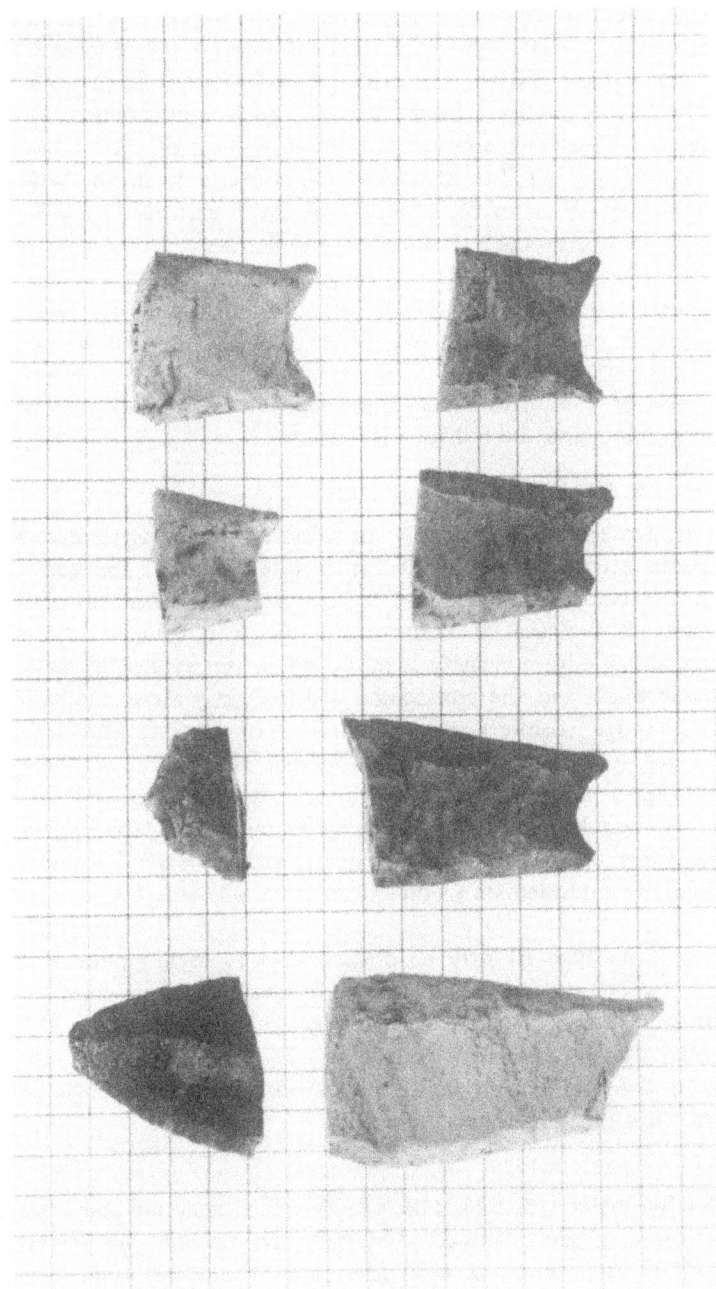

Figure 2. Subtype II, and Groups A, F, G, Subtype III
Top Row L to R: Tip FC 512, Tip FC 506; Base FC 130 Group F, Base FC 118 Group A.
Bottom Row: FC 511 probably the base of FC 512, FC 56 probably the base of FC 506, both Subtype II; FC 126 Group G, FC 254 Group A.

3 basal thinning. The two "good" bases have a pronounced taper of the lateral basal edges (ca. 18-20 degrees). Lateral basal edges are straight on one; the other has a slight fishtail. The basal concavity of FC 56, the only specimen with both ears relatively intact, is 4 mm deep, well rounded, and slightly asymmetrical. Illustrated subtype II artifacts include FC 511, a base with a slight fishtail, and tip FC 512 which is probably from the same point (ca. 70 mm long, 24 mm MW, 17 mm BW, and 6 mm thick). FC 56, a base without a fishtail, probably belongs in another style group. The 1a flute is overridden by a 1b flute 30 mm long. It is made from a reddish brown chalky chert, as is FC 506 which may be the tip of 56. Other illustrated subtype II points include two fluted point blades, FC 87 and 374.

For a discussion of wear patterns on these artifacts see the sections on Reworked Fluted Points and the Subtype II Cluster.

*Style Groups Subtype III—Bifacially Fluted Points*

These style groups are based primarily on relatively minor attributes of basal shape. These attributes are divided into three sets: 1. the lateral basal edges; 2. the basal concavity; and 3. the ears. The edges are first classed as straight or concave. If concave, the point is said to have a fishtail. The amount of edge concavity is measured in mm as the difference between the basal width and the constricted width slightly above the base. The curve of the edge (fishtail) may be gradual or abrupt. The angle between the edges is measured above the fishtail. The depth of basal concavity is measured in mm. It is classed as rounded, squared, or "vee" shaped; regular or irregular; and symmetrical or asymmetrical. The ears are classed as long, short or medium; their shape is either knobby, rounded (both edges rounded), intermediate (rounded on the inside edge), square, or pointed.

Grid B points in subtype III may be divided into 12 style groups. Five of these contain two or more points each, while seven are represented by only one point each. Some of the grid B style groups also occur on grid C and D. Additional style groups not found on grid B occur in grid E, C, and D. Twenty-six of the grid B subtype III bases were complete enough for style group identification; three bases were not.

Style Group A

This includes five bases (FC 524, 118, 47, 79, 153). They are characterized by pronounced abrupt fishtails. Although the fishtails are plainly noticeable, there is only about 2 mm difference (1 mm on each edge) between the basal width and the constricted width. The basal concavities are shallow (ca. 3 mm), rounded, slightly irregular, and symmetrical. The ears are short and rounded (See Fig. 2).

Style Group B

This includes three good examples (FC 74, 94, 158) and one possible one (FC 62). They have very slight gradual fishtails. Edge concavity varies from .25 to .50 mm per edge. Basal concavities are deep (ca. 5 mm), rounded with slight squaring, regular, and symmetrical. Ears are medium length, and intermediate to slightly rounded (Fig. 3).

Style Group C

This includes three good examples (FC 48, 285, 338) and one possible (FC 320). They have slight abrupt fishtails. Edge concavity is about .5 mm per edge. The basal concavities are quite deep (ca 6 mm) rounded, irregular, and somewhat asymmetrical. The ears are of medium length and knobby, (Fig. 3). These points are similar to Debert Points, especially in the depth of basal concavities. Might they be the work of a visitor from the East?

Style Group D

This includes only two examples (FC 177, 197). They have very slight gradual fishtails. Edge concavity is on the order of .1 to .2 mm on each edge. One edge is slightly more concave than the other which is almost straight. The basal concavities are deep regular asymmetrical "vees" (ca. 4.5 mm deep). The ears are long and pointed (Fig. 3).

Style Group E

This includes three good examples (FC 65, 294, 313), a possible (FC 168), and a basal half that appears to be in the group. A base from grid D probably belongs in the group. The three best examples from grid B and the one from D were either found in a fire and/or show the effects of being in a fire. Their workmanship is somewhat cruder than most of the other style groups, both lateral edges and basal concavities being somewhat irregular. They have slight, gradual fishtails with about a .5 mm concavity on each edge. Basal concavities are shallow (ca. 3.4 mm) and rounded. Ears are of medium length and intermediate outline (Fig. 3).

Style Group F

This consists of one example FC 130 (Fig. 2). It has a very pronounced taper (23 degrees) and no fishtail; an irregular shallow basal concavity (3.4 mm) and a pointed ear. Two other bases, one earless and the other with only one lateral edge intact might be in this class. They were in the same cluster around Feature 6/8 and are of material very similar to FC 130.

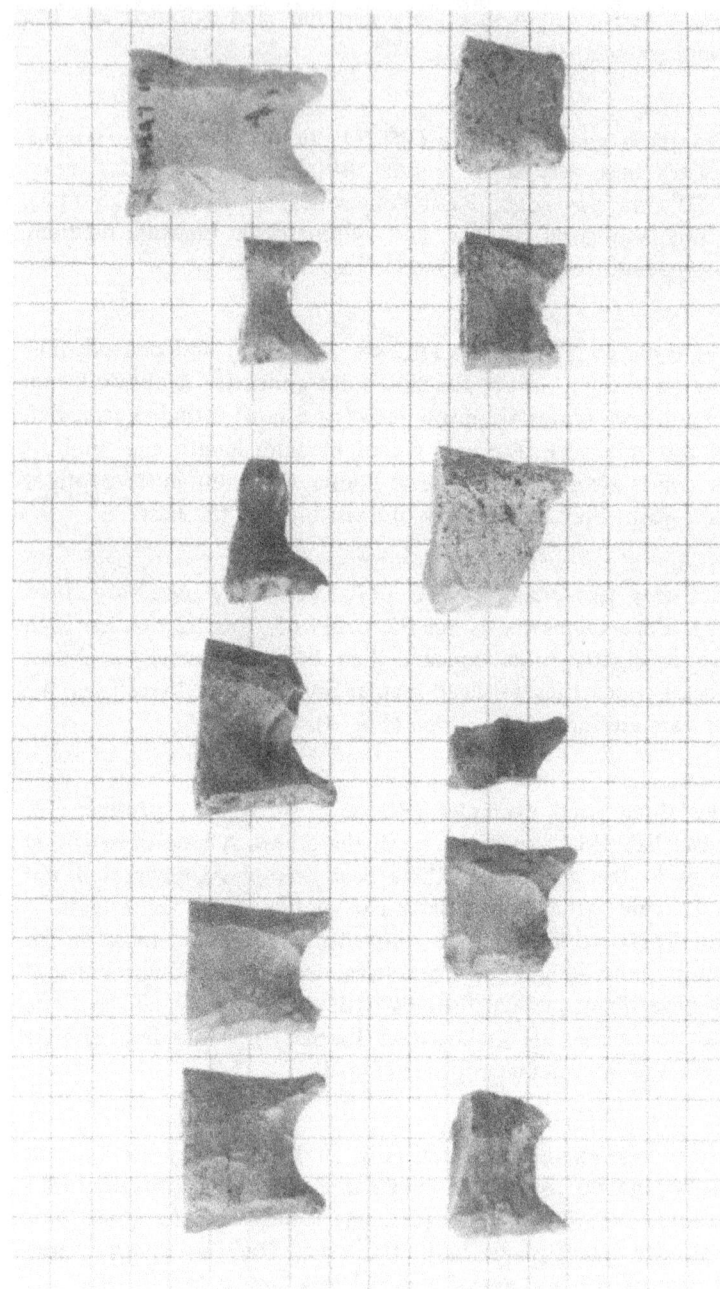

Figure 3. Style Groups B-K Grid B.
Top Row L to R: FC 94, FC 158 both Group B; FC 48, FC 285 both Group C; FC 177, FC 197 both group D.
Bottom Row: FC 146 Group H; FC 294, FC 294, FC 293 both Group E; FC 375 Group I; FC 339 Group J; FC 263 Group K. FC 294 was in Feature 9, FC 177 was in Feature 9A.

## Style Group G

This consists of FC 126. This point and the style group A and B points have the finest workmanship of any of the style groups (Fig. 2). It has a very slight gradual fishtail. Edge concavity is about .5 mm per edge. The basal concavity is 4.2 mm deep, rounded, and regular. The one complete ear is very rounded. Material is the same rainbow-hued chert as midsection FC 151 from the same cluster around Feature 6/8. This color may be the result of heat treatment. The general outline of FC 126 is very similar to that of FC 56 of subtype II, and it is possible that both were made by the same person.

## Style Group H

This includes FC 146 (Fig. 3). This point has no fishtail. The basal concavity is deep (5.5 mm) and squared. The ear is pointed.

## Style Group I

This includes FC 375, which is part of the same point as blade FC 127/280 (two fragments that fit). It has a very slight gradual fishtail. The basal concavity is difficult to characterize, because a big piece including one ear is missing. The remaining ear is short and intermediate. It does not seem to belong in any of the other style groups in subtype III (Fig. 3), but the outline shape is similar to FC 511 in subtype II.

## Style Group J

This is FC 339. It has a slight gradual fishtail with ca .1 mm edge concavity. Basal concavity is only 2.8 mm and rounded. The ears are short, very wide, and of intermediate outline (Fig. 3).

## Style Group K

This is FC 263 (Fig. 3). It is a real anomaly. If it were not for the edge grinding and the fishtail, I would suggest that it is probably the snapped tip of a preform. The basal edge is almost straight, i.e., it has no concavity and therefore no ears as such.

## Style Group L

This is FC 102 (Fig. 5). It has a gradual pronounced fishtail with ca .75 mm concavity on each edge. The basal concavity is 4.7 mm deep and rounded to squared. The ears are unusually long and narrow with square outlines.

If we assume that each style group is (by definition) the work of an individual this means twelve individuals were present on grid B. The distribution of the points in each style group and their associations with

Figure 5. Major artifacts from three Mini Clusters. Artifacts are on 5 mm grid. Left (A) large subtype I fluted knife FC 92–in Fea 5; Top Row L to R (B) large end scraper FC 53, (C) blade from subtype II point reworked into an end scraper FC 87, (D) base of a subtype II point or knife FC 56, (E) small subtype II fluted knife FC 85; Bottom Row L to R (F) small side scraper or groover FC 55, (G) base of fluted preform FC 107, (H) base of subtype III point FC 102, (I) base of subtype III point FC 47. The first mini cluster included A, B, and D; the second included F, G, and I; while the third consisted of C, E, and H. Each mini cluster also included three or four channel flakes, plus a small cluster of flakes of bifacial retouch and pressure flakes—all byproducts of making and fluting points. Each mini cluster apparently represents a two man work area where old points were discarded and two new ones made.

various feature clusters in grid B will be discussed later. In some cases points in subtypes I and II might represent the work of other individuals. However, because the differences between subtypes may be functional, any given individual could have made artifacts in all three subtypes.

*Reworked Fluted Points, Especially Fluted Point Blades*

This category crosscuts subtypes and style groups. It includes broken fluted points that have been reworked for a number of secondary uses, usually as knives or scrapers. Resharpened fluted points that were reused as projectile points are technically in this category, but they do not interest us here.

Many reworked fluted points are fluted point blades—fluted points that have had their bases snapped off. They often lack part of their original tips, and many have been resharpened to give them new tips. Lateral basal edges of some were modified to reduce the width at the break, presumably to facilitate hafting.

A common functional modification of reworked fluted points that is often found on fluted point blades is that of conversion to heavy duty knives. These blades have been resharpened with an intermittent unifacial pressure chipping which gives them sharp sinuous cutting edges. Many of them have "hard" or demi-quina wear (step wear) patterns on the blade edges indicating that they were probably used as knives or scrapers on substances such as bone or antler. They were probably hafted.

FC 374 is a subtype II fluted point blade 38 mm long which lacks both base and tip. It is made of a chalky gray chert. It has sinuous retouch on one edge and heavy demi-quina wear on the other. Apparently it was used as a heavy duty knife. It is too small to have been used effectively without hafting (Fig. 1).

FC 87 is a subtype II fluted point blade 39 mm long also without base or tip and is made of a creamy chocolate chert. It does not have the sinuous edges found on heavy duty knives. However, it shows slight demi-quina wear on one edge indicating a possible use as a knife or scraper. The tip has been reworked into an end scraper with a graver spur in the middle. One edge of the scraper has some light demi-quina wear, the graver has been polished from use (Fig. 5).

FC 207 is 50 mm long. An estimated 10 to 15 mm of the base is missing. Heavy lateral basal edge grinding is present for 10 mm on each edge. The face illustrated (Fig. 1) has type 1a fluting that runs out the tip. The other face has double (possibly triple) fluting that hinges out. Sharp sinuous blade edges show that it was resharpened with intermittent unifacial pressure chipping. Demi-quina wear on the blade edges indicates its possible use as a knife.

FC 208 is 38 mm of the midsection of a large subtype III point with 1b fluting on both faces and it is made of a chalky pink and gray chert very similar to FC 207. It is the only point on grid B that definitely has 1b-1b fluting. (Many of the short bases with 1-1 fluting could come from points with 1b-1b fluting.) The basal end of FC 208 was narrowed and tapered after the base had broken off. It may have seen use as a knife. The other two subtype III fluted point blades from B were used as knives. Apparently they, 207, and 208 were all knives, but not heavy duty ones.

FC 506 is a tip fragment only 12 mm long. It probably is the tip of FC 56, a subtype II base. Both are a dark reddish brown chalky chert. FC 506 has the sinuous resharpening of a heavy duty knife. Part of the blade between the base and tip is missing. Without the intervening section it is impossible to say whether the blade of 56/506 was used as a heavy duty knife by itself or with the point still intact. The base appears to have been reworked to narrow it. FC 56/506 may have been reworked from a wider point for use as a heavy duty knife (Fig. 2).

FC 24 of grid E is also a heavy duty knife. It is a fluted point blade of chalky white chert and is a subtype II point (Fig. 1).

The reworked fluted points and especially all the fluted point blades from grids B and E are made either of a chalky chert or were subtype II points or both. The three heavy duty knives from B and E are both chalky chert and II points. Apparently this chert is tougher; unifacially fluted subtype II points are tougher; therefore, both tended to survive in reusable form as reworked fluted points. The subtype II and III fluted point blades are also slightly thicker at the break than the bladeless subtype III bases from grid B. This might help to explain their survival.

*Fluted Point Preforms*

FC 107 is a unifacially fluted type B preform base from the second feature 5 cluster (Fig. 5). Three squared-off type B preform tips are also from grid B. These are similar to the "snapped" Folsom preform tips noted by Judge (1970). Two were in the feature 9-9A cluster complex, and one was in the feature 21 cluster.

*Miscellaneous Fluted Points*

This miscellaneous category includes three bases that are too fragmentary for style group identification, plus two midsections and three tips.

*Bits and Pieces of Fluted Points*

Ears of 14 fluted points were found in grid B; 13 of these are from finished points. The one ear from an unfinished point matches the material of two fluted point tips from the 9-9A cluster complex. There are also nine miscellaneous fragments of fluted points from B. This brings the possible ones to 73 fluted points from B.

Three half-bases, all from the 9-9A cluster complex, are in this category. FC 293 appears to be in style group E; it was in feature 9. FC 171 and 260 appear to be from unidentified style groups.

*Channel Flake Points*

Two tips and two midsections of points made from channel flakes came from the 9-9A and 6/8 clusters. I would suggest that they probably were toys—tips for toy spears. A very small "mini" end scraper was also found in this area of grid B, and this could also have been a child's toy.

*Unfluted Points*

These are represented in grid B by one artifact from the 9-9A cluster complex. It could be the tip of a point with 1b-1b fluting, although it has no evidence of fluting. The tip of an Archaic or Woodland point was found on the surface to the east of the major concentration of artifacts.

## Grid E: Fluted Points

Grid E, which centers in a slight depression ca. 860 N – 70 E, is just south of grid B. It yielded a surface collection of two end scrapers and three fluted points. The area was tested briefly in 1974 and was found to be almost sterile. A coronet graver came from the test pits.

Fluted point FC 24 (Fig. 1) is from just south of the low ridge that separates grid B from grid E, at about 970 N. It is a subtype II fluted point blade. An estimated 10 to 15 mm of the base is msssing. It has full-length type 1a fluting offset slightly to the left on one face and very short type 1b fluting on the other. The full 1a fluting is overridden by very short type 1b fluting. It is made of chalky white chert and is 38 + mm long (estimated at 48 to 53 mm). The remnants of the lateral basal edges are heavily ground and highly tapered. It appears to have been resharpened. Battering, splitting, and heavy demi-quina wear on the blade edges indicate that it was used as a knife (or scraper) on some hard substance such as antler or bone.

FC 206 (Fig. 4) is a very well-made subtype III point with type 1a fluting and type 3 basal finishing on each face. It is 40 mm long; an

Figure 4. Miscellaneous Artifacts Grids C, D, E, and elsewhere.
Top Row L to R: FC 19–Group O; FC 538–Group N (Grid C); FC 206 Grid E, FC 13 Grid D both Group M; FC 365 Point Made from Channel Flake.
Bottom Row: FC 543, FC 205 Both Grid C, FC 286 Grid D–Fluted Knives; FC 194 Fluted Drill, Grid D.

estimated 10 mm of the tip is missing. It appears to have been resharpened and/or used as a knife. The tip may possibly have been used as an end scraper. (Dave Woodside thinks it was used as a scraper, but I am skeptical.) It belongs in style group M along with FC 209 of grid C and FC 13 of grid D. Points in this style group may be characterized as having very noticeable gradually flaring fishtails. Basal concavities are moderately deep, rounded, and slightly irregular. Ears are long, narrow, and rounded. The difference between the BW and the CE of FC 106 is 1.7 mm or .85 mm per edge, while the basal concavity is 4.2 mm deep. The third point from grid E is FC 200, a tip only 16.7 mm long and 14.4 mm wide. It has unifacial 1a fluting, and may belong in subtype II. It seems to have been resharpened and may have been used as a knife.

## Clusters of Artifacts in Grid B.

From a rough preliminary study of clusters in grid B it was apparent that there were possible clusters of artifacts associated with features 2, 4, 5, 6/8, 9-9A, 17, 20 and 21 or 36. Each cluster includes fluted points, channel flakes, flakes of bifacial retouch and pressure flakes.

A detailed study of grid B was made for this report. A map of grid B showing features was made with 10 cm (about four-inch) squares representing the five-foot squares of the actual grid. The locations of the artifacts were plotted in the squares as accurately as possible. From this map it became obvious that the feature 5 cluster actually includes three small clusters, the feature 9-9A cluster complex is composed of at least three smaller clusters, the feature 17 cluster is probably two smaller clusters, and feature 21 (not 36) is the focal point of that cluster.

This scale map was then converted to a model of the site by placing the artifacts themselves on their proper locations. The 1/15 scale model provided us with information not obtainable in any other way, although it is a bit small, and some of the four-inch squares are rather cluttered. We are planning another map with six-inch squares (1/10 scale) for photographic purposes.

*Feature 5: Mini Clusters*

Feature 5 is a rather vague dark stain in the subsoil of 1030 N and 1035 N – 40 E. Apparently it was not a fire. At one time we thought that it might have been a rodent burrow, but while we cannot entirely discount the idea, there is little evidence to support it. What we took for the outline of a pit in the west wall of 1035 N – 40 E was probably the natural interface of the upper sandy loam and the underlying waterlaid clay that had been subjected to considerable loading, producing a very convoluted surface. The same phenomena also occurred in 1035 N – 35 E without any of the dark staining in the loam. It continued on west into 1035 N – 30 E.

The first feature 5 mini cluster is primarily in 1030 N and 1035 N – 40 E. It includes a large subtype I knife which was in the feature, a big end scraper, and the base of a subtype II point. They and two channel flakes were in an area about six feet NS by 1.75 feet EW. Two more channel flakes and a fragment of a preform were some five feet to the west in 1030 N – 35 E (Fig. 5). N.B. This and all other grid B clusters also include flakes of bifacial retouch and pressure flakes.

The second feature 5 cluster is primarily in 1025 N – 45 E. A fluted preform base, a side scraper and four channel flakes were in an area about four feet NS by four feet EW. A style group A base is a surface find from 1025 N – 45 E.

The third feature 5 cluster centers in 1030 N – 50 E which contained a subtype I knife, subtype II fluted point blade made into an end scraper, and three channel flakes. The group L base was just over the line in 1035 N – 50 E.

These three mini clusters have a number of things in common. Each contains two discarded fluted artifacts (either a fluted point and a fluted knife, or a fluted point and a fluted preform), three or four channel flakes, and a scraper. In each case the points (or knives) are in different subtypes or style groups and could have been made by two different people. Each mini cluster may represent the activities of two men. In each case they discarded two fluted artifacts and fluted two new ones (none of the channel flakes fits any of the discarded artifacts). A similar two-man pattern appears to be present at feature 2, at feature 4, and at feature 21. It may also occur at feature 17, perhaps at feature 9, and possibly at feature 20. Each of these mini clusters has two points (or knives) of different subtypes or different style groups, plus three or four channel flakes that do not match the points, and usually either a scraper or a used flake. The cluster in 1020 + 1025 N – 55 E is very similar except that the two point bases may be in the same style group.

In discussing the possible significance of these "two-man" clusters Chris Ellis suggested that they could be an indication that two men were required to flute a point. This assumes that indirect percussion was used and that the preform was either held in the hand (wrapped in hide, etc.) or placed in some sort of handle that was held in the hand. One man might hold the preform, while the other held the punch and the hammer and did the actual fluting (see Crabtree, 1966: especially p. 12).

As to feature 5, there are other similarities, the first and third cluster each has a nearly perfect subtype I fluted knife and part of a subtype II point. The material of the preform fragment in the first cluster is identical with that of the fluted preform base in the second cluster and the subtype II fluted point blade (the end scraper) in the third cluster. The material of the scrapers in the first two clusters is identical with that of the small subtype I knife in the third cluster. This suggests that the maker of the subtype II points (and possibly the scrapers) was present at each cluster.

*Other Mini Clusters in the North End of Grid B*

Feature 4 is a small dark charcoal (?) stain in the NW corner of 1040 N - 80 E. It may represent a small Paleo-Indian hearth. The mini cluster centers in 1040 N - 75 E which had a group C base and a group E base that appear to have been in a fire. The cluster includes three channel flakes (one of which fits the fluted preform base from the second feature 5 cluster), a fragment of a point or preform that matches the material of the channel flake and preform; and two ears. Several other channel flakes occur in adjacent squares.

Most of the ears found were recovered by three people, Gary Laye, Randy Laye, or Reynold Welke. These ears are quite small. Most of them pass through the quarter-inch mesh readily—in contrast to point bases, channel flakes, scrapers, and flakes of bifacial retouch. The distribution of ears recovered from the site is partly a function of who it was who excavated a given area.

Feature 2 is an area of hard-packed charcoal stained sand in 1025 N - 70 E. It may be a small Paleo-Indian hearth. Feature 3 in the two squares just to the west is by contrast a very loosely packed area of charcoal stained sand with a number of burrows or root channels also filled with loosely packed dark stained sand leading to or from it. Feature 3 is probably not a Paleo-Indian feature. The artifact cluster in the feature 2 area includes a subtype I knife and a group A point base from 1025 N - 65 E. A group B base is from a disturbed area in the subsoil in 1025 N - 70 E. This square also yielded a large worked flake. The cluster includes four channel flakes; other channel flakes were in adjacent squares.

There apparently was no feature associated with a cluster of two point bases, one of group B and the other possibly of group B, and four channel flakes in 1020 N - 55 E and 1025 N - 55 E. Material of the two points is the same as that of two points from the feature 2 cluster.

*Mini Clusters in the South End of Grid B*

A small cluster of subtype II points occurred in and near the south end of feature 20. Feature 20 is a very large area of charcoal stained sand that dominated at least eight squares. Several sherds (probably Late Woodland) were in the plowzone over this feature with one at the interface on it. There was also some rotten wood in the feature, which is probably not of Paleo-Indian origin. The base of a large subtype II point is from the plowzone of 1010 N – 75 E. The tip of the same point is from feature 20 in the subsoil on the line between 1010 N 70 and 75 E. What appears to be the tip of feature 5 subtype II point base is from 1010 N – 70 E. This rather diffuse cluster also includes part of the blade of a subtype II point that has been used as a small end scraper, four channel flakes, and a used flake. The two points may represent two style groups in subtype II.

Feature 21 is in the NW corner of 1010 N – 65 E. It is a dark charcoal stained area bordered on one edge by a very hard dark red ochre stained area. A group A base was just over the line in 1015 N – 65 E. It has hard cemented dark red ochre on one face. The only group J base was in 1010 N – 65 E. The cluster also includes the snapped tip of a fluted preform, two channel flakes, and two worked flakes (one of which may be of Archaic origin).

There are two channel flakes and two used flakes in 1005 N – 60 E and a channel flake in 1010 N – 60 E that could be part of the feature 21 cluster. They may belong in the feature 9 cluster.

The snapped preform tip is one of three from grid B. There is good evidence that about seventy old points were discarded here and replaced by new points made (and especially fluted) here. This low percentage of snapped preform tips (ca. 4 percent) suggests that the technique of snapping the tip of the preform after fluting occurred on only a few of the Parkhill site Barnes points. Judge (1970) has suggested that this technique is a standard part of Folsom point making. From my own knowledge of central New Mexico Folsom sites (see Roosa, 1967) I would estimate that this technique occurs on ca. 10 to 20 percent of New Mexico Folsom points.

*The Feature 9-9A Cluster Complex*

Feature 9 appears to be a large hearth in the NE corner of 1000 N – 60 E and the adjoining areas of 1005 N – 60 E and 1000 N – 1005 N – 65 E. It is almost certainly of Paleo-Indian origin. It contained a fluted point base, half the base of a fluted point, and a channel flake. The pollen sample comes from just below this feature. Several distinct artifact clusters appear to lie around feature 9 and 9A, which is a smaller hearth in the SW corner of 1000 N – 60 E. It was linked to feature 9 at the plowzone subsoil interface but was distinct from it a little way down in the subsoil.

The first cluster in the feature 9 complex is a very small cluster ca. 4.5 feet EW by two feet NS in feature 9 and just to the east of it, mainly in 1000 N + 1005 N – 65 E. This cluster includes a style group E base that was *in situ* in the feature, and a group C point base from the plowzone near its edge. This cluster also includes the snapped tip of a fluted point preform, three channel flakes, a probable guide flake, and an ear.

Half a fluted point base, probably of a style group E, was on the north edge of feature 9 in 1005 N – 60 E. As noted, two channel flakes and two used flakes were in 1005 N – 60 E, and a channel flake was in 1010 N – 60 E. Some of these, especially the half base from the feature, may be part of the first feature 9 cluster.

The feature 9A cluster is primarily in 1000 N – 55 + 60 E, and 1005 N – 55 + 60 E west of feature 9. It is ca. 10.5 feet NS by 5.5 feet EW and vaguely elliptical. It includes the base of a style group D point from feature 9A, and the only group K base from 1005 N – 55 E, a fluted point blade, a midsection of a fluted point, two fluted point tips, a preform tip, and a basal half. The cluster also includes the proximal end of a small snapped end scraper, two worked flakes, an unfluted point tip, and 19 channel flakes including a worked channel flake.

The third cluster in the feature 9 area is an ellipse ca. seven feet NS and six feet EW centering in the eastern half of 995 N – 60 E and the western half of 995 N – 65 E, with a slight overlap to the north and south. This cluster is south of feature 9. It includes six fluted point bases, one in each of style groups A, E, H, and I (plus two unclassified); two pieces of a fluted point blade from the style group I point, a basal half, four ears, a point fragment, and 22 channel flakes. All the major pieces of fluted points (except the group A base and part of the group I blade which were in the middle) are from the edges of the cluster. The 22 channel flakes (including a midsection and a tip of two projectile points made from channel flakes) were on the inside of the cluster with the ears and the fragment. On the 1/15 scale model the whole cluster is virtually paved with channel flakes. This cluster is also the locus of a very high concentration of flakes, mostly of bifacial retouch and pressure retouch. The flake concentration here is the highest of any place on the site excavated to date.

## *The Feature 6/8 Cluster*

Feature 6 was first noted in the north edge of 985 N – 60 E. Feature 8 was first seen in 990 N – 55 E. They joined in 990 N – 60 E forming feature 6/8. Feature 6 contained some wood fragments and could be relatively recent. Feature 8 might be a Paleo-Indian hearth.

The artifact cluster centers in and around 985 N - 55 E. This square contained four fluted point bases of style groups A, F, G, and possibly F in an area ca. 1.5 feet EW by 2.5 feet NS. A group B point base was in 980 N - 55 E, a subtype II tip was in feature 8 in 990 N - 55 E, while what may be the base of the same point was in 985 N - 50 E. The midsection of a fluted point was in 990 N - 55 E. The cluster also includes two ears and 16 channel flakes, including a midsection and a tip of small points made from channel flakes.

## The Feature 17 Clusters

Feature 17 appears to be a relatively recent rodent burrow that may have intersected a hearth. Square 995 N - 70 E yielded a style group C base, a fluted point tip, a large snapped end scraper, and three channel flakes along the western edge in an area ca. 4.5 feet NS by two feet EW, plus a subtype II base in the NE corner. A used flake from the NE corner of 990 N - 65 E is in the same cluster. A possible group E base and a mini scraper from 1000 N - 70 E may also be part of this cluster.

Squares 990 + 995 N - 75 E held a subtype II fluted point blade and a group C base plus four channel flakes. A small end scraper-cum-graver from 990 N - 70 E may be part of this cluster. Both Ross and Sheppard believe this is an Archaic scraper for various reasons: the material, the flake type, and possibly scraper type.

Another cluster worthy of mention occurs in 985 N - 65 E east of the 6/8 cluster. This square contained six channel flakes, an ear, two other fragments of fluted points, a used flake, and a possible mini graver.

## Possible Significance of Grid B Clusters

The significance of these clusters has been the subject of much conjecture. It is obvious that grid B is a point making area. The mini clusters may be explained as two-man work areas.

Some of these two-man mini clusters, i.e., features 2, 4, and 21, have possible Paleo-Indian hearths in association; while others, i.e., the three feature 5 clusters and the 1020 + 25 N - 55E clusters, do not. The absence of fire at some of these may indicate that they were only temporary work areas. On the other hand, the evidence of fire at the feature 2, 4, and 21 clusters may indicate that they were overnight camps of two men, men who may have been scouting for game. The ochre at feature 21 may indicate some special activity, such as pre-hunting magic. The fire for the 1020 + 25 N - 55 E cluster is probably feature 2. The feature 5 clusters may have been associated with a fire in the immediate area, but there is presently no good evidence for it.

The feature 9-9A cluster complex clearly represents something much more complex than a two-man work area. The small feature 9 cluster itself may be a two-man work area; however, the 9A cluster and the ellipse south of feature 9 are also associated with feature 9. The three feature 9 clusters include the following subtype III style groups: A, C, D, E, K, H, and I; but no subtype I or II points. Of the style groups represented by two or more artifacts, only B is absent from the feature 9 complex. The feature 9-9A complex apparently represents a camp of at least seven men. Judging from the size of the hearth and the amount of associated material including flakes, it was a camp of some duration, possibly three or four days and nights.

The feature 6/8 cluster is also more complex than a two-man work area. Individuals here include A, B, F, G, and at least one of the two subtype II point makers, and it apparently represents a camp of at least four or five men. Judging from the amount of material, I would suggest that it was used as a camp for two or three days and nights. The feature 9 complex and the 6/8 cluster probably represent scouting parties looking for game. The channel flake points (which could be toys) in the 6/8 cluster and the feature 9-9A complex may indicate that at least one boy was present in each party. If we assume that the presence of scrapers, especially in quantity and in variety, is an indication of women's work areas, then we may say that there is little evidence of women at B.

Apparently the man who made the style group A points was a special case. He left points at five loci—four of them near possible hearths. One of his points was probably originally in the ochre of feature 21. Assuming that feature 21 was the locus of pre-hunt magic, "A" is a good candidate for the status of shaman.

Taken together, the first two feature 5 clusters include a possible triad of artifacts, i.e., a whole point and two whole scrapers similar to the triads found at Bull Brook (Jordan, 1960), there thought to represent possible burial offerings although the skeletons had long since decomposed. The feature 5 clusters might have been associated with a burial. Note that the shaman "A" was there.

Feature 5 might be a very old woodchuck (*Marmota monax*) burrow. If so, it is possible that Paleo-Indians (probably while looking for bigger game) may have killed a groundhog there. The big scraper could have been used to dig it out. The feature 17 may be (in part) a woodchuck burrow. There are similarities in the scrapers from the feature 5 clusters and the feature 17 cluster. Would you believe two Paleo-Indian woodchuck kills??

## Grids C and D Parkhill Site

*Grid C*

Grid C is south of Grid B. The C baseline is at 710 North. The artifact concentration at C (like that at B) is just north of a low east-west ridge. Grid C was extensively tested in 1974. One area of C was excavated in 1975. At the time of writing (September 1975) further excavations were planned in C. Not all the excavated grid C material has been tabulated or analyzed.

Surface finds from grid C include six fluted points (i.e., one almost whole, two bases, and three blades), three end scrapers and one channel flake. Excavated material includes a whole fluted knife, ten fluted point bases, a fluted preform base, a reworked fluted point blade, three end scrapers, two coronet gravers, about 20-25 channel flakes, and 30-40 scraper retouch flakes. Some of this material appears to be clustered around a possible Paleo-Indian hearth. In contrast to grid B, no major flake concentrations were located in C.

*Grid D*

Grid D is on a low hill to the south and east of grids B and C. Paleo-Indian surface finds from D include six fluted points (one almost whole point, two blades, two bases, and one blade fragment), fifteen end scrapers, three side scrapers, one unfluted "plano" point base, a fluted drill, and an almost whole channel flake point. Our 1974 excavations in a small area of D yielded three fluted point bases, fifteen channel flakes, six end scrapers, three side scrapers, two coronet gravers, 72 scraper retouch flakes, and miscellaneous Paleo bits and pieces. Most of these, along with hundreds of Amabel chert flakes of bifacial retouch and pressure flakes, were concentrated in two features which are in small natural depressions in a natural micro drainage channel on the hillside. Judging from the nature of these features and a C-14 date of 3400±210 years BP (I-8866) from one feature, this material probably washed in from a camp higher on the hill at about the time of Lake Nipissing. The variety of artifacts present on grid D suggests that it probably represents the remains of a base camp (Judge, 1973).

A late Archaic hearth is located just west of the two above-mentioned features on D. Two C-14 dates from this hearth are 2980 ± 105 BP (I-8867) and 2485 ± 100 BP (I-8868). The associated Archaic tool kit is functionally similar to the Paleo tool kit from D. The Archaic material is a gray chert that contrasts markedly with the Paleo Amabel chert.

Another small area of D was tested in 1975. Finds here include five Paleo side scrapers and some flakes of Amabel chert. An Archaic hearth with associated artifacts was also found here. This material has not been tabulated or analyzed.

The above three C-14 dates may all be too recent, due to possible contamination resulting from the use of an ammonia sprayer on the corn crop in the area. This sprayer, which sounds innocent enough at first, cuts grooves into the subsoil. Pollen samples from the dated Archaic hearth were contaminated with modern pollen including corn pollen. A third C-14 date from this hearth of $1725 \pm 100$ BP (I-8865) is undoubtedly the result of such contamination. Fire-cracked rock in the upper part of the hearth where this C-14 sample was found was neatly aligned in a north-south orientation, apparently by the action of the sprayer.

## Comparison of Grids B, C, and D.

The Paleo-Indian tool kits represented by our samples from grids B, C, and D have some strong resemblances. Most of the artifacts are of Amabel chert. The same point type occurs on all three grids. All three point subtypes occur at B and C. Only subtype III points have been found at D. Some style groups occur on more than one grid. Channel flake points occur on both grid B and D. Two channel flakes from B fit points from D. Some scraper types and subtypes occur on more than one grid. The gravers are all quite similar.

Differences in the tool kits from the three grids involve the presence or absence of some artifact classes and substantial differences in the percentages of fluted points, fluted knives, scrapers, and scraper retouch (re-sharpening) flakes present.

The strongest contrast is between grids B and D. Grid B has fewer classes of tools than D, and a much higher percentage of points and channel flakes than D. Grid D has a much higher precentage of scrapers and scraper retouch flakes than B and has a much greater variety of scrapers than either B or C. Grids C and D have a higher percentage of fluted knives and heavy duty knives than B; they both have gravers, while B has none. (However, one was found in grid E just south of B.) Grid D has the only Paleo drill from the site.

Grid B is almost exclusively a point making area where old points were discarded and replaced with new points shaped from preforms, then fluted and finished on the spot. The presence of a few scrapers and used flakes at B suggests that activities like the shaping of weapon shafts or foreshafts and the fitting of points into them took place here on a limited scale.

Grid D by contrast appears to represent a base camp where a much wider range of activities, involving the use of many types of scrapers and gravers, took place. Some point making also occurred at D, but it was less important than at B (or C).

The grid C tool kit is somewhat intermediate between the one from B and the one from D. While it has a higher percentage of scrapers and scraper retouch flakes than B, the grid C sample lacks the wide range of scrapers present at D.

The distribution of material at grids B and C apparently approximates the original camp layouts fairly closely, but the material from the 1974 excavations at grid D was apparently washed in and thus cannot give a good approximation of the layout of the base camp.

## Relationship of the Parkhill Complex to Other Paleo-Indian Complexes

As noted above, I have classed the Parkhill site points as Barnes points. The Barnes site sample is small, and many of the points are preforms, i.e., unfinished. The Parkhill sample, which is much better, consists almost exclusively of finished points, primarily bases. Thus, a comparison of the two samples is a bit tricky. Type 1a fluting is the most common Barnes site technique; some type 1b fluting also occurs there. Type 3 basal thinning is present in both site samples. It occurs as basal thinning on the opposite face from type 1 fluting or as a basal finishing technique that overrides type 1 fluting.

Only three Barnes site points are definitely finished, while only two of these are relatively whole and one of them has been resharpened (Wright and Roosa, 1966). The measurements of two whole Barnes site points are: 85 mm long (est), MW 25, BW is 17 mm; 36.4 mm long, MW 23, BW is 19 mm (resharpened). The big one has full-length type 1a fluting on one face and type 3 basal thinning on the other. The short one has type 1 fluting on one face and what appears to be type 1 fluting on the other, overridden by two large finishing flakes.

None of the three finished Barnes site points has a fishtail. It should be noted that points with and without fishtails occur at the Shoop site (Witthoft, 1952) and the Bull Brook site (Byers, 1954; Jordan 1960). Points with and without fishtails also occur at Parkhill. Their absence at Barnes is probably a function of the very small sample of finished points. Shaping of the fishtail was one of the last steps in finishing a fluted point; it was done after the point was fluted. Fishtails do not occur on the preforms.

Several of the Barnes site preforms have narrow bases in the 15 mm range. There are no finished Barnes site points in this size range. This, and the fact that one unfluted Barnes site preform is 92 mm long, led Wright and me to the conclusion that Barnes site points are fairly large. This may have been erroneous. I now believe that the Barnes site and Parkhill site probably represent the same culture complex and that the seeming difference in point size is a function of the nature of the two samples.

The Barnes site sample includes fluted preforms or knives with type 1b fluting. Their bases are missing. They belong in the category of fluted point blades. Some may be heavy duty knives as found at the Parkhill site, but I do not recall whether they have sinuous edges, or demi-quina wear on the edges. The major difference between the Barnes and Parkhill site artifacts in this class is the preference for 1a fluting at Parkhill and for 1b fluting at Barnes and this may easily have been a matter of individual preference.

Since the name "Barnes points" is already in the literature, I shall call the Parkhill site fluted points Barnes points and designate the cultural complex found at the Barnes and Parkhill sites as the Parkhill complex.

Fishtail Barnes points as found at the Parkhill site and elsewhere in the Great Lakes (Michigan, New York, and Ontario) look very much like small Cumberland points from the Ohio Valley and souteastern U.S. Most of the Cumberland points I have seen or have seen in photographs are much larger; many specimens are in the 75 to 150 mm length range. The few I have examined apparently do not have the type 3 basal finishing technique. The fishtail Parkhill site Barnes points are closely related to Cumberland points, but they are probably products of another group with a closely similar cultural tradition.

In terms of total tool assemblages, the Parkhill complex has its nearest counterpart in the Bull Brook complex. This complex, best known from the type site in Massachusetts, also occurs in the Great Lakes (Byers, 1954; Jordan, 1960; Roosa, 1965.). Although the two types are different, they share the same fluting and finishing techniques. The overall range of scraper and graver types is quite similar.

There are also strong resemblances in scrapers and gravers among the Parkhill complex, the Bull Brook complex, and the Debert complex of Nova Scotia. The latter has been securely dated at ca. 10,600 years BP (MacDonald, 1968). Three of the points from the Parkhill site, which are probably the work of the same person, have the deep basal indentation so characteristic of Debert points. Except for these three points the two point samples are distinct.

There are also a number of specific resemblances in points and scrapers between the Parkhill complex and the well-known Folsom complex. Folsom points are securely dated at between 10,600 and 10,800 years BP (Haynes, 1964). The two point types are distinct, although they do share the Folsom fluting technique. Both the Folsom and Parkhill complexes include very small points made from channel flakes. Folsom points are a very neat type with little variation; Banres points have a much greater range of variation. Folsom points are noticeably wider than Barnes points and may have been hafted on a different type of weapon.

The Parkhill complex appears to be fairly localized in the eastern Great Lakes area. Based on resemblances with the Folsom complex and the suggested antiquity of the Parkhill site pollen, an age of ca. 10,500 years ago seems reasonable for the Parkhill complex. Clovis-like Enterline points (Witthoft, 1952), which also occur in the Great Lakes area, may predate the Parkhill complex. Their lowest known occurrence is at the Lux site in Michigan at some 630 feet on the Lake Lundy shoreline (Roosa, 1965).

The Holcombe complex (Fitting et al., 1966) may postdate the Parkhill complex. Holcombe points have several strong similarities to Midland points which are post-Folsom at the Hell Gap site (Irwin-Williams, et al., 1970). Holcombe points are also known from sites slightly lower than the Lake Algonquin shoreline (B. Deller, personal communication).

## Acknowledgments

University of Waterloo excavations at the Parkhill site in 1973, 1974, and 1975 were financed by research grants from the Canada Council. The site was called to my attention in 1973 by Brian Deller of Mount Byrdges, Ontario. He located it as part of his intensive site survey of Paleo-Indian and Early Archaic sites in Middlesex County. The site was discovered by three Parkhill boys (Ray Baxter, Gary Laye, and Randy Laye) who brought it to Brian's attention. His subsequent investigation revealed that others, including Ed McLeod, had found fluted points on or near the site. However, it was not until the Layes and Ray Baxter found six fluted points and several scrapers on the site that it was recognized as a potentially important site.

It should be noted that over the past five or six years Brian Deller has developed a system for locating Paleo-Indian and Early Archaic sites. This system makes certain assumptions about the nature of Paleo-Indian cultures—i.e., that they were hunting big game (probably caribou) and that they frequented Pleistocene beach ridges—which are similar to those developed by Judge and Dawson (1972) for central New Mexico sites. The

Parkhill site is only one of many located by Brian in the course of his survey.

Several of my students from the University of Waterloo have assisted me in the field and in the laboratory. These include Chris Ellis (flakes), Debbie Ross (Paleo scrapers), Peter Sheppard (statistics and Archaic), and Dave Woodside (edge wear).

Geologists who have assisted include Andy Cooper of the Geological Branch of the Division of Mines of the Ontario Ministry of Natural Resources, who has been engaged in mapping Pleistocene features in the area and Dr. Al Morgan of the Earth Science Department, University of Waterloo, who is analyzing the stratigraphy. His wife, Mrs. Ann Morgan, is working on beetles from the site. Dr. John McAndrews and his assistants at the Royal Ontario Museum are doing the pollen analysis.

## References Cited

Byers, Douglas
    1954    Bull Brook—A fluted point site in Ipswich, Massachusetts. American Antiquity 19:343-51.

Crabtree, Don E.
    1966    A stoneworker's approach to analyzing and replicating the Lindenmeier Folsom. Tebiwa 9(1):3-39

Fitting, James E., Jerry DeVisscher, and Edward J. Wahla
    1966    The Paleo-Indian occupation of the Holcombe Beach. University of Michigan Museum of Anthropology, Anthropological Papers No. 27.

Haury, Emil W.
    1953    Artifacts with mammoth remains, Naco, Arizona. American Antiquity 19:1-14.

Haynes, C. Vance, Jr.
    1964    Fluted projectile points: their age and dispersion. Science 145: 1408-13.

Irwin-Williams, Cynthia, Henry Irwin, George Agogino, and C. Vance Haynes
    1973    Hell Gap: Paleo Indian occupation on the high plains. Plains Anthropologist 18 (59).

Jordan, Douglas F.
    1960    The Bull Brook site in relation to "fluted point" manifestations in eastern North America. Unpublished Ph.D. Dissertation, Harvard University.

Judge, W. J.
    1970    Systems analysis and the Folsom-Midland question. Southwestern Journal of Anthropology 26 (Spring).

Judge, W. J., and Jerry Dawson
   1972   PaleoIndian settlement technology in New Mexico. Science 176: 1210-16.
Lahren, Larry, and Robson Bonnichsen
   1974   Bone foreshafts from a Clovis burial in southwestern Montana. Science 186:147-50.
MacDonald, George F.
   1968   Debert: a PaleoIndian site in central Nova Scotia. Anthropology Papers National Museum of Canada No. 16.
Roosa, William B.
   1965   Some Great Lakes fluted point types. The Michigan Archaeologist 11(3-4).
   1967   Data on early sites in central New Mexico and Michigan. Unpublished Ph.D. Disseration, Ann Arbor: The University of Michigan.
Witthoft, John
   1952   A PaleoIndian site in eastern Pennsylvania: an early hunting culture. Proceedings of the American Philosophical Society 96: 464-95.
Wright, Henry T., and Wm. B. Roosa
   1966   The Barnes site: a fluted point assemblage from the Great Lakes region. American Antiquity 31 (6).

# AN EXAMINATION OF LATE ARCHAIC DEVELOPMENT IN THE FALLS OF THE OHIO RIVER AREA

*Donald E. Janzen*
Centre College

The Falls of the Ohio River are located in the lower part of the Middle Ohio Valley approximately six hundred miles downstream from the confluence of the Allegheny and Monongahela Rivers. In reality, the Falls consisted of a series of rapids approximately four miles long which interrupted the flow of the Ohio, and in pioneer times the need to portage around this part of the river was responsible for the location and early settlement of Louisville, Kentucky. Today, as a result of a locks and dam system, the water level at Louisville has been raised and the Falls no longer exist.

This portion of the Ohio River is rich in prehistoric antiquities, yet it has received little attention from the professional archaeologist. In an attempt to rectify this situation, a research project termed The Falls of the Ohio River Archaeological Project was initiated by the author in 1969. Since that time, six summers of excavation, representing fifty-six weeks of fieldwork and over fifteen thousand hours, have been invested in the project. The primary focus of the research is on Archaic period sites located within a thirty-mile radius of the Falls of the Ohio River (Fig. 1). This spatial unit was selected since five distinct physiographic provinces merge within this zone (Fig. 2). From east to west, these regions are as follows: The Outer Blue Grass (Ky.)–Muscatatuck Regional Slope (Ind.); the Scottsburg Lowland; the Knobs (Ky.)–Norman Upland (Ind.); Mississippian Plateaus (Ky.)–Mitchell Plain (Ind.); and the Alluvial Plain of the Ohio River, which transects the area from northeast to southwest. (The need to hyphenate certain names of provinces indicates that different names are used in Kentucky and Indiana for the same physiographic unit.) A portion of the Indiana Scottsburg Lowland extends into Kentucky where it is classified as a subdivision of the Outer Blue Grass province. For the purpose of this research the Kentucky Scottsburg Lowland is considered a

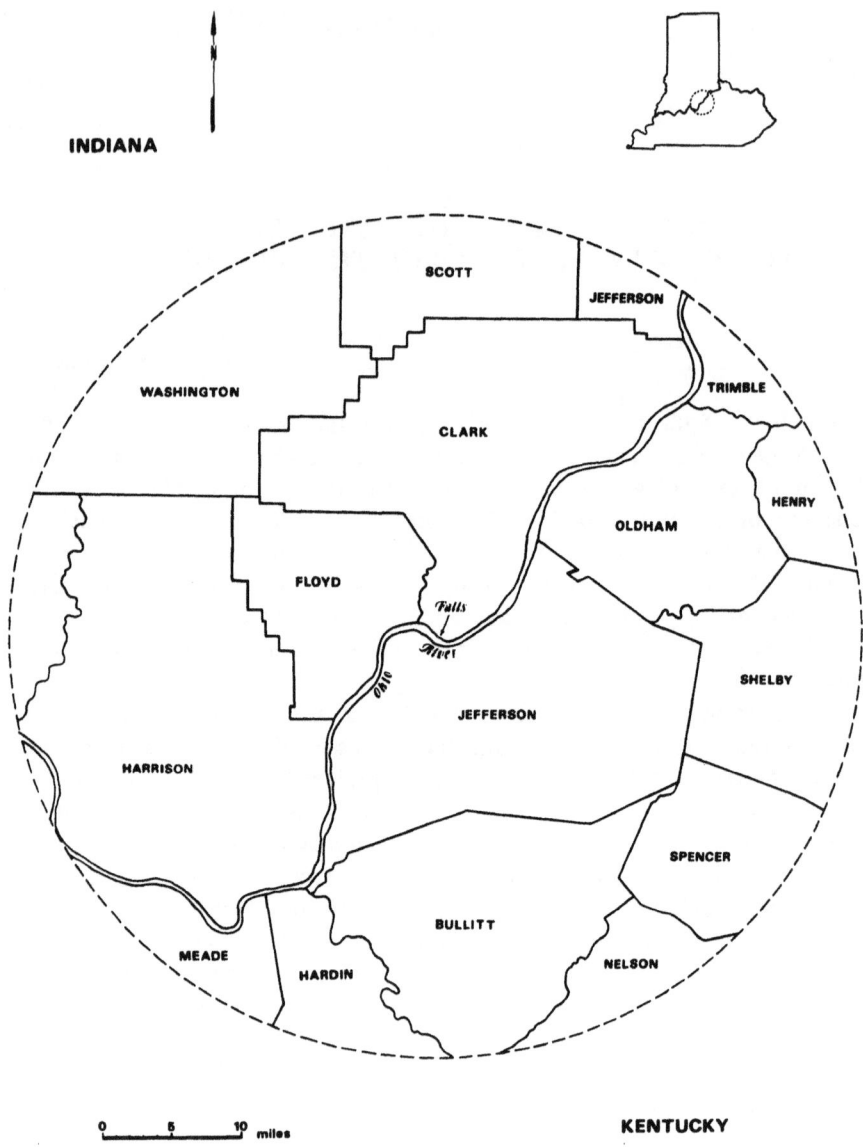

Figure 1. Map of the area to be investigated by the Falls of the Ohio River Archaeological Project, as described by a circle of 30 mile radius centered on the Falls of the Ohio River.

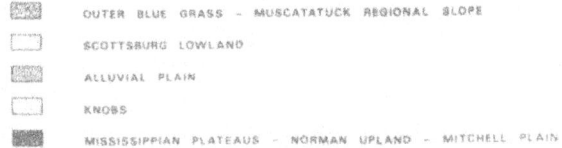

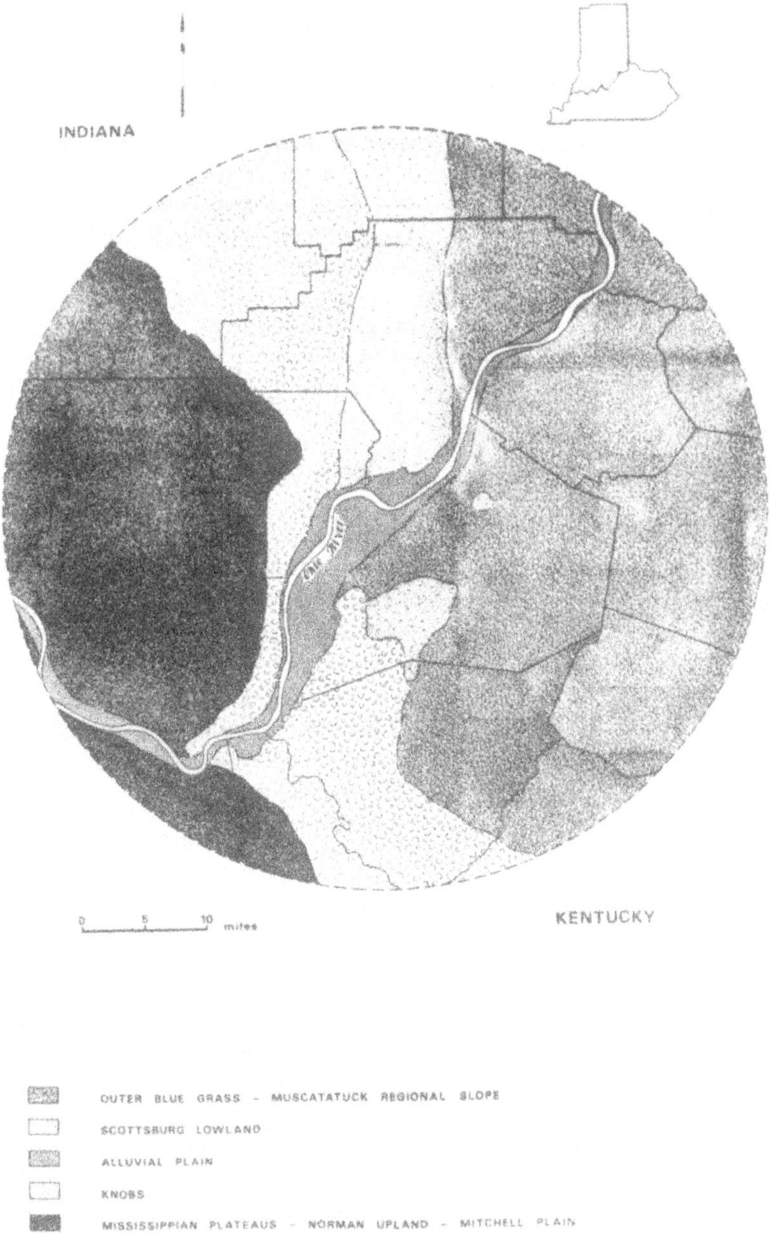
INDIANA
KENTUCKY
0 5 10 miles
OUTER BLUE GRASS - MUSCATATUCK REGIONAL SLOPE
SCOTTSBURG LOWLAND
ALLUVIAL PLAIN
KNOBS
MISSISSIPPIAN PLATEAUS - NORMAN UPLAND - MITCHELL PLAIN

Figure 2. Physiographic Provinces in the Falls of the Ohio River Area.

distinct physiographic unit like its Indiana counterpart. Since the Falls of the Ohio represents a unique physical setting it is probably also valid to consider it as a separate microenvironmental area. Naturalists such as Constantine Rafinesque, R. Ellsworth Call, and Thomas Lea studied the fauna at the Falls, and many species of fish and mollusca were first described at this locality.

The topography of this region varies from the rugged hill country of the Knobs to the gentle undulating terrain of the Outer Blue Grass—Muscatatuck Regional Slope and the Mississippian Plateaus—Mitchell Plain, to the flat plain of the Scottsburg Lowland. Associated with these zones are different drainage patterns which range from small streams and major tributaries in the Knobs and Blue Grass country to underground drainage systems in the karst topography of the Mississippian Plateaus—Mitchell Plain. In the Scottsburg Lowland drainage is impeded by the low gradient and shale bedrock, and a swamp-like condition is maintained throughout most of the year.

Within this region of diverse physiographic characteristics a variety of plant communities can also be expected. The Falls area lies within the Western Mesophytic Forest region and four of the six sections of this region are found within a thirty-mile radius of the Falls of the Ohio River (Braun 1972:128-56). Areas of mixed mesophytic, xerophytic and hydromesophytic forest occur within the research area, and the Scottsburg Lowland which Gunn (1968:5-6) has identified as a unique botanical area for north central Kentucky is of particular interest. This degree of geographical and floral diversity, concentrated within such a relatively small area, seemed ideal for examining Archaic settlement patterns, and as a starting point the research has concentrated on this subsystem.

Historically, our understanding of the Archaic in this portion of the Ohio Valley has been extrapolated from the work of William Webb and his associates along the Green River in western Kentucky. Indeed, sites like Indian Knoll (Webb, 1946) have tended to give the impression that the Green River drainage was the heartland of the midwestern Archaic and that areas like the Falls were marginal to the main centers of cultural development. Such an attitude was certainly reinforced by Webb and Funkhouser's survey of prehistoric sites in Kentucky (1932), although it was not their intention to slight the Falls area. For Jefferson and the adjacent four counties, which include an area in excess of 1,500 square miles, only sixteen sites were listed. Prior to our work, no professionally directed excavations of prehistoric sites had been conducted in this portion of Kentucky. In Indiana, the situation was much the same, although E. Y. Guernsey, working in conjunction with the Indiana Historical Society, excavated several Archaic sites in the Indiana segment at the Falls area in the late 1930s. It appears that Guernsey kept no formal fieldnotes describing his work, and no manuscripts dealing with specific sites were prepared. Our main knowledge of his work comes from three modest reports that appeared in the *Proceedings of the Indiana Academy of Science* (1937, 1939, 1942). Supplementing Guernsey's articles were several descriptive accounts of Archaic sites published by amateur archaeologists in state archaeological journals (Burnett, 1963; Matthews, 1958a) and these, along with a handful of reports that have appeared in the non-archaeological literature (Borden, 1874:184-86) provided the foundation for our knowledge of Archaic culture in the Falls area. In general there is little information from which the prehistoric cultural development can be synthesized, and the following is a brief summary of our knowledge prior to the Falls Project.

Evidence from the Paleo-Indian period is limited to fluted projectile points found in the private collections of amateur archaeologists, in almost all cases from surface finds. Only the Schafer site, located near Henryville, Indiana in Clark County, has produced a substantial number of fluted points (ten points are in the Glenn Black Laboratory for Archaeology at Bloomington, Indiana), and this is the best candidate for a possible Paleo-Indian habitation site. The following unsupported statement of a discovery in Louisville may serve as additional evidence of Big-Game Hunters in the Falls area:

> ... and in a gravel pit at the corner of Fourteenth and Kentucky Streets, at a depth of twenty-five feet below the surface, was found the tooth of a mastodon, among human bones and implements of the Stone Age. Here we have facts from which the ethnologist might infer that men had been contemporary with the mastodon (Durrett, 1893:10-11).

Following the Paleo-Indian period, there is extensive evidence of Archaic sites and these far outnumber the sites from any other period. They occur along the Ohio River, its major tributaries, and even in areas where the only water source is from small secondary streams. From the variety of projectile points that have been found on these sites, it may be inferred that there was a continuous habitation from Early to Late Archaic times. The transition from Archaic to Early Woodland is based on the occurrence of mounds, thick, grit-tempered pottery, and Adena type projectile points. Today there are few mounds left in the area, although a fair number are documented in literary accounts (Durrett, 1893:9-10). The best examples of Early Woodland pottery have come from the Zorn Avenue site (Matthews, 1959a), and Schwartz has proposed a ceramic type, Zorn Punctate, which shows a strong Adena influence (Schwartz, 1961:84).

Of all periods, the ensuing Middle Woodland is the most difficult to define; except for the occurrence of an occasional Snyders-type point, Hopewellian influence is difficult to establish. Actually, so little research has been done that this may merely reflect our ignorance of what constitutes Middle Woodland in the Falls area.

There is a definite decrease in the frequency of sites from Archaic to Early Woodland and this decline seems to be attenuated during Middle Woodland times. During the final period of prehistoric habitation in the Falls area, there appears to be an increase in site density and size. Cultural influences seem to have been derived primarily from the downstream Mississippian groups rather than from Fort Ancient peoples to the northeast. The most noteworthy sites of this period in the Falls area are the Prather, Newcombe, Elrod, and Clark's Point sites, all located in Clark County, Indiana; the last three were located adjacent to the Falls. Today remnants of a Mississippian component can be found only at the Newcombe and Prather sites.

Based on this limited data, two overall impressions have emerged regarding Falls area prehistory. First, it was felt that the prehistoric cultural development reflected cultural manifestations whose foci were elsewhere in Kentucky, Indiana, or Ohio. Lying downstream were the famous Green River Archaic sites and Mississippian centers like the Angel mounds, while upstream were the impressive centers of Adena, Hopewell, and Fort Ancient development. The second impression was that, although the Falls area could be considered peripheral to the mainstream of prehistoric cultural development, the area had undergone continuous, uninterrupted growth from Paleo-Indian to Mississippian times.

Against this background, the Falls of the Ohio River Archaeological Project was launched in 1969 and a major statement of the research goals and a description of the environmental setting was prepared (Janzen, n.d.). Because of the large number of Archaic sites distributed throughout the various physiographic provinces in the Falls area, a high priority was given to obtaining radiocarbon dates for a sample of these sites. Although emphasis on temporal-spatial archaeology has decreased in recent years, an understanding of these dimensions must complement any study of the cultural systems. When the project started, there was not a single site that was dated absolutely in the entire region, and it seemed vital to obtain this kind of information for a settlement pattern study. With some grasp on the temporal dimension, we could start to learn whether site distribution represented units within a pattern of shifting seasonal settlement or changes in adaptation and utilization of the different physiographic regions through time.

By the end of the 1974 field season, a total of nineteen radiocarbon dates had been obtained from nine different Archaic sites in the Falls area. The location of these sites, as well as the Riverwood rockshelter site where a charcoal sample associated with Early Woodland ceramics was dated, is shown in Figure 3. As these dates accumulated, a trend began to emerge from which it was tempting to infer a pattern. First, the dates from sites in the alluvial plain all clustered from 3500 B.C. to 2200 B.C., and second, no dates from 2200 B.C. to 1000 B.C. were present. This twelve-hundred year gap was intriguing, but it was generally assumed that this hiatus reflected only our sampling and not prehistoric population shifts. A number of different hypotheses had been developed to explain the distribution of dates, but these have been temporarily abandoned in the light of new research data on radiocarbon. Recent studies have demonstrated that, for certain time periods, there is a noticeable deviation between C-14 dates and the corresponding true calendar dates, and correction tables have been published by the Museum Applied Science Center for Archaeology of the University Museum, University of Pennsylvania (Ralph, Michael and Han, 1974). All Archaic dates and the Early Woodland date from the Riverwood rockshelter have been adjusted according to the MASCA tables; these are listed in Table 1 and shown diagrammatically in Figure 4. These conversions were computed according to MASCA procedures which require that the C-14 B.P. date be multiplied by 1.03 to convert to the 5730-year half-life and that ten years be added to the standard deviation. After these steps had been taken, and the date rounded off to the nearest ten years, the MASCA tables were consulted for the corrected dates. In some cases, these tables give a range of dates for a particular C-14 date; this information is incorporated into Figure 4 by showing two horizontal dashes connected by a vertical line. The standard deviation is then added to and subtracted from the original date and the resulting numbers adjusted according to the tables. In Figure 4, solid vertical lines extending from the dashes indicate ± one standard deviation and if a portion of these lines is dashed, it indicates that the tables converted a single date into a range of dates.

As a result of these corrections, every date was pushed back in time from 700 to 900 years, and what had been a 1200-year gap expanded to almost a 2000-year gap. In order to obtain a better geographical sampling of sites, the 1974 excavations were centered inland from the alluvial plain on the Salt River in eastern Bullitt County and Spencer County, Kentucky.

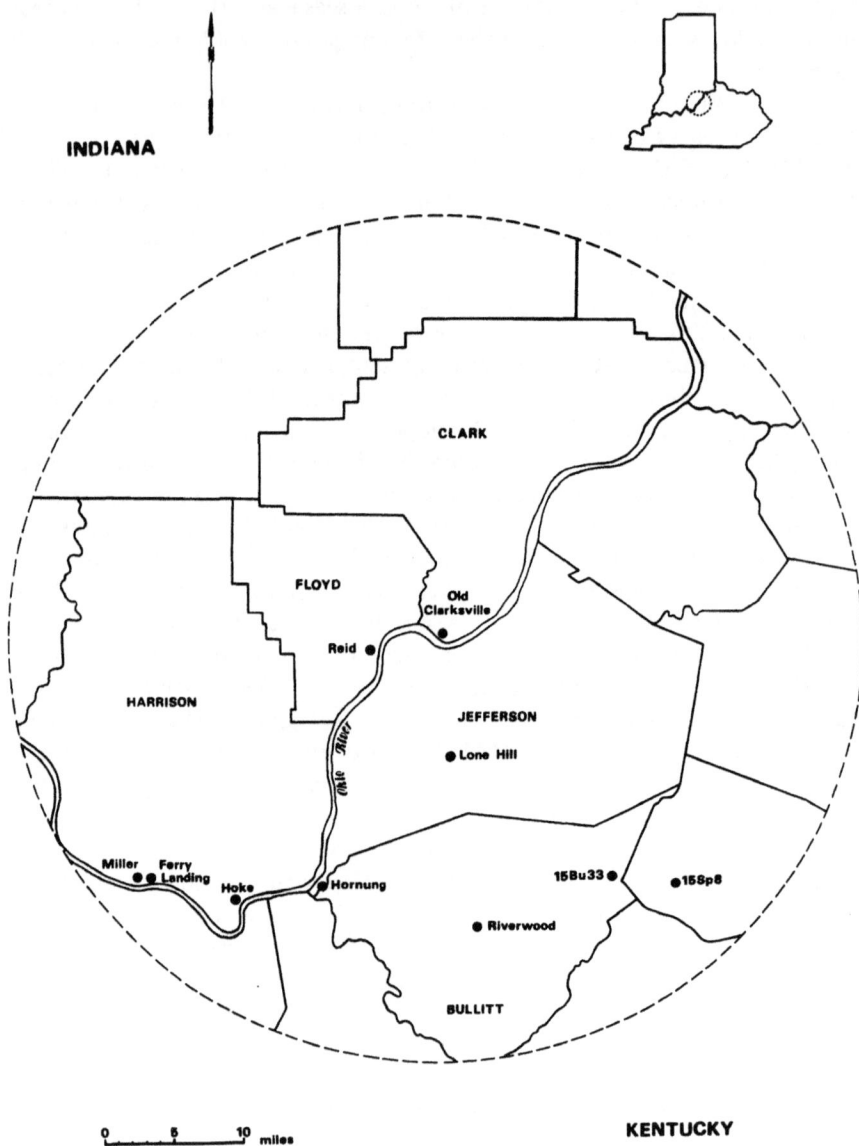

Figure 3. Archaic sites excavated by the Falls Project from 1969-1974.

## TABLE I
### Radiocarbon dates from the Falls of the Ohio River Area

| Site | Sample No. | Date B.P. 5568 half-life | Date B.P. 5730 half-life | Date B.C. (MASCA) |
|---|---|---|---|---|
| Old Clarksville | M-2307 | 4180±180 | 4305 180 | 2920±190 |
| | M-2308 | 4460±180 | 4594±180 | 3210-3310±190 |
| | M-2309 | 4460±180 | 4594±180 | 3210-3310±190 |
| Reid | UGa-267 | 4555±70 | 4692±70 | 3350-3370±80 |
| | UGa-309 | 5480±90 | 5644±90 | 4400±100 |
| Hornung | M-2460 | 4900±200 | 5047±200 | 3710±210 |
| | M-2461 | 5220±230 | 5377±230 | 4040-4060±240 |
| | UGa-261 | 4240±95 | 4367±95 | 2970±105 |
| | UGa-262 | 4315±60 | 4444±60 | 3010-3110±70 |
| | UGa-390 | 5085±85 | 5238±85 | 3890±95 |
| | UGa-401 | 5100±75 | 5253±75 | 3900±85 |
| Hoke | UGa-823 | 4400±185 | 4532±185 | 3160±195 |
| Ferry Landing | UGa-843 | 4365±120 | 4496±120 | 3150±130 |
| Miller | M-2389-2391 | 5220±200 | 5377±200 | 4040-4060±210 |
| Lone Hill | UGa-841 | 4365±185 | 4496±185 | 3150±195 |
| | UGa-842 | 3935±95 | 4053±95 | 2550±105 |
| Riverwood | M-2462 | 2870±150 | 2956±150 | 1110±160 |
| 15Bu33 | UGa-806 | 5690±70 | 5861±70 | 4550±80 |
| 15Sp8 | UGa821 | 5390±220 | 5552±220 | 4330-4350±230 |
| | UGa-820 | 4550±85 | 4687±85 | 3350-3370±95 |

The purpose of the project was to test a number of Archaic sites to see if cultural deposits dating between 1000 and 2000 B.C. could be found. Such sites might provide evidence of a shift to an inland adaptation during the latter part of the Late Archaic. The results were somewhat disappointing, since only two sites, 15Bu33 and 15Sp8, produced sufficient charcoal for dating, and in both cases the dates were too early.

Before an attempt is made to interpret the significance of the Archaic dates derived from this project, a brief description of each site will be given, as background against which the validity of the inferences and speculations can be assessed. (The reader is referred to Figure 3 for site location.)

### Old Clarksville Site (12CL1)

As a result of the great flood of 1937, of the land-fill operations for the New Albany, Indiana floodwall, and of the erosion caused by the positioning of the McAlpine Dam, the Old Clarksville site has been almost totally destroyed. We were fortunate to locate a small undisturbed portion of this site in 1969 and 1970, and fifteen five-by-five foot units were

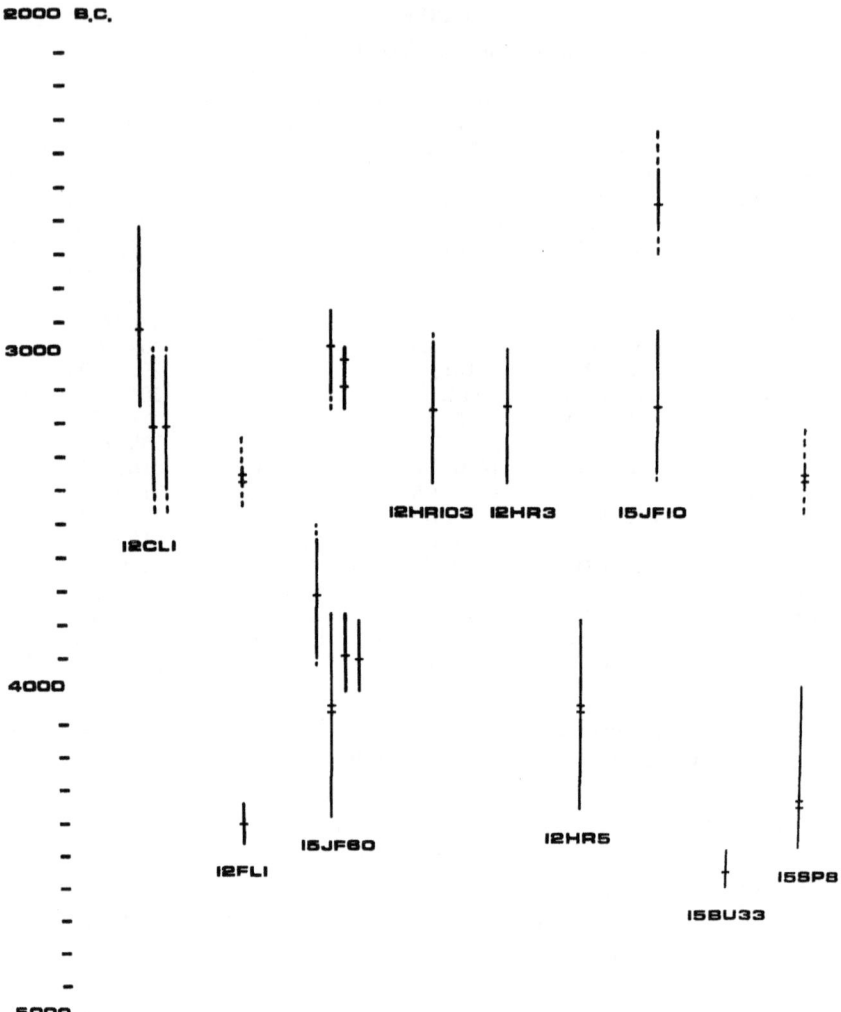

Figure 4. Radiocarbon dates from the Falls of the Ohio River area.

excavated. The most informative data was derived from a ten-by-twenty-foot trench where the cultural deposits were three feet in depth. The midden was homogeneous, showed no discontinuities, and produced only an Archaic component. The radiocarbon dates listed in Table I were derived from the 15–18 inch level (M-2307) and the 24–47 inch level (M-2308 and M-2309). Although the cultural material from these excavations can be considered highly selective in terms of site sampling, the faunal remains were consistent with those found in erosion areas throughout the site. The molluscan fauna was relatively dense with a variety of freshwater bivalve and univalve species present. The frequency of the latter far exceeds the numbers encountered at other sites—one five-by-five foot unit, three feet deep, yielded over 24,000 specimens.

*Reid Site (12FL1)*

The Reid site is located on the alluvial plain of the Ohio River less than ten miles downstream from the Old Clarksville site. The site covers several acres and consists of a huge mound that rises abruptly from the floodplain. Its size can be appreciated from an aerial photograph that appeared on the last page of *Life Magazine* in March 27, 1964. The picture was taken during a flood and the alluvial plain is underwater except for the very top of the mound which still provided sufficient space for a two-story farmhouse, farm implements, and about fifty head of cattle.

In 1971, while excavations were being conducted at the Prather site (12CL4) in Clark County, Indiana, a small crew was sent to the Reid site to dig a five-by-five foot test pit. According to the tenant farmer, mussel shell extending to a depth of fourteen feet had been found on top of the mound when pilings for a new barn were driven. In order to avoid deposits of this thickness, the test pit was located 155 feet south of the top of the mound where shallower deposits could be expected. Even in this area, the midden was extensive; the excavation revealed six feet of cultural deposits with three distinct stratigraphic zones. The first zone consisted of twenty-one inches of dark brown soil laced with fire-cracked rock, chippage, and twenty-seven fragments of badly eroded Early or Middle Woodland pottery. The second zone started at the 18 to 21-inch level and was composed of a dense layer of mussel shell that continued to a depth of six feet. Finally, the basal zone was an orange-brown clay which was sterile of cultural material.

Two radiocarbon dates were obtained from this test pit: the first from the top of the shell zone and the second from the basal six inches. The dates respectively were, 4,555±70 radiocarbon years: 2605 B.C. (UGa-267; MASCA correction: 3350-3370 B.C.) and 5,480±90 radiocarbon years: 3530 B.C. (UGa-309; MASCA correction: 4400 B.C.).

*Hornung Site (15JF60)*

The Hornung site is located near the confluence of the Ohio and Salt Rivers on the alluvial plain. From 1970 to 1972 twenty-eight five-by-five-foot units were excavated, making this the most extensively studied prehistoric site in the Falls area. The most conspicuous feature on the site is a small, elliptical mound approximately five feet high and 110 feet long along the major axis. Excavations on the top of the mound revealed a thin layer of mixed Early and Middle Woodland materials beneath which was an Archaic component that extended to a depth of forty-two inches. The mound appears to have been formed by the dumping of trash and later to have been used as a burial area. Features were difficult to detect, and the only ones positively identified intruded from the lower levels into the orange-brown clays. A large amount of bone was recovered, but mussel shell was sparse and occurred in isolated concentrations instead of in a uniform layer. Stratigraphically the Archaic and Woodland components could not be distinguished, although they could be roughly separated on the basis of the relative frequency of different kinds of chert (Janzen, n.d.)

In 1970, two radiocarbon dates were obtained from the Archaic component and dates of 4,900±200 radiocarbon years: 2950 B.C. (M-2460; MASCA correction: 3710 B.C.) and 5,220±230 radiocarbon years: 3270 B.C. (MASCA correction: 4040-4060 B.C.) were derived from the 27-30 and 33-36 inch levels respectively. The most unexpected find in 1970 was a fragment of charred corn cob that was 6-9 inches deep in the Woodland component (Ford, 1971). In 1971 a test pit was excavated adjacent to the unit that had yielded the corn cob and adequate charcoal samples were collected from level 4 (9-12 inches). This sample dated 4,240±95 radiocarbon years: 2290 B.C. (UGa-261; MASCA correction: 2970 B.C.) and from level 5 (12-15 inches) a date of 4,315±60 radiocarbon years: 2365 B.C. (UGa-262; MASCA correction: 3010-3110 B.C.) was obtained. The difference between these dates seems logical for adjacent three-inch levels but their absolute values are much earlier than expected.

In 1972, excavations were conducted away from the mound to see if a habitation area could be located. An Archaic component was exposed which yielded several fire pits. Radiocarbon dates from two of these pits were 5,085±85 radiocarbon years: 3135 B.C. (UGa-390; MASCA correction 3890 B.C.) and 5,100±75 radiocarbon years: 3150 B.C. (UGa-401;MASCA correction 3900 B.C.)

*Hoke Site (12HR103)*

During the 1972 field season, a surface collection was made from the Hoke site in Harrison County, Indiana. Most of the artifacts collected dated from the Late Archaic, although there was some evidence from the Early Woodland period. The site was selected for study in 1973, and a controlled surface collection was made and eight five-by-five-foot units were excavated. Our findings showed that the cultural deposits seldom exceeded fifteen inches and that most of the cultural material was in the plow zone. Since charcoal was extremely sparse, a sample of bone from the basal level was submitted for dating. Even though the margin of error in dating bone is greater than for charcoal, and bone usually dates later in time than the "true" date (personal communication with the Geochronology Laboratory, University of Georgia), it would be sufficiently accurate to indicate if the Hoke site were terminal Archaic. A date of 4,400±185 radiocarbon years: 2450 B.C. (UGa-823; MASCA correction: 3160 B.C.) was obtained; thus the initial habitation of the Hoke site falls approximately into line with other Archaic sites on the Alluvial plain.

## Ferry Landing (12HR3)

Within the greater Falls region, no locale displays a greater concentration of sites than the area around Mauckport, Indiana. The traditional focal point for the collection of relics in this area has been the Ferry Landing site and, in 1968, several individuals leased the site and dug a trench at least fifty feet long. According to a reliable source, the midden extended to a depth of at least six feet, and the lower levels consisted of a dense layer of mussel shells. The finds most frequently discussed, and verified to be true, are the atlatl weights and occasional atlatl hooks, which were associated with the burials. No charcoal was saved during this operation, but bone found on the surface was submitted for dating. It was realized that such a date would have a limited value but it was felt that some temporal tag should be placed on the site. The date was 4,365±120 radiocarbon years: 2415 B.C. (UGa-843; MASCA correction: 3150 B.C.).

## Miller Site (12HR5)

In recent years, sand and gravel operations have been intensified along the alluvial plain of the Ohio River near Mauckport, Indiana. The procedure is to remove twenty or thirty feet of fill, exposing old channels of the Ohio River. One such operation was about to destroy an Archaic site totally, and a quick salvage plan was instigated. Four five-by-five-foot units were excavated and deposits ranging from eighteen to thirty-six inches were encountered. When a fifty-foot cut was made through the site with a bulldozer to expose a profile, a shell lens approximately one foot thick was found to underlie a layer of dark brown midden. Dense areas of shell were exposed during the sand and gravel operations but it was impossible to measure the thickness of these deposits. Only one C-14 date could be obtained for the site, and charcoal from three levels had to be combined for an adequate sample. From Test Pit A, levels 3-5 (6-15 inches) a date of 5,220±200 radiocarbon years: 3270 B.C. (M-2389-2391; MASCA correction: 4040-4060 B.C.) was obtained.

### Lone Hill (15JF10)

In 1953, a large Archaic site was destroyed in the Kentucky Scottsburg Lowland area by the construction of a Ford Motor Company assembly plant. The site proved to be large in spatial extent, and extensive artifact collections were made, as earthmoving equipment distributed the cultural deposits over a vast area. As dates accumulated from our excavations in the alluvial plain we wondered how inland sites like Lone Hill would fit into the Archaic settlement system. An attempt was made in 1969 to locate an undisturbed portion of the site that had survived construction activities, but our efforts failed. To obtain a temporal fix on the site, two samples of bone were submitted for dating. The dates were; 4,365±185 radiocarbon years: 2425 B.C. (UGa-841; MASCA correction 3150 B.C.) and 3,935±95 radiocarbon years: 1985 B.C. (UGa-842; MASCA correction 2550 B.C.); both fall directly into the pattern of dates for other sites in the Falls area.

### 15Bu33 and 15SP8

As a result of five seasons of fieldwork, no MASCA corrected radiocarbon dates had been recorded from approximately 3000 B.C. to 1000 B.C. (the Lone Hill date of 2550 B.C. was derived from bone and can therefore probably be pushed back to around 3000 B.C.). In 1974, our attention was directed to sites inland along the Salt River in the Outer Blue Grass of Bullitt and Spencer counties, Kentucky. A number of sites were examined so that plans for future excavations might be formulated. Four different Archaic sites were tested; in all cases the deposits were shallow, seldom exceeding one foot. At only two sites were we fortunate enough to find features, and a total of three dates were obtained. They were: 5,690±70 radiocarbon years: 3740 B.C. (UGa-806; MASCA correction: 4550 B.C.) from 15BU33 and 4,500±85 radiocarbon years: 2600 B.C. (UGa-820; MASCA correction: 3350-3370 B.C.) and 5,390±220 radiocarbon years: 3440 B.C. (UGa-821; MASCA correction; 4330-4350 B.C.) from 15SP8. Mussel shell was absent from all the Archaic sites that were tested, and they lacked the dark brown midden and large quantities of fire-cracked rock that characterized sites in the alluvial plain.

The artifact assemblages from all of these sites, along with surface collections from several dozen other sites, have been studied and some projectile point typologies have been established. The total number of points under examination is estimated to be in excess of one thousand. It has been difficult to divide the collection into traditional classes of artifact types, and the projectile point assemblages, even from the same level at a site, are characterized by a diversity in size, shape, hafting configuration, and material. Research presently being conducted by Stephen R. Claggett (n.d.), on approximately 1,500 projectile points, from the Salt and Rolling Fork River drainages of Bullitt and Nelson counties, Kentucky, has encountered this same situation.

One definite pattern relating to the utilization of chert sources in the Falls area has emerged from a study of the lithic material. Six different chert types were identified in 1969 (Janzen, 1971:376), and these have now been reduced to five types. What has been designated Types I and II are found in the Knobs—Norman Upland, Type III is from the Mitchell Plain and is commonly called Harrison County chert, Type IV occurs in the Outer Blue Grass—Muscatatuck Regional Slope area and at the Falls, and Type V specimens are glacially derived pebble cherts that are found along the alluvial plain of the Ohio River. What was originally called Type VI has now been classified as a variation of Type I. An examination of over 100,000 pieces of chippage from the Clarksville, Reid, Hornung, Lone Hill, Hoke, and Miller sites has indicated that during the initial period of habitation at these sites the chert sources closest to the sites were predominately utilized. Through time there was a steady decline in the use of local chert sources and in the later Archaic deposits, particularly in the Woodland levels at the Hornung site, the high quality Galconda cherts from Harrison County, Indiana (Type III) were extensively utilized.

At all of the sites investigated in the alluvial plain bone preservation was excellent and a variety of bone tools, such as awls, needles, hairpins, beads, and atlatl hooks have been recovered. In a few cases examples of engraved bone have been found and the design motifs are exactly identical to those illustrated by Miller (1941:43, 46-47) from the McCain site. At two sites, Hornung and Old Clarksville, bone fishhooks were found and, although all other bone tools from these sites displayed a high degree of similarity, the fishhooks were different. Fishhook residues indicated that at both sites fishhooks were fashioned from the long bone of deer, small mammals, and birds. Only at the Hornung site was there evidence of manufacturing fishhooks from deer phalanges. The difference between the fishhooks at these two sites was the configuration at the top of the hook where the line was fastened. In some cases a groove was cut below the top of the hook while in others a small protruding overhang was left on one side of the shaft. Of the 36 whole or partially whole fishhooks excavated at the Old Clarksville site, 35 had the protruding overhang while only one was grooved. From the sample of 19 hooks obtained from the Hornung site 18 were grooved and one had the protruding overhang. Since the layers that produced these hooks at both sites were broadly contemporary this difference in fashioning the top of the hook is not attributed to a change in style through time.

On the basis of the radiocarbon dates derived from these nine sites it is possible to make some generalizations about Late Archaic development in the Falls area. In the alluvial valley, Late Archaic sites display considerable midden accumulation and these deposits rest on sterile orange-brown clays. Radiocarbon dates from the basal levels of Reid (12FL1) and Hornung (15JF60, 15BU33) indicate that these sites were inhabited at least by 4000 to 4500 B.C. Therefore it is assumed that this range of dates can be used to bracket the initial period of Late Archaic occupation in the area. A date of 4000 B.C. has been used as a lower temporal limit for the Late Archaic (Griffin, 1967:178), but it may be necessary to push this date back now that errors in radiocarbon have been recognized. The MASCA correction for 4000 B.C. is 4600 B.C.

With the exception of 15BU33 all sites have yielded C-14 dates that cluster between 4000 and 3000 B.C. From the extensive cultural deposits encountered at most of these sites, and the homogeneous and stratigraphically uninterrupted nature of the midden, it can be inferred that the millennium following 4000 B.C. was a period of unparalleled prehistoric cultural growth in the Falls region. The radiocarbon dates from Hoke (12HR103), Ferry Landing (12HR3) and Lone Hill (15JF10) are all based on bone samples and, with the exception of one date from the latter site, are all of similar ages (see Table I). Since dates based on bone tend to shift toward the present, it is safe to assume that the three sites have habitation zones dated around 3500 B.C.

Relatively little is known about the terminal phase of the Late Archaic in the Falls area, and, after six seasons of fieldwork, there is not a single MASCA corrected C-14 date between 2920 and 1110 B.C. The date of 2550 B.C. from Lone Hill is based on bone and therefore probably too recent. The Riverwood rockshelter date of 920 B.C. (MASCA correction 1110 B.C.) is the earliest Early Woodland date the project has recorded, and it is used to mark the initial phase of the Woodland period in the Falls area. The date was obtained from charcoal found in a feature associated with plain, thick, grit-tempered pottery.

## Late Archaic in the Falls of the Ohio River Area

Although the spatial extent of the Falls project is relatively large and the testing procedures cannot be called extensive, it is tempting to speculate about the missing dates from the terminal phase of the Late Archaic. At two sites, Reid (12FL1) and Hornung (15JF60), the Archaic component was capped with a thin zone of Early and Middle Woodland material. The first eighteen inches of midden at the Reid site contained sparse amounts of Woodland pottery, while level 7 (18-21 inches), which was the transition level into the shell zone, dated 3350-3370 B.C. (MASCA corrected). At the Hornung site, level 4 (9-12 inches) dated 2970 B.C. (MASCA corrected), while level 3 (6-9 inches) contained Early and Middle Woodland pottery.

There is good evidence of cultural continuity from about 4000 B.C. to 3000 B.C., but thus far there are no dated deposits showing a development from Late Archaic into Early Woodland. Instead, the data suggest that after 3000 B.C. the vigorous development of the Shell Mound Archaic in the Falls region declined rapidly, and the area witnessed a sharp decrease in population density.

In attempting a settlement pattern study of a hunting and gathering culture like the Shell Mound Archaic, certain models come to mind. One that has been applied to this culture is a settlement system called Central-Based Wandering (Meggers, 1956:139). This scheme is presently referred to as shifting seasonal settlements, and Winters' (1969) Riverton Culture is the most recent application of this approach to the midwestern Archaic. This particular model has proved so useful that it now seems to be accepted as a reality. It is assumed that sufficient testing and the recovery of the right kinds of data will yield information on seasonal habitation of a site. Even with the recovery of abundant faunal remains it has been difficult to extract this kind of information from the Archaic sites excavated in the Falls area. Sites like BU-33 and SP-8 appear to be logical candidates for season-specific sites, but the absence of faunal remains makes this difficult to substantiate. At Old Clarksville, Hornung, and Hoke an analysis of the faunal assemblage has shown white-tailed deer to be the major source of animal food. Evidence has not been found at these sites which would permit a season of the year to be excluded as a time of habitation.

Based strictly on logical considerations, the frequency and distribution of sites do not follow the expected pattern of a shifting settlement system. The largest sites are found in the alluvial valley, and it is assumed that these represent central-base camps. Such sites as Old Clarksville, Reid, Hornung, and Ferry Landing, with midden deposits ranging from four to twelve feet, clearly fall into this category. To consider that these sites represent different seasonal loci does not seem logical since they are located within the same geographical region and the exploitative potential at each appears to be identical. If these sites dated from different time periods within the Late Archaic then perhaps it could be argued that they represent focal activity centers within a shifting settlement system. However, the radiocarbon dates indicate that they all have similar temporal levels, and considering that these are not the only large sites in the alluvial valley, the concentration of major contemporaneous sites seems unusually dense.

A second factor to consider is the location of sites in the alluvial valley. They are all situated near the juncture of at least two physiographic provinces where several microenvironments are accessible. The Old Clarksville site is located at the Falls, which can be considered a unique ecological zone, and nearby are the Scottsburg Lowland and the Norman Upland. The Reid, Hornung, and Hoke sites are on the alluvial plain at the juncture of the Knobs (Ky.)–Norman Upland (Ind.) zones, and the Ferry Landing and Miller sites are on the alluvial plain adjacent to the Mitchell Plain. The physiographic diversity within the Falls area is also reflected in the variability of the plant communities that merge in this region. This in turn means that the seasonal movements of animal populations need not extend over large distances. For example, white-tailed deer usually move into the Knobs-Norman Upland during the autumn and winter months, but since this physiographic province merges into the alluvial valley they can also be found here during those months. Similarly, the large quantities of charred nut fragments found in the midden deposits of most alluvial valley sites indicate that prehistoric people exploited the nut-bearing forests of the Knobs-Norman Upland.

The Central-Based Wandering and shifting settlement model is based on the efficiency of seasonal mobility as a means of utilizing food resources from different microenvironmental zones. Assuming that the various physiographic regions in the Falls area could produce different exploitative potentials at different times of the year, and given the compression of these natural zones in the Falls area, it may have been possible to locate sites in such a way as to minimize seasonal movements. Moreover, it is suggested that in such a setting, and with abundant food resources, a residual population might have remained at the same location throughout most of the year. In this case a hub and spoke model, or semi-sedentary with wandering, might better describe the settlement pattern. The Archaic is defined as a period of adaptations to regional environments and, considering the environmental variation in the Eastern United States, it is questionable if all settlement systems would fall into a pattern of seasonal mobility.

In conclusion, after six years of research in the Falls of the Ohio River region, the data have produced some unexpected results. On the basis of excavations at seven sites, the evidence indicates a rapid decline in Late Archaic development after 3000 B.C. with not a single deposit so far dating from around 2900 to 1110 B.C. If additional research reinforces this picture, it will be necessary to seek an explanation for this decline, and one source of information that may prove useful is in the data accumulating on post-Pleistocene oscillations in climate.

Finally, our research was started with a shifting settlement system in mind, and the data has been analyzed in an attempt to extract seasonal information. The results have not been encouraging and suggest that a settlement model based on seasonal mobility may not be totally adequate. An alternative hub and spoke model, or semi-sedentary with wandering, has been proposed. This model has been developed on logical grounds for situations where there is a high degree of geographical variability concentrated in a small area. If sites are located near the junction of several different microenvironmental zones, the need for seasonal movements may have been reduced to the point where a residual population could remain at the site for an entire year, with splinter groups breaking away to exploit seasonal food resources. This model is presently being considered along with the more conventional shifting settlement approach, and its validity will be accepted or rejected on the basis of additional research.

# References Cited

Borden, William
    1874   Report of a geological survey of Clarke and Floyd Counties. Fifth Annual Report of the Geological Survey of Indiana made during the Year 1873:184-87.

Braun, E. Lucy
    1972   The deciduous forests of eastern North America. New York.

Burnett, Richard
    1963   Lone hill. Central States Archaeological Journal 10:84-90.

Claggett, Stephen R.
    n.d.   Seriation of projectile points from Archaic sites in central Kentucky. Master's dissertation in preparation. Wake Forest University.

Durrett, Reuben T.
    1893   The centenary of Louisville. Filson Club Publications No. 8. Louisville.

Ford, Richard I.
 1971 Corn from the Hornung Site, Jefferson County, Kentucky. University of Michigan Museum of Anthropology, Ethnobotanical Laboratory Report No. 459.
Griffin, James B.
 1967 Eastern North American archaeology: A summary. Science 156: 175-91.
Guernsey, E. Y.
 1937 Certain southern Indiana sources of lithic artifact material. Proceedings of the Indiana Academy of Science 46:47-52.
 1939 Relationships among various Clark County sites. Proceedings of the Indiana Academy of Science 48:27-32.
 1942 The culture sequence of the Ohio Falls sites. Proceedings of the Indiana Academy of Science 51:60-67.
Gunn, Charles R.
 1968 The flora of Jefferson and seven adjacent counties, Kentucky. Annuals of the Kentucky Society of Natural History 2:5-6.
Janzen, Donald E.
 1971 Excavations of the Falls of the Ohio River. The Filson Club Historical Quarterly 45:373-80.
 n.d. An archaeological study of the falls of the Ohio River region. Submitted and awaiting publication by the Filson Club of Louisville.
Matthews, James J.
 1958a Shell mound incised bone and stone artifacts. Ohio Archaeologist 9:42-43, 46.
 1958b The Zorn Village site, Louisville, Kentucky. Ohio Archaeologist 8: 114-26.
Meggers, Betty J., editor
 1956 Functional and evolutionary implications of community patterning: Item *in:* Seminars in archaeology: 1955, The Society for American Archaeology, Memoir 11.
Miller, Rex
 1941 McCain Site, Dubois County, Indiana. Prehistory Research Series, Indiana Historical Society II(1):43, 46-47.
Ralph, E. K., H. N. Michael, and M. C. Han
 1974 Radiocarbon dates and reality. Archaeology of Eastern North America 2:120. Eastern States Archaeological Federation.
Schwartz, Douglas W.
 1961 A key to prehistoric Kentucky pottery. Transactions of the Kentucky Academy of Science 22:82-85.
Webb, William S.
 1946 Indian Knoll, site Oh2, Ohio County, Kentucky. University of Kentucky Reports in Anthropology and Archaeology IV (3) pt. 1.

Webb, William S. and William D. Funkhouser
 1932 Archaeological survey of Kentucky. University of Kentucky Reports in Archaeology and Anthropology II.

Winters, Howard D.
 1969 The Riverton culture. The Illinois Archaeological Survey, Monograph No. 1, Springfield.

# SOME OBSERVATIONS OF THE GOODALL FOCUS

*Richard E. Flanders*
Grand Valley State Colleges

In 1935, James B. Griffin and George I. Quimby began a study of Hopewellian material from Michigan and Indiana, which Quimby continued with Glenn Black in 1937 and which resulted in Quimby's Master's degree from the University of Michigan. The material was classified as the Goodall Focus, Elemental Aspect of the Hopewellian Phase, Pattern Unknown (Indianapolis Archaeological Conference, 1935).

Quimby attempts a detailed record of finds although he admits that "haphazard" recovery methods of much of it hampered his efforts (Quimby, 1941a:63). The fact that particular emphasis was placed on ceramic analysis was no doubt due at least in part to Griffin's influence. Since the publication of the first attempt to discover order in the Western Michigan Hopewellian manifestation, a large store of data has been recorded by record search, excavation and analysis. Perhaps it is time to look again at those "impoverished Hopewell outliers" (Fitting, 1970:98) to see what they can contribute to knowledge of northeast United States prehistory. It is clear that the model of a gradual expansion of Hopewellian traits northward from the Kankakee drainage to the Muskegon River is no longer tenable because of new evidence. It is also clear that Quimby's original concept of a close connection between early stages of Illinois Valley Hopewell and the Michigan manifestation is supported. It has been proposed by Griffin that the term Goodall "Focus" be dropped because of the relatively long time span involved (at least four hundred years) and the fact that material from early to late Hopewell is included in Goodall, using the Illinois Valley sequence (Brown, 1964:110; Griffin et al., 1970:189). Griffin has suggested that there may be at least two phases involved, an early Norton phase and a later Converse phase (Griffin, 1970). James Brown's observation that the hypothesis of a Goodall development out of Illinois Havana has not yet been tested in the field (Brown, 1964:122) is no longer applicable after the field work of the last ten years (Gillis and Davis, 1954, 1956; Prahl, 1966, 1970; Flanders, 1965; Fitting, 1972). There is a closer relationship between Goodall sites and Illinois Havana than was apparent from the original Goodall sample.

Evidence of Early Woodland in western Michigan comes in the form of Marion Thick-like pottery (Flanders, 1963) and from radiocarbon dates from a burial complex that included cremation, grave-pit and mound construction and distinctive projectile point styles (Prahl, 1970). It is interesting to note that the best authenticated sites for an Early Woodland burial complex are in the Muskegon River Valley, considered the northern limit of Hopewellian influence in western Michigan. This complex is contemporary with similar developments in other parts of the northeastern United States and in Eastern Michigan (Prahl, 1970:124; Fitting, 1972). There seems to be no clear continuity from Early to Middle Woodland mortuary practices in Michigan, although it might be noted that one item of grave furniture, a ground slate gorget, shows up in seven of the original ten Goodall components. This item would ordinarily be associated with a Late Archaic or Early Woodland complex, but it seems to reappear in a late Hopewell context in this area (cf. Flanders, 1965).

The earliest evidence for Hopewell in western Michigan would appear to be the Norton Mounds burial complex (Griffin et al., 1970) which is an example of what James Brown has termed the "northeastern extension of Havana" (Brown, 1964). The grave goods in this complex include pottery vessels very similar to vessels from the Adler Mounds (Winters, 1962) and the Utica group in northern Illinois (Hendricksen, 1965). These Norton vessels belong to Quimby's category of Goodall dentate-stamped (Quimby, 1941b) and are very close in vessel form and decorative technique to the Naples type of Havana Ware in the Illinois Valley. A radiocarbon date of 10 B.C. ± 120 from Norton Mound C (M-1493) should mark the advent of the Hopewellian burial complex in this part of the Upper Great Lakes. Included in this complex are several caches of the Norton type of projectile point (White, 1965), locally manufactured effigy pipes, Gulf coast *Busycon* shells and a unique Michigan engraved turtle carapace container (Flanders, 1965; Griffin et al., 1970).

Probably the most sensitive marker for stages in Hopewell development is the ceramic burial vessel manufactured in most cases specifically as part of the grave furniture. Radiocarbon dates from the Norton Mounds do not give a clear picture of the extent or kind of contact with the Illinois Valley because the range of error in dates is great enough to obscure the introduction of new decorative techniques or the acquisition of a "model" vessel from the Illinois center. How rapidly did the initial movement take place? The majority of burial vessels from the Kankakee drainage and from the Grand River Norton Group are certainly "Havanoid," with zoned bodies and thick dentate stamping (Quimby's Type 11-B or Goodall dentate-stamped). Havanoid sherds also show up in village sites to the north of the Grand at the Toft Lake site (Losey, 1967), at the Jancarich village site near the Brooks Mounds (Prahl, 1970) and further north in Antrim County (William Lovis, personal communication), although none of these are in burial context. On the basis of the one charcoal radiocarbon date from Norton (M-1493)—and ignoring the later dates (M-1488 and M-1490) from Norton Mound H, taken from decomposed pine bark in the burial pit (Funke, 1972)—this initial movement of Havana traits is believed to have happened during the end of the first century before the Christian era. The whole question of the relationship of the Hopewellian materials from eastern Michigan, like the Schultz Site material (Fitting, 1970), is not considered here, although this eastern manifestation may have received some influence from Ohio which is not clear in western Michigan.

Following close on the heels of the Havanoid complex was the "classic" Hopewell style burial vessel (Griffin, 1952) with its limestone temper, zoned body treatment and both "fine" dentate rocker stamping and plain rocker stamping. The Goodall sites that have yielded these vessels include the Goodall type site with at least two vessels, Sumnerville on the St. Joseph with at least one vessel, both Norton and Spoonville on the Grand River (two vessels apiece), the Gratton Component in Kent County with possibly one vessel, and the Brooks Mounds on the Muskegon River with at least one vessel (Prahl, 1970: Pl. XVL). In the case of Norton, the limestone tempered vessels were represented only by a few sherds in a "burial cache" situation. It is reasonable to assume that the finely polished, limestone tempered vessels were trade items from the Illinois Valley and functioned as models for the locally made, grit-tempered Sumnerville types. Another decorative technique that probably accompanied the classic Hopewell style was plain rocker stamping, which appears in sites from the St. Joseph, Grand and Muskegon valleys but not in the Goodall type site. This decorative technique seems to persist as a decorative motif on a small proportion (ca. 2-5 percent) of village material in what is tentatively identified as Late Middle Woodland in this area, including the Spoonville and Zemaitis sites in Ottawa County, Michigan (Flanders, 1965, 1970). There is a question about the radiocarbon dates from features at the Spoonville site (M-1428, A.D. 110 ± 120 and M-1427, A.D. 215 ± 110 years) which would appear to date Wayne Ware-like utilitarian pottery. The whole question of the temporal position of this cordmarked, everted-rim ware will certainly be the subject of some debate in the near future (c.f. Fitting, 1970: Ch. V; Rogers, 1972, on Allegan Ware; and Brashler, 1973). The advent of the classic Hopewell ware and plain rocker stamping nevertheless would appear to belong somewhere in the first century A.D. The majority of mortuary ware from Michigan Hopewell sites would fall into Quimby's original categories IIA, B or C, a grit-tempered copy of Illinois classic Hopewell or of the Baehr derivative. The familiar cross-hatched rim (incised or at times dentate stamped) bordered by hemiconical punctates, a plain neck zone and a zoned body appears in all Michigan Hopewell sites. It is interesting to note that at all sites where there is at least one Sumnerville incised or Norton cross-hatched vessel there is also at least one Type I (Hopewellian Zone-stamped) vessel present, although this was not clear from the original sample.

All four of the major river valleys involved in the original Goodall Focus also yield a type of burial vessel first defined by Quimby as "generalized Woodland" (Quimby, 1941b), which appears to be close to Fitting's Wayne Ware (Fitting, 1965) in vessel form, rim style and decorative techniques. This would appear to occur toward the end of Middle Woodland burial ceremonialism and perhaps be equivalent to the Weaver and Fox Creek phases in the middle and lower Illinois Valley. No equivalent phase has been suggested for northern Illinois (Griffin et al., 1970:10). It would also seem to match the activity at the Springwells Mound Group where Wayne Ware, slate gorgets and Snyders, *affinis* points were present (Halsey, 1968).

Borrowing from the Illinois Valley sequence as proposed by Griffin et al. 1970, we might attempt a correlation between phases of Hopewell development in Michigan and the centers to the south. Table 1 suggests a possible arrangement of the sequential development of Michigan Hopewell. Several points might be noted here:

1. There is no phase name proposed for the Early Woodland material from Western Michigan—including the presence of Marion Thick ceramics and Prahl's Muskegon River material, with early radiocarbon dates—until more evidence, particularly in the form of ceramics, has accrued.
2. The initial Hopewellian intrusion into Michigan was evidently a rapid one, quickly covering those areas that later yielded the established "classic" material, including both the Norton and Converse phases. There is a distinct differentiation between the material from the Muskegon Valley and that from further north which would belong to

TABLE I

Proposed Phases for Western Michigan Woodland

| Time | Illinois Valley Phases | West Michigan Sites | Phases |
|---|---|---|---|
| A.D. 600 | | Carrigan Intrusive | ? |
| A.D. 400 | Fox Creek, Weaver | Palmiteer | |
| A.D. 200 | Pike, Steuben, LaPorte | Converse, Brooks, Late Norton | Converse |
| A.D. 100 | | Norton Md. D. J. | |
| A.D. 1 | Bedford, Ogden | Norton Mds. M, H, C, I Goodall Md.21 | Norton |
| 200 B.C. | Calhoun, Fulton | | |
| | Peisker, Morton, Black Sand | Croton Dam Carrigan | ? |

the Lake Forest Middle Woodland at the same time period with a different adaptive mode. It might be noted that there is almost no evidence of "intrusive" or trade ceramics between the two biotic zones. If trade occurred, it may have been concerned with substances that would not require pottery storage.

3. Following the initial movement of Hopewellian traits into Michigan, there seems to have been a period of consolidation and continued contact with the Illinois center as evidenced by the presence of trade items (*Busycon* conch shells, mica, Illinois and Indiana flint) in amounts comparable to other sites in the Illinois center. The burial at Spoonville with the copper celts (Flanders, 1969) may furnish an example of the trade items involved in the contact. This continued contact would apply to the proposed Converse Phase and would include Prahl's Mallon Mound B (Prahl, 1970) near Muskegon.

4. The "breakdown" in Hopewellian funerary ceremonialism can be noted in Michigan as it has been noted for Illinois, and the evidence indicates that it happened at the same time for the "outliers" as it did for the "center." Whatever climatological or cultural changes were

involved in this breakdown would appear to have spread as rapidly as the initial development.

Although this is admittedly a simplification of a very complex situation in the Upper Great Lakes and does not take into consideration such studies as Wilkinson's (1971) which indicates that there may not have been an actual physical migration of people from Illinois into western Michigan, perhaps Griffin's proposed phases will make western Michigan Middle Woodland more manageable for future work.

## References Cited

Brashler, Janet
    1973    A formal analysis of prehistoric ceramics from the Fletcher site. M.A. Thesis, Michigan State University.

Brown, James A.
    1964    The northeastern extension of the Havana tradition. Item *in*: Hopewellian Studies, J. R. Caldwell and R. L. Hall, eds. Illinois State Museum Scientific Papers, (4) Springfield.

Fitting, James E.
    1965    Late Woodland cultures of southeastern Michigan. University of Michigan, Museum of Anthropology, Anthropological Papers No. 24.
    1970    The archaeology of Michigan. Garden City: The Natural History Press.
    1972    The Schultz site at Green Point. University of Michigan, Memoirs of the Museum of Anthropology No. 4.

Flanders, Richard E.
    1963    Marion thick pottery in Michigan. The Coffinberry News Bulletin, 10:47-9.
    1965    Engraved turtle shells from the Norton Mounds near Grand Rapids, Michigan. Papers of the Michigan Academy of Science, Arts and Letters 50:361-64.
    1965    A comparison of some Middle Woodland materials from Illinois and Michigan. Ph.D. Thesis, the University of Michigan.
    1969    Hopewell materials from Crockery Creek. Michigan Academician 1: 147-51.
    1970    The Salad site. The Coffinberry News Bulletin 17:30-32.

Funke, James and Richard Flanders
    1972    Norton radiocarbon samples. The Coffinberry News Bulletin 19: 66-67.

Gillis, Edward V. and George W. Davis
  1954   Archaeological excavations of the Parson Mound group, Brooks Township, Newaygo County, Michigan. Ms. on file, Museum of Anthropology, University of Michigan.
  1956   Field notes: excavation of the Palmiteer Mound group. Ms. on file, Museum of Anthropology, University of Michigan.

Griffin, James B.
  1952   Some Early and Middle Woodland pottery types in Illinois. Item *in:* Hopewellian Communities in Illinois. Illinois State Museum Scientific Papers V:93-130.

Griffin, James B., Richard E. Flanders and Paul F. Titterington
  1970   The burial complexes of the Knight and Norton Mounds in Illinois and Michigan. The University of Michigan, Memoirs of the Museum of Anthropology No. 2.

Halsey, John R.
  1968   The Springwells Mound group. Item *in:* Contributions to Michigan archaeology. University of Michigan, Museum of Anthropology, Anthropological Papers No. 24.

Henricksen, Harry C.
  1965   Utica Hopewell. A study of early Hopewellian occupation in the Illinois River Valley. Illinois Archaeological Survey Bulletin 5: 1-67.

Indianapolis Archaeological Conference
  1935   Committee on state archaeological surveys. National Research Council.

Losey, Timothy C.
  1967   Toft Lake Village site. The Michigan Archaeologist 13:126-29.

Prahl, Earl J.
  1966   The Muskegon River survey. Item *in:* Edge area archaeology, edited by James E. Fitting. The Michigan Archaeologist 12: 183-209.
  1970   The Woodland Period of the lower Muskegon Valley and the northern Hopewellian frontier. Ph.D. Thesis, The University of Michigan.

Quimby, George I.
  1941a  The Goodall focus: an analysis of ten Hopewellian components in Michigan. Indiana Historical Society 2:(2).
  1941b  Hopewellian pottery types in Michigan. Papers of the Michigan Academy of Science, Arts, and Letters 26:489-95.
  1943   The ceramic sequence within the Goodall focus. Papers of the Michigan Academy of Science, Arts, and Letters 28:543-48.

Rogers, Margaret B.
  1972   The 46th Street site and the occurrence of Allegan ware in southwestern Michigan. Michigan Archaeologist 18:47-108.

White, Anta M.
   1965   Typology of some middle Woodland projectile points from Illinois and Michigan. Papers of the Michigan Academy of Science, Arts, and Letters 50:355-60.

Wilkinson, Richard G.
   1971   Prehistoric relationships in the Great Lakes region. University of Michigan Museum of Anthropology, Anthropological Papers No. 45.

Winters, Howard D.
   1961   The Adler Mound group, Will County, Illinois. Chicago area archaeology. Illinois Archaeological Survey Bulletin 3:57-88.

# PREHISTORIC CULTURE AREAS AND CULTURE CHANGE ON THE GULF COASTAL PLAIN

*William H. Sears*
Florida Atlantic University

From "Proceedings of the 22nd Southeastern Archaeological Conference–1965": Griffin: "Now, Bill, you may be looking at it very clearly, but you haven't said yet what kind of materials they are–I'm lost."
Sears, 1974: "O.K., Jimmy, here it is."

## Introduction

This essay is based on the premise that prehistoric culture areas may be spatially and temporally bounded by the distribution of ceramic complexes. Changes through time in the ceramic complex in the defined area may be comparatively gradual, in which case we are talking about traditions (Willey, 1945:53). Complexes and traditions allow us to keep track of changes in the spatial distribution of cultures through time and to perceive their replacement.

While the useful tool for this purpose is the complex (Willey, 1949:6), representing as it does a tremendous number of modal choices agreed on by a lot of potters, it is of course based on the type, itself a modal cluster of varying dimensions and content. Culture contact, so important in giving us our first view of cultural interaction, is perceptible through "trade" sherds.

The concept of series (Willey, 1949:6) will also be used, but this requires care. A series may be the sole product of a culture at one point in space and time and only a part of a complex at another point.

The data used in this essay is restricted to pottery collections from village sites. The necessity for this restriction, the elimination of collections from mounds and cemeteries, has been discussed at some length in another paper (Sears, 1973). We have enough information to tell us where the heads and tails of a few of our cultural animals are in time and space. Except for some minimum information on settlement pattern and ceremonial complex, we do not know much about most of the animals. It is often difficult to tell whether we are dealing with cats or rats. But, perhaps a point which needs emphasis is that you cannot select a problem, work on a culture or any part of it, until you know where the critter is.

A fair amount of data is reported, or referred to, for the first time in this paper. In either case, full site descriptions and reports of complete artifact analyses are available in the survey files of the appropriate states. This material comes from a survey of the Gulf Coastal plain from the bend of Florida to the Mississippi delta which I did with the aid of National Science Foundation Grant 5019 between 1957 and 1960. During its course, I visited most of the mound sites excavated by C. B. Moore and made collections from the associated midden areas. Many of these of course supplement collections made and reported by Gordon Willey (1949). Many of his sites were also revisited.

Some neighboring areas were visited, and collections from them as well as from the defined area were reanalyzed, often on a sampling basis. I offer here my sincere appreciation to the archaeologists at the Universities of Texas, Oklahoma, and Louisiana State, and to Clarence Webb, E. Bruce Trickey, and William Lazarus, in whose homes their collections were studied.

I wish, when working on problems of relationship between my area of interest and the lower part of the Mississippi Valley that I could use, even frequently refer to, the superb classification of Phillip Phillips (1970). My reason for not doing so is not our terminological disagreement about types and varieties (Sears, 1960; Phillips, 1958) but simply because work of comparable quantity and quality is not available in my area. Too, period complexes from the Red River mouth area as described by Ford in a series of publications (1951, 1952) appear to have been particularly involved with cultures to the east.

The CMVAS A-G framework (Phillips, Ford and Griffin, 1951) is used for relative chronology and a structural outline. Some adjustment has been made following Ford (1952) for the particularly important Red River area, and Phillips (1970) for the D-F period in the lower valley and the Issaquena complex. This framework, constantly readjusted as new information becomes available by students working in the Mississippi Valley, does not serve my purposes perfectly of course, any more than it has those of others. It is serviceable, and helps in visualization of central Gulf Coastal Plain-Mississippi Valley relationships. Some comments, suggestions, concerning the absolute dates offered will be found further on in this paper.

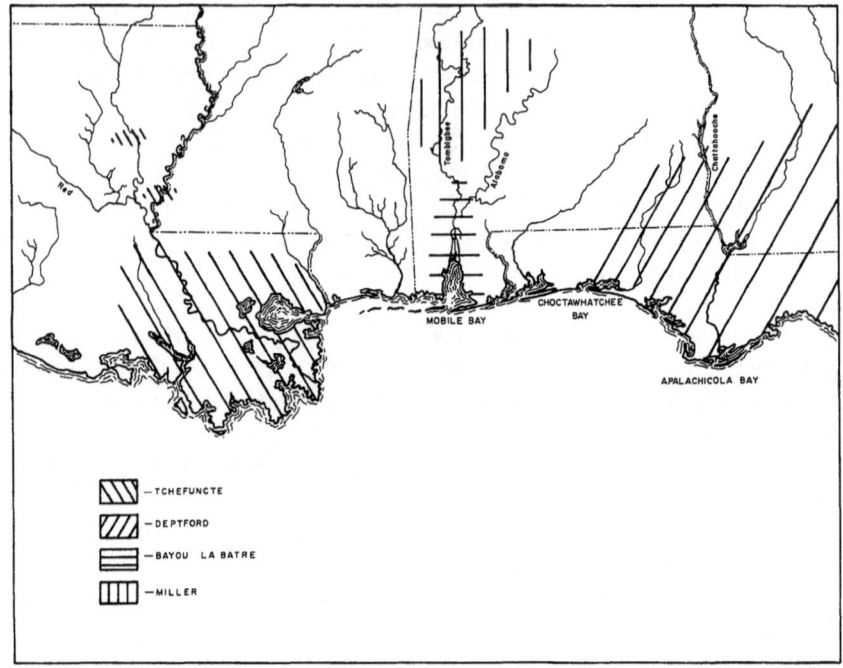

Figure 1. Period F-G.

## Period F-G

*Ceramic Series*

*Deptford:* Types Deptford Check Stamped (*not* Bold Check Stamped, Deptford Linear Check Stamped, Deptford Simple Stamped). (Sears and Griffin, 1950; Sears 1957:23).

*Bayou La Batre:* Bayou La Batre Stamped, Bayou La Batre Scallop Impressed (Wimberley, 1953).

*Tchefuncte:* Tchefuncte Stamped, Tchefuncte Incised, Tammany Pinched, Lake Borgne Incised (Ford and Quimby, 1945).

*Miller:* Saltillo Fabric Marked, Furrs Cord Marked. Tishomingo Cord Marked which is clay tempered is a later member of the Miller complex (Jennings, 1941:201).

Most of the foregoing types, and all of the series excepting possibly Miller, use the tetrapod based jar form to some extent. Other evidence for contemporaneity of these complexes demonstrates that the tetrapod form is a horizon marker. Simultaneously, if obviously, it also indicates cultural relationship between them. Unfortunately, I do not know of any data which demonstrates, or even suggests, who got tetrapods first. A Poverty Point origin which has been suggested (Ford, 1966:181-2) seems unacceptable for many reasons, not least of which is the surface context of the specimens involved. *Deptford Complex:* The Deptford series developed from fiber-tempered ancestors in the Savannah River Area (Waring, 1968:207-8; Sears and Griffin, 1950). It moved into the area we are considering which was virtually uninhabited until the culture ear-marked by Deptford pottery in middens and the Yent ceremonial complex in mounds (Sears, 1962) came in around the beginning of the Christian era. There was some use of the Central Gulf Coastal Plain by populations with Archaic cultures, and some fiber tempered pottery appears to have been made there before the appearance of Deptford (Phelps, 1965). Both are represented by very few small sites. Willey (1949) lists half a dozen sites in the northwest coast which have Deptford components, demonstrated either stratigraphically, or by surface collections with the total Deptford complex. To these we may add the initial, and intense, occupation of the Mandeville site in south Georgia (Kelly, Kellar and McMichaels, 1962) and the Deptford complexes, Deptford series sherds plus consistently associated types from other series, from the following new sites or new collections. The Florida sites are in the eastern part of the northwest Florida coast as indicated by the county designations. Some of these collections are particularly important since they demonstrate the presence of "trade" sherds generally not listed in earlier published accounts of Deptford components.

| *Wa-47* | | *Wa-1 (Mashes Island)* | |
|---|---|---|---|
| Dept. Check | 4 | Dept. Check | 2 |
| Dept. Linear Check | 1 | Dept. Simple Stpd. | 2 |
| Bayou La B. Stpd. | 7 | Crooked River C.S. | 1 |
| B. La B. Shell Stpd. | 4 | (last type occurs in Dept.-Swift Creek transition.) | |

| *Wa-43-Ochlockonee Bay area* | | *Fr-2 (Carabelle)* | |
|---|---|---|---|
| Dept. Check | 2 | Dept. Check | 15 |
| Dept. Linear Check | 4 | Dept. Linear Check | 14 |
| Dept. Simple Stpd. | 2 | Deptford Simple Stpd. | 1 |
| Lake Borgne Inc. | 5 | Brewton Hill C.S. | 15 |
| Tchefuncte Plain | 4 | (last type late Deptford. Quantities Early Swift Creek C.S. also present.) | |

*Wa-4. Hall Site*
Dept. Linear Check 2
Deptford Check 2
Bayou La Batre Stpd 1
(22 other check stpd.
Sherds, some Deptford)

*Fr-3. (1 Mi.W. of Carabelle)*
Deptford Check 31
Dept. Simple Stpd. 12
Dept. Linear Chk. 1
Mossy Oak Simple Stpd. 1

*East Bay Site-Franklin Co.*
Deptford Check 61
Dept. Linear Check 8
Dept. Simple Stpd. 21
Brewton Hill C. S. 18
Brushed, sand temper 3
(All other sherds plain.
Brewton Hill and brushed
demonstrated to be part of
complex)

*Bryan Sand Pit, Geneva Co., Ala.*
Dept. Check 6
Dept. Simple Stpd. 2
(other sherds plain or later)

A final reference for this period is the large collections from the Tucker Site (Sears, 1963:39). A major Deptford component there has associated with it, besides a few Norwood Plain fiber-tempered sherds, Santa Rosa Stamped, which does not occur with later units; cord marked specimens, sand-tempered brushed ware, Bayou La Batre Stamped, and a series of the Check to Complicated stamped transitional variants.

The Tchefuncte and Bayou La Batre sherds in these collections document contact of some intensity along the coast. As we will see, this works both ways. The West Florida Cord Marked and, at Tucker, Dunlap Fabric Marked sherds may well be traded from Miller I, to the north and west.

Deptford components occur with considerable frequency from the eastern end of the northwest Florida Coast to Choctawhatchee Bay. From there to Mobile Bay, very few Deptford sherds, let alone components, have been found, nor are there other materials to suggest occupation in this period. There was a gap then between the western edge of Deptford spread to the west and the area occupied by the Bayou La Batre culture around Mobile Bay.

Bits of evidence in these collections and in published reports on the Tucker and Mandeville sites supports my thesis of twenty-five years ago (Sears, 1952) that Deptford develops into Early Swift Creek, a type and complex to be considered in the next time interval. The presence of such types and variants in Deptford and/or Early Swift Creek association as Crooked and New River Complicated Stamped, the odd sherds in the Deptford Complex (Waring, 1968:140), and Brewton Hill Complicated Stamped (Caldwell and Waring, 1939) are evidence for this. The transition must have been rather abrupt, a thesis supported by one stratigraphic cut in the Chattahoochee Basin which I have seen but which remains unreported. Again, there isn't much involved except carving some new paddles and making smaller tetrapods.

*Bayou La Batre Series*

All the distribution data for this complex has been published by Wimberly and Trickey (Wimberly, 1960; Trickey, 1958). The small size of the area is really surprising, but it is verified by my own survey and other work, published and unpublished.

This series, with no perceptible ancestors or descendants, is a variant of the general form-surface treatment style characteristic of this period. Bayou La Batre sherds in Deptford, Miller, and, I suspect, Tchefuncte context document contemporaneity. This is also demonstrated by associations at several Bayou La Batre sites or levels such as the Myers site (Trickey, 1958) and the Bayou La Batre shell midden (Wimberly, 1960). Both have quantities of Deptford sherds and the type site also has Tchefuncte sherds associated. There are also sand-tempered fabric and cord marked sherds which almost certainly came downstream from the Miller I culture. I see no reason then to accept the very early C-14 date which has been advanced (Trickey and Holmes, 1967:25). There are no ceremonial sites which can be definitely, or even probably, associated with this culture.

*Tchefuncte Complex*

The area characterized by this complex is heavily slanted toward the Mississippi Delta (Gagliano, 1967:9-22; Phillips, 1970:880-86). Evidence suggests that the late fiber tempered and early St. John's complexes to the east were major contributors to Tchefuncte development (Sears and Griffin, 1950; Bullen, 1970:67-8). Some stylistic elements may well have come from the north, suggested by the many sherds in the type site of the Alexander series (Ford and Quimby, 1945) which has many Hopewellian characteristics.

Evidence for contemporaneity with Deptford and Bayou La Batre has already been presented. It is strengthened by the presence of occasional Deptford sherds in the Tchefuncte area (Gagliano, 1967:17).

*Miller Complex*

The discovery that this complex, occurring in multiple mound sites as well as midden deposits, dominates the Tombigbee River drainage above the junction with the lower Alabama and extends across to the lower Alabama was one of the surprises of the survey. Most of the culture area is north of the fall line, assuming continuity between the area originally defined (Jennings, 1941:214-8) and the northernmost sites I have. This assumption appears to be supported by current survey work in the intervening area (DeJarnette, personal communication).

This is but another variant of the fabric marked to cord marked or check stamped complexes characteristic of the Appalachians during this and the next period from the northeast to the Mississippi Valley. Probably the Miller complex, in this and the next two periods, is responsible for most of the cord and/or fabric marked sherds which appear in coastal sites. Some of the collections listed below will demonstrate that the communications ran both ways.

Probably, here as elsewhere, the fabric marked pottery appeared first, was then supplemented by cord marking, and then disappeared about when the clay tempered Tishomingo Cord Marked began to replace the sand-tempered Furrs Cord Marked. Tishomingo is apparently identical to Mulberry Creek Cord Marked.

With the difficulty in drawing a Miller I-II dividing line, I have listed complete collections in most cases. There is no excavated material from the area except for C. B. Moore's references to cord marked sherds in a few holes dug into small mounds which were uniformly a disappointment to him.

*Dunns Creek* – Wilcox Co., Alabama, on Alabama River

| Miller Complex | | McLeod Series | |
|---|---|---|---|
| Furrs Cord Mkd. | 7 | McLeod Linear Chk. Stpd. | 15 |
| Tishomingo Cord Mkd. | 12 | Wakulla Chk. Stpd. | 17 |
| Pensacola Series | | | |
| Pensacola Incised | 5 | Great variety plain ware | |
| Moundville Incised | 3 | includes sand, grit, shell and clay temper. | |

This site is dominantly Miller II period and later. It is listed here because of the presence of Furrs Cord Marked. The inclusion of Wakulla Check Stamped in the McLeod series appears to be the most reasonable choice.

*MacDuffie* – Wilcox Co., Alabama

| Miller Complex | | Weeden Island – Wakulla Complex | |
|---|---|---|---|
| Saltillo Fab. Mkd. | 4 | Wakulla Check Stpd. | 179 |
| Furrs Cord Mkd. | 15 | Weeden Is. Pl. Rims | 11 |
| Tishomingo Cd. Mkd. | 6 | Carrabelle Inc. | 5 |
| McLeod Series | | Weeden Is. Inc. | 1 |
| McLeod Lin. Chk. Stpd. | 5 | Weeden Is. Punct. | 1 |
| McLeod Simple Stpd. | 13 | Weeden Island Red. | 1 |
| | | Carrabelle Punct. | 1 |
| Pensacola Inc. | 1 | | |

(348 plain sherds. All sand tempered excepting 16 with shell and 3 with clay temper.)

The site is listed here because initial occupation was clearly in the Miller I period. Most of the material, in a very clearly defined square midden, is later. The complex with Wakulla Check Stamped, which I am sure also includes the McLeod series as well as the Weeden Island specimens, here reaches its western limit inland, just west of the Alabama River. The few shell tempered sherds probably came from a small, separate site some 50 yards away. A conical mound 300 yards to the northeast presumably relates to the main period of occupation.

*Clifton Landing* – Wilcox Co., Alabama, on Alabama River

| Miller Complex | | Historic Creek | |
|---|---|---|---|
| Furrs Cord Mkd. | 3 | Chatahoochee Brushed | 15 |
| Tishomingo Cord Mkd. | 2 | Ocmulgee Fields Inc. | 3 |
| Wakulla Check Stpd. | 17 | | |

Site reported here for consistency, since it began in later period.

## KIMBROUGH GRAVEL PIT, WILCOX CO., ALABAMA

Commercial gravel operations have removed large areas of this site, but some 5-10 acres remain. It is about midway between the Alabama and Tombigbee Rivers, just south of the fall line. All sherds from the site are reported, by complexes as far as possible. Projectile points demonstrate an even longer period of use since there are Archaic points and a fragment of a fluted, Clovis type.

| Miller Complex | | Deptford Series | |
|---|---|---|---|
| Saltillo Fabric Mkd. | 34 | Deptford Check Stpd. | 3 |
| Furrs Cord Mkd. | 7 | Deptford Simple Stpd. | 1 |
| Tishomingo Cord Mkd. | 56 | | |
| This period, either of above. | | | |
| Santa Rosa Stpd. | 7 | Sand tempered brushed | 1 |
| Flint River Brushed | 1 | Wright Check Stpd. | 1 |

| Weeden Island Complex and associated specimens | | | |
|---|---|---|---|
| Weeden Island Red | 1 | Weeden Island Pl. rims | 5 |
| Keith Inc. | 1 | Swift Creek C.S., late | 5 |
| Rhinehard Punct. | 1 | Wakulla Check Stpd. | 8 |
| Troyville Pl. rim | 1 | | |

| McLeod Series | |
|---|---|
| McLeod Simple Stpd. | 5 |
| McLeod Linear Chk. Stpd. | 1 |

(480 plain sherds divided by temper into 341 sand, 113 clay, 12 shell and 14 grit.)

The 7 Santa Rosa Stamped are, here as elsewhere, associated with the early horizon, with this time period rather than the next one. If clay tempered, they would be classified as Tchefuncte Stamped.

### BLUE ROCK, MARENGO COUNTY, ALABAMA, TOMBIGBEE RIVER

| Furrs Cord Mkd. | 2 | Sand tempered plain | 13 |

### BRICKLEY LANDING, MARENGO COUNTY, ALABAMA, TOMBIGEE RIVER

| Furrs Cord Mkd. | 14 | Sand tempered plain | 5 |
| Wakulla Check Stpd. | 1 | | |

This site is one of the multiple mound sites visited by C. B. Moore. Plowing has almost flattened all of the mounds. The sherds came from a slight rise where they were associated with human bone scrap.

### SMITH LUMBER COMPANY, MARENGO COUNTY, ALABAMA, TOMBIGBEE RIVER

A group of 10 mounds, each 30-40 feet in diameter and 3-5 feet high. There is no evidence that the site, in heavily timbered country overlooking a small creek, has ever been plowed. C. B. Moore reported testing in one mound and his pit is still visible. He found cord marked pottery and human bone. The site is assigned to the Miller complex on this basis, and because of its obvious relationship to other groups with midden areas associated with sherds from the mounds.

### CARTERS OLD FIELD, MARENGO COUNTY, ALABAMA

Near same creek as site above, 8 mound group on terrace, somewhat flattened by agriculture. Same comments by Moore on testing one mound.

### MCALPIN, MARENGO COUNTY, ALABAMA, TOMBIGBEE RIVER

The site stretches along about a mile of bluff on an old natural levee of the river. There are 2 clusters of about 40 small mounds each ranging in height from 2 to 8-10 feet, at the north and south ends of the site. Most of the area in between has midden deposit in 2 one-quarter mile or longer by 100-yard-wide stretches. The midden may be continuous and extend through an intervening wooden strip. Collecting was by areas, but lack of differentiation permits combination here.

| Miller Complex | | Other – Trade | |
|---|---|---|---|
| Saltillo Fabric Mkd. | 72 | French Fork Inc. | 4 |
| Furrs Cord Mkd. | 54 | Yokena Inc. | 4 |
| Tishomingo Cord Mkd. | 35 | Weeden Island Pl. rims | 6 |
| | | McLeod Simple Stpd. | 1 |

(1,230 plain sherds almost entirely sand tempered)

Most of the projectile points are kinds which elsewhere are associated with Troyville and Weeden Island, but there are some larger Archaic points. A local collector has an ovoid Weeden Island Plain bowl and two obtuse-angle elbow pipes from one mound in the north group.

The dominance of Miller I is clear, as is the lack of any non-Miller occupation. The few Troyville and Weeden Island sherds must relate to the period in which Tishomingo Cord Marked was made.

I have visited 3 other small groups of mounds on the Tombigbee. Each had 4-8 of the low structures and all of them had once been plowed but are now in forested country. Presumably they are all Miller sites.

EUBANKS – GREEN COUNTY, ALABAMA, TOMBIGBEE RIVER

This site is just north of the fall line, but it is well known locally and sounded worth a visit. It is large, well over 40 acres, and contains a great deal of shell which alone differentiates it from other Miller sites. No mounds were observed or reported, but there is little doubt about the complex.

| Miller Series | | Other – Trade | |
|---|---|---|---|
| Saltillo Fabric Mkd. | 121 | Napier Comp. Stp. | 2 |
| Furrs Cord Mkd. | 54 | Weeden Island Pl. rims | 2 |
| Tishomingo Cd. Mkd. | 2 | Porter Zone Stpd. | 1 |
| | | Swift Creek C.S., late | 2 |
| (75 plain sherds all sand- | | Pickwick C.S. | 1 |
| tempered) | | Basin Bayou Inc. | 2 |

The complicated stamped sherds and the other trade sherds are definite anomalies in this predominantly Miller I complex. Probably they are to be associated with the Furrs Cord Marked-Tishomingo Cord Marked transition.

## Period F-G Summary

Culture areas marked by the distribution of the Deptford, Bayou La Batre, Miller, and Tchefuncte series or complexes are clearly delineated. Borders are clear, with that between Deptford and Bayou La Batre especially so with the absolute minimum Deptford penetration of the area between Choctawhatchee and Mobile Bays. Contact between all of them is equally clear from the distribution of trade sherds. Miller contact with the coast was probably as intense as that between the coastal complexes, but is masked by typological problems.

A ceremonial complex—which is needed to do much more with settlement pattern than to say that small villages, coastal or inland, are the rule— is known only for Deptford. This is the Yent complex (Sears, 1962). However, the large clusters of small mounds in the Miller area document intense ceremonial-mortuary activity there. Assuming that the data for the northern Miller sites applies (Jenning, 1941), some of the mounds should have been built in the Miller I period and should contain Hopewellian artifacts.

The Hopewell affiliations of the Yent complex, the ceremonial aspect of Deptford culture, is important in many ways, one of which is dating. The relationship of Yent to mid-to-late Ohio Hopewell is clear enough. Not only are there classic Hopewell artifacts in Yent, but the bulk of the check and simple stamped sherds in Prufer's Southeastern Complex (Prufer, 1968) are late Deptford, and the balance appear to be Cartersville. This relationship makes the large series of dates in the 0-500 A.D. range for mid-to-late midwestern Hopewell applicable to Deptford. This is supported by my own as yet unpublished work in South Florida where a complex with Deptford, Cartersville, St. Johns I and Crystal River series trade sherds dates in this range. I will comment further here only to point out that Deptford is at the very least stratigraphically before Early Swift Creek. Early Swift Creek, to be discussed in the next section, has very definite ties with the Issaquena complex and the Issaquena dates (Phillips, 1970:957 and 960, Fig. 450), without modification, are later than the 0-500 A.D. range.

We can see here then, particularly on the coast, the beginning development of intercultural relationships on the Gulf Coastal Plain, clearly present in midden context. This is supplemented by the appearance of western ceramic concepts in the Yent ceremonial complex (Sears, 1962).

## Period E-F

In the Central Gulf Coastal Plain, the ceramic series and complexes assigned to this period, and consequently the cultures, seem to be of relatively short duration. Increasing speed of culture change with an increase in culture complexity and population density should not surprise us, of course. It may be further noted that developmental trends involving the entire area become clear in this period, and become even more obvious in

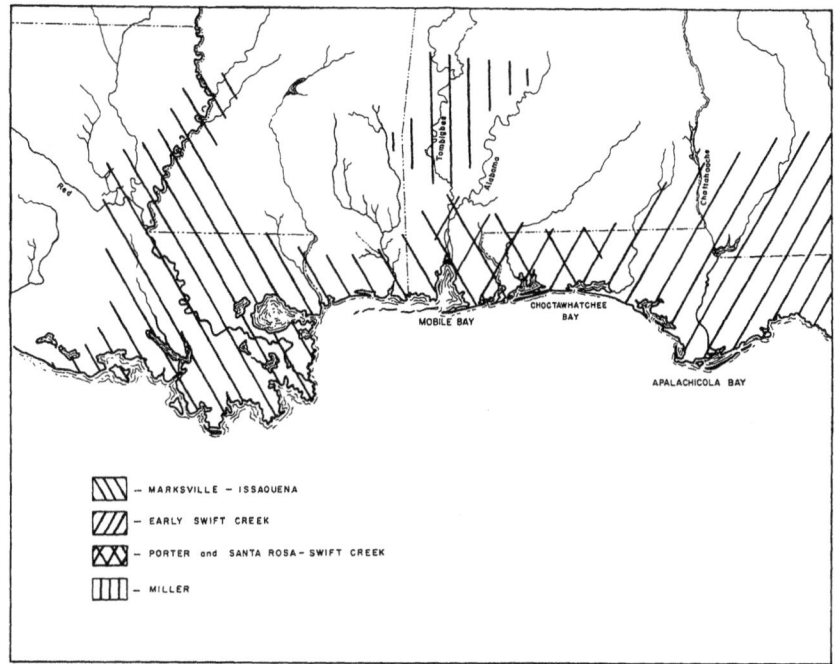

Figure 2. Period E-F.

the next, a fact that led some of us at one time to adopt a concept of a "Gulf Tradition."

*Ceramic Complexes*

*Early Swift Creek:* Types Swift Creek Complicated Stamped, Early Variety. Franklin Plain, which has distinctive notched lip and Tetrapod bases, and, with overlap back into preceding period, early varieties of Crooked River, St. Andrews, and New River Complicated Stamped (Willey, 1949:378-86).

*Santa Rosa:* Alligator Bayou Stamped, Santa Rosa Punctated, Basin Bayou Stamped and possibly Santa Rosa Stamped although most specimens of this type are assignable to Deptford period (Willey, 1949:372-78).

There are several problems here, particularly in connection with handling the mass of data presented by Willey. One is that Swift Creek sherds are not consistently assigned to the "Early" or "Late" categories. My own collections and analyses help, but there are blind spots. In the western part of the area, between Choctawhatchee and Mobile Bays, precisely that area with little or no Deptford occupation, there is another way of handling the problem. In sites with the Santa Rosa series and few or no Weeden Island specimens, complicated stamped sherds are either Early Swift Creek or they are the Crooked River, New River and St. Andrews types which consistently have late Deptford or early Swift Creek associations.

The other problem which I pointed to some years ago in connection with sacred assemblages (Sears, 1962) is that some sacred pots, and I now add midden sherds, of the Santa Rosa series are technically Marksville-Issaquena types. The Florida descriptions allow both clay and sand temper. In my classification Florida types are restricted to sand temper, and the type name is used which conveys the most information.

*Marksville-Issaquena:* Types of either of these complexes as defined (Ford and Willey, 1940:59-87; Greengo, 1964:35-62; Phillips, 1970) will be referred to as appropriate. Their "home" areas are indicated on the map. Further description and discussion is not necessary for our purposes here, although the complexes are most important in discussion further on.

*Porter Hopewell:* Demonstrated to be a consistently recurring complex by the excavations which Wimberly (1960) reports, although most of the types are also parts of the Marksville-Issaquena, Santa Rosa, and Early Swift Creek complexes or series, discussed above or below. There is one new type, Porter Zone Incised (Wimberly, 1960:98-101). It appears to represent the transition between the zoned rocker-stamped types and the later, zoned, Weeden Island-French Fork styles.

In the Porter Hopewell collections, which I have worked on for many days, I would have to argue about clay tempered sherds being trade sherds. In some decorative styles, there seems to have been a free choice between clay or sand temper. Franklin Plain and Swift Creek Complicated Stamped are the only absolute exceptions.

I rather suspect that the period represented by this complex is a lengthy one, superimposed as it is directly on the unrelated Bayou La Batre and continuing until it is replaced by one of several Weeden Island complexes. There is a hint of change in the material as reported stratigraphically in tabular form by Wimberly (1960). In levels in which the Porter Complex occurs with heavy concentrations of Bayou La Batre, as at the type site, definitely clay-tempered wares seem to be more important, whereas in sites and levels with just Porter, or with Weeden Island series specimens, the sand tempered types are more frequent. Possibly then, in terms of the northwest coast, the later material with more sand temper overlaps Weeden Island. Obviously this is subjective, and the suggestions made, based on collections which the Indians unfortunately left mixed stratigraphically, may be based as much on geography, coastal or inland location.

*Miller I-II:* Precise ceramic diagnostics for this time interval are not known. I would expect domination by Furrs Cord Marked, with little fabric marking and, perhaps, the clay tempered cord-marked just beginning. Since Tishomingo Cord Marked is, at best, a regional variant of Mulberry Creek, it should fall in the next time period. However, in the Mississippi Valley, it does appear in Marksville and Issaquena contexts (Phillips, Ford and Griffin, 1951:87; Phillips, 1970:136-9).

I will then have little to say about the Miller Complex in this time interval. All of the sites that could be relevant were noted in the section on the previous period.

*Early Swift Creek and Santa Rosa Complexes*

These are best discussed in one section since their relationship is highly significant. Although there are problems with typology, one major trend can be observed in the collections reported by Willey (1949). With collections reported by me below, and by others, with more precise classification, the trend is well documented. It is that from Choctawhatchee Bay west, precisely the area with little or no occupation during the Deptford period, the quantities of Santa Rosa types increase proportionately with distance west and Early Swift Creek decreases. From the Apalachicola delta area east, and north up the river, collections increasingly—almost entirely in most instances—emphasize the complicated stamped ware. Phelps commented on this in 1969 (Phelps, 1969) and preferred, or suggested, a straight Swift Creek period terminology for the eastern area.

A good, if small, example of the western variety of this complex may be found at site Sa-2, with 3 Swift Creek, 3 Basin Bayou, and 1 Alligator Bayou Stamped sherds. In line with the variability noted is Sa-6, where all 15 decorated sherds are complicated stamped and specifically Early Swift Creek. But, a few miles away, Sa-4 has 14 Santa Rosa series sherds and 46 complicated stamped including St. Andrews and Crooked River types. Absence of any later materials, and the presence of 11 Franklin Plain sherds, demonstrate that this is a single, early complex. It is quite similar to one further east at Ok-2. Here 2 of 23 specimens are Weeden Island series and 1 is classified as Deptford Check Stamped. The balance of the collection is distributed between 18 complicated stamped, 4 Franklin Plain and 2 Santa Rosa Stamped.

Now, to look to the east, just west of the mouth of the Apalachicola, we find in site By-10 31 Swift Creek sherds, with a note that they are "mostly early" (Willey, 1949:236), and no other decorated specimens except a red painted sherd. Another collection from the same site has 74 stamped specimens, 70 of which are "Swift Creek," 4 Franklin Plain, and only 2 sherds of Alligator Bayou Stamped. In Franklin County, adjacent to the mouth of the Apalachicola, Fr-1 has no Santa Rosa sherds. There are 3 from the Fort Walton complex and 5 of the Weeden Island series. These are accompanied by 42 complicated stamped, 2 Franklin Plain, and 5 Deptford specimens. 10 Gulf Check Stamped could be in this period or earlier.

Phelps study of 3 sites, 2 in Wakulla County, the eastern end of the coastal distribution of the Early Swift Creek complex and one in Santa Rosa County (Phelps, 1969) strongly reinforces this thesis.

A few collections of my own contain pertinent data. Collections from 2 Wakulla County sites, Marsh Island and Hall, contain Early Swift Creek, New River and Crooked River Complicated Stamped sherds, but none of the Santa Rosa complex. Carabelle, Fr-1, produced 17 Early Swift Creek, 3 Crooked River, and only 1 Santa Rosa Punctated.

One site collected by William Lazarus, Sa-16, serves as a nice counterbalance to the Santa Rosa County site above with too much complicated stamped ware for the western area. My analysis produced:

| | | | |
|---|---|---|---|
| Early Swift Creek | 2 | Sand-tempered "copy" of | |
| Brewton Hill Com. Stpd. | 1 | Marksville Inc. | 1 |
| Basin Bayou Inc. | 2 | Indeterminate Check Stpd. | 2 |
| Marksville Stamped | 2 | (16 of 36 plain sherds clay-tempered, possibly Marksville Plain) | |

This collection would be almost unnoticed if it were just a bit nearer Mobile Bay, such as a site near Moore's Bear Point Mound, Ba-1. This small, thin site produced:

| | | | |
|---|---|---|---|
| Early Swift Creek | 5 | Manny Stamped | 1 |
| Basin Bayou Incised | 6 | Franklin Plain | 1 |
| Yokena Incised | 1 | Troyville Stamped | 2 |

(Plain sherds include sand and clay tempered)

One last midden collection of some importance here is one of mine from the Aspalage site, Gd-1, well up the Apalachicola River. In the midden adjacent to mounds excavated by C. B. Moore (1903:481-8) the pre-Weeden Island complex consisted of 44 Early Swift Creek and 1 St. Andrews Complicated Stamped sherds.

The Mandeville site in Georgia is important here too. By combining some earlier mimeographed reports with the final report (Kelly, Kellar and McMichaels, 1961, 1962), it is very clear that a complex characterized by Early Swift Creek Complicated Stamped and such earlier relatives as Crooked River, in mound fill or midden, is associated with only trace quantities of Santa Rosa types. There is also no doubt, basing this on memory and correspondence as well as the reports, that the earliest material here is Deptford, even though illustrated vessels in the final report, from a sacred context, are Cartersville Check Stamped. It is also quite clear that the Deptford-Swift Creek transition takes place at this site.

*South Mississippi*

This is of course an area rather than a complex. However, some survey work was done, and some of the data is relevant for the first time in this period. Many small collections and a few large ones are almost invariably dominated by quantities of shell tempered plain pottery and decorated ware of the Pensacola series. However, and this is true from virtually the Mississippi border to the Pearl River delta, there is no trace of eastern influence. Pre-Mississippian specimens do occur regularly, but in small quantities. They include plain ware and decorated types of the Marksville, Troyville, and Coles Creek complexes, excluding Coles Creek Incised and its relatives. All of the data say that the area is part of the Mississippi Valley culturally until the local cultures are replaced by the Pensacola culture. Maps for this and the next period then have the line for the eastern boundary of the Red River tradition complexes drawn near the eastern border of Mississippi. The most doubtful areas are inland, but a few small sites up to the fall line are the same as the coastal ones.

## Period E-F Summary

The major feature of this period in our area is the movement eastward from the Mississippi Valley of a late Marksville-Issaquena complex which meets and interpenetrates the westward movement of the Early Swift Creek complex. East of Mobile Bay, the Red River tradition specimens and local copies are defined as the Santa Rosa complex. There appear to be fairly even gradients with the western tradition diminishing in importance as it moves eastward and the complicated stamping diminishing as it moves west. In the key area just east of Mobile, both are entering an area which had little, or very light, occupation in the preceding period.

The Porter Hopewell complex, as much Issaquena as it is anything else, is the best known example of the western end of this phenomenon. It does represent, in its area, a new culture, since there are no indications that it developed from the temporally precedent Bayou La Batre.

In the previous period, culture areas were distinct, and contact was demonstrated by trade sherds. Now we have, from Mobile Bay to Choctawhatchee Bay, a culture using elements that came from two ceramic complexes, distinct in the previous period and still distinctive in this one east of Choctawhatchee Bay and west of Mobile Bay.

This leads directly to events of the next period when western ceramic ideas, as the Weeden Island series, become of great importance and an integral part of culture complexes as far to the east as northern Florida and southern Georgia. There is no evidence either in this E-F period or in the next, Weeden Island dominated one, for any real influence from the east penetrating west of the Mobile Bay area. The only exception may be in the form of rare complicated stamped-like designs executed in a different medium on a different paste.

The Miller culture does not seem to be involved in any of this complexity. There are trade sherds from both east and west in Miller sites but no suggestion of significant adoption of any foreign ideas.

## Periods C-D-E

Our consideration of cultures in this period will be restricted to a smaller area and the ceramic complexes present in it. Essentially, we will be concerned with what Gordon Willey defined as the Weeden Island area (Willey, 1949). As indicated on the map, the area is extended a bit north to the fall line, and the west coast of peninsular Florida, where Weeden Island is almost entirely a sacred ware (Sears, 1973), is left out.

This restriction is based on the premise, not fully discussed nor documented in this paper, that interaction with areas west of the present Mississippi state line is insignificant in this period of time. The central gulf Coastal Plain, the Weeden Island area if you will, develops and changes in part from its own resources and in part as the result of new influences from the north.

Unfortunately, while the total data available demonstrate clearly that the period is one of extreme cultural complexity and is thus highly significant for our eventual understanding of cultural processes, we do not control the data at all well at this time. Variation in both space and time is perceptible but cannot be well ordered. Some suggestions will be made. In part because of the tremendous amount of data and its complexity, and in part because of our lack of adequate control, my discussion of this period covers a long time range, and will be more general than it was for earlier periods.

Prehistoric Culture Areas & Change on the Gulf Coastal Plain  169

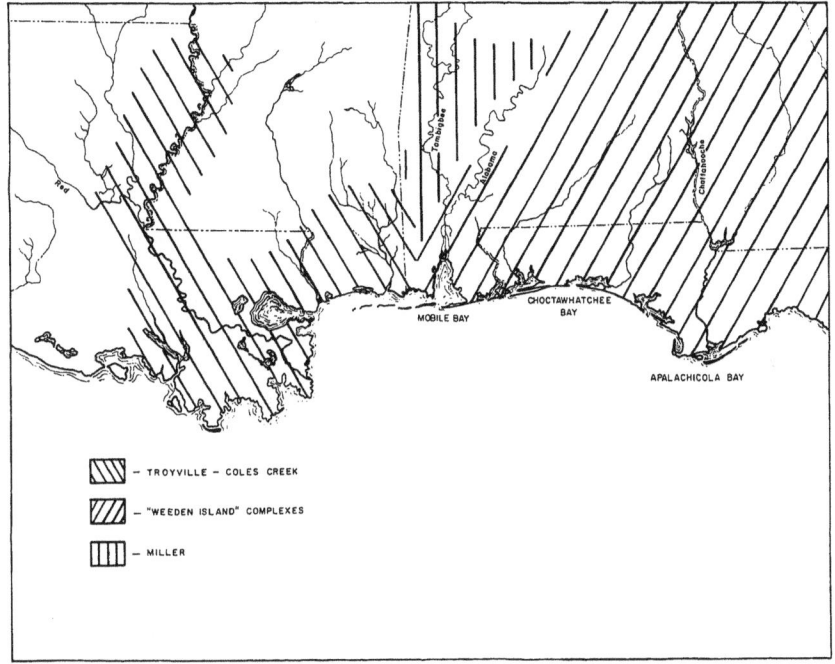

Figure 3. Periods C, D, E.

Village, "secular" pottery is certainly characterized, most of the time and in most places, by total complexes which are mixtures of two or three series. These in preceding periods had separate areas and some may continue to have, at least on the tradition level. These are as follows:

*Weeden Island Series:* (Willey, 1949). Punctated, incised and red painted types with some close analogues in the Troyville-Coles Creek complexes, so that we can speak of continuation of the Red River mouth tradition.

*Complicated Stamped Series:* Swift Creek Complicated Stamped, Late Variety (Willey, 1949:429-35) is the only member of the series which has been both defined and used, except for Kolomoki Complicated Stamped (Sears, 1951:9-16), technically a subdividion of the Late Swift Creek type. I have offered several other subdivisions (Sears, 1956:15-18), but these have not been used. Certainly there must be changes in complicated stamping between the end of Early Swift Creek and the appearance of the sloppily applied Lamar style, but they are difficult to perceive. Modal analysis of large collections, aided by stratigraphy, should provide answers about temporal and spatial variation.

Kolomoki Complicated Stamped is of some interest. The type has clearly been influenced by Troyville-Coles Creek concepts that are apparent in overall vessel form, the flat bases which may be discs or squares, and in the area of decoration, which is often limited to the shoulder but is below a plain band under the upper rim.

*Check Stamped, or Wakulla Series:* A single type, Wakulla Check Stamped (Willey, 1949:437-38). No efforts at analysis of large collections have been made except treatment as a mode and breakdown of rim forms at Tucker (Sears, 1963).

Plain ware associated with all of the foregoing series is indistinguishable, with two exceptions, both at the mode rather than at the type level of analysis. Plain bases associated with Kolomoki Complicated Stamped are usually flat, disc-shaped or square. Many of these specimens may be from the bases of the stamped type, of course. Weeden Island plain can be a useful tool but can be identified only in rim sherds, bowl rims which are thickened in one way or another.

In the standard system, assemblages with specimens from these series have been arranged in time into an earlier Weeden Island I period, with the Weeden Island and Complicated Stamped Series, and a later Weeden Island II period with Weeden Island and Wakulla Check Stamped specimens (Willey, 1949). This doesn't work in many instances. The kinds of assemblages we must really deal with are much more complex than suggested, a complexity intensified by their areal and spatial distribution. Some examples follow. Unless other references are provided or new data tabulated, the site descriptions and analyses are from Willey (1949). Some relevant collections were described in the period E-F section.

### "Weeden Island" Complexes

*Late Swift Creek and Weeden Island:* Carabelle, Pits I and II. W1-2, W1-11, By-7. St. Andrews Point, Lev. 5 (Trickey 1958:Fig. 3). Units at Kolomoki (Sears 1956:Chart I, p. 41). Fairchilds Landing (Caldwell 1958:58).

*Complicated Stamped and Wakulla Check Stamped:* No Weeden Island Series. Fr-12, 10 complicated stamped, 10 check stamped, and 40 plain.

*King Site, Houston County,* Alabama, Choctawhatchee River.

| | | | |
|---|---|---|---|
| Swift Creek Comp. Stpd. | 13 | Wakulla Check Stpd. | 17 |
| West Florida Cord Mkd. | 1 | | |
| Ft. Walton Complex | | | |
| Ft. Walton Inc. | 2 | Pinellas Inc. | 8 |

(104 sand and grit tempered plain sherds).

This site has a small platform mound and a small conical mound about three hundred feet apart, with midden area between them.

*Wakulla Complex and Plain Ware:* Wa-2, Ok-5, Fr-13, Wa-6. Many sites could be added to these, but, simply to document distribution, I would add only the upper levels at Tucker (Sears, 1963) in some units, the upper levels of the St. Andrews Point site on Mobile Bay (Trickey, 1958:Fig. 3) and a site in Franklin County where I collected 39 Wakulla Check Stamped specimens which were accompanied by 13 McLeod series sherds, simple and linear check stamped, and 49 plain sherds.

The distribution of this complex is clearly across the entire area from east to west. It is also present well up the Apalachicola River.

*Kolomoki Complicated Stamped and Plain Ware:* Small or no quantities Weeden Island Series. Units at Kolomoki (Sears, 1956:Chart I, p. 41). Ja-63 (Bullen, 1958:327:31). Fairchilds Landing (Caldwell, 1958:58). Mound Field Site, Wa-8, lower levels of Pits I and II based on my reanalysis of Willey collections (Willey, 1949:55,64), Hall Site, Wa-4 (Allen, 1953).

Occurrence of this complex outside the immediate Kolomoki area is rare. There are sites where it is barely represented, as at Tucker (Sears, 1963). It is not then, over the entire area, representative of a "Period" as I once thought (Sears, 1956). My 1956 sequences are as invalid as any others offered.

*Weeden Island and Plain Ware:* Only a few sites and test pit levels have such a complex. There are levels approaching this at the Tucker site and in a few of the test pit collections described by Willey. There is a hint of it at Kolomoki too. Its real existence would be doubtful if it were not for my surface collection from a large site in Alabama, on the Conecuh River north of Choctawhatchee Bay. This site is a ceremonial center with a low platform mound, a burial mound, and a well-defined plaza area with midden defining its sides. Collection is:

| | | | |
|---|---|---|---|
| *Weeden Island Complex* | | | |
| Weeden Island Pl. rims | 58 | Weeden Island Red | 29 |
| Carabelle Incised | 4 | Keith Incised | 3 |
| Carabelle Punctated | 10 | Indian Pass Incised | 7 |
| Weeden Island Punct. | 7 | Weeden Island Inc. | 1 |
| Mound Field Net Mkd. | 2 | Swift Creek Comp. Stpd., late | 14 |
| Napier Comp. Stpd. | 2 | Larto Red Filmed | 2 |
| French Fork Incised | 2 | Churupa Punctated | 1 |
| McLeod Simple Stpd. | 2 | McLeod Lin. Check Stpd. | 19 |
| | | Wakulla Check Stpd. | 7 |
| *Pensacola Complex* | | | |
| Pensacola Incised | 1 | Mercier Check Stpd. | 1 |

*Plain Wares*

| Sand-tempered | 424 | Clay-tempered | 14 |
| Chalky | 4 | Grit-tempered | 2 |
| Shell-tempered | 5 | | |

Some comments at the end of this section will apply to the few McLeod series and the Wakulla sherds found here.

*Wakulla Check Stamped, Weeden Island Series:* Varying in quantity. No complicated stamped. Sites with this sort of complex are very numerous throughout the area. In many sites, stratigraphic relationships with plain ware and complicated ware in association with the Weeden Island series have been noted. There is little point in listing all, or even a sample, of them here. They extend from Mobile Bay and Jackson County, Alabama, where occasional Pontchartrain Check Stamped and Mulberry Creek Cord Marked sherds are found in the same levels, to Wakulla County at the east end of the area. In some sites there is a definite overlap with the McLeod series. In that area there are also enough cord marked specimens, sand and clay tempered, to demonstrate that contact with the Miller culture was being maintained.

*McLeod-Deptford Complex:* McLeod Check Stamped, McLeod Simple Stamped, and McLeod Linear Check Stamped (Wimberly, 1953).

I suggest that this complex, a puzzle to all who have worked with it (Trickey, 1958:392, Wimberly, 1960:26), is one major key that can help unravel some of this confusion. All types use the simple jar form. The check-stamped type is indistinguishable from Wakulla, except for a few rim forms. This results in most specimens being put into an "indeterminate" category in the Mobile Bay area except in pure sites.

The Cartersville Complex (Fairbanks, 1953), related on formal stylistic grounds, is the obvious earlier developmental stage for McLeod. It is a long way off in northwestern Georgia and is unknown elsewhere except, if I read the peculiar classificatory terminology correctly, in the Chattahoochee drainage around Columbus, Georgia (McMichael and Kellar, 1960). The only significant differences between the two are that the McLeod complex does not have tetrapods, making it later than the Early Swift Creek-Marksville level, nor the plain zone or band below the lip and above the shoulder which occurs frequently in the Cartersville types.

McLeod Deptford, called the McLeod complex hereafter to avoid further compounding of semantic problems, appears in the inland, Jackson County area at the very end of Porter Hopewell in several sites. There is considerable evidence for this in the material presented by Wimberly (1960). It is still present, in great quantities, with the full Weeden Island, or, as Wimberly calls them, Weeden-Island-Coles Creek assemblages. It dominates all other material, even all other decorated sherds if one totals all check-stamped pottery, in some sites and levels. Since it dominates some components at its first appearance and apparently appears in pure components, it may well be representative of an intrusive culture, with acculturation both ways producing increasingly difficult and complex blends through time and space.

Down on the coast, it is not present at all in the earliest levels and sites with the Weeden Island complex. Levels 4 and 5 of the St. Andrews Point site, with some Swift Creek Complicated Stamped, late variety, is a good example. After this, the coastal complexes are swamped with Wakulla Check. This can be explained rather easily, with stratigraphic support in Clarke County, by viewing this as a continued spread of McLeod, with the simple and linear variants dropped out. This would be at about the end of the Troyville period to the west, or the beginning of Coles Creek.

## Period C-D-E Summary

I have described above some of the great variety of "Weeden Island" complexes that exists and its spatial distribution. Some explanation for the check-stamped phenomenon, in the western end of the area, was offered. Before going on with a summary, we need to look back at developments here outlined as taking place in the area from the Alabama-Mobile Rivers east.

We started with distinct cultures, each ceramic complex or series occupying a distinct area from Deptford on the east to Tchefuncte to the west and Miller to the north. Contact among all of them is demonstrated by trade sherds. This situation changes rapidly. At, and just after, the time of development of Early Swift Creek from Deptford, the complicated stamped type and accompanying plain ware continues to dominate the eastern area and spreads west to Mobile Bay. But, in an area from Mobile Bay to somewhere near Choctawhatchee Bay, an area with little or no Deptford period occupation, elements from the west, originating in the Red River Mouth area of the Mississippi Valley, are added to the Swift Creek material moving from the east.

In the Mobile Bay country, and upriver to the forks of the Alabama and Tombigbee Rivers, the distinct Bayou La Batre culture is replaced by Porter Hopewell, dominantly a late Marksville-Issaquena complex, but, as the western edge of the cultural mix, it makes consistent use of some Early Swift Creek and more of the eastern sand temper. West of Mobile Bay, there are no eastern ideas at this time nor are there even trade sherds. From the eastern point of view, the complicated stamped tradition, very little affected by western ideas, maintained its strength, particularly around Apalachicola Bay and up the river system to the Mandeville site on the Chattahoochee.

A definite trend for Mississippi Valley concepts to move eastward, accepted and used by eastern cultures, is then established. This tendency is even stronger in the next, Weeden Island period. Since we cannot control time or space in the lengthy and widespread Weeden Island period, with the many variant complexes, it is difficult to document increasing spread and importance of the western concepts in any kind of time-space framework. Hypotheses can be advanced, with some support for them.

I suggest that the Red River Mouth tradition, accompanied by an increasing emphasis on plain ware, moved further eastward rapidly, and constantly gained in importance. As it was adopted in both sacred and secular contexts by cultures which made complicated stamped pottery, it produced some of the mixtures, the complexes, we call Weeden Island. Eventually, it moved all the way across southern Georgia to the Altamaha and the Ocmulgee. In this same period, complicated stamping maintained much of its strength in the east, and there are sites and components with very little western influence in total complexes. The continuation of the South Appalachian tradition, east of the Chattahoochee at least, is of course a logical necessity or it would have had to be reinvented to produce the Lamar horizon which extends into the historic period over most of Georgia.

It is suggested that check stamping, the other part of our problem, developed from the McLeod complex, itself a simple development out of the Cartersville complex. Although we have seen this only to the west, particularly in Clarke County, Alabama, it may well have taken place across a broad zone just north of the fall line. After establishing itself as the McLeod complex at the end of Porter Hopewell, the variants were dropped, and, as Wakulla Check Stamped, it spread south to the coast and east to the edge of the Florida West Coast. The variety of complexes with Wakulla Check Stamped suggests that the type was accepted by some cultures, and that the culture typified by it and a plain ware also moved eastward. Only such a complex hypothesis can account for the variety we can see.

In this "Weeden Island" period then, lasting some six to eight hundred years and stretching across space from Mobile Bay to central Georgia, real understanding will be reached only when we understand, and work out regionally, the permutations involved in three distinct complexes moving at different rates, sometimes alone, with single series representing cultures, sometimes combining into complexes, apparently in all possible ways. The problems are going to require a lot of field work and a lot more sophistication in artifact analysis than has recently been characteristic of work in the area. We made a very good start with the work published by Gordon Willey in 1949. With the data I have at present, it does not seem possible to go much further without new work.

There is one consistent element in all the varying culture complexes, and I think cultures, over this huge area and long time span. Except for pure check-stamped complexes, all of them seem to have participated in the same kind of ceremonialism, eventually resulting in the burial mounds with the east side pottery deposits. Each of them, and there really are not a lot in the total area (one per site except at Kolomoki), represents ceremonialism during the entire time period in which that side was "Weeden Island" of any kind. The pottery deposits are apparently an accumulation of ceremonial vessels produced and used during the entire period. Most of these accumulations contain complicated stamped, check-stamped and Weeden Island variant pots. We have no really good way of telling when an accumulation started and when it ended, since, in these single east side deposits, almost all vessels—perhaps all—were specially made for ceremonial function.

## Period A-C

Starting slightly before time B, two new ceramic series appear in the Gulf Coastal Plain. Each represents a culture which, in its area, replaced one or more earlier Weeden Island complexes. Because I regard these cultures as invaders, and not as producers of the normal processes of in-place cultural development that we have been concerned with, this discussion will be brief and general. It is based on all data available to me, with most of it coming from Willey (1949; Trickey, 1958 and personal communication; Wimberly, 1960) and my own survey. The two series are:

Fort Walton: Types Lake Jackson Plain, Fort Walton Incised, Point Washington Incised (Willey, 1949:458-63), Pinellas Incised (Willey, 1949:482), Cool Branch Incised, Lake Jackson Incised (Sears, 1967:32-39). The last two types were included by Willey in Pinellas Incised. Cool Branch Incised is a grit-tempered variant of Moundville Incised (Heinlich, 1952:24-25).

Pensacola: Types Pensacola Plain, Pensacola Incised (Willey, 1949:463-66), Moundville Incised, and Moundville Engraved. Trickey has pointed out a matter of some importance, that designs in his area classified as Pensacola Incised are often "broken down Southern Cult motifs" (Trickey, 1958).

There has been some confusion, which I will not detail here, caused by reference to sites with only the Pensacola Series as Fort Walton period. Being careful to keep midden and cemetery or mound context separated, since weird types and combinations as well as complex mixtures of the two series do occur in sacred context, the two series do not overlap in space significantly. They are similar, but separate late Mississippian cultures.

*Fort Walton*

Coastal distribution eastward is about the same as for the preceding Weeden Island complex. Inland, the heaviest concentration is around Tallahassee, with large temple mound sites such as the Lake Jackson site. Large sites with large mounds continue up the Apalachicola, an area of concentration, and up the Chattahoochee to near Fort Benning. In most cases, the east side of the Chattahoochee is Lamar territory, the west side Fort Walton. The western boundary, on the coast, seems to lie about halfway between Choctawhatchee Bay, with the Fort Walton site, and Pensacola. Inland, the story is somewhat different. Only Fort Walton materials have been found in this period, and, while sites are generally small and only a few have small platform mounds, they do run all the way to the eastern edge of the valley of the Alabama River. As soon as one reaches the valley itself, all material is Pensacola complex.

The center for the culture is definitely in an area from Tallahassee to the Apalachicola and the upper Apalachicola. All of the large sites, with large temple mounds, and there are many of them, are in this area. While the coastal occupation is widespread, there is, and apparently was, a coastal site with a large temple mound only at Fort Walton.

I agree completely with Willey (1949:580) that the Fort Walton culture is intrusive. There have been theories concerning Fort Walton derivation from Weeden Island, based on pottery design similarities and the occurrence of Wakulla Check Stamped on Fort Walton sites. These arguments do not appear convincing, and I have not seen any good intermediate or developmental complexes. The most probably ancestral complex in the entire area, remembering that Fort Walton, part and parcel, is very late Mississippian in all its characteristics, is the little-known Averett complex (Chase, 1963) from the Fort Benning area. This complex, with big plain pots, is in the right place and is demonstrably late enough since Etowah II period sherds are frequently associated. Etowah II is definitely late Mississippian, with strap handles and an incised ware very similar to Moundville Incised. The earliest Fort Walton anyone has referred to, with some stratigraphy, is at the Rood Plantation site. The earliest levels here

(Caldwell, 1955) contain sherds of Moundville Incised classified as Pinellas Incised "A".

*Pensacola Series*

The Pensacola series with the sharp boundary between it and Fort Walton, noted above, has a peculiarly limited distribution in our area. Inland, it is very narrowly restricted to the Valley of the Alabama River. The coast is a different matter indeed. Coastal sites, all shell middens, spread east to the boundary with Fort Walton, and west to the Mississippi delta. Some of these sites are very large and complex, covering acres with midden debris many feet thick. Examples are the Bottle Creek site, a huge midden in downtown Pascagoula and a very large site on Dauphin Island in Mobile Bay. As plotted, the culture seems to tumble down the Alabama Valley and splash when it hits the coast. The analogy is not, I suspect, too far-fetched.

The origins of the Pensacola series are obviously in the Moundville complex, but it is later. There is no Southern Cult material known even in cemeteries, except for a very occasional engraved bottle, and the designs on the common bowls that are qualitatively very poor "cult" designs. In the Pensacola series, while the major Moundville decorated utility ware, Moundville Incised, is present, decoration is largely on the incised bowl forms so typical of this immediately prehistoric-early historic horizon through the entire southeast, including finally historic Creek and Cherokee ceramic complexes.

## Period A-C Summary

The two series, Fort Walton and Pensacola, are very similar in virtually all aspects of ceramic style. The only consistent difference is in choice of temper. The Fort Walton series is sand and grit tempered while the Pensacola is shell tempered. Obviously the Indians knew the difference, since the distributions of these series are discrete, although occasional sherds and, in mortuary association, even pots were exchanged.

Each of them appears suddenly in our area. Their ancestry is elsewhere, seemingly to the north in both cases, toward areas of Mississippian development. In both cases, and at very nearly the same time, they replace resident Weeden Island people. The data suggests, here as further north, Mississippian expansion by conquest. Very probably Mabila, somewhere near Pensacola but inland, was the last fortified outpost of Mississippian expansion to the sea.

There is a good deal of scattered documentation from mounds and cemeteries for the continued existence of both these complexes into the sixteenth century. Coins, iron spikes, beads, and all sorts of odds and ends in middens, mounds and cemeteries are Spanish in origin when the point is determinable, but are not the kind of things found in the later Mission sites. Rather, they are what one might expect from the sixteenth-century exploration efforts.

The final occupations are those of the historic Creek and Choctaw. Creek material throughout the coastal plain is characterized by the ceramic complex found in the eighteenth-century Chattahoochee River towns (Bullen, 1958; Willey and Sears, 1952). This is true of all sites inland from the Alabama to the Chattahoochee, including several in the Alabama River area with nineteenth-century Caucasian ceramics associated. It is interesting that this is essentially the Fort Walton area. To the north, where ill-defined shell tempered material, similar at least to the Pensacola complex, characterizes the earlier periods, the historic Creek material is shell tempered. I have suggested elsewhere (Sears, n.d.) that we may well speak of shell tempered and grit tempered Creeks instead of upper and lower.

## Time

The chart above presents the relative temporal relationships of the various complexes in the several areas. It is based on contemporaneity demonstrated by trade sherds and/or by use of the same combinations of modes for the cultures considered in this essay in any detail. The Red River and Lower Valley columns represent my attempt, obviously affected by my interpretation of data from eastern Mississippi eastward, at a fit between them and between any of them and "Central Gulf Coastal Plain" cultures.

The "threat of the Atom" is long since upon us, so calendar, or absolute, dates are offered. Documentation for these is not offered, in some part because I have no desire to participate in the game of "good" and "bad" dates. In most instances, trends or averages of clusters of dates, and interpolation between them, were used. A variety of sources and compilations has been used and some external relationships enter into this. As explained earlier, I have considered dates for mid-Western Hopewell in the mid-to-late range as applicable to Deptford and the other coastal plain cultures which are demonstrated to be coexistent, and dates for the Issaquena complex, clearly coeval with Early Swift Creek as shown by the Porter Hopewell complex. Sources range from Phillips' compilation (Phillips, 1970) to Ford's (Ford, 1969).

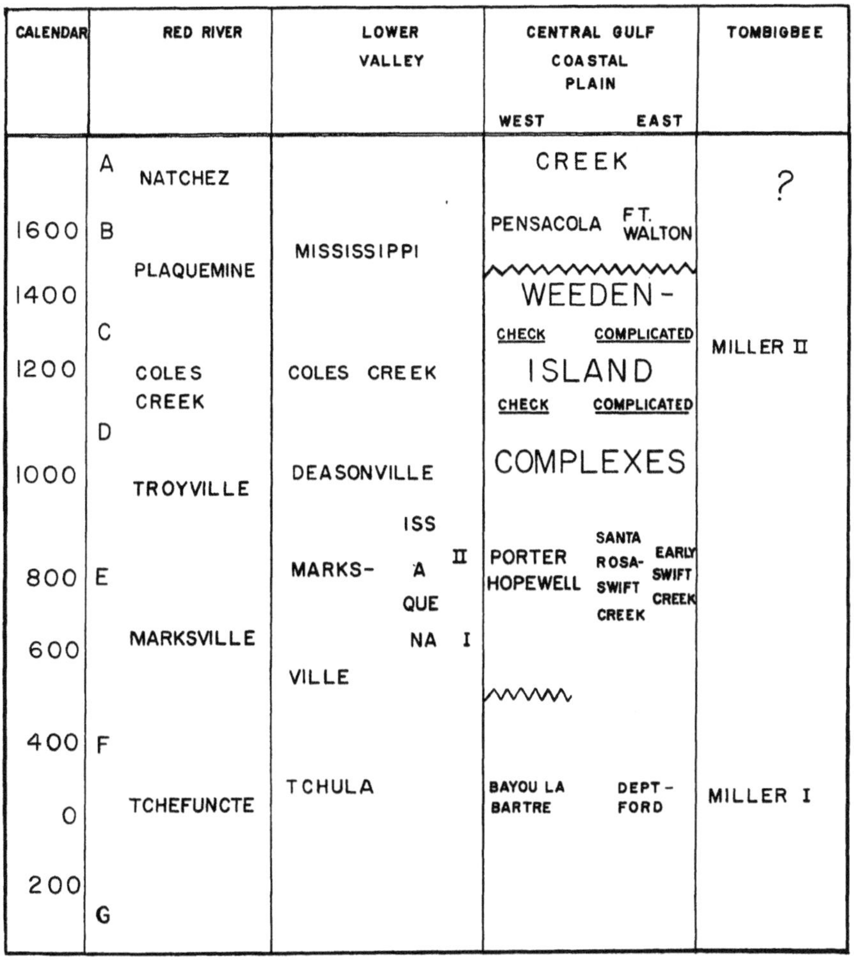

| CALENDAR | RED RIVER | LOWER VALLEY | CENTRAL GULF COASTAL PLAIN | | TOMBIGBEE |
|---|---|---|---|---|---|
| | | | WEST | EAST | |
| | A NATCHEZ | | CREEK | | ? |
| 1600 | B | MISSISSIPPI | PENSACOLA | F.T. WALTON | |
| | PLAQUEMINE | | ~~~~~~~~~~ | | |
| 1400 | | | WEEDEN- | | |
| | C | | CHECK  COMPLICATED | | MILLER II |
| 1200 | COLES CREEK | COLES CREEK | ISLAND | | |
| | | | CHECK  COMPLICATED | | |
| | D | | | | |
| 1000 | TROYVILLE | DEASONVILLE | COMPLEXES | | |
| | | ISS | | SANTA | |
| 800 | E | MARKS- A  II | PORTER | ROSA- EARLY | |
| | | QUE | HOPEWELL | SWIFT  SWIFT | |
| | | | | CREEK CREEK | |
| 600 | MARKSVILLE | NA  I | | | |
| | | VILLE | ~~~~~ | | |
| 400 | F | | | | |
| | | TCHULA | BAYOU LA | DEPT- | MILLER I |
| 0 | TCHEFUNCTE | | BARTRE | FORD | |
| 200 | | | | | |
| | G | | | | |

Figure 4. Chart of relative temporal relationships of complexes.

The crowding at the top of the chart, very similar to that which bothered Phillips (1970:960) seems to me reasonable. This is based on two premises. First, there is no truly Early Mississippi complex in the area, with loop handles, etc. Second, culture change does occur with increasing rapidity as cultures increase in complexity.

## Summary and Conclusions

Pottery-using cultures appear across the entire area approximately simultaneously, discounting the slight and very scattered occupation earlier by people using fiber-tempered pottery. These first cultures, Deptford, Bayou La Batre and Tchefuncte, are related in common use of the tetrapod based small jar. Each of them has a distinct, well-defined area, and culture contact is indicated by trade sherds. The very different Miller culture, well inland on the Tombigbee, is our only "Woodland" representative, with fabric and cord marked ware. It participated in culture contact at the same "trade sherd" level.

In place development of the coastal cultures continues after time F, except that Bayou La Batre is replaced. Miller remains aloof. In period E-F, the Marksville-Issaquena periods of the Mississippi Valley, established cultures begin a much more intensive interchange of ideas, and ceramic complexes are produced which are blends of earlier distinct series.

The Red River Mouth tradition, probably with some variation, is areally extended to the Mississippi border and, almost, to the Tombigbee-Mobile drainage. From the forks of the Alabama and Tombigbee down the Mobile River and Mobile Bay to the coast, the late Marksville-Issaquena complex, modified by some eastern concepts, takes over, defined as Porter-Hopewell. At the eastern end of the coastal plain, Early Swift Creek Complicated Stamped and a few relatives represent a culture that extends to the western end of Choctawhatchee Bay. The area from there to Mobile Bay has increasingly less complicated stamped pottery as one moves westward, with the final minimum in the Porter complex, and there is increasingly less Red River Mouth tradition kinds of material as one moves east to its disappearance at Choctawhatchee Bay. The variant complexes in this Mobile Bay-Choctawhatchee Bay strip are classifiable as representatives of the Santa Rosa-Swift Creek complex.

In this E-F period, cultural interaction is very clear. Total ceramic concepts at the type level are moving, as well as many smaller clusters of modes and single modes. This interaction is not shared by Miller, a woodland culture with obviously unrelated ceramics.

The interaction intensifies in what we can only, at present, call the Weeden Island period, covering the entire C-E interval. In this interval, with Miller, obviously by now a completely foreign culture not participating again, Red River tradition concepts of how to make and decorate a pot, but locally interpreted in sand instead of clay temper, move all the way across our area and beyond as the definitive element in a considerable variety of Weeden Island complexes.

The data suggests that the processes involved through time and space were:

1) Continued increase in use, with eastward movement, of Red River tradition concepts.

2) Continued development of complicated stamping and at least continued dominance in many sites and areas in the Apalachicola-Chattahoochee drainage, the coastal areas adjacent to the Apalachicola, and eastward into southern Georgia.

3) The introduction of a very strong element of check stamping as the Cartersville series derived McLeod series at the beginning of the period in the forks of the Alabama and the Tombigbee. Simple stamping and linear check stamping were dropped at a point in time, leaving the check stamping as Wakulla Check Stamped. It moves to the coast and then east, increasingly dominating a variety of complexes.

In each instance, the ceremonial assemblages either precede the movement of the concepts in secular context or move with them. In Weeden Island, with only one mound produced in one ceremony containing all of the ceremonial vessels assembled during the Weeden Island occupation of the site, it is hard to tell who moved which way when.

Restricting ourselves now to the area from the east edge of the Tombigbee Valley and the Mobile Valley and bay system, two distinct, very late post-Southern Cult Mississippian cultures, Fort Walton and Pensacola, cut off and replace the Weeden Island development. West of this area, the derived Mississippian Plaquemine culture is dominant. To the east the complicated stamped South Appalachian tradition, across the Chattahoochee, continues its development into the Lamar horizon. Both of these are in-place developments. Fort Walton and Pensacola are not.

Fort Walton, with the major sites centered in the Apalachicola-lower Chattahoochee-Tallahassee area is now, period A-B, the only culture present inland between the boundaries noted. On the coast, it extends westward to just west of Choctawhatchee Bay. The Pensacola complex, very similar but with normal Mississippian shell instead of grit temper, represents another Moundville derived culture. It dominates the Alabama River Valley, the sides of Mobile Bay, and on the coast, with some very large sites, spreads east through the Pensacola area and west along the Mississippi coast to the Mississippi delta. In both cases, Fort Walton and Pensacola, we are witnessing the final spread of Mississippian cultures to the sea, barely complete when Hernando DeSoto arrived.

At some point after this, developing from Fort Walton, the entire area inland is occupied by the lower Creek, with their ceramic trademarks of brushed and incised grit tempered pottery. They continue in the area, documented by trade materials, well up into the nineteenth century, particularly in the western part of the area where there are many people of Creek descent today.

## References Cited

Allen, Glenn T., Jr.
    1953    A stratigraphic investigation of the Hall site, Wakulla County, Florida. Notes in Anthropology 1(2).

Bullen, Ripley P.
    1970    The transitional period of southeastern United States as viewed from Florida, or the roots of the Gulf tradition. Southeastern Archaeological Conference. Bulletin No. 13.
    1958    Six sites near the Chattahoochee River in the Jim Woodruff Resevoir Area, Florida. River Basin Surveys Papers No. 14, Bureau of American Ethnology Bulletin 169.

Caldwell, Jospeh R.
    1958    Trend and tradition in the prehistory of the eastern United States. Memoirs of the American Anthropological Association, No. 88.
    1955    Investigations at Rood's Landing, Stewart County, Georgia. Early Georgia 2 (1).

Caldwell, J. and A. J. Waring, Jr.
    1939    Type description Deptford series. Newsletter, Southeastern Archaeological Conference, edited by W. Haag.

Chase, David W.
    1963    A reappraisal of the Averett complex. Journal of Alabama Archaeology 9(2).

Fairbanks, Charles H.
    1953    Excavations at site 9 HL 64, Buford Reservoir, Georgia. Florida State University Studies Anthropology 16:1-26.

Ford, James A.
    1969    A comparison of formative cultures in the Americas. Smithsonian Contributions to Anthropology, vol. II.
    1966    Early formative cultures in Georgia and Florida. American Antiquity 31:781-99.
    1952    Measurements of some prehistoric design developments in the southeastern states. Anthropological papers of the American Museum of Natural History 44 (pt. 3)
    1951    Greenhouse: A Troyville-Coles Creek Period site in Avoyelles Parish, Louisiana. Anthropological papers of the American Museum of Natural History 44 (pt. 1).

Ford, J. A., and George I. Quimby, Jr.
    1945    The Tchefuncte culture: an early occupation of the lower Mississippi Valley. Society for American Archaeology, Memoir No. 2.

Ford, J. A., and Gordon Willey
    1940    Crooks site, a Marksville period burial mound in LaSalle Parrish,

Louisiana. Anthropological Study, No. 3. Dept. of Conservation, Louisiana Geological Survey.

Gagliano, Sherwood M.
1967 Late archaic-early formative relationships in south Louisiana. Proceedings of the 23rd Southeastern Archaeological Conference, Bulletin No. 6.

Greengo, Robert E.
1964 Issaquena, an archaeological phase in the Yazoo Basin of the lower Mississippi Valley. American Antiquity 30 (pt. 2). Memoirs of the Society for American Archaeology, No. 18.

Heimlich, Marion Dunlevy
1952 Guntersville Basin pottery. Geological Survey of Alabama, Museum Paper No. 32.

Jennings, J. D.
1941 Chickasaw and earlier Indian cultures of northeast Mississippi. The Journal of Mississippi History 3:135-226.

Kelly, A. R., J. H. Kellar, and E. V. McMichael
1962 The Mandeville site in southwest Georgia. American Antiquity. 27:336-55.

McMichael, Edward V., and James Kellar
1960, Archaeological salvage in the Oliver Basin. University of Georgia Laboratory of Archaeology Series.

Moore, Clarence B.
1903 Certain aboriginal mounds of the Apalachicola River. Journal of the Academy of Natural Sciences of Philadelphia 12: 440-92.

Phelps, David S.
1969 Swift Creek and Santa Rosa in northwest Florida. Paper presented to Society for American Archaeology, Annual Meeting, 1969 (mimeographed).
1965 The Norwood series of fiber-tempered ceramics. Proceedings of the 20th Southeastern Archaeological Conference, Bulletin No. 2.

Phillips, Phillip
1970 Archaeological survey in the lower Yazoo Basin, Mississippi 1949-1955. Papers of the Peabody Museum of American Archaeology and Ethnology, Harvard University, vol. 60.
1958 Application of the Wheat-Gifford-Wasley taxonomy to eastern ceramics. American Antiquity 24:117-25.

Phillips, P., J. A. Ford, and J. B. Griffin
1951 Archaeological survey in the lower Mississippi Alluvial Valley, 1940-1947. Papers of the Peabody Museum of American Archaeology and Ethnology, Harvard University, vol. 25.

Prufer, Olaf H.
1918 Ohio Hopewell ceramics. An analysis of the extant collections.

University of Michigan, Museum of Anthropology, Anthropological Papers No. 33.

Sears, William H.
- 1973 The sacred and the secular in prehistoric ceramics. Variation in Anthropology—Essays in Honor of John McGregor. Illinois Archaeological Survey, pp. 31-42.
- 1971 Food production and village life in prehistoric southeastern United States. Archaeology 24:322-29.
- 1967 The Tierra Verde burial mound. The Florida Anthropologist 20: 25-73.
- 1963 The Tucker site on Alligator Harbor, Franklin County, Florida. Contributions of the Florida State Museum—Social Sciences No. 9.
- 1962 The Hopewellian affiliations of certain sites on the Gulf Coast of Florida. American Antiquity 28:5-18.
- 1960 Ceramic systems and eastern archaeology. American Antiquity, 25: 324-29.
- 1957 Excavations on the lower St. Johns River, Florida. Contributions of the Florida State Museum—Social Sciences, No. 2.
- 1956a Excavations at Kolomoki—a final report. University of Georgia Series in Anthropology, No. 5.
- 1952 Ceramic development in the south Appalachian Province. American Antiquity 18(2).
- 1951a Excavations at Kolomoki. University of Georgia Series in Anthropology, No. 2.
- n.d. Southeastern U.S.—400 B.C.-1,000 A.D. Handbook of North American Indians, Smithsonian Institution.

Sears, William H., and James B. Griffin
- 1950 Type descriptions, Deptford Series pottery and Mossy Oak Simple Stamp. Prehistoric pottery types of eastern United States. Ceramic Repository, University of Michigan.

Trickey, E. Bruce
- 1958 A chronological framework for the Mobile Bay Region. American Antiquity 23:388-96.

Trickey, E. Bruce, and N. H. Holmes
- 1967 The Mobile Bay chronology. Bulletin No. 6. Proceedings of the 23rd Southeastern Archaeological Conference.

Waring, Antonio J.
- 1968 The Waring papers. The collected works of Antonio J. Waring Jr., edited by Stephen Williams. Papers of the Museum of Archaeology and Ethnology, Harvard University.

Willey, Gordon R.
- 1949 Archaeology of the Florida Gulf Coast. Smithsonian Miscellaneous Collections, vol. 113.

1945 Horizon styles and pottery traditions in Peruvian archaeology. American Antiquity 2: 49-56.

Willey, Gordon R., and William H. Sears
1952 The Kasita site. Southern Indian Studies, vol. IV.

Wimberly, Steve B.
1960 Indian pottery from Clarke Co. and Mobile Co., southern Alabama. Alabama Museum of Natural History, Museum Paper 36.

Wimberly, Stephen B.
1953 Bayou La Batre Tchefuncte pottery series. Prehistoric pottery types of eastern U.S. Museum of Anthropology, University of Michigan.

# THE PENETRATION OF NORTHEAST ARKANSAS BY MISSISSIPPIAN CULTURE

*Dan Franklin Morse*
Arkansas Archeological Survey

Sometime around A.D. 900-1100 a Mississippian chiefdom migrated into extreme northeast Arkansas. Its ultimate roots appear to be in the Fairmount phase at Cahokia, located near St. Louis, but the immediate area of origin would seem to be the Cairo Lowlands. The migration meant an intrusion of a strongly structured chiefdom into an area consisting of a weakly structured segmentary tribe. The indigenous population reacted by amalgamation with or acculturation to the dominant society. The ultimate result was a third society patterned after a central Mississippi Valley chiefdom.

The term "Mississippian" refers here to a particular kind of socioeconomic adaptation of human society in much of the Eastern United States between around A.D. 700 and 1700 (Fig. 1). For convenience, we use early, middle and late Mississippian to refer to the general time periods in the central Mississippi Valley: A.D. 700-1100; A.D. 1100-1400; and A.D. 1400-1700. Most early Mississippian references in this paper are to the period A.D. 900-1050, during which Mississippian culture first appeared within much of the southeast and midwest. The term "Middle Mississippi" refers to a geographical region based on Holmes' (1903:80) description of the pottery of the Middle Mississippi Valley region and was continued by Griffin (1967:Fig. 5) to describe an area of broad ceramic similarity and hence a contiguous region of cultural similarity. Illustrations of Middle Mississippi ceramics are usually of specimens from southeast Missouri and northeast Arkansas.

There are three very major problems associated with Middle Mississippi events: 1) The specific sociological and technological nature of Mississippian culture: 2) the points and causes of origin of Mississippian; and, 3) the cause and nature of the spread of Mississippian culture within the Middle Mississippi region and into the remainder of the midwest and

Penetration of Northeast Arkansas by Mississippian Culture 187

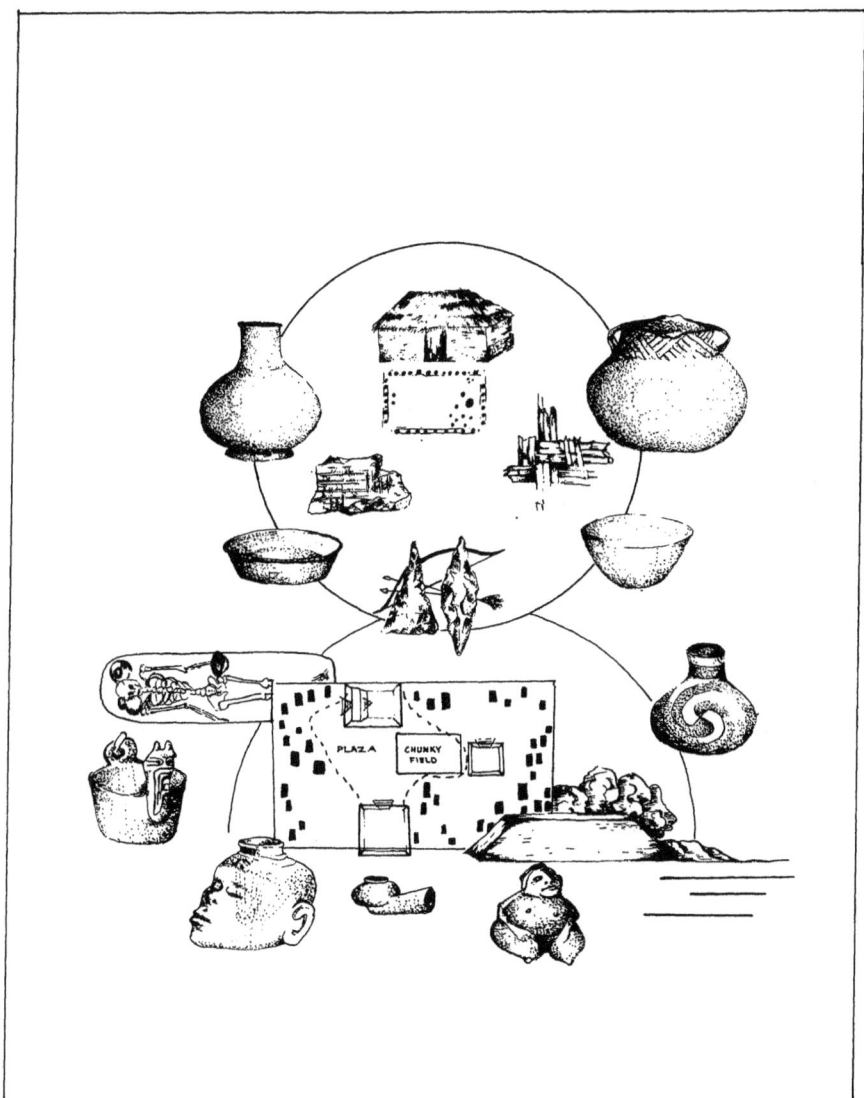

Figure 1. Mississippian culture. The two spheres of household and pantribal artifacts and features are based on the Nodena phase of A.D. 1400-1700.

southeast. This paper will study the third problem, with particular emphasis upon the spread of Mississippian culture within the southwestern portion of the Middle Mississippi region; that is, down the Mississippi River Valley into the north Delta of Arkansas known as the St. Francis Basin (Fig. 2).

## Introduction: Mississippian Culture

> I don't know much about the Middle Mississippi Phase, and I would like to have someone define it (Griffin, 1937:49).... The amorphous agglomeration of traits known as Middle Mississippi (Griffin, 1943:257).... It is decidedly unfortunate that we do not have any modern analytical and interpretive monographs on any Middle Mississippi cultural division (Griffin, 1946:91).

The most noticeable archaeological inference about Mississippian is the very significant increase in population. This inference is based on the presence of larger sites spaced closer together and a tremendous increase in the quantity of broken ceramics over anything seen in the previous periods of human occupation in the central Mississippi Valley. In addition, literally thousands of Mississippian graves have been dug, mostly by "pot hunters," to obtain exotic vessels for sale or for curio cabinets (Morse, 1973a, 1973b).

Traditionally, "prevailingly shell-tempered" pottery has been one of the diagnostic traits of Mississippian culture (McKern, 1939:309). Certainly Mississippian culture is not necessarily shell-tempered pottery, but tempering with burned shell was apparently a Mississippian innovation which allowed the manufacture of a large number of relatively exotic vessels from easily accessible montmorillinite clay (Million, 1974). In the Valley, most local clay is not good pottery clay. Recent work by Michael Million (1974) has demonstrated that when backswamp clays were modified by the addition of lime (burned shell in much of this area), it caused clay particles to flocculate, producing less shrinkage and better workability. Better pottery clay, such as that used for Bell Plain, had minute grog tempering added to the paste. Other pottery clay from upland sources may not have required any lime modification. The immediate effect of Million's discovery—that shell-tempering is basically a technological tool and not merely a diffusionist style—is almost revolutionary to archaeological theory in this area. It frees archaeologists from having to make purely sociological explanations for variations or similarities in temper. Yet, some archaeologists tend to continue to do so. The assumption that cultural behavior such as pottery making is "woman's work" and not relevant to "sweeping changes in sociopolitical and ceremonial orientations which ordinarily come about through means that are mainly in the control of men" (Phillips, 1970:569) is a traditionally strong, albeit false, archaeological premise.

The economic basis of Mississippian culture involves intensive agriculture. It is intensive to the extent that large, closely-spaced populations locate adjacent to or upon areas of prime agricultural lands. An impressive number and variety of cultigens have been recovered from Mississippian sites (Cutler and Blake, 1973) including an improved breed of corn developed during this time period (Cutler and Blake, 1969:134-35). There is some evidence of large-scale land clearing and of slash and burn preparation of land areas. For example, at the Upper Nodena site in Mississippi County, Arkansas, in 1973, evidence was found for a cyclical pattern of surface burning and localized soil erosion predating the construction of this ceremonial center village. There is continuing evidence of significant wild animal and plant exploitation (Smith, 1975), and the concept of "intensive agriculture" has to be modified to include natural exploitation on a wide scale.

The usual and logical sociological classification of Mississippian culture is as a chiefdom (Sahlins, 1968:20-27), but this is more clearly the case in some situations than in others. There is no evidence of state organization except possibly a secondary state coincidental with European contact and interaction. Evidence for the chiefdom nature of Mississippian culture is considerable. Sites are internally well organized and there is a clear indication of the central direction of conscripted labor to build pyramidal mounds and even whole villages or towns, to promote economic production and to encourage specialized production. There is evidence of a settlement hierarchy and an overall plan to position sites within a single sociological sphere, in order to exploit a region containing a variety of microenvironmental zones spread over one hundred or more square miles. A variety of domestic and wild resources apparently were gathered at distribution centers to be subsequently redistributed back to all parts of the society. Houses within a village tend to be constructed at the same loci through time (Morse, 1973d:7, 1974a; Firth, 1957:82, 87, 316). In addition, there is good evidence of lithic specialization beyond a normal household economy. This evidence is both site specialization, for example in basalt adzes (Morse, 1974b), and in individual knapping specialization, for example in exotic chert forms (Don Crabtree, personal communication). However, field verification of the chiefdom hypothesis in Arkansas has not been completely accomplished. For instance, evidence of a pattern of "status burials" is absent and so-called Southern Cult items are not prevalent.

## Problem: Origin of Mississippian Culture in the Middle Mississippi Region

By 1939, when the present Lower Mississippi Valley Survey was first discussed, an immense amount of data on Middle Mississippi had accumulated, but the problem of its origins and development appeared to be as far from resolution as ever. There was a general impression, shared by many students of Southeastern culture, that this was because the "central" Mississippi Valley, the assumed center of distribution of the culture, had not been sufficiently investigated. It was primarily to make good this lack that the present Survey was undertaken (Phillips, Ford and Griffin, 1951:39).

Phillips, Ford and Griffin did not "solve" this problem concerning the origin and development of Mississippian culture. Actually, they concluded:

We are even more certain that *the* center for its development is not in the Survey Area at all. In fact, we are becoming increasingly doubtful that a single center for this development exists anywhere. We envisage rather a number of centers in which this culture was developing more or less simultaneously along parallel lines with continuing interaction between them (1951:451).

They did outline five major "elements" thought to be important in the development of Mississippian culture in the Central Mississippi Valley. These included continuity from Baytown, influences from the north, Mesoamerica and the Southwest and a category of elements called the "X-factor" which embraced such things as new cultigens, population increase, a new socio-political system, and others.

One difficulty in this approach to the problem is that the problem has never been very clearly defined. Each major topographic zone in the Central Mississippi Valley such as the Malden Plain or Big Lake Highlands contains a relatively distinctive kind of Mississippian culture. Each zone also reflects an unique history of the development of that particular Mississippian culture. However, the very specific similarities of cultural behavior as reflected by artifacts and sites indicate a common history and the basic problem we wish to outline is how this came about.

To merely define a center and delimit a region within which strong similarity to that "center" exists is not an explanation of the process involved in creating this situation. Descriptions of phase sequences in a specific region also are not an explanation. Phase sequences help generate the recognition of a problem and a reexamination of the phase sequences from the standpoint of specific hypotheses may help test those hypotheses.

There has been a pendulum swing from site unit intrusion to simultaneous areal development in interpreting Mississippian culture development in the eastern United States. Even now, we do not have adequate control over the initial phases of development within each major region. What can happen is well exemplified by the recognition that "Old Village," thought at one time to be the initial Mississippian expression at Cahokia, is actually quite a bit later in time than what now is called the Fairmount phase. We now suspect that the initial phases of Mississippian culture occurred "almost simultaneously" in wide-spread areas. What we do not know is what is meant by "simultaneous" when we are operating with dating methods which cannot give us even generational control over time.

Since 1951, it has become increasingly clearer that Cahokia was a primary center for the development of the Middle Mississippian, an opinion apparently long held by Griffin (1952:362). Whether the lowlands adjacent to the Illinois, Missouri and Kentucky borders where the Mississippi and Ohio Rivers meet is another primary center, as thought, is obscured by the concept of the Cairo Lowland "phase" (Williams, 1954) because it lumps together a great deal of Mississippian diversity covering a long period of time. It is now apparent that the area south of the St. Francis Basin was a secondary rather than a primary center as previously believed by Phillips, Ford, Griffin and others (Willey, 1966:293).

The Cahokia site near East St. Louis is 5.8 square miles of refuse and more than 100 mounds including one (Monks Mound) which covers 15 acres and is over 100 feet high. Four other large sites are located within about a 200-square-mile area (Fowler, 1969). The construction of Monks Mound began soon after the crystallization of the Cahokia chiefdom, called the Fairmount phase. Elaborate status burials and areas defined by large upright cypress logs, probably astronomical calendars, were present by around AD 1000. Porter (1969:54) hypothesizes that Cahokia Mississippian culture developed as a secondary state in response to Mesoamerican trade, but there is no evidence of objects such as obsidian blades, copper bells, or whelk trumpets which would be indicative of such trade.

The traditional archaeological approach to the ordering of data recovered from the Cahokia area has hampered efforts to resolve the problem of how Mississippian culture could have evolved there. In particular, the expectation that a simple unilinear sequence, stylistically flowing from one stage to another, seems oversimplified when we consider the complexity of a chiefdom organization. The two or three hundred years preceding the beginning of Mississippian culture at Cahokia have been classified as a single "phase" (Fowler and Hall, 1972). The diversity of these remains at Cahokia and in the surrounding loess-covered bluff, which include elements of Bluff or Jersey Bluff (Munson, 1966:19); Raymond (Maxwell, 1951:278); Embarrass (Winters, 1969:101-104), Maples Mills or Tampico (Cole and Deuel, 1937:195), and other complexes, should be emphasized and not camouflaged. It is difficult to view the developing chiefdom as having its roots in a single Late Woodland complex. Rather, the degree of social diversity reflected by the Cahokia site implies roots in several autonomous Woodland traditions. Through time more communities would then be incorporated in the developing Fairmount phase chiefdom. In fact, community incorporation seems to have continued subsequent to the Fairmount phase period (Perino, 1971).

From Middle Woodland to Mississippian, the American Bottoms underwent a tremendous population increase (Munson and Harn, 1971:Figs. 28 and 32). The number of villages and camps increased by at least 150 percent during the Late Woodland (Munson and Harn, 1971:9-14, 30-36). Population pressure (Meyers, 1971) may account for a shift to intensified agriculture in the American Bottoms and for a new social order. It may also account for the rapid establishment of regular trade with societies exploiting other microenvironments or involved in other exploitative patterns. This kind of trade would be expected were the people of the developing chiefdom concentrating on food production and the exploitation of bottomland resources. Craft specialization would be encouraged as part of a diversification program to produce exotic artifacts. Lineages involved in different patterns of exploitation and production would be linked together in a much stronger pan-tribal solidarity. These lineages would not have to originate from the same Woodland tribe; presumably a sort of lineage-ranking system would develop within the chiefdom, based on time of joining and original distance of kinship.

Trade to neighboring groups would tend to stabilize those groups in a single exploitative system with subsequent acculturation or amalgamation. Trade is functional for peace reinforcement (Harding, 1967:59-60; Sahlins, 1972:168-70), as well as for resource procurement. The potentially fragile nature of a developing chiefdom would call for the stronger political control necessary to the centralized direction of a redistribution system involving thousands of people. Trade with peripheral groups would involve those groups in a peaceful system without their having to be amalgamated within it. The earliest foreign stone recognized at Cahokia is Mill Creek chert (Munson and Harn, 1971:35-36), mined in Union County, Illinois, and ideal for spades and hoes. Mill Creek chert artifacts, particularly spades are found throughout the Mississippian period in the central regions and probably functioned to cement inter and intra chiefdom relationships. Salt and shell beads (whelk and *Anculosa* shell) were primary trade items important in Mississippian culture.

Archaeologists, confused over the meaning of shell tempering, have been unable to define fully the Cahokia sequence. An expanding population would have placed stress on pottery clay sources and specialized shapes would require a better clay than that available in the backswamp areas of a large meandering river. The addition of lime, first as limestone and then increasingly as burned shell, would solve this problem (Million, 1974): i.e., the chemical effect of the lime, not the shell *per se*, is the important thing. A rapid changeover in ceramic technology would mean that older stylistic attributes should disappear quickly. Indeed, the rapidity with which cord-marking is phased out with the new ceramic technology is most impressive. Handles were first riveted (as loops) and later appliquéd (as straps) much like modern stoneware handles, and this is an indication of the kind of experimentation that was going on during these first few generations of Mississippian culture.

## Hypotheses: Cultural Competition and Colonization

> The details of the cultural development in Eastern North America are unique, but the general trend may be regarded as a common one in human society, and the patterns of behavior, as analogous to those developed by other peoples in other areas of the Old World and the New (Griffin, 1967:191).

If we accept the fact that Mississippian culture in the Middle Mississippi Region began at Cahokia (or there and in the Cairo Lowlands simultaneously), our immediate problem is to explain its infiltration into the remainder of that region, particularly southward into Arkansas. The solution of this problem may indicate a solution of how Mississippian culture spread into other regions. We do not automatically equate the presence of agriculture with the very significant changes associated with Mississippian culture as has been done with the Neolithic in Europe (Piggott, 1965:26, 35-39). Our problem is not so much the spread of agriculture itself as the spread of a cultural system *based* upon intensive agriculture.

In Europe, the spread of pottery making and agriculture is explained in terms of colonization and acculturation as two separate events (Clark, 1969:128-29, 132). The implicit assumption is that cultural contact and possibly even competition is involved and that local traditional behavior as well as introduced innovative techniques and traits will influence the outcome. In an attempt to isolate meaningful factors in contact, Wauchope (1956:8) and others classified "culture contact situations." Two major divisions—"site-unit intrusion" and "trait-unit intrusion"—were each subdivided into four categories. The emphasis here is upon trait retention or change rather than on cultural processes. For example, in Type A2:

> In an area of more or less homogeneous culture, Culture A, a different culture, Culture B, appears as one or more site-units. Subsequently only one culture is identifiable in the area, representing a fusion of elements found in both of the earlier cultures but with elements of Culture A predominating.
> The Early Middle Mississippi culture of North America appears in intrusive site units in outlying areas from Wisconsin to Georgia.... The clearest of these [examples] occurs around the Macon Plateau site in Georgia where Early Middle Mississippi culture came in contact with Swift Creek culture.... The end result of the fusion process was the widespread and uniform culture known as Lamar.... There is more of Middle Mississippi in the settlement patterns and subsistence patterns of Lamar, and more of Swift Creek in the pottery style (Wauchope, 1956:11-12).

A more sophisticated approach, attempting explanation rather than simply classification, is possible with archaeological data. When we speak of site-unit intrusion and downriver drift (Phillips, 1970:912-13), we are not only not explaining anything, but the classification is not particularly meaningful. If we assume that cultural processes are the same, wherever and whenever *Homo sapiens* has existed, then there is the possibility of formulating or at least reviewing hypotheses pertinent to the problem of the origin of Mississippian culture in northeastern Arkansas and testing or further specifying those hypotheses. The specific hypotheses to be reviewed here were published by Sahlins (1961) and Willey (1953). The archaeological data to test them were obtained in Arkansas between 1968 and 1973 (Morse, 1973c, 1975) and pertain to contact both between neighboring segmentary tribes and between a resident segmentary tribe and an intruding chiefdom.

Sahlins' (1961) hypotheses concerning cultural expansion and confrontation, based on the Tiv, Dinka and Nuer, are that:

1) A tribe moving into an uncontested or uninhabited territory will grow by segmentation but these segments will not fuse into larger segments.

2) A tribe moving into a contested territory will grow by segmentation and these segments will fuse into larger segments.

3) A tribe described in hypothesis 1 will tend to remain weakly structured; that is, it will not fuse into larger segments even when confronted by competition for its territory.

4) A tribe described in hypothesis 2 confronting another such as that described in hypothesis 3 will conquer and absorb its competition. It may migrate by continuous "pushing" or it may "leap frog."

5) A strongly structured segmentary lineage system will not develop when confrontation is with a band and will be ineffective when competing with a chiefdom.

Willey's hypotheses (1953) concerning cultural expansion are based on archaeological examples in Central Georgia, northern Yucatan and north coastal Peru:

1) Upon migration of a dominant alien culture as a colony into an area already occupied by a less dominant recipient culture, there will be a period of acculturation by the recipient culture, now limited to refuge regions.

2) A third culture will develop out of a merging of both the alien and recipient cultures which will occupy both the colony and refuge regions.

3) Cultural colonization will be achieved whether the cultures involved are of similar or of different economic bases.

4) "The success of the process of final acculturation is facilitated by the background of a common cultural tradition and by similar cultural-environmental adjustments of the merging cultures" (Willey, 1953:382).

## Tests: The Zebree Site and the Big Lake Phase

> I'm very sorry that I don't know of any material from Wisconsin that would substantiate Griffin's position (McKern, in Orr, 1950:17).... My reconstruction was what Radcliffe-Brown used to call hypothetical (Griffin, in Orr, 1950:18).

All the cultural innovations that have occurred in the eastern United States through time are reflected in northeast Arkansas. It is a primary area during the early hunting-gathering period and in the late prehistoric period of intensive agriculture. Throughout this period of human activity, investigation of each stage can contribute something to our understanding of cultural processes. We are particularly fortunate in tracing the beginnings of Mississippian culture in northeast Arkansas. An initial expression occurred in the Big Lake Highlands at the Zebree site where only sporadic occupation had taken place previously. Just before the construction of this site, the area had been exploited by open communities of incipient agriculturalists. The contrast both in settlement and ceramics is striking. The later developments of Mississippian culture were concentrated elsewhere; and there was minimal mixture with these early deposits. The weak points in a northeast Arkansas test are: dependence upon artifact grab samples; lack of systematic sampling of different micro-ecological zones; and inability to differentiate between multiple componency and amalgamation in shallow sites.

## Environmental Background

Northeast Arkansas (Fig. 2) is an area of rich alluvial soils and hardwood forests adjacent to the Mississippi River in the lower, deltaic part of its course. This is an area of warm summers and mild winters; average annual rainfall is some 48 inches, with winters being generally wetter and falls

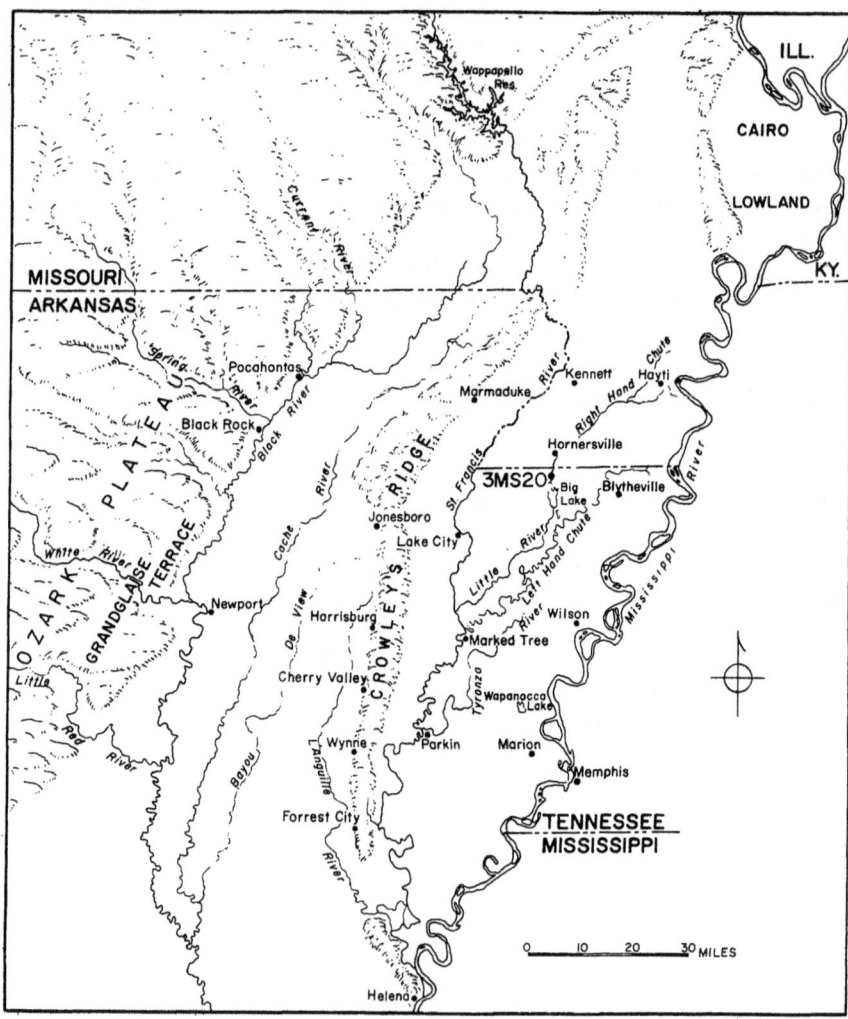

Figure 2. Map of northeast Arkansas and southeast Missouri. The Zebree site is marked 3MS20 and is in the right center of the figure.

drier than the rest of the year. The average growing season is 220 days (Morse, 1969).

Two lowlands are defined by a high, north-south erosional remnant called Crowley's Ridge. The lowlands have no stone, but Pleistocene chert gravels and "ironstone" (a sandstone) abound on Crowley's Ridge. Good quality Boone and Pitkin chert are found in the Ozark Highlands to the west. In the Missouri Ozarks to the north there are a variety of stone resources, including basalt (Branson, 1944).

Saucier (1970:Fig. 2) indicates two basic divisions within the Eastern Lowlands. There is a series of four relict braided stream surfaces on the west and two Mississippi River meander belts, one of which is relict, on the east. These braided stream surfaces originated sequentially through time, from west to east. It is not known exactly when the St. Francis River broke through Crowley's Ridge (it drains out of the Western Lowlands) but it may have been subsequent to the abandonment of Braided Surface C.

The meander belt area is divisible into two major parts. On the west is the abandoned Mississippi River Meander Belt and on the east is the present Mississippi River Meander Belt. Intruding from the present meander belt across Braided Surface D along the boundary with Braided Surface C and then joining the abandoned meander belt system opposite Memphis is a relatively large relict Mississippi River Channel now occupied by the Left Hand Chute of Little River (Saucier, 1970). This interrupts the Right Hand Chute of Little River and the St. Francis River. In both cases the rivers were dammed by natural levee construction and water backed up to form Lake St. Francis and Big Lake. The event is thought to have occurred around A.D. 900.

The soil between the two lakes, the Big Lake Highlands, is sandy. It is within the Amagon-Dundee-Crevasse soil association (Ferguson and Gray, 1971). The Dundee soil capability unit is considered I-1 unless frequently flooded. In other words, this is about the best farming soil available in the country and needs the least management. Its only real drawback is the risk of flooding. The soil association of the area immediately around Big Lake itself is Sharkey-Steele. These soils are considered generally well suited for wildlife habitat and in addition provide pottery clay. The wooded environment of Big Lake provides food, water, and protection for wildlife and the lake itself provides abundant wild fowl and fish. In speaking of the Mississippi River corridor, Bellrose (1968:8) states: "Because of its narrowness, this corridor has the greatest density of dabbling duck passage of any migration corridor east of the Rocky Mountains." Wintering mallards in northeast Arkansas are estimated at 400,000 (Bellrose, 1968:8), and an estimated 150,000 blue and lesser snow geese pass near Memphis, Tennessee, on their way to the Gulf Coast in the fall (Bellrose, 1968:19). Between the two lakes there was a prairie in historic times (Stephenson and Crider, 1916:29). That it also existed in prehistoric times is demonstrated by the finding of the thirteen-lined ground squirrel and prairie chicken at the Zebree site (Guilday and Parmalee, 1971).

*The Late Woodland Period of A.D. 700-900*

In much of northeast Arkansas there is a break in habitation evidence between about 500 B.C. and A.D. 700, except for the south of this area and possibly along the meander belt areas in the eastern portion. The area was marked, during the period A.D. 700-900, by populations expanding into it. A sand-tempered Barnes pottery which is more at home in southeast Missouri occurs in the northern part of this region, while a grog-tempered Baytown pottery occurs more often in the southern and eastern portions of the deltaic basin. The two styles seem to represent movement toward each other of two tribes with expanding populations. Most Barnes pottery is found west of the Left Hand Chute of Little River and Baytown pottery is primarily found east of Little River and to the south. There is an exception near Blytheville where Barnes pottery extends eastward almost to the Mississippi River. East of Blytheville is found grog-tempered Tchula pottery dated to around 500 B.C. to A.D. 1. However, no grog-tempered Marksville ceramics are known in this immediate area from between A.D. 1 and A.D. 700, although such ceramics are found north and south of this area. This pattern suggests that the two late pottery traditions are new to the area and that the inferred movement toward each other ceased around the time the crevasse channel came into existence, around or just prior to A.D. 900.

Sahlins' hypothesis concerning the movement of a segmentary tribe into an uncontested area predicts that these segments will not fuse. Archaeologically, large nucleated village sites should be absent. The Late Woodland sites surveyed to date within the Big Lake Highlands are small and characterized by small amounts of Crowley's Ridge debitage, an occasional point or scraper and Barnes pottery (Fig. 3). The pattern seems to be a diffused community, or "neighborhood," and each locus probably related to a single house as indicated by excavations at the Zebree site itself. It is a general pattern characteristic of much of northeast Arkansas.

Sahlins also predicted that fusion would result when a tribe moved into a contested territory. Beneath large Mississippian villages dating to the Nodena phase period of A.D. 1400-1700 are Late Woodland villages with Baytown pottery. South, between Memphis and Little Rock, there is

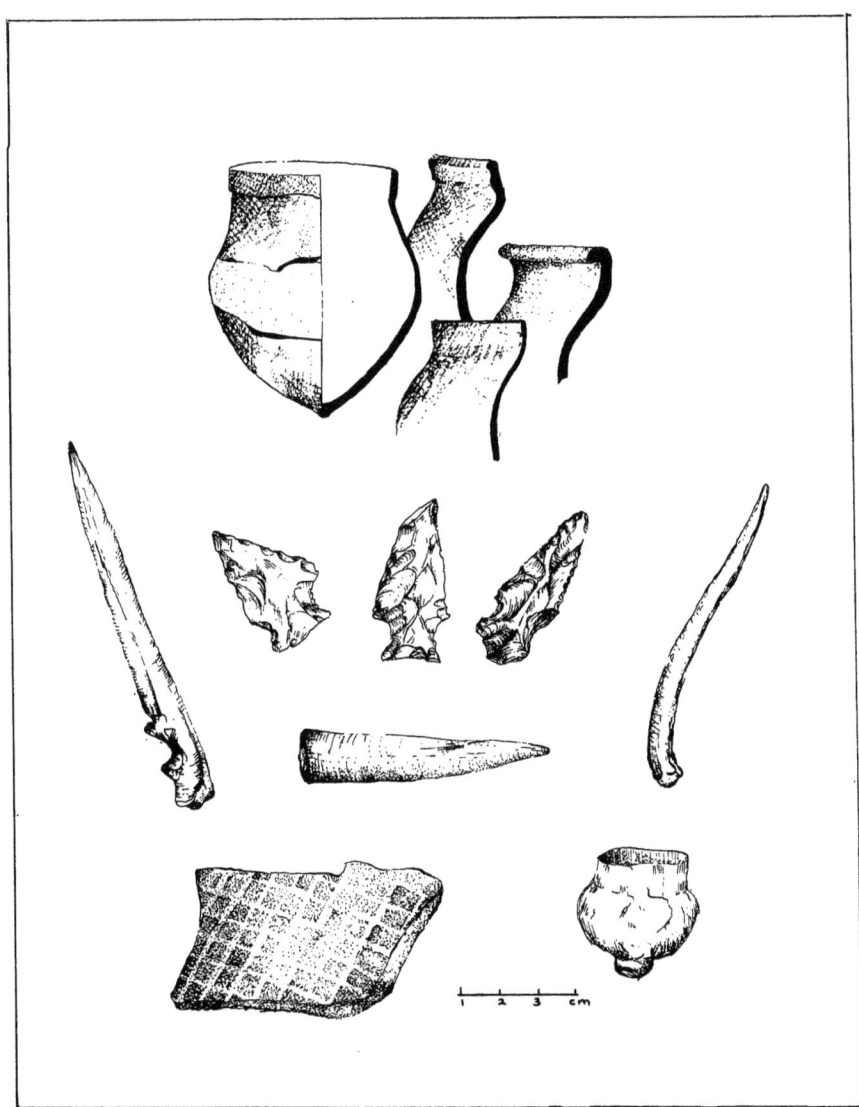

Figure 3. Barnes complex. This figure is based on the component at the Zebree site.

further evidence of Baytown fusion in the form of larger sites and exotic artifacts, such as boatstones, thought to be functional in cementing inter-village relationships. Fusion defined this way is a characteristic of Baytown; it exists where there may have been contests for land with Barnes or other Baytown pottery people. Sahlins' prediction seems to be valid.

Large Barnes pottery sites have not been found in Arkansas or Missouri even where there should have been considerable competition. Barnes sites are noteworthy for the absence of exotic artifacts or any evidence of long-range trade. The third Sahlins hypothesis seems to hold up.

Also to be expected from Sahlins' hypotheses is an encroachment of the Baytown complex upon land occupied by Barnes sites. Two tests are possible: first, a stratigraphic test. At site 23NM269, just west of the southern end of the Cairo Lowlands, Baytown pottery supersedes Barnes pottery (R. Williams, 1972:46), but additional stratigraphic tests should be made. A second test of Baytown expansion depends on the horizontal distribution of four pottery types. Cord-marked and plain surfaces are the major treatments for the Baytown and Barnes complexes. In Barnes pottery, which develops about the end of the Middle Woodland period, a plain surface treatment is the predominant style (Phillips, Ford and Griffin, 1951:436; Hopgood, 1969:190). This is similar to the situation in central Illinois (Morse, 1963:Table II) where plain pottery is preeminent until, or shortly after, the end of the Illinois Hopewell period. Subsequently, cord-marked pottery predominates until, as at Cahokia in the Patrick phase, pottery is "cord-marked to the rim ... [at a time thought to be] ... just prior to the crystallization of the Mississippian cultural pattern" (Fowler and Hall, 1972:3). It seems clear that by about A.D. 700 or slightly later cord-marked pottery significantly outnumbers plain pottery. At the edge of the known Barnes pottery distribution, then, plain Barnes pottery should have been superseded by cord-marked Baytown pottery. Just such a situation seems to be the case in the Cairo Lowlands (R. Williams, 1968:40-43) and along the Tyronza River east of Marked Tree, Arkansas. The samples involved, however, are very small.

## *The Initial Mississippian of A.D. 900*

At about A.D. 900, the Barnes pottery sites (probably the Dunklin phase) were apparently decreasing in number and being amalgamated into one or two Baytown pottery phases from the south and from the northeast. The fusion mechanisms for resisting this encroachment were absent, as predicted by Sahlins. Additionally he predicted that a segmentary tribe, even if strongly structured, could not compete with a chiefdom, and the events subsequent to A.D. 900 in northeast Arkansas bear this out. Willey hypothesized that cultural colonization involved a period of contact and acculturation, followed by a merging into a third distinct culture. The Late Woodland data cannot be used to test this concept since encroachment by Baytown onto Barnes territory was a continuous process of amalgamation of societies, as well as one of land acquisition. Nevertheless, these data underscore Willey's fourth hypothesis that acculturation is facilitated by a common cultural background. Willey's hypotheses are not fully relevant here since they relate to colonization by chiefdoms and states rather than by one segmentary tribe over another.

According to the "law of cultural dominance" (Sahlins, 1968:2), a more successful system expands at the expense of less successful systems. There is a

> rule—or 'law' as some are pleased to call it—that cultural dominance goes to technical predominance: the cultural type that develops more power and resources in a given environmental space will spread there at the expense of indigenous and competing cultures (Sahlins, 1968:2).

The conical clan chiefdom can divide and multiply. "More often it is divided into several independent chiefdoms" (Sahlins, 1968:25). This provides a built-in mechanism for site intrusion as lesser-ranked lineages move into new, less competitive niches. Trading relationships would tend to be retained in order to keep external peace and for the receiving of exotic goods to ensure internal peace and security.

Both the cultural and natural environment in the Big Lake Highlands constitute a ripe setting for a migration. Big Lake had just come into being. The prairie, Crowley's Ridge, relict and active Mississippi River meanders and the lowland topography associated with a major delta are all similar to the Cairo Lowlands. S. Williams' (1954:114-16) fauna list for the Crosno site in Missouri is very similar to that prepared by Guilday and Parmalee (1975) for the Zebree site in Arkansas. The Cahokia environment is similarly diverse. Although able to compete with a fused segmentary lineage organization, the migrating lesser independent chiefdoms would have been funneled along the Left Hand Chute of Little River (then an arm of the Mississippi River from near Hayti, Missouri, to Marked Tree and Parkin, Arkansas) and Big Lake into the Big Lake Highlands where population was sparse and resistance minimal.

Intrusion of Mississippian culture into northeast Arkansas about A.D. 900 is supported by considerable evidence. There is no local developmental background for the Big Lake phase (Fig. 4) either culturally or demographi-

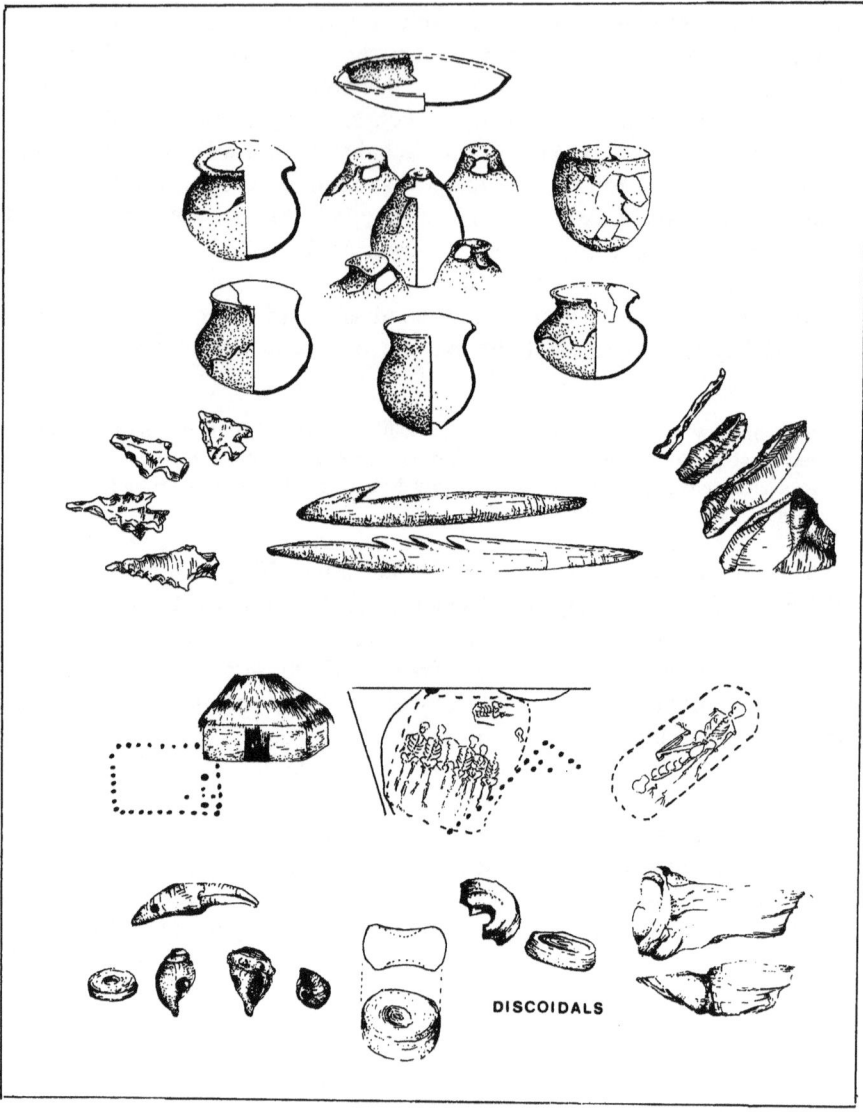

Figure 4. The Big Lake phase as represented by the Zebree site. Traits suggesting Fairmount phase affiliation are emphasized.

cally; there is a very clear relationship to the Fairmount phase at Cahokia dating between A.D. 900 and 1050, including the use of Illinois cherts at the Zebree site; the Zebree site component of the Big Lake phase is stratified directly upon the Barnes component; and the Zebree site was palisaded when first constructed as a village, an indication of potential or actual indigenous hostile reaction.

Similarities in features and artifacts to the Fairmount phase at Cahokia (Fowler, 1969) tend to place occupation at the Zebree site (Morse, 1975) between A.D. 900 and 1050 (Fowler and Hall, 1972:4-6). The large number of overlapping features and the possibility that the village was reconstructed at least once during this period indicate that occupation continued for almost the entire 150 years. In the southeast corner of the Zebree site, the spoil from a borrow pit was deposited directly upon the Barnes midden, and occupation of that artificial surface began immediately after its deposition. A stockade ditch has been defined as existing around most or all of the site. The basal fill of this ditch contained only Barnes sherds, an indication that the ditch was excavated before much, if any, Big Lake phase occupation had occurred at the site.

The small single-post rectangular house pattern characteristic of the Big Lake phase at the Zebree site is associated at Cahokia with pre-Fairmount and early Fairmount deposits (Fowler and Hall, 1972:5) and has not been associated with later deposits in either Illinois or Arkansas. At the Zebree site a rectangular burial group of eight extended skeletons (four males and four females) over a partial bed of mussel shells was found. This is similar to but less spectacular than graves found at the edge of Mound 72 at Cahokia (Fowler, 1969:19). The entire Zebree site is similar to, but not nearly so complex as, Cahokia during the Fairmount phase.

Indications of the Cahokia Microlith Industry, characteristic of an unknown period at Cahokia, are prevalent at the Zebree site, and indeed the same cherts are involved. Burlington (also called Crescent and Dupo) chert is the main raw material, although Mill Creek chert and Illinois Novaculite were used as well. This industry, oriented around bone and shell working (Morse, 1974c), would seem to fit a situation where shell beads are in demand, and at both loci, whelk and *Anculosa* shell are used to make beads. In addition, both sites produced single and triple barbed bone and antler harpoons during this time. Small serrated points, probably arrow points, are found at both sites; in Arkansas, this may be the initial introduction of the bow and arrow.

Although a definite plaza-mound has not been identified at the Zebree site, there is evidence of ceremonies not previously known in Arkansas.

Discoidal chunky stones are found at both Zebree and Cahokia. At the Zebree site the "Jersey Bluff" type discoidal (Perino, 1971:112-16) is represented; in Illinois, this is considered a Late Woodland type. At the Zebree site there were also small crude pottery discoidals, associated in Illinois with Woodland sites as well. A similar pottery discoidal has been found in northwest Florida and may belong in Weeden Island II (Morse, Morse, and Morse, 1973).

A total of 46,708 sherds were recovered in 1969 at the Zebree site. There are a number of ceramic similarities to Cahokia, particularly to O'Brien's "Period V" at the Powell tract (1972). The basic red filmed jar shape for the Big Lake phase is included in the Powell ceramics. Both contemporary phases are characterized by shell tempering, a high incidence of red filming, and gourd effigy bottles. The Wickliffe Thick funnel and the large pan, both dated to post-Fairmount times at Cahokia (Fowler and Hall, 1972:8, 11) were found at Zebree. However, the funnel and pan may not have been functionally necessary to the Fairmount phase. An experiment was conducted (North, 1975) to determine whether salt could be made from leaching the ashes of *Nelumbo lutea* (American lotus) in order to test the idea that the funnel and pan may have been components of a salt-making system similar to that described by Schultz (1962:124-25). The success of the experiment indicated that salt can be produced without salt springs.

Both the Wickliffe funnel and Varney Red Filmed are later characteristics of the Cairo Lowlands. The overwhelming similarity to the Fairmount phase indicates that the Big Lake phase originated from Cahokia itself or from some part of the Cahokia sphere, which may include part of the Cairo Lowlands not now recognized. The use of Mill Creek chert, *Anculosa* (Baker, 1941:61) and the Wickliffe funnel would tend to indicate that part of the Cairo Lowlands might logically be involved in the intrusion of the Big Lake phase.

## The Barnes Amalgamation to Mississippian Culture After A.D. 900

A review of possible Big Lake phase sites can be found elsewhere (Morse, 1975). The Zebree site appears to be the major one in the phase, while up to sixteen other sites in Arkansas and Missouri are now considered as possibly belonging to the phase. All these sites, including Zebree, either have been destroyed or are in the process of being destroyed; thus it is difficult to relate them to each other and to Zebree. Only four sites, two located south of Zebree along the edge of Big Lake, contain any elements of the Zebree ceramic complex except for red filmed and plain jars. At least three sites (and perhaps a fourth, although it seems to have been relatively insignificant in comparison to the other three) were probably colonies. The other thirteen sites may either be farmsteads in the Big Lake or a later phase of acculturating Barnes groups. In addition to the noted lack of ceramics, all the sites are characterized by an absence of microliths and the presence of Barnes ceramics and Woodland points. *Anculosa* beads occur at some sites, and like the jars are a possible indication of trade with Zebree.

The thirteen small sites located within the Big Lake Highlands may be an indication of Barnes amalgamation. If these sites were involved in the process of amalgamation, then they should be located differently in the Big Lake Highlands from the "pure" Barnes sites. In particular, these postulated later sites should be on or near significant concentrations of the Dundee soil which is best suited for the intensive agriculture practiced by Mississippian culture. This seems to be the case, at least on the basis of our present grab sample. In addition, we need better environmental reconstruction of the highlands for greater control over Barnes sites, which may reflect seasonal hunting and gathering and a quasi-agriculture. The data so far reflect precisely the sort of situation predicted by the Willey hypothesis of cultural colonization.

*Mississippian Culture After A.D. 1200*

By around A.D. 1100, there is no evidence of any Woodland tradition in northeast Arkansas and from this we conclude that amalgamation of Barnes and Baytown groups by Mississippian culture was completed by this time. There is no evidence of any Mississippian migration after this time. At this time or shortly afterwards, ceramic innovations are introduced which include cord-marked surface treatment (rare), the plate form, the "bean pot" form, longer necks on bottles, effigy bowls, lugs and strap handles, Mound Place Incised, O'Byam Incised, Matthews Incised and Carson Red on Buff. In addition, the wall-trenched house pattern appears around A.D. 1100-1200. Sites include pyramidal mounds, and there is an indication based on settlement pattern that the previous need for compact villages with palisade ditches no longer exists.

The development of the Lawhorn phase (Moselage, 1962) over much of the eastern lowlands of northeast Arkansas took place around A.D. 1100-1200. There was a population shift away from the Big Lake Highlands west to the St. Francis River area, largely abandoned after A.D. 1300, and east to a few selected areas, later the location of the intensive Nodena phase of A.D. 1400-1700 (morse, 1973b). Population growth southward, particularly between Marked Tree and Parkin, is little understood since the intensive Parkin Phase (Davis, 1966) developed after about A.D. 1300-1400 and obscured the earlier events. The only good example of a Middle Mississippian period phase is the almost completely excavated Snodgrass site associated with the Powers phase (Price, 1973). This site is divided into wards, a reasonable expectation given the events postulated to have occurred at and shortly after A.D. 900.

## Conclusion

The Mississippian culture of A.D. 1541 in eastern Arkansas is the one that the DeSoto expedition encountered after crossing the Mississippi River. This is basically the Mississippian of Holmes and of Phillips, Ford and Griffin (1951). This late Mississippian culture is the product of a series of events initiated at Cahokia about A.D. 700-900. A Mississippian colony was established near Big Lake around A.D. 900, followed by the amalgamation of indigenous Woodland peoples. The result (A.D. 1100-1200) was the Lawhorn phase, a Middle Mississippi chiefdom typical of the central Mississippi Valley. The later development around A.D. 1400 into the Nodena and Parkin phases was a localized intensification of the socio-political competition of chiefdoms involving greater populations in the southwestern portion of the Middle Mississippi region.

## Acknowledgments

Several individuals and institutions provided assistance for the excavations and for the analyses of archaeological data leading to the interpretations presented here (Morse, 1975). The National Park Service (Contract No. 14-10-7:911-21) and the Arkansas Archeological Survey gave financial aid. Arkansas Archeological Survey personnel who have helped directly in the preparation of this paper are Louis Gregorie, D. D. Dowden-Million, Ruby C. Chittenden, and Phyllis A. Morse, who edited the preliminary and final drafts.

## References Cited

Baker, Frank C.
    1941   A study in ethnozoology of the prehistoric Indians of Illinois. Item *in:* Contributions to the archaeology of the Illinois River Valley, edited by James B. Griffin and Richard G. Morgan. Transactions of the American Philosophical Society 32:51-77.

Bellrose, Frank C.
- 1968 Waterfowl migration corridors east of the Rocky Mountains in the United States. Illinois Natural History Survey, Biological Notes 61.

Branson, E. B.
- 1944 The geology of Missouri. University of Missouri Studies, vol. 19 (3).

Clark, Grahame
- 1969 World prehistory. Cambridge: Cambridge University Press.

Cole, Fay-Cooper and Thorne Deuel
- 1937 Rediscovering Illinois. Chicago: Univ. of Chicago Press.

Cutler, Hugh C. and Leonard W. Blake
- 1969 Corn from Cahokia sites. Item *in:* Explorations into Cahokia archaeology, edited by Melvin L. Fowler. Illinois Archaeological Survey, Bulletin 7:122-36.
- 1973 Plants from archeological sites east of the Rockies. Missouri Botanical Garden, (mimeographed).

Davis, Hester A.
- 1966 An introduction to Parkin prehistory. Arkansas Archeologist 7:1-40.

Ferguson, Dick V. and James L. Gray
- 1971 Soil survey of Mississippi County, Arkansas. United States Department of Agriculture, Soil Conservation Service, Washington.

Firth, Raymond
- 1957 We, the Tikopia: kinship in primitive Polynesia. Boston: Beacon Press.

Fowler, Melvin L.
- 1969 The Cahokia site. Item *in:* Explorations into Cahokia archaeology, edited by Melvin L. Fowler. Illinois Archaeological Survey, Bulletin 7:1-30.

Fowler, Melvin L. and Robert L. Hall
- 1972 Archaeological phases at Cahokia. Illinois State Museum Research Series, Papers in Anthropology 1.

Griffin, James B.
- 1937 Saturday afternoon session, December 7, 1935: general. Item *in:* The Indianapolis archaeological conference, edited by Carl E. Guthe. National Research Council, Washington, (mimeographed).
- 1943 The Fort Ancient aspect: its cultural and chronological position in Mississippi Valley archaeology. University of Michigan Press, Ann Arbor.
- 1946 Cultural change and continuity in eastern United States archaeology. Item *in:* Man in northeastern North America, edited by F. Johnson. Papers of the Robert S. Peabody Foundation for Archaeology 3:37-75.

1952  Culture periods in eastern United States archaeology. Item *in:* archaeology of eastern United States, edited by James B. Griffin, pp. 352-64. Chicago: University of Chicago Press.

1967  Eastern North American archaeology: a summary. Science 156: 175-91.

Guilday, John E. and Paul W. Parmalee

1971  Thirteen-lined ground squirrel, prairie chicken and other vertebrates from an archaeological site in northeastern Arkansas. The American Midland Naturalist 68:227-29.

1975  Appendix I: faunal remains from the Zebree site. Item *in:* Report of excavations at the Zebree site 1969, by Dan F. Morse. Arkansas Archaeological Survey, Research Report 4.

Harding, Thomas G.

1967  Voyagers of the Vitiaz Strait: a study of a New Guinea trade system. Seattle: University of Washington Press.

Holmes, William H.

1903  Aboriginal pottery of the eastern United States. Bureau of American Ethnology 20th Annual Report for 1898-99:1-237.

Hopgood, J. F.

1969  Continuity and change in the Baytown pottery tradition. M.A. thesis, University of Missouri.

McKern, W. C.

1939  The midwestern taxonomic method as an aid to archaeological culture study. American Antiquity 4:301-13.

Maxwell, Moreau S.

1951  Woodland cultures in southern Illinois. Logan Museum Publications in Anthropology, Bulletin 7.

Meyers, J. Thomas

1971  The origins of agriculture: an evaluation of three hypotheses. Item *in:* Prehistoric Agriculture, edited by Stuart Struever, pp. 101-21. Garden City: Natural History Press.

Million, Michael G.

1974  Ceramic technology of the Nodena phase peoples (ca. A.D. 1400-1700). Paper presented at the 1974 meeting of the Southeastern Archaeological Conference, Atlanta.

Morse, Dan F.

1963  The Steuben village and mounds: a multicomponent late Hopewell site in Illinois. University of Michigan Museum of Anthropology, Anthropological Papers 21.

1969  Introducing northeastern Arkansas prehistory. Arkansas Archeologist 10:12-28.

1973a  Natives and anthropologists in Arkansas. Item *in:* Anthropology beyond the university, edited by Alden Redfield. Southern Anthropological Society, Proceedings 7:26-39.

1973b Nodena: an account of 75 years of archeological investigation in southeast Mississippi County, Arkansas. Arkansas Archeological Survey, Research Series 4.
1973c Zebree: a frontier site in the penetration of northeast Arkansas by the Mississippi stage. Arkansas Archeological Survey, University of Arkansas, (xeroxed).
1973d The 1973 field school excavations at Upper Nodena. Arkansas Archeological Society, Field Notes 106:3-8.
1974a Excavation strategy at the Armorel site. Arkansas Archeological Society, Field Notes 117:3-6.
1974b Armorel site lithics. Arkansas Archeological Society, Field Notes 117:10-11.
1974c The Cahokia microlith industry. Newsletter of Lithic Technology 3:15-19.
1975 Report of excavations at the Zebree site. Arkansas Archeological Survey, Research Report 4.

Morse, Dan F., Daniel G. Morse, and Daniel A. Morse
1974 A biconcave pottery discoidal from northwest Florida. Florida Anthropologist 27:59-61.

Moselage, John
1962 The Lawhorn site. Missouri Archaeologist 24.

Munson, Patrick J.
1966 An archaeological survey of the Wood River Terrace and adjacent bottoms and bluffs in Madison County, Illinois. Illinois State Museum, Preliminary Reports 8.

Munson, Patrick J. and Alan D. Harn
1971 An archaeological survey of the American Bottoms and Wood River terrace. Illinois State Museum, Reports of Investigation 21.

North, F. Chester
1975 Appendix II: determination of sodium and potassium in Nelumbo lutea. Item *in:* Report of excavations at the Zebree site, 1969, by Dan F. Morse, pp. 235-37. Arkansas Archaeological Survey, Research Report 4.

O'Brien, Patricia J.
1972 A formal analysis of Cahokia ceramics from the Powell tract. Illinois Archaeological Survey, Monograph 3.

Orr, Kenneth G. (Editor)
1950 Symposium on northern Mississippi Valley archaeology. Department of Anthropology, University of Chicago, and Illinois State Museum, Springfield, (mimoegraphed).

Perino, Gregory
1971 The Mississippi component at the Schild site (no. 4) Greene County, Illinois. Illinois Archaeological Survey, Bulletin 8:1-148.

Phillips, Philip
  1970 Archaeological survey in the lower Yazoo Basin, Mississippi, 1949-1955. Papers of the Peabody Museum of Archaeology and Ethnology, vol. 60.
Phillips, Philip, James A. Ford, and James B. Griffin
  1951 Archaeological survey in the lower Mississippi Alluvial Valley, 1940-1947. Papers of the Peabody Museum of Archaeology and Ethnology, vol. 25.
Piggott, Stuart
  1965 Ancient Europe from the beginnings of agriculture to classical antiquity. Chicago: Aldine.
Porter, James W.
  1969 The Mitchell site and prehistoric exchange systems at Cahokia: A.D. 1000±300. Item *in:* Explorations into Cahokia archaeology, edited by Melvin L. Fowler. Illinois Archaeological Survey, Bulletin 7:137-64.
Price, James E.
  1973 Settlement planning and artifact distribution on the Snodgrass site and their socio-political implications in the Powers phase of southeast Missouri. Ph.D. dissertation, University of Michigan.
Sahlins, Marshall D.
  1961 The segmentary lineage: an organization of predatory expansion. American Anthropologist 63:322-45.
  1968 Tribesmen. Englewood Cliffs: Prentice-Hall.
  1972 Stone age economics. Chicago: Aldine-Atherton.
Saucier, Roger T.
  1970 Origin of the St. Francis sunk lands, Arkansas and Missouri. Geological Society of America, Bulletin 81:2847-54.
Schultz, Harald
  1962 Brazil's big-lipped Indians. National Geographic 121:118-33.
Smith, Bruce
  1975 Middle Mississippian exploitation of animal populations. University of Michigan Museum of Anthropology, Anthropological Papers 57.
Stephenson, Lloyd W. and Albert F. Crider
  1916 Geology and ground waters of northeastern Arkansas. United States Geological Survey, Water Supply Paper 399.
Wauchope, Robert
  1956 Seminars in archaeology: 1955. Society for American Archaeology, Memoir 11.
Willey, Gordon R.
  1953 A pattern of diffusion-acculturation. Southwestern Journal of Anthropology 9:369-84.
  1966 An introduction to American archaeology, vol. 1: North and middle America. Englewood Cliffs: Prentice-Hall.

Williams, Raymond
    1968    Southeast Missouri land leveling salvage archaeology: 1967. National Park Service, Omaha, and Archaeological Research Division, University of Missouri, (offset).
    1972    Land leveling salvage archaeology in Missouri: 1968. National Park Service, Omaha, and Archaeological Research Division, University of Missouri, (offset).

Williams, Stephen
    1954    An archaeological study of the Mississippian culture in southeast Missouri. Unpublished Ph.D. dissertation. Department of Anthropology, Yale University.

Winters, Howard D.
    1969    An archaeological survey of the Wabash Valley in Illinois. Illinois State Museum, Reports of Investigations 10.

# THE EIGHTEENTH-CENTURY OVERHILL CHEROKEE

*Alfred K. Guthe*
University of Tennessee

For several anthropologists whose speciality is eastern North America, a perennial concern has been the explanation of the presence of the Cherokee in the Southern Appalachian area. The recognition of a linguistic relationship between the Cherokee and the northern Iroquois is probably the principal stimulus for this concern. Mooney was satisfied that tradition and historical evidence identified the early homeland of the Cherokee as the region around the headwaters of the Ohio River, or just south of the northern Iroquois region (Mooney, 1900:17). Archaeologists have not been able to support this view. Arthur Parker, from the available data, postulated that the Iroquois-speaking peoples had formerly lived in the middle Mississippi Valley near the mouth of the Ohio River and had migrated to the locations occupied when European contact took place (Parker, 1916: 503). A review of the more recent theories of Cherokee origins has been presented by Coe (1961:53-60).

Archaeologists and ethnologists believe that a linguistic relationship indicates an affinity that should be demonstrable in other cultural characteristics. Efforts to define the characteristics of each culture to permit comparative studies have been made. Students of the northern Iroquois met annually from 1945 to 1957 to share their research. A summary of these meetings was prepared by Fenton and Gulick (1961:3-7) in the foreword to papers presented during a symposium on Cherokee and Iroquois culture, held in 1958 to determine where such studies had led and to seek a consensus as to the direction of future studies. In evaluating the symposium, Fenton set forth the research needs in this field (1961:273-4). One of these was to document Iroquoian culture history, and emphasis was given to that of the northern Iroquois, but it was noted that it applied to Cherokee culture history as well. A part of this documentation will come from archaeology. It is the intent of this paper to present some data of value in ascertaining the culture history of the Cherokee.

Before summarizing data recovered through excavations in eighteenth-century Cherokee settlements, at least four significant contributions must be noted. In 1958, Caldwell defined several cultural traditions in the eastern United States. He also presented data in support of his premise that these traditions influenced one another even though each had developed in a separate region. The Middle Eastern Tradition was introduced into the southern piedmont from the north early in the first millenium B.C. (Caldwell, 1958:22-27); at about the same time the Southern Appalachian Tradition was developing in the southeast (Caldwell, 1958:34-52). These traditions interacted and modified each other. Caldwell concluded that the East, since the Archaic, "had been essentially a grand diffusion sphere." (1958:71). The diffusion indicates cultural contact and possibly population movements.

A second significant contribution was the hypothesis that the ceramic traditions of the northern Iroquois groups were derived from prehistoric types defined for the Lower Great Lakes region (MacNeish, 1952:89). This hypothesis could lead to the interpretation that the northern Iroquois had occupied their historic area since Woodland times. Of course, the language spoken at that prehistoric time cannot be determined; the identification of a cultural complex with a specific social unit that can be said to be ancestral to a social unit hundreds of years later is mere conjecture. However, cultural developments within the Lower Great Lakes area, although exhibiting variations, can be traced over a considerable period of time and are manifested in historic northern Iroqouis cultural assemblages. No migration of peoples or culture is needed to explain the presence of ceramic complexes in the area that are attributed to the Iroquois.

The third significant contribution relates to prehistoric cultural development in the historic Cherokee area. Dickens briefly summarized the development of thought leading to the premise that the Cherokee culture developed within the Southern Appalachian region (Dickens, 1974). He also described the three regional developments, some traits of which were present during A.D. 600-800, which were important in the synthesis of Cherokee culture. He concludes:

> I do not mean to imply that these developments can be identified solely with the Cherokee, nor that they were the only contributors to Cherokee culture as it was defined historically. I do propose, however, that within these three developments lies a Cherokee material-culture tradition, and that each development represents an important strain in that tradition (Dickens, 1974:30).

It has been suggested that the linguistic relationship between the northern Iroquois and the Cherokee was probably the principal reason for a concern with Cherokee origins. A report on a linguistic analysis constitutes the final significant contribution. An evaluation of the extent of phonetic, grammatical, and lexical change accruing to the Cherokee language has been made and, on the basis of glottochronologic counts, it is estimated that an effective split between Cherokee and other Iroquoian languages took place some 3,500 to 3,800 years ago (Lounsbury, 1961:11).

The implication of these several contributions is that a considerable period of time has elapsed during which cultural complexes developed in widely separated areas retaining some similarities and undergoing many changes. The determination of a basic Iroquois complex will have to follow studies of the culture histories in each of the regions. Perhaps, as Fenton says, determining the ultimate origin of the Cherokee and the northern Iroquois is not worth the effort. Rather, the focus should be on the parallel processes to be found in the history of the two groups (Fenton, 1961:258). In either case it is necessary to determine the complexes that constitute the prehistoric cultural complexes in these histories.

In the Southern Appalachian region traits that are found in the Cherokee culture at the time of European contact appeared about A.D. 600-800. By approximately A.D. 1000, three distinct regional developments were occurring in the historic Cherokee area (Dickens, 1974:10-11). These developments need to be defined with greater precision, and each one should be studied separately to determine its history before a comparison is attempted. Their relationship to the historically recognized Cherokee groups remains to be clearly demonstrated. During the eighteenth century three major Cherokee groups could be identified, referred to as the Lower Settlements, the Middle Settlements and the Overhill Settlements (Mooney, 1900:16-17; Swanton, 1952:215-29).

In accord with this concept, the characteristics of the Overhill Cherokee cultural complex, as based upon excavations conducted by the University of Tennessee in the lower valley of the Little Tennessee River, will be discussed here. The excavations began in 1967 and will continue until the Tellico Dam is completed by the Tennessee Valley Authority in 1977. Although the total range of Indian occupation in the valley is being investigated, a principal concern has been to identify a cultural complex attributable to the Overhill Cherokee who occupied the area during the eighteenth century. Other Overhill Cherokee settlements were located along the Tellico and Hiwassee Rivers at that time (Swanton, 1952:215-29). It does not appear that the Cherokee were in this area much before the beginning of the eighteenth century. The settlements seem to have been late extensions from the heart of Cherokee country (Lewis and Kneberg, 1946:16).

*The Eighteenth-Century Overhill Cherokee* 215

It was during this century that the British and their colonists were moving westward. The Overhill Cherokee were on the frontier, and British traders and military personnel were anxious to establish peaceful relations with them. In 1756, it was decided to build Fort Loudoun just above the mouth of the Tellico River to protect the settlements from possible French assault (Kelley, 1958:8). As on several frontiers, skirmishes between the Indian and British colonists took place; Fort Loudoun was destroyed by the Cherokee in 1760. One year later Henry Timberlake, a British colonial officer, was sent to reestablish peaceful relations. He spent part of 1761 and 1762 living in Overhill Cherokee villages and located several of them (Williams, 1927), on a map that he prepared. The sites of Citico (40MR7), Chota (40MR2) and Tomotley (40MR5) have been verified archaeologically. This paper is based on data obtained through excavations at the site of Chota, occupied from 1725 to 1798. Chota served as the capital of the Overhill Cherokee from 1755 to 1788 and was considered a "peace town," or town of refuge, wherein one guilty of a crime would be safe so long as he remained in the town (Mooney, 1900:207).

## Settlements

Overhill Cherokee towns were located in the broad bottom lands of the Little Tennessee River. The structures were placed on the natural levees, or river terraces, which run roughly parallel to the river, some of them being 500 to 700 feet from the stream. On the land side of the terraces there are lower lands which even today are flooded during wet seasons. Obviously, the Cherokee had selected the best drained land in the bottoms for their settlements. Because of the terrain the larger villages were stretched out along the river—the structures at Chota were distributed over a distance of almost a mile. The townhouse, or social center, was not located in the geographical center of the community at Chota, but there was a plaza just west of the townhouse.

No alignment of structures has been noted. Our findings support those of contemporary observers who wrote of "scattered Indian dwellings" (Williams, 1928:464). The concentrations of postmolds that have been recorded doubtless mark the locations of structures, but there are overlapping patterns and obvious intrusions of one pattern into another. The historic records indicate that the number of structures in a village varied through time. At Chota there were 52 houses in 1761, 30 in 1784 and only five houses by 1797 when many Cherokee had moved westward (Royce, 1886:144, 151, 204).

216                     *Alfred K. Guthe*

The scattered placement of structures has made it difficult to determine the limits of a village. A glance at the topography would lead one to expect a community to be identified with one relatively flat section of the alluvial bottomland. Timberlake's map, however, indicates that two villages, separated by streams of modest size, existed simultaneously in some of the extensive bottoms.

## Structures

The Overhill Cherokee were familiar with more than one type of structure, and different structural types may have served different purposes. Circular structures were recorded at Chota and Tomotley. Indeed, preliminary data from the 1974 effort at Chota suggests that circular structures were favored. Some of them served as dwellings (Fig. 1). Structure 5 was 23 feet in diameter, with four central support posts set in a square eight feet on a side and with a central hearth. The walls were once covered with daub placed over split wooden lath-like elements. Broken pottery vessels were recovered on its floor (Gleeson, 1970:122-23).

Figure 1. Postmold Pattern of Circular Structure, Chota.

A structure judged to be the townhouse was located on what is now the highest land in the Chota village area. In the center of an octagonal postmold pattern almost 60 feet in diameter there was a hearth, which seems to have been the site of a fire over a long period, since the soil was fire-reddened within a circle about five feet in diameter. An open area surrounded the hearth. Then eight large support posts had been placed about 10 feet apart to form a rough circle. At least one of these posts had been replaced or stabilized, for several large stones had been placed in a hole adjacent to it. The area between these support posts and the walls was filled with smaller postmolds, which probably supported bench-like seats to form an amphitheater (Gleeson, 1970:124-27). Henry Timberlake, who visited Chota in 1761-62, describes the townhouse he saw as follows:

> The townhouse, in which are transacted all public business and diversions, is raised with wood, and covered over with earth, and has all the appearance of a small mountain at a little distance. It is built in the form of a sugar loaf, and large enough to contain 500 persons, but extremely dark, having besides the door, which is so narrow that but one at a time can pass, and that after much winding and turning, but one small aperture to let the smoak out, which is so ill contrived that most of it settles in the roof of the house. Within it has the appearance of an ancient amphitheatre, the seats being raised one above another, leaving an area in the middle, in the center of which stands the fire; the seats of the head warriors are nearest it (Williams, 1927:59).

Laboratory inspection of the postmold plot led to the identification of a second, smaller structure, its hearth only 5.5 feet from that of the larger structure. Archeomagnetic samples collected by David Thorn, Earth Sciences Observatory, Norman, Oklahoma from each of these hearths indicated that they were separated by 25 years in time. An important fact is that there was no evidence of any attempt to build a mound of earth over the earlier floor. The Cherokee, in this instance, did not adhere to the usual Mississippian practice of separating one floor from another by clean soil (Fig. 2).

Log cabins were situated in the area by 1784 (Williams, 1928:260). Malone boldly states that the aboriginal house had been replaced by the log cabin in 1775 (Malone, 1956:12). Postmold patterns and other evidence at Chota may indicate the location of two such structures close to the river (Gleeson, 1970:120-21). One pattern consisted of 8 postmolds forming a 10x15 foot rectangle (Fig. 3). The Starnes Site (40MR32), occupied during the late eighteenth and early nineteenth centuries, also provided evidence of what was probably a log cabin (Salo, 1969:177).

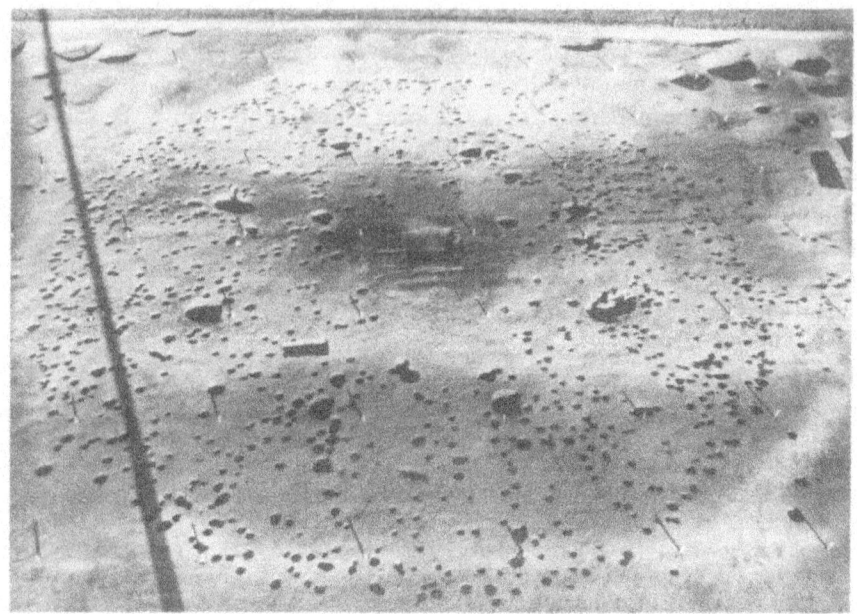

Figure 2. Postmold Pattern of Chota Townhouses. Stakes are at Ten Foot Intervals.

Several structures were surrounded by additional features. These included small shallow pits containing charred corn cobs, pits filled with refuse, and burial pits. An oval pit form which recurred near several structures had a postmold in the bottom at each of the narrow ends. In one of these, at Chota, the articulated skeleton of a dog was found. Its back was against one of the longer sides of the pit. The pits may have been used for food storage, with vertically placed posts serving as supports for a ridgepole. Smaller poles could then have been placed against the ridgepole to form a roof.

The location of this cultural data suggests that family life was centered around the structure in which they lived. Refuse found in the pits included corn and the bones of deer, bear, birds, turtle and fish as well as cow and pig. Additional refuse consisted of abandoned or lost utensils such as iron clasp knives, axes and gun parts. Articles associated with horsemanship were recovered. An abundance of pottery fragments testifies to the continuing production of fragile native-made vessels despite the introduction of more durable metal kettles.

Figure 3. White Spots Mark the Postmold Pattern of Log Cabin. Strucure 2, Chota.

## Ceramics

The native pottery recovered from Overhill Cherokee sites and attributable to the Cherokee occupation is predominantly shell-tempered; these types are referred to as the Overhill Series. Grit-tempered types which occur are mainly of the Qualla Series. Some sherds exhibit shell-grit-clay tempering.

The ceramic sample recovered at the Chota Site during two field seasons (1969 and 1970) can be used to characterize the eighteenth-century ceramic complex at Overhill Cherokee sites. The Overhill Series consisted of 51,728 sherds, or 97 percent of the sample; the Qualla Series is represented by 1,186 sherds or two percent of the sample; shell-grit-clay tempered sherds totaled 167, or less than one percent of the sample. Within the Overhill Series 98 percent of the sherds were classified as Overhill Plain (Gleeson, 1971:Table 1). The surface treatment consisted of scraping or smoothing. Vessel forms include bowls, jars and pans. The rim treatment

Figure 4. Overhill Plain Rim Sherd.

varies, but a folded rim strip with notching at its base is the most common (Fig. 4; King, 1970:61-64).

Additional Overhill types are distinguished primarily on the basis of surface treatment and decorating techniques. These include: Check Stamped, Complicated Stamped, Residual Stamped, Roughened, fabric impression, cane impressions and incised lines (Fig. 5; Gleeson, 1970:53-56).

The Qualla Series is a minority series in the Overhill Cherokee ceramic sample. Its presence in the lower portion of the Little Tennessee Valley may indicate a continuation of a ceramic tradition or contact with the Cherokee in the Lower and Middle Settlements (Fig. 6).

Figure 5. Overhill Complicated Stamped Sherds.

Figure 6. Qualla Check Stamped Rim Sherd.

Of the small sample (167 sherds) of shell-grit-clay tempered pottery recovered during two field seasons at Chota, 20 sherds represent the Fatherland Incised type (Quimby, 1942:263-64), a type associated with the Natchez of Mississippi.

## Burials

Data on Cherokee burial customs was obtained from the sites of Citico and Chota. Inhumation in the flesh in an elongated oval pit was the usual practice. The burial position was partly flexed. Usually the knees were bent so that the feet were under the pelvis. The arms were placed with the hands by the face, or near the knees. Three individuals buried near the townhouse had been placed in the fully extended position, and it is thought they reflect Christian influence. One of these may be a noted war chief, Oconastota, who died in 1783 and requested burial at Chota in a dugout canoe (King and Olinger, 1972). A demographic analysis of the burials indicates that the sexes were equally represented. A number of burials were those of children (Gleeson, 1971:Table 17).

Burial accompaniments were frequent. Children were more frequently found with grave goods than adults. Both trade and native items including tools, weapons and ornaments were placed in the graves. One interesting grave association was a cluster of twelve brass points which had been cut from kettles and attached to shafts. Evidently the shafts were of arrows since the placement leads to the conclusion that a quiverful had been placed at the shoulder of the deceased (Fig. 7).

There was no evidence to indicate that burials were confined to a specific area, or cemetery, for Cherokee burials were encountered in or near structures.

## Stone

An inventory of the chipped stone artifacts from the sites occupied by the Overhill Cherokee would be misleading because a large portion of the specimens were recovered in the plow zone. On a typological basis the projectile points range from Archaic to Historic. Of the 292 identifiable projectile points recovered during the 1969 and 1970 seasons at Chota, only 36 were recovered from features, postmolds, burials or burial pit fill. Only five knives were found in a useful context.

The projectile points have been classified as Madison or Mississippian Triangular types. The Madison point is triangular with straight to excurvate edges and a base which ranges from incurvate to excurvate. The Mississippian Triangular point displays a long, narrow blade with excurvate edges (Fig. 8). The fact that chipped stone artifacts were not numerous can be readily explained by the presence of gun parts and equipment and of cutting implements of metal.

Additional stone articles of native manufacture associated with the Cherokee occupation include pipes for tobacco fashioned from slate or steatite. Many fragments were found in the townhouse area, but at least one accompanied a burial (Fig. 9). Two chunky stones were found in the townhouse area at Chota (Gleeson, 1970:76).

## Floral and Faunal Material

The analysis of this material remains to be completed. Corn, beans and peaches were represented. Deer and bear, small mammals, birds, turtles and some fish have been identified. Domesticated forms include dogs, pigs and cows. The recovery of metal objects which were parts of bridles may indicate the presence of horses.

Figure 7. Burial 5, Chota, with Brass Points at Shoulder.

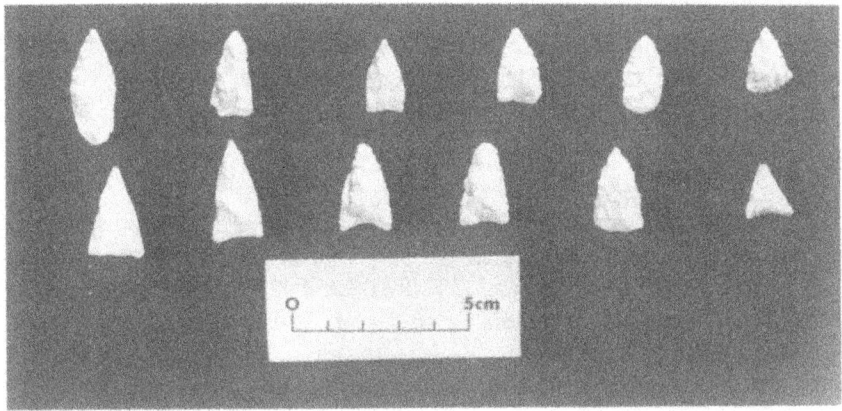

Figure 8. Projectile Points from Chota. Top Row: Mississippian Triangular. Bottom Row: Madison. A Coat of White Gouache was applied with Air Brush to Heighten Contrast.

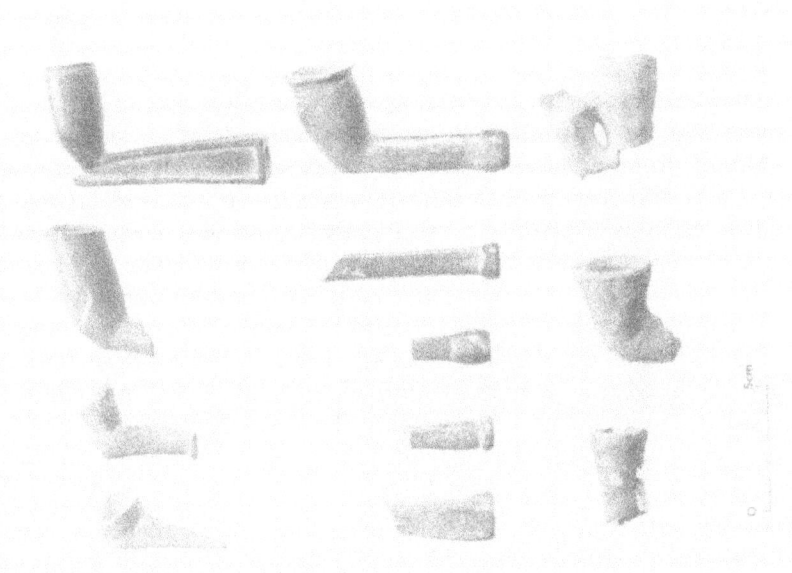

Figure 9. Stone and Pottery Pipes. The Pottery Pipes are in the right hand column.

The three most common types of shell found with the occupational debris were *Obliquaria reflexa, Pleurocera* (snail), and *Pleurobema* (mussel). Conch shell beads and oyster shell beads were also recovered (Gleeson, 1970:100-102; Gleeson, 1971:79-80).

## Trade Materials

An itemized list and description of the variety of artifacts and fragments received in trade with the British can be found in the published reports by Salo (1969:50-52) and Gleeson (1970:81-96; 1971:59-74). These can be grouped in terms of materials: iron, glass, brass, silver, pewter, lead, European ceramics and kaolin; or by artifact types, including axes, gun parts, kettle fragments, buttons, ornaments, needles, fishhooks, nails, scissors, jews'-harps, bracelets, projectile points, knives, and containers. The artifact types conform to those from the period 1725-1800, with the exception of some European ceramics that date to the early nineteenth century (Gleeson, 1971:59). Many of these were utilitarian objects selected by the Cherokee as replacements for their less efficient and less durable native products. The gun, for example, was readily adopted for use in hunting.

## Summary

A review of some studies relating to the development of the northern Iroquois and the Cherokee indicates that characteristics of each group can be derived from prehistoric cultural complexes in their respective areas. This review also suggests that cultural trends in the southeast as well as a linguistic analysis support the premise that these two Iroquoian-speaking groups became separated during the first millenium B.C. The long-held view that the Cherokee were recent immigrants into Southern Appalachia is no longer tenable. Instead of a study to seek evidence of the ultimate origin of the Cherokee and the northern Iroquois, one concerned with the processes which produced the Southern Appalachian culture and the culture of northern Iroquois should be undertaken. However, further work is required to determine the culture histories of both groups, considering the regional developments which took place in each of the respective areas, before a comparison of them can be undertaken. The persistence of a linguistic relationship has contributed to the formulation of an oversimplified hypothesis.

In order to comprehend the regional developments in each area it will be necessary to examine and define carefully the several stages of development. This paper has attempted to define the eighteenth-century stage of Overhill Cherokee culture. It summarizes information recovered during several field seasons in the eastern Tennessee area and provides some comparative material on settlements, structures, ceramics and burial practices. Overhill Cherokee villages were located in the river bottoms where the soil was well drained and the adjacent land suitable for the cultivation of corn. Nearby higher terrain provided other food resources. Structures were placed at random throughout the settlement. Dwellings were of two types. One was a circular structure built of vertically-placed poles covered with a latticework and then local clay. Four centrally-placed posts served as roof supports. A second structure was rectangular and may have resembled an arbor, or shade, in appearance. At least one townhouse was octagonal and conformed with those observed among the Creek by Bartram (Swanton, 1946:402). Native pottery was almost exclusively shell-tempered. The majority of the vessels were prepared with a plain surface finish, although some check stamping and complicated-stamping occurs. Burials were flexed inhumations placed in oval pits near dwellings.

It is evident that the Cherokee were long resident in the Southern Appalachian region and shared in the development of the typical Southeastern cultural pattern. The process by which this developed must be determined before attempts to define a common cultural origin for Iroquoian-speaking peoples are begun.

## References Cited

Caldwell, J. R.
    1958   Trend and tradition in the prehistory of the eastern United States. Memoirs of the American Anthropological Association 88.
Coe, J. L.
    1961   Cherokee archaeology. Item *in:* Symposium on Cherokee and Iroquois cultures, edited by W. N. Fenton and J. Gulick. Bureau of American Ethnology, Bulletin 180:53-60.
Dickens, R. S., Jr.
    1974   The origins and development of Cherokee culture. Paper presented at Ninth Annual Meeting of the Southern Anthropological Society, Blacksburg, Virginia.
Fenton, W. N.
    1961   Iroquoian culture history: a general evaluation. Item *in:* Symposium on Cherokee and Iroquois cultures, edited by W. N. Fenton and J. Gulick. Bureau of American Ethnology, Bulletin 180: 257-77.

Fenton, W. N., and J. Gulick (Editors)
　1961　Symposium on Cherokee and Iroquois culture. Bureau of American Ethnology, Bulletin 180.
Gleeson, P. (Editor)
　1970　Archaeological investigations in the Tellico Reservoir, interim report, 1969. Department of Anthropology, University of Tennessee Report of Investigations 8.
　1971　Archaeological investigations in the Tellico Reservoir, interim report, 1970. Department of Anthropology, University of Tennessee Report of Investigations 9.
Kelley, P.
　1958　Historic Fort Loudoun. Fort Loudoun Association, Vonore, Tennessee.
King, D. H.
　1970　Pottery. Item *in:* Archaeological investigations in the Tellico Reservoir, interim report, 1969, edited by P. Gleeson. Department of Anthropology, University of Tennessee Report of Investigations 8, pp. 52-64.
King, D. H. and D. E. Olinger
　1972　Oconastota. Item *In:* Reports. American Antiquity 37:222-28.
Lewis, T. M. N., and M. Kneberg
　1946　Hiwassee Island. Knoxville: Univ. of Tennessee Press.
Lounsbury, F. G.
　1961　Iroquois-Cherokee linguistic relations. Item *in:* Symposium on Cherokee and Iroquois cultures, edited by W. N. Fenton and J. Gulick. Bureau of American Ethnology, Bulletin 180:9-17.
MacNeish, R. S.
　1952　Iroquois pottery types: A technique for the study of Iroquois prehistory. National Museum of Canada Bulletin 124.
Malone, Henry T.
　1956　Cherokees of the Old South. Athens, Georgia.
Mooney, J.
　1900　Myths of the Cherokee. Bureau of American Ethnology, Annual Report 19 (pt. 1):3-548.
Parker, A. C.
　1916　Origin of the Iroquois as suggested by their archaeology. American Anthropologist, n.s. 18:479-507.
Quimby, G. I.
　1942　The Natchezan culture type. American Antiquity 7:255-75.
Royce, C. C.
　1887　The Cherokee nation of Indians. Bureau of American Ethnology Annual Report 5:121-378.
Salo, L. V. (Editor)
　1969　Archaeological investigations in the Tellico Reservoir, Tennessee,

1967-1968, an interim report. Department of Anthropology, University of Tennessee.

Swanton, J. R.
1946 The Indians of the southeastern United States. Bureau of American Ethnology, Bulletin 137.
1952, The Indian tribes of North America. Bureau of American Ethnology, Bulletin 145.

Williams, S. C. (Editor)
1927 Lieut. Timberlake's memoirs. Johnson City: The Watauga Press.
1928 Early travels in the Tennessee country, 1540-1800. Johnson City: The Watauga Press.

# WOMEN ON THE LOWER COLUMBIA RIVER IN THE EARLY NINETEENTH CENTURY

*George I. Quimby*
The University of Washington

A number of different cultural groups lived in the Lower Columbia River Valley in the early nineteenth century. There was not only the local indigenous culture of the Lower Chinook tribes (Chinook, Clatsop, and Shoalwater Chinook) but also the European culture manifested by the Scottish, Irish, English, French Canadian, and American (United States) fur traders. Other exotic additions were the cultures of Plateau Indians, French Canadian voyageurs, Iroquois Indians from Eastern Canada, Algonkian and Siouan speaking Indians from the Upper Mississippi Valley and the northern Great Lakes region, and, most exotic of all, the Polynesian culture of the Hawaiians (Quimby, 1972).

Elsewhere and in other frames of reference I have written of people, things, and events in the Columbia River Valley in the era of the fur trade. In the course of my research I became aware of the unusually abundant (considering the time and place) amount of information about women. Here, it is my intent to assemble and to order data concerning women and their various roles among the people of the Lower Columbia River in the period from 1811 to 1821. These data are found principally in the narratives of educated employees of Canadian and American fur companies operating out of Astoria.

Astoria, the center of the fur trade on the Columbia, was established in 1811 by representatives of the Pacific Fur Company owned by the New York merchant, John Jacob Astor. In the autumn of 1813, a time of war between England and the United States, the North West Company, owned by Canadians, was able to purchase on excellent terms the trading establishment and all the supplies of the Pacific Fur Company. The North West Company men promptly changed the name of Astoria to Fort George.

In the vicinity of Astoria—Fort George there lived the aforementioned Chinook Indians. Ross Cox, an Irishman in the employ of Astor's Pacific

Fur Company saw these Indians for the first time in 1812 and recorded a highly prejudiced view of them, one probably typical of the European fur traders.

> They were most uncouth-looking objects; and not strongly calculated to impress us with a favourable opinion of aboriginal beauty, or the purity of Indian manners. A few of the men were partially covered, but the greater number were unannoyed by vestments of any description. Their eyes were black, piercing, and treacherous; their ears slit up, and ornamented with strings of beads; the cartilage of their nostrils perforated, and adorned with pieces of *hyaquau* [dentalium shells] placed horizontally; while their heads presented an inclined plane from the crown to the upper part of the nose, totally unlike our European rotundity of cranium; and their bodies besmeared with whale oil [fish oil], gave them an appearance horribly disgusting. Then the women,—Oh ye gods! With the same auricular, olfactory, and craniological peculiarities, they exhibited loose hanging breasts, short dirty teeth, skin saturated with blubber, bandy legs, and a waddling gait; while their only dress consisted of a kind of petticoat, or rather kilt formed of small strands of cedar bark twisted into cords, and reaching from the waist to the knee. This covering in calm weather, or in an erect position, served all the purposes of concealment; but in a breeze, or when indulging their favourite position of squatting, formed a miserable shield in defence of decency: and worse than all, their repulsive familiarities rendered them objects insupportably odious; particularly when contrasted with the lively eyes, handsome features, fine teeth, open countenance, and graceful carriage of the interesting islanders [Hawaiian women] whom we had lately left (Cox, 1832: 69-70).

The French-Canadian fur trader, Gabriel Franchère, who served with the Pacific Fur Company for three years and was one of the founders of Astoria, also recorded his observations of the local Indians. He seems to have been more perceptive and less prejudiced than Ross Cox. Moreover, Franchère had learned enough of the language to communicate directly with the Indians.

According to Gabriel Franchère (1854: 240-45),

> The natives inhabiting on the Columbia ... are, generally speaking, of low stature, few of them passing five feet six inches, and many not even five feet. ... we were exceedingly surprised to see that they had almost all flattened heads. This configuration is not a natural deformity, but an effect of art, caused by compression of the skull in infancy. It shocks strangers extremely, especially at first sight; nevertheless, among these barbarians it is an indispensable ornament: and when we signified to them how much this mode of flattening the forehead appeared to us to violate nature and good taste, they answered that it was only slaves who had not their heads flattened. The slaves, in fact, have the usual rounded head, and they are not permitted to flatten the foreheads of their children. The natives ... procure these slaves from the neighboring tribes and from the interior, in exchange for beads and furs. They treat them with humanity while

their services are useful, but as soon as they become incapable of labor, neglect them and suffer them to perish of want. The Indians ... are of a light copper color, active in body, and, above all, excellent swimmers ... they make no scruple of laying hands on whatever suits them in the property of strangers. ... The goods and effects of European manufacture are so precious in the eyes of these barbarians, that they rarely resist the temptation of stealing them.

The men go entirely naked, not concealing any part of their bodies. Only in winter they threw over the shoulders a panther's skin, or else a sort of mantle made of the skins of wood-rats sewed together. In rainy weather I have seen them wear a mantle of rush mats, like a Roman toga, or the vestment which a priest wears in celebrating mass; thus equipped, and furnished with a conical hat made from fibrous roots and impermeable, they may call themselves rain-proof.

The women, in addition to the mantle of skins, wear a petticoat made of the cedar bark, which they attach round the girdle, and which reaches to the middle of the thigh. It is a little longer behind than before, and is fabricated in the following manner: They strip off the fine bark of the cedar, soak it as one soaks hemp, and when it is drawn out into fibres, work it into a fringe; then with a strong cord they bind the fringes together. With so poor a vestment they contrive to satisfy the requirements of modesty; when they stand it drapes them fairly enough; and when they squat down in their manner, it falls between their legs, leaving nothing exposed but the bare knees and thighs. Some of the younger women twist the fibres of bark into small cords knotted at the ends, and so form the petticoat disposed in a fringe, like the first, but more easily kept clean and of better appearance.

Cleanliness is not a virtue among these females, who, in that respect, resemble the other Indian women of the continent. They anoint the body and dress the hair with fish oil, which does not diffuse an agreeable perfume. Their hair (which both sexes wear long) is jet black; it is badly combed, but parted in the middle ..., and kept shining by the fish-oil before mentioned. Sometimes, in imitation of the men, they paint the whole body with a red earth mixed with fish oil. Their ornaments consist of bracelets of brass, which they wear indifferently on the wrists and ankles; of strings of beads of different colors (they give a preference to the blue), and display in great profusion around the neck, and on the arms and legs; and of white shells called *Haiqua* [Dentalium shells], which are their ordinary circulating medium.

Although a little less slaves than the greater part of the Indian women elsewhere, the women on the Columbia are, nevertheless, charged with the most painful labors; they fetch water and wood, and carry the goods in their frequent changes of residence; they clean the fish and cut it up for drying; they prepare the food and cook the fruits in their season. Among their principal occupations is that of making rush mats, baskets for gathering roots, and hats very ingeniously wrought. As they want little clothing, they do not sew much, and the men have the needle in hand oftener than they.

Franchère had more to say about the women's preparation of food:

The kitchen utensils consist of plates of ashwood, bowls of fibrous roots, and a wooden kettle; with these they succeed in cooking their fish and meat in less time than we take with the help of pots and stewpans. See how they do it! Having heated a number of stones red-hot, they plunge them, one by one, in the vessel which is to contain the food to be prepared; as soon as the water boils they put in the fish or meat, with some more heated stones on top, and cover up the whole with small rush mats, to retain the steam. In an incredibly short space of time the article is taken out and placed on a wooden platter, perfectly done and very palatable. The broth is taken out also, with a ladle of wood or horn (1854:248).

The foreign women who visited or lived for some time in the Lower Columbia Valley were a most interesting lot. Among them were Indian women from the Inter Mountain tribes east of the Cascades, Iroquois, Siouan, and Algonkian women from eastern North America, at least one Hawaiian woman, and an English woman from Bath.

The Hawaiian lady's visit was brief. She accompanied a man in the employ of Astor's American Fur Company. Fur trader Ross Cox wrote of this as follows: "Mr. Wadsworth, of whom I have already spoken, was also engaged for the Company's service, to act as an officer on sea or land, as occasion should require. He brought his [Hawaiian] lady with him, not being accustomed, as he declared, to live in a state of single blessedness" (Cox, 1832:51). The *Beaver* left Hawaii April 6, 1812 and came to anchor in Baker's Bay near Astoria on May 1. The Hawaiian lady and Mr. Wadsworth left the Columbia River aboard the *Beaver* on August 4.

The English woman from Bath was unique in the annals of Astoria. She arrived at Astoria (then Fort George) on April 17, 1813 after a thirteen-month voyage from England aboard the North West Company Ship, *Isaac Todd*. Other passengers included the proprietors, Donald M'Tavish and John M'Donald and four clerks.

Ross Cox recorded many interesting aspects of her visit.

> The two [proprietors] ... brought out another object which more strongly recalled to our semi-barbarized ideas the thoughts of our "dear native home," than all the other *bonnes choses* contained in the vessel. This was neither more nor less than a flaxen-haired, blue-eyed daughter of Albion, who, in a temporary fit of erratic enthusiasm, had consented to become *le compagnon du voyage* of Mr. Mac-.
>
> Miss Jane Barnes had been a lively bar-maid at an hotel in Portsmouth, at which Mr. Mac- had stopped preparatory to his embarkation. This gentleman being rather of an amorous temperament, proposed the trip to Miss Jane who, "nothing loath," threw herself on his protection, regardless of consequences, and after encountering the perils of a long sea-voyage, found herself an object of interest to the residents at the fort, and the greatest curiosity that ever gratified the wondering eyes of the blubber-loving aboriginals of the north-west coast of America. The Indians daily thronged in numbers to our fort, for the purpose of gazing on and admiring the fair beauty, every article of whose dress was examined with the most minute scrutiny. She had rather an extravagant wardrobe, and each day exhibited her in a

new dress, which she always managed in a manner to display her figure to the best advantage. One day, her head decorated with feathers and flowers, produced the greatest surprise; the next, her hair, braided and unconcealed by any covering, excited equal wonder and admiration.

The young [Indian] women felt almost afraid to approach her, and the old were highly gratified at being permitted to touch her person. Some of the chiefs having learned that her protector intended to send her home, thought to prevent such a measure by making proposal of marriage. One of them in particular, the son of Comcomly, the principal chief of the Chinooks, came to the fort attired in his richest dress, his face fancifully bedaubed with red paint, and his body redolent with whale oil. He was young, and had four native wives. He told her, that if she would become his wife, he would send one hundred sea-otters to her relations; that he would never ask her to carry wood, draw water, dig for roots, or hunt for provisions; that he would make her mistress over his other wives, and permit her to sit at her ease from morning to night, and wear her own clothes (meaning that he would not insist on her wearing the light covering of the Indian females); that she should always have abundance of fat salmon, anchovies, and elk, and be allowed to smoke as many pipes of tobacco during the day as she thought proper; together with many other flattering inducements, the tithe of which would have shaken the constancy of a score of the chastest brown vessels that ever flourished among the tribes of the lower Columbia.

These tempting offers, however, had no charms for Jane. Her long voyage had not yet eradicated certain Anglican predilections respecting mankind, which she had contracted in the country of her birth, and among which she did not include a flat head, a half-naked body, or a copper-coloured skin besmeared with whale oil. Her native inamorato made several other ineffectual proposals; but finding her inflexible, he declared he would never more come near the fort while she remained there. We shortly afterward learned that he had concerted a plan with some daring young men of his tribe to carry her off while she was walking on the beach (her general custom every evening while the gentlemen were at dinner), a practice which, after this information, she was obliged to discontinue.

Miss Barnes was fond of quotations; but she was no *Blue*. One of the clerks was one day defending the native and half-bred women, whose characters she had violently attacked, and he recriminated in no very measured language on the conduct of the white ladies: "O Mr. Mac!" said she, "I suppose you agree with *Shakespeare*, that 'Every woman is at heart a rake?' " – "Pope, ma'am, if you please." – "Pope! Pope!" replied Jane. "Bless me, sir! you must be wrong; *rake* is certainly the word. I never heard of but one female pope." Then in order to terminate the argument, she pretended to read an old newspaper which she held in her hand. He quickly discovered by her keeping the wrong end uppermost that she did not know a syllable of its contents. He quitted her abruptly; and as he was coming out I met him at the door, a wicked and malicious grin ruffling his sunburnt features. "Well, Mac," said I, "what's the matter? You seem annoyed." – "What do you think?" he replied; "I have just had a conversation with that fine-looking damsel there, who looks down with such contempt on our women, and may I be d-d if she understands B from a buffalo!" Her supposed education was the only excuse in his opinion to justify her usurpation of superiority; that gone he judged her "poor indeed."

"Mr. Mac [the proprietor, not the clerk] at first intended to have brought her with him across the continent to Montreal; but on learning the impracticability of her performing such an arduous journey, he abandoned that idea, and made arrangements with the captain for her return to England by way of Canton [China]. ... On the arrival of the vessel at Canton, she became an object of curiosity and admiration among the inhabitants of the "Celestial Empire." An English gentleman of great wealth, connected with the East India Company, offered her a splendid establishment. It was infinitely superior to any of the proposals made by the Chinook nobility, and far beyond anything she could ever expect in England: it was therefore prudently accepted, and the last account I heard of her stated that she was then enjoying all the luxuries of eastern magnificence (1832:140-41).

Miss Barnes and the aforementioned Hawaiian woman, each of whom was basically an ornament and an entertainer, are in sharp contrast with the skillful and hard-working Indian women of the Lower Columbia. Less of a contrast but perhaps of greater interest were the Iroquoian, Siouan, and Algonkian women from eastern North America and two particular Plateau Indian women, one of whom played the role of a man.

The manly-hearted woman and her female companion were of the Kutenai nation in the northern Plateau area. Their visit to Astoria was recorded by Gabriel Franchère:

On the 15th [June, 1811] some natives from up the river, brought us two strange Indians, a man and a woman. They were not attired like the savages on the river Columbia, but wore long robes of dressed deer-skin, with leggings and moccasins in the fashion of the tribes to the east of the Rocky Mountains. We put questions to them in various Indian dialects; but they did not understand us. They showed us a letter addressed to *"Mr. John Stuart, Fort Estekatadene, New Caledonia.."* Mr. Pillet than addressing them in the *Knisteneaux* [Cree] language, they answered, although they appeared not to understand it perfectly. Notwithstanding, we learned from them that they had been sent by a Mr. Finnan M'Donald, a clerk in the service of the Northwest Company, and who had a post on a river which they called *Spokan*; that having lost their way, they had followed the course of the ... Columbia, that when they arrived at the Falls, the natives made them understand that there were white men at the mouth of the river and not doubting that the person to whom the letter was addressed would be found there, they had come to deliver it.

We kept these messengers for some days, and having drawn from them important information respecting the country in the interior, west of the Mountains, we decided to send an expedition thither, under the command of Mr. David Stewart; and the 15th July was fixed for its departure (1854:118-19).

Their departure was interrupted by the arrival of Mr. David Thompson of the Northwest Company in a canoe bearing the British flag and manned by eight voyageurs. According to Franchère, Mr. Thompson "recognized the two Indians who had brought the letter addressed to Mr. J. Stuart, and told us that they were two women, one of whom had dressed herself as a man, to travel with more security" (Franchère, 1854:122).

The manly-hearted Kutenai woman (whose name was Qánqon) played the roles of courier, guide, husband, prophet, and warrior. Anthropologist Claude E. Schaeffer (1965:193-236) has written a detailed account of her life from 1811 to 1837. "During these years, according to Schaeffer, "she dressed in masculine garb and lived as 'husband' of a succession of individuals of her own sex." She was a person of prominence among the Kutenai and a peace mediator between the Flathead and Blackfoot in 1837, in which year she was killed by Blackfoot.

Qánqon and wife were among the traders and explorers who left Astoria on July 22, 1811 and started up the Columbia River. Alexander Ross of the Pacific Fur Company wrote of them:

> In accompanying us, they sometimes shot ahead, and at other times loitered behind, as suited their plans. The stories they gave out among the nonsuspecting and credulous natives as they passed, were well calculated to astonish as well as to attract attention. ... they were capable of practicing all the arts of well-instructed cheats; and to effect their purpose the better, they showed the Indians an old letter, ... and told them that they had been sent by the great white chief, with a message to apprize the natives in general that gifts, consisting of goods and implements of all kinds, were forthwith to be poured in upon them; that the great white chief knew their wants, and was just about to supply them with everything their hearts could desire; that the whites had hitherto cheated the Indians, by selling goods in place of making presents to them, as directed.... These stories, so agreeable to the Indian ear, were circulated far and wide; and not only received as truths, but procured so much celebrity for the two cheats, that they were the objects of attraction at every village and camp on the way; nor could we, for a long time, account for the cordial reception they met with from the natives, who loaded them for their good tidings with the most valuable articles they possessed— horses, robes, leather, and higuas [Dentalium shells]; so that, on our arrival at Oakinacken, they had no less than twenty-six horses, many of them loaded with the fruits of their false reports (1849:144-45).

To reap these rewards of her message and oratory the manly-hearted Kutenai woman must have been able to communicate in a number of languages, among which would have been Cree, Blackfoot, Chinook, Kutenai, Flathead, Okanagon, and various other Salish languages of Indians in the Plateau area. With their newly acquired riches Qánqon and wife disappeared, temporarily at least, into the hazy mists of history.

In 1825 Qánqon was recognized as a person of importance in a band of Kutenai who were trading at a Hudson's Bay Company post among the Flathead. The Bay Company trader knew that she was a woman in male attire and noted that, as interpreter, she spoke Flathead well (Schaeffer, 1965:213-14).

The manly-hearted woman died in 1837 while attempting to save a party of Flathead outnumbered and surrounded by the Blackfoot. As mediator between the Flathead and Blackfoot, she made a number of trips back and forth to both camps; in the end she was killed because she had deceived the Blackfoot while the Flathead were making their escape to Fort Hall (Schaeffer, 1965:214-15).

We have another example of great bravery and strength of character in an Iowa Indian woman from the Upper Mississippi Valley. She was the wife of Pierre Dorion, son of a French Canadian "Creole" and a Sioux woman. Dorion and his wife were part of Wilson P. Hunt's party that went overland from St. Louis to Astoria in 1811-12, Dorion serving the Astor party first as interpreter and hunter and later as a trapper. Of his hiring, Washington Irving (Vol. I, 1836:233-34) worte, "The greatest difficulty was to procure the Sioux interpreter. There was but one man to be met with at St. Louis who was fitted for the purpose ... The individual in question was a half-breed named Pierre Dorion. . . ." Pierre agreed to serve only if he could bring his Indian wife and child along and this was agreed to.

On the 29th of December, 1811 Mrs. Dorion gave birth to a child, an event also described by Washington Irving:

> Early in the following morning the squaw of Pierre Dorion, who had hitherto kept on without murmuring or flinching, was suddenly taken in labour, and enriched her husband with another child. As the fortitude and good conduct of the poor woman had gained for her the good will of the party, her situation caused concern and perplexity. Pierre, however, treated the matter as an occurrence that could soon be arranged and need cause no delay. He remained by his wife in the camp, with his other children [child] and his horse, and promised soon to rejoin the main body, who proceeded on their march.
> In the course of the following morning the Dorion family made its reappearance. Pierre came trudging in the advance, followed by his valued, though skeleton steed, on which was mounted his squaw with the newborn infant in her arms, and her boy of two years old, wrapped in a blanket and slung at her side. The mother looked as unconcerned as if nothing had happened to her; so easy is nature in her operations in the wilderness, when free from the enfeebling refinements of luxury, and the tamperings and appliances of art (1836: Vol. II, pp. 235-37).

Irving was writing of events he had not actually witnessed, although he did have the advantage of documents and journals supplied to him by John Jacob Astor. In any case he overrated the "ease of nature in her operations" because the Dorion baby died some ten days after birth. The mother subsequently had another baby, one of two children who were with her in her great ordeal of 1814. In the winter of that year she and her husband and children were members of a party of trappers under the command of John Reed in the lands of the Shoshones. The Indians killed the whole party, except for Mrs. Dorion and her two children, in early January of 1814. She was reunited with a brigade of traders upward bound on the Columbia on April 17, 1814. Ross Cox wrote the most detailed account of these events:

> shortly after Mr. Read had built his house, she proceeded with her husband and other hunters named Peznor and LeClerc, between four and five days march from the post to a part of the country well stocked with beaver, of which they succeeded in trapping a considerable quantity. One evening about the beginning of January, while the poor fellows were thus occupied LeClerc staggered into her hut mortally wounded. He had merely strength sufficient to acquaint her that the savages had suddenly fallen on them while they were at their traps and had killed her husband and Peznor: —he was then proceeding to give her directions as to the best means of effecting her escape; but ere he had concluded, death terminated his existence.
>
> With that courage and self-possession of which few Indian women are devoid in times of necessity, she at once determined on flying from a spot so dangerous. With considerable difficulty she succeeded in catching two horses. On one she placed her clothes, a small quantity of dried salmon, and some beaver meat which remained in the hut. She mounted on the other with her two children, the elder of whom was only three years old and the other did not exceed four months. Thus provided, she commenced her journey towards Mr. Read's establishment. On the third day she observed a number of Indians on horseback galloping in an easterly direction: she immediately dismounted with the children, and was fortunate enough to escape unnoticed. That night she slept without fire or water. Late in the evening of the fourth day, on which she expected to have arrived at Mr. Read's house, she came in sight of the spot on which it had stood; but was horror-struck at beholding there only a smoking ruin, with fresh marks of blood scattered all around. Her fortitude, however, did not forsake her, and she determined to ascertain whether any of the party were still living.
>
> Having concealed the children and horses in an adjoining cluster of trees, she armed herself with a tomahawk and a large knife, and after night-fall she cautiously crept towards the scene of carnage. All was silent and lonely, and at every step fresh traces of blood met her view. Anxious to ascertain if any had escaped the massacre, she repeatedly called out the various names of the party, but no voices responded. By the expiring glare of the smouldering timbers she observed a band of prairie wolves engaged in a sanguinary banquet. The sound of her voice scared them, and they fled. Fearful that they might bend their way to the spot in which she had deposited her precious charge, she hastened thither, and arrived just in time to save her children from three of those ferocious animals which were then approaching them.
>
> From thence she proceeded the following morning towards a range of mountains not far from the upper parts of the Wallah Wallah river, where she intended to remain the rest of the winter. This place she reached on the next day in a state

of great exhaustion from the want of food. Fortunately she had a buffalo robe and two or three deer skins, with which, aided by some pine bark and cedar branches, she constructed a wigwam that served to shelter her tolerably well from the inclemency of the weather. The spot she chose was a rocky recess close by a mountain spring. She was obliged to kill the two horses for food, the meat of which she smoke-dried, and the skins served as an additional covering to her frail habitation. In this cheerless and melancholy solitude the wretched widow and her two poor orphans dragged on a miserable existence during a severe season. Towards the latter end of March she had nearly consumed the last of her horseflesh, in consequence of which she found it necessary to change her quarters. During the whole of this period she saw none of the natives, or any indication of human habitations. Having packed up as much covering and dried meat as she could carry, she placed it with her younger child on her back, and taking the elder by the hand, she bade adieu to her wintry encampment. After crossing the ridge of mountains she fell on the Wallah Wallah river, along the banks of which she continued until she arrived at its junction with the Columbia. Her reception and treatment by the tribe at that place was of the most cordial and hospitable description; and she had been living with them about a fortnight when the canoes passed, and took her up to Oakinagan (1832:136-38).

Thus ended the ordeal of the widow Dorion. It is regrettable that we do not have more information about her. We don't even know her name, and, if it were not for naturalist John Bradbury who traveled part of the way from St. Louis to the Pacific with the Astor brigade under Wilson Hunt, we would not have known her tribal affiliation, since it was not mentioned either by the fur traders or Washington Irving. Bradbury, writing of events when the party was traveling up the Missouri River stated,

In our return to the boat we met the squaw belonging to our interpreter [Dorion], who being of the Ayauway [Iowa] nation, appeared to be much afraid of the Osages during our passage up the river, and it was thought with reason, as on our first interview with the commandant, it had been debated whether or not it would be prudent to send a file of men to conduct her from the boat to the fort during our stay. On enquiry we found that she had been invited up to the village by some of the Osages, and of course, according to Indian custom, would be as safe with them as in the fort (1817:38-39).

If the Iowa Indian widow of Dorion remained on the Columbia River, she may have been employed by the North West Company or may have returned to eastern North America with a fur brigade bound for Fort William and Montreal.

This brief survey of women on the Columbia River in the early nineteenth century is indicative of the range of information about the status and role of females of various cultures and in differing contexts. The primary sources of available data are the written records or recollections of the literate clerks of the Pacific Fur Company and the North West Company, namely Gabriel Franchère, Ross Cox, and Alexander Ross. I have chosen to quote them at length because I consider each printed statement a document or artifact representative of its time and place. Each of these documents simultaneously manifests the historical datum, the bias of the utterer, and my bias inherent in the selection.

It is regrettable that these women could not speak for themselves. But it seems to be characteristic of ethnohistory that the people concerned do not speak for themselves and thus are perceived historically only by means of the preserved records of literate foreigners.

I have used Linton's (1936:113-14) concept of status—the rights and duties of an individual in a particular cultural context—and role—the dynamic aspect of a status, an individual's performance of his or her rights and duties in a particular cultural context. Since there is no status without a role, I have inferred the status of the women from their roles.

## References Cited

Bradbury, John
    1817   Travels in the interior of America in the years 1809, 1810, and 1811; including a description of upper Louisiana, together with the states of Ohio, Kentucky, Indiana, and Tennessee, with the Illinois and western territories, and containing remarks and observations useful to persons emigrating to those countries. London: Sherwood, Neely, and Jones.

Cox, Ross
    1832   Adventures on the Columbia River including the narrative of a residence of six years on the western side of the Rocky Mountains among various tribes of Indians hitherto unknown together with a journey across the American continent. New York: J. & J. Harper.

Franchère, Gabriel
    1854   Narrative of a voyage to the northwest coast of America in the years 1811, 1812, 1813, and 1814 or the first American settlement on the Pacific, trans. and edited by J. V. Huntington. New York: Redfield.

Irving, Washington
    1836   Astoria; or enterprise beyond the Rocky Mountains. (3 vols.) London: Richard Bentley.

Linton, Ralph
    1936   The study of man. New York: Appleton-Century Co.

Mason, Otis T.
- 1889 The human beast of burden. Report of the United States National Museum under the Direction of The Smithsonian Institution 1887, pt. 2:237-95.
- 1894 Woman's share in primitive culture. New York: Appleton-Century Co.

Quimby, George I.
- 1972 Hawaiians in the fur trade of Northwest America 1785-1820. The Journal of Pacific History 7: 92-103.

Ross, Alexander
- 1849 Adventures of the first settlers on the Oregon or Columbia River. London.

Schaeffer, Claude E.
- 1965 The Kutenai female Berdache: courier, guide, prophetess, and warrior. Ethnohistory 12:193-236.

# PART III

Foreign Studies

# THE CERAMIC SEQUENCE AT KAMINALJUYU

*Ronald K. Wetherington*
Southern Methodist University

In 1968 an ambitious program of excavations and analysis at the site of Kaminaljuyu in the central highlands of Guatemala was begun. Through the Pennsylvania State University Kaminaljuyu Project (Sanders and Michels 1969; Michels and Sanders 1973), an interdisciplinary team of senior scholars and graduate students conducted a four-year major effort in the field to define and interpret the culture history of this important Highland Mayan capital.

The project had as its principal objectives 1) the definition of the cultural sequence, in terms of the major and minor changes through time, 2) the definition of the socio-political, religious, and economic character of Highland Mayan society during these time periods, 3) the determination of the geographic extent of primary control and influence generated by Kaminaljuyu, particularly the nature of rural-urban cultural relationships within the immediate sustaining area, and 4) the clarification of the nature and extent of external contacts, including the important question of influences from the Valley of Mexico, and their changes through time.

To recover the data necessary to reach these objectives, a three-component field program was initiated: 1) an extensive test-pit operation at Kaminaljuyu to provide both settlement pattern data and information on residential and special activity areas, 2) selective mound-group excavations to provide information on civic architecture and political-ceremonial organization, and 3) extensive surface collections and digging of selected test-pits in the Guatemala Valley to provide information on the distribution and patterns of settlement in the sustaining area of Kaminaljuyu.

Concurrently with these field operations, laboratory analysis of artifacts was conducted. The final field season, 1971, was devoted exclusively to completing the ceramic analysis. During the subsequent year, with additional funding from the National Science Foundation, the author and several graduate students continued work on interpreting the ceramic sequence and distribution.[1]

Because of the sheer quantity of ceramics, this facet of the project was the most demanding and time-consuming, while also promising the greatest potential returns for time investment (Fig. 1). Approximately one and one-half million of the two million artifacts catalogued were ceramic vessels and sherds. Well over 100,000 of these were individually examined and analyzed in the laboratory. Samples of this magnitude require restriction of recorded attributes to manageable size and reduction of observations to a relatively simple code. The attribute categories and attribute states utilized, as well as the resulting ceramic classification, are discussed elsewhere (Wetherington, n.d.) and will be available in published form shortly. The purpose of this paper is to present a general picture of the emerging sequence and distribution of vessel forms, specific attribute clusters (modes), and ceramic types at Kaminaljuyu. Their relationships to the general archaeological picture, and the resulting implications for understanding Precolumbian cultural development in the Guatemalan Highlands, are beyond the scope of this paper.

## Previous Work on the Cultural Sequence

Despite the fact that systematic excavations in the early 1940s began to reveal a long and complex sequence of prehistoric cultural achievements and changes in the central highlands of Guatemala, few descriptions of this sequence have been published. The excellent Carnegie reports on Miraflores Mound E-III-3 (Shook and Kidder, 1952) and Esperanza Phase Mounds A and B (Kidder, Jennings and Shook, 1946) give quite detailed information on tomb furnishings, but neither presents a clear picture of the general ceramic characteristics of these important phases. Moreover, both studies dealt only with upper status mortuary ceramics.

The Formative sequence was briefly characterized by Shook (1951a) and subsequently the entire sequence from Formative through Postclassic was assigned phase names and given approximate datings (Shook, 1952). Brief mention of ceramic examples from particular phases have appeared in occasional reports (Berlin, 1952; Kidder, 1945, 1948, 1961, Kidder and Shook, 1946; Shook, 1945, 1947, 1948, 1949, 1950, 1951b; Shook and Proskouriakoff, 1956). More recently, the chronology and phase designations initially proposed by Shook have been revised, but with little elaboration of the ceramic characteristics (Coe, 1961, Fig. 12; Parsons, 1967, Fig. 16; Borhegyi, 1965, Table 1; Warren, 1961). The most comprehensive attempt to synthesize the highland ceramic sequence, based primarily on the earlier reports, is that of Rands and Smith (1965).

# The Ceramic Sequence at Kaminaljuyu

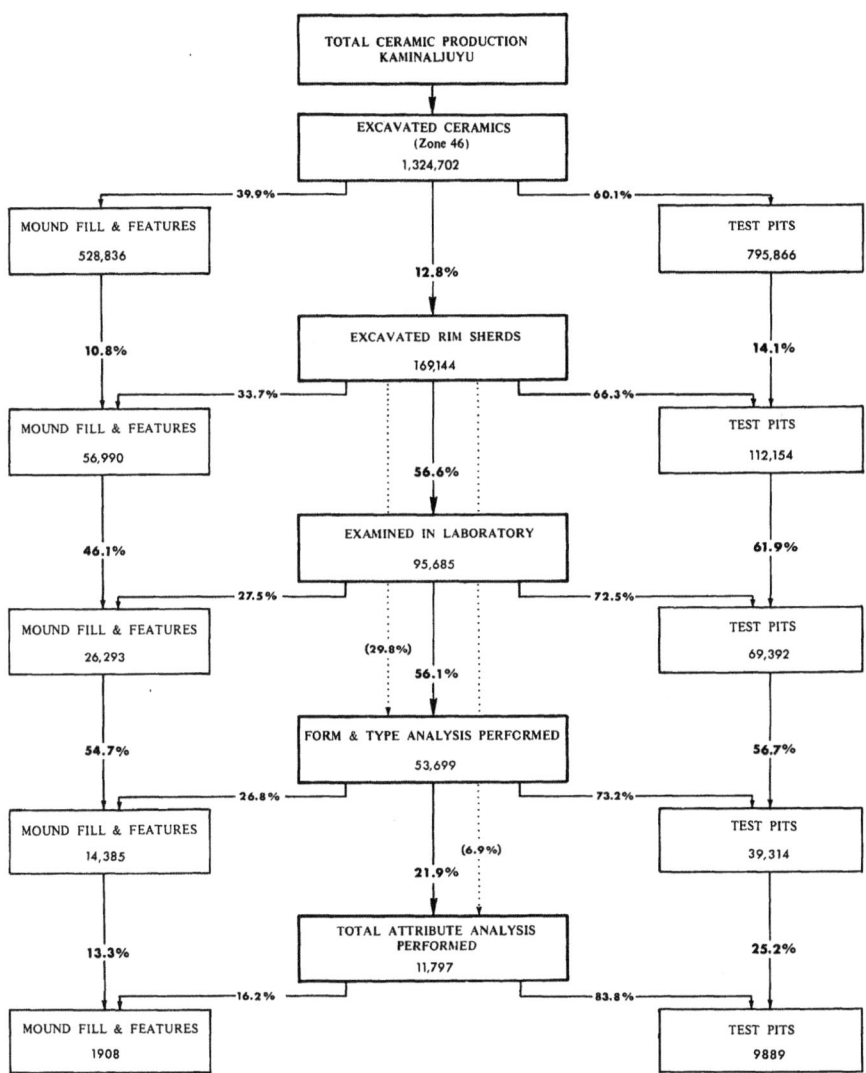

Figure 1. Sample sizes and proportions, Kaminaljuyu ceramic analysis.

Our point of departure in ceramic analysis and interpretation was the assumption that the general sequence and its ceramic diagnoses, as previously reported, was correct in its bold outlines. However, allowances in research design were made for both minor refinements and major revisions and inversions as careful stratigraphic control dictated. Specific attempts were made to verify each portion of the sequence, while both chronometric and taxonomic procedures were undertaken to establish a sequence *de novo*. Results have been exhausting, but hardly exhaustive of the analytical rigor now available through computer technology.

## Cultural Periods and Ceramic Taxonomy

Culture change through self-generated developmental events is a relatively continuous process. The designation of discrete time-specific stages, periods and phases is to this extent an arbitrary but convenient procedure designed more to facilitate interpretation and comparison than to reflect major watersheds in culture history. That is, transitions from one period to another are not equally abrupt from one region to another; such transitions may not always signify the same kinds of causes and events; and the same terms may not be equally descriptive of the societies to which they are applied.

For convenience we have retained the designations Formative, Classic and Postclassic to identify the cultural periods which subdivide the many regional sequences in Mesoamerica. At Kaminaljuyu, each of these periods has its own characteristics in architecture, settlement pattern, and ceramic and non-ceramic artifacts. Such characteristics, however, are not uniform throughout each period, nor are they uniform in their relationships to one another. The Formative, moreover, witnesses a genuine florescence and elaboration prior to its conclusion which belies its name. Furthermore, a greater magnitude of culture change, whether assessed qualitatively or quantitatively, occurs during the Formative—even within its latter half—than during the long Classic period.

The subdivisions of these periods have corresponding ceramic phases, named again for convenience and, in most cases, to achieve continuity with previous designations. For the most part types, varieties and their expressive modes help to characterize more than one ceramic phase. The phase is thus identified as a cluster of particular ceramic attributes in frequencies and proportions which have a statistically reliable uniformity across spatial units, and which may be distinguished by a reasonably concise temporal unit. The case for greater scientific objectivity in this approach than in approaches previously utilized in phase-naming is moot. It is best handled under a rubric not feasible in this paper. Suffice it to say that the phases discussed here have been identified in separate excavations having pure components which are stratigraphically distinct and temporally ordered.

## TABLE I
### Cultural Chronology at Kaminaljuyu

| | | |
|---|---|---|
| Postclassic | Late | 1200 - 1500 A.D. |
| | Early | 1000 - 1200 A.D. |
| Classic | Late | 600 - 1000 A.D. |
| | Middle | 400 - 600  A.D. |
| | Early | 200 - 400  A.D. |
| Formative | Terminal | 200 B.C. - 200 A.D. |
| | Late | 500 - 200  B.C. |
| | Middle | 1000 - 500 B.C. |

The cultural sequence is presented in Table 1. The corresponding dates are supported by obsidian hydration and radiocarbon analyses (Michels and Sanders, 1973).

The classification of the ceramic inventory at Kaminaljuyu involved the simultaneous procedures of recording the variable expressions (states) of some 16 attributes and coding the presence of particular modes of form, stylistic treatment, and vessel technology (Wetherington, 1969; n.d.). The former procedure was performed on 11,797 sherds and vessels, with all data keypunched and subsequently stored on magnetic tape. These data provided the basis for the resulting typology. The latter procedure was performed on a total of 53,699 sherds and recorded on data sheets filed by excavation unit. These data amplified the typology through information on the temporal and spatial association of the types and modes.

Analysis of these data resulted in the designation of 51 ceramic types with 85 varieties bracketing the sequence from Early Formative through Late Postclassic. The subsequent grouping of comparable types reduced the number of ceramic wares to 20. Illustrated in Figure 2 are the frequencies of 19 of these wares within each phase (Utatlan Ware, diagnostic of the Providencia phase, is omitted). Several types without formal ware designations, as well as the stylistic mode represented by Usulutan treatment, are also included. Figure 3 indicates the frequencies within each phase of the more common form modes in the sequence. The predominant ceramic characteristics of each phase, with illustrative examples, are presented in Figure 4. This provides an abbreviated picture of the diagnostic as well as the more ubiquitous wares, types, varieties, and modes. Names in capital letters are either wares (designated as such) or types. The single exception

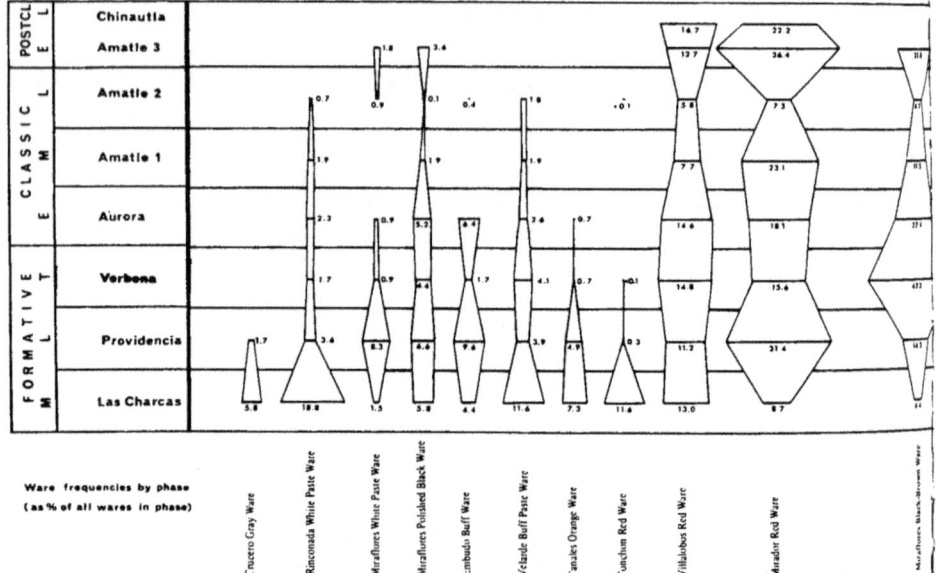

Figure 2. Frequencies of wares and selected types within ceramic phases.

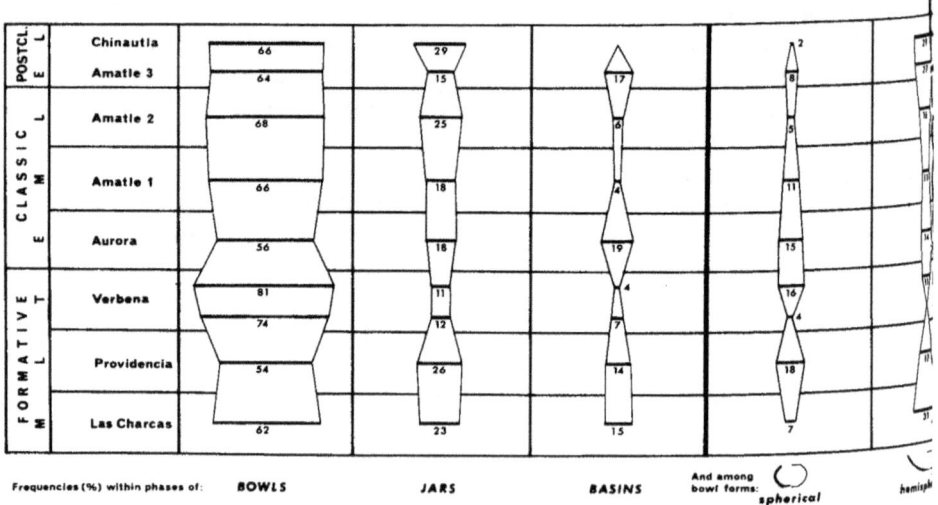

Figure 3. Frequencies of selected vessel forms within ceramic phases.

# The Ceramic Sequence at Kaminaljuyu

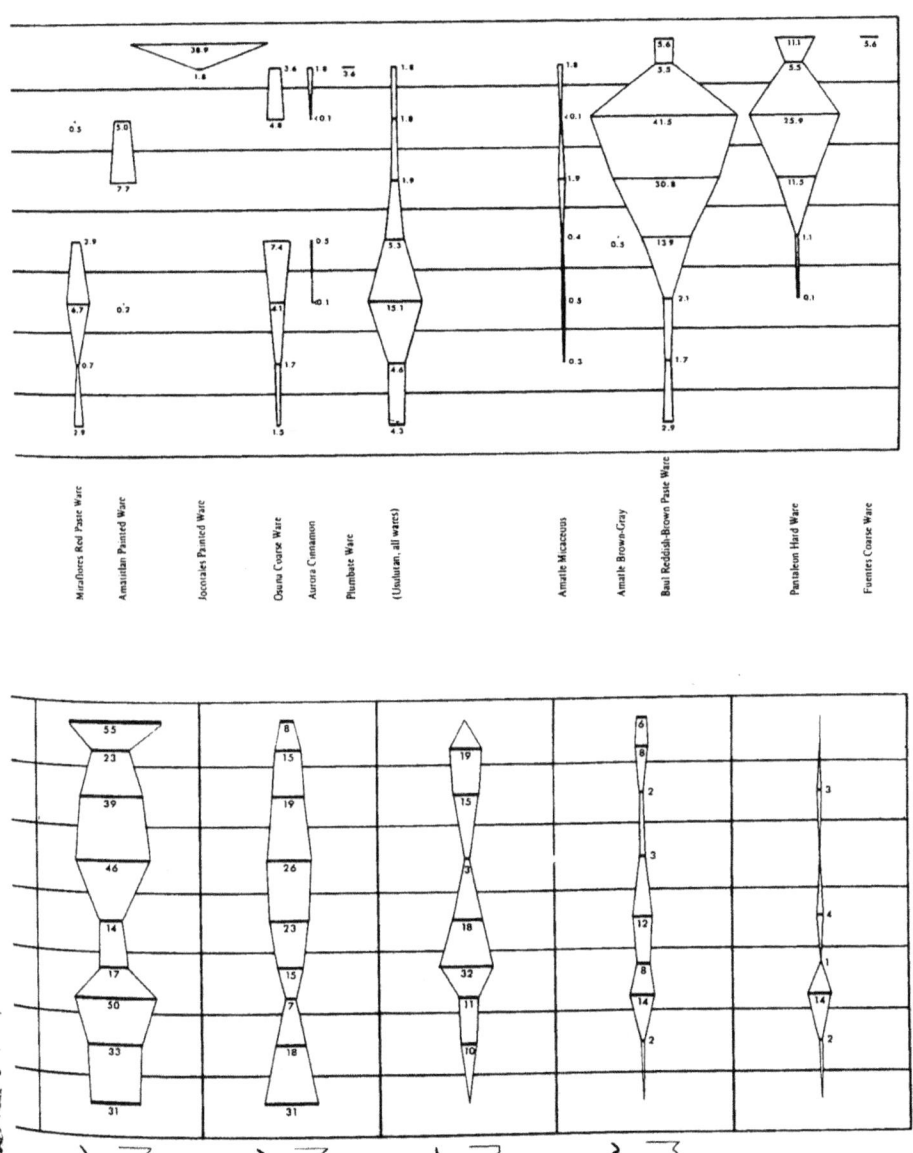

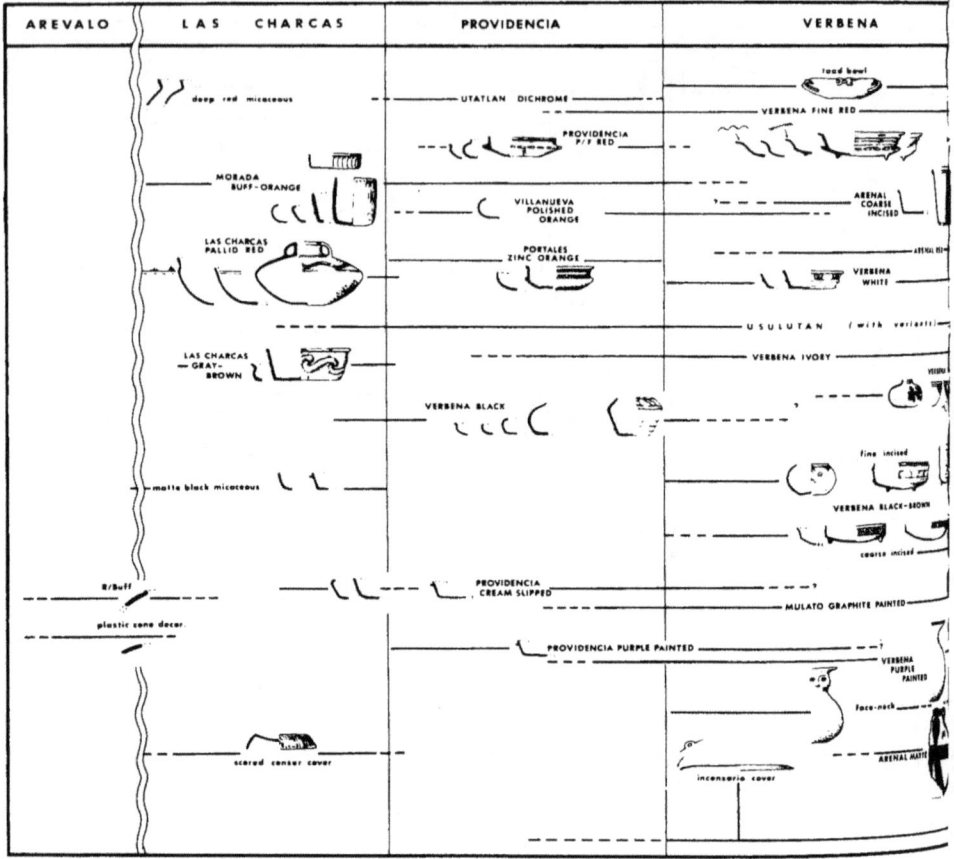

Figure 4. General characteristics of the ceramic sequence at Kaminaljuyu. (See text for key to designations).

is Usulutan, a stylistic mode represented in several wares and types. Lower case names are either formal varieties or general descriptions.

The ceramic taxonomy should be derived independently of the ceramic sequence. The definition of that sequence depended upon identifying single-phase ceramic components with stratigraphic integrity, while the recognition of a component which was unmixed depended upon some knowledge of the sequence. Avoiding interpretive circularity of this sort is a procedural dilemma frequently encountered but infrequently exposed. Three objectives converge at this point: 1) to minimize the likelihood that

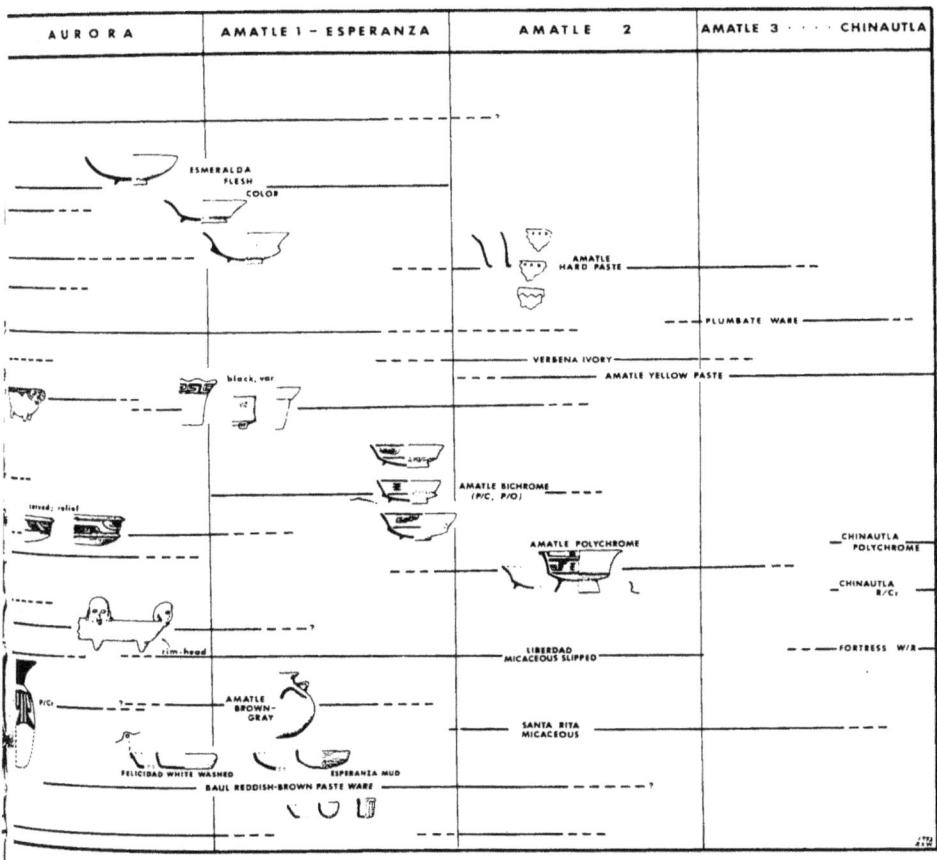

any ceramic types will acquire an *a priori* positive or negative value in diagnosing a particular phase; 2) to maximize the analytical power of the total attribute inventory; 3) to optimize the size of the component samples to validate the sequence.

Our procedure in meeting these objectives was first to choose those excavation units having the strongest likelihood of representing a single temporal unit. Mound excavations and surface collections were omitted and, from the more than 500 test pits, only those with an internal stratigraphic consistency were examined. Ceramic attributes having strong association were provisionally set aside. These were then applied to test pits having stratigraphic units whose contents suggested multiple time periods. Attribute associations were again set aside. At this point those units which, as a result, were felt to represent single components were tabulated by the presence (and frequency) of ceramic types, varieties, and modes, and those that were more consistent or had high frequencies were compared with others. Stratigraphic sequences from several hundred test pits were compared in this manner to determine which ceramic attributes were the most appropriate indices at particular points in the sequence. The final number of "usable" test pits in this analytical phase was less than 100. At the same time, those types, varieties and modes which, from previous investigations, were the strongest indicators of particular complexes were examined in our sequence. For example, the fine-incised black-brown ceramics diagnostic of Miraflores, the Zinc Orange from Providencia, the Pallid Red of Las Charcas, the Hard Ware of the Classic, were all tabulated by stratigraphic unit. Among those previously accepted "index types," those found to be consistent, both in positive or negative association with others and in their stratigraphic relationships, were accepted as ceramic keys to particular phases.

These procedures allowed both recognition of the general sequence and identification of ceramic changes through that sequence. In the process, specific associations with newly recognized types, varieties and modes introduced new diagnostics, while the usefulness of some previously recognized indices (e.g., Usulutan, Fine Red) was put in doubt. Some previously recognized phases (e.g., Majadas) were eliminated as having insufficient validity.

The final decisions regarding the ceramic sequence, and the phase designations which it reflects, necessarily involved some subjective judgment. For example, the decision to include or omit a ceramic inventory of a particular test pit level may have significant effects upon the ceramic frequencies (such as are represented in Fig. 2) which subsequently define the phase represented. This is particularly true for the earliest and latest phases, poorly represented to begin with. Yet, the decision to omit a particular level may have been based on the presence in that level of a ceramic type which in the author's judgment clearly "did not belong." In such a case we eliminated that and all higher levels and sometimes the entire excavation unit. Parsimony dictated that to err on the side of omission was the better part of discretion. Consequently, while there were probably several levels of many test pits which could have been included in a particular phase documentation, I believe there were none included that should have been omitted.

Having established the ceramic classification and sequence in their broad outlines as previously described, we next sought to refine the sequence and expand our knowledge of its spatial distribution. The most appropriate means was through independent verification of the sequence by chronometric dates. A very extensive series of obsidian hydration dates had been processed, along with several carbon-14 dates, representing stratigraphic levels of virtually all the test pits and mound excavations.

Utilizing our ceramic records for all excavation units, ceramic phases and chronometric dates were compared. Surprisingly few conflicts in assessment occurred: the majority of obsidian and/or carbon dates were supported ceramically both by the presence of types and varieties appropriate for the date and by the absence of types and varieties inappropriate for the date. Where no conflicts were present in the unit (usually a test pit level or series of levels) and where associated units (earlier or later) were consistent, the unit and its ceramic phases were designated as a valid component. Where there was inconsistency between chronometric and ceramic data from a unit, it was omitted.

The results of this procedure not only confirmed the general ceramic sequence but have permitted finer analysis of associated ceramics in each phase, the partitioning of phases into earlier and later components based on subtler ceramic distinctions, and the identification of settlement distribution and densities through time.

What follows, then, is a narrative description of the ceramic character of the sequence, with its patterns of emphasis, as illustrated in Figure 4 and as derived from the procedures discussed above. The number of excavation units (test pits and mounds) containing components of a period or phase is given in parentheses.

## The Formative Period (142)

This important cultural period, divided into Early, Middle, Late and Terminal subdivisons, spans the time from initial occupation of the region though the emergence of Kaminaljuyu as a strong center of social and ceremonial activity. It thus covers a great deal of cultural development, reflected in changes in the quantity and the diversity of the ceramics.

### Early Formative (Arevalo Phase)

The Arevalo Phase is not represented by any component at Kaminaljuyu, and it is almost totally absent in the sustaining area. In the lowest levels of several Middle Formative occupations are scattered ceramics indicating this phase. The well-made ceramics, primarily of thick-walled, unslipped tecomates, frequently have painted rims and plastic body decoration. Varieties of punctation, striation and rocker-stamping have been recorded. The sparse sample shows a resemblance to some Ocos Phase material at La Victoria (Coe, 1961), and suggests a Pacific coastal source or influence for these initial ceramics in the Guatemala Valley.

*Middle Formative (Las Charcas Phase) (5)*

This phase is better represented than the former, but in surprisingly few pure (occupational) components. Less than thirty test pits contained Las Charcas material, and only five had unmixed Las Charcas components. Even when material from mound fill and samples from the museum collection are included, our knowledge of this important ceramic phase is quite restricted.

Well-made wares and simple forms characterize Las Charcas. Bowl forms predominate, but relatively less so (62 percent) than in other phases. Almost 70 percent of the bowls are simple silhouette and all are flat-based. No secondary vessel supports occur. The basin form in this phase is a large, thick-walled hemispherical bowl shape which, together with the common jar form, comprises almost all of the Pallid Red ceramic type. The jar is characteristically vertical-necked with bolstered lip. Its squat form, with the largest diameter mid-way on the vessel wall, is distinctive.

The vase form is commonly cylindrical with grooved or modeled lines and curvilinear designs, a decorative technique equally common in bowls. Incensario covers are predominately heavily scored during Las Charcas.

Surfaces are almost uniformly well-smoothed, frequently with a high, waxy burnish. Unslipped vessels are rare (there are a few red-on-unslipped buff bowls), and slips are generally hard. Colors are typically muted, darker values of buff, buff-orange, red, and grayish-brown. Some use of deep red, black and especially white slip pigments occurs. Firing is frequently irregular and splotches and streaks are common.

None of the ceramic wares or types is exclusive to Las Charcas. Most continue in reduced frequencies into Late Formative, or comprise the initial appearance of types more diagnostic of later phases. The most nearly exclusive is Conchon Red Ware with its single Las Charcas Pallid Red type. Three-fourths of this ware occurs here. Crucero Gray Ware, with its single Las Charcas Gray-Brown type, is likewise common, about half occurring in Las Charcas times and half in Providencia, although sample sizes for both these wares are really too small to allow statistical confidence in the distribution. Providencia Purple Painted, one of two types within Rinconada

White Paste Ware, has the highest frequency of all wares during Las Charcas, occurring late in the period as matte or low-polished unslipped bowls. These flat-based, angular walled vessels have rim flanges with purplish-red lips and occasionally painted flange edges. They continue through the subsequent phase. A superficially similar white-slipped type (Providencia Cream Slipped, Miraflores White Paste Ware) with identical forms and decoration appears here and continues through Verbena, where it achieves more variety and is accompanied by the related Verbena Ivory.

The earliest examples of Usulutan treatment occur during Las Charcas, a "cloudy" example of undiagnosed type and the Usulutan Cream Slipped type belonging to Mirador Red Ware.

*Late Formative (Providencia Phase) (28)*

Providencia and the presumably related Sacatepequez Phase briefly continue the characteristics of Las Charcas and, more significantly, establish the ceramic character of the following Terminal Formative. It was at first thought that Borhegyi's (1965) distinction between Providencia as the ceremonial elite facet and Sacatepequez as the provincial rural facet of this part of the Formative Period had merit. However, mound-associated ceramics of this period are significantly different from either occupational debris elsewhere at Kaminaljuyu or collections from the valley survey. Kidder's (1961) suggestion that Sacatepequez represents a western facet of the Late Formative merits investigation. Our present attempts to distinguish consistent temporal patterns within this period, however, may well allow recognition of early and late aspects. In the meantime, the term Providencia is used to designate the Late Formative ceramic complex.

Previous types continue and new types of the same wares reflect a growing elaboration. New forms are introduced, including the standing-wall bowl so common during the following phase. Small shouldered bowls, larger medial-flange and labial-flange bowls, and spherical bowls characterize the new variety, with a significant reduction in simple hemispherical bowls. Modeled and grooved decoration is still common, to which is added some limited incising and an intermediate groove-incising. The vertical-grooving and fluting common in Las Charcas seems to decrease in favor. Painted decoration increases in frequency, including red-on-buff, purple-on-red, and red-and-black treatments with zones separated by grooving and incising. Among the significant examples of this are Utatlan Dichrome, a new ware restricted to this phase, and Providencia Purple-on-Fine Red. The occasionally faceted flange on the latter, with grooved designs filled with purple paint, anticipates the faceted flange and rim of Verbena Fine Red, also belonging to Mirador Red Ware.

Two new polished orange types extend the orange ware of the preceding phase. One, Portales Zinc Orange, is highly diagnostic of the Providencia Phase, with its bright hue and groove-incised stepped and zigzag decoration on the upper segment of bowls. Fine white-paste wares, slipped and unslipped, continue without change with one exception: a jar variety with outflaring neck and purple/red painted lip is introduced, Verbena Purple Painted, which is elaborated in the succeeding phase.

Finally, the polished black and black-brown wares characteristic of Verbena Phase ceramics occur sporadically in the form of small hemispherical and spherical bowls. Some of the typical Verbena fine-incising is introduced, apparently late in the sequence.

Two significant developments seem to characterize the ceramics of Providencia Phase. The first is an expansion of pre-existing wares into new types and varieties, rather than any change towards greater standardization or restriction. Plastic decoration is no more common than before, although decorative modes change, and painting becomes more common. The second is a change in form modes, particularly in bowls, with the introduction of a firm distinction between the upper and lower portions of the vessel. This is reflected most simply in the standing-wall bowl and more elaborately in the flanged, shouldered, and other composite silhouette forms. The S- and Z-angle forms occasionally seen in Las Charcas are supplemented by modes in which the vessel wall occasionally has distinct basal, medial, and rim zones, frequently further set apart by decoration. This three-zone concept characterizes the red and orange wares, and it is the former which becomes quite standardized in the subsequent phase.

*Terminal Formative (Verbena Phase) (109)*

As in the Late Formative, the two commonly cited component phases, here Verbena and Arenal, cannot yet be distinguished temporally. Moreover, no differences in distribution are found when various types and varieties are plotted by test pit provenience to suggest functional distinctions in ceramic assemblages during this sub-period. Only in vessel forms (Fig. 3) are there significant differences, and these and other modes are currently being studied in more detail.

This period witnesses a cultural florescence: occupation expands greatly, ceramic quantities indicate a significant increase in production, many new types are introduced, and certain varieties acquire a standardization suggesting occupational specialization and mass-production. There is little question of continuity from the previous period, particularly in some of the forms seen in black-brown and fine red. Painted decoration becomes less frequent, and is largely restricted to red or purple on white bowls and jars of Rinconada and Miraflores White Paste Wares. Incised decoration, with or without modeled rim effigies and modeled appliques, reaches truly elaborate heights and occurs in frequencies which far overshadow alternate modes. This is all the more significant in view of the relative absence of incising during the Classic Period.

The division of the vessel into horizontal zones and decorative fields reaches its greatest elaboration during the Terminal Formative. This occurs principally in three wares: Mirador Red Ware, especially Verbena Fine Red; Miraflores Red Paste Ware, particularly the Incised Variety of Verbena White; and Miraflores Black-Brown Ware. In the latter, the Verbena Black-Brown Fine Incised type commonly occurs on both bowls and vases with the three-part division. The medial portion is frequently framed by modeled horizontal ridges and occasionally even further sub-divided in the same way. Between these ridges a number of alternative but highly standardized design motifs occur in fine incisions into the slip. The Coarse Incised type is largely restricted to standing-wall bowls, with the wall divided into horizontal panels by repeating coarsely-incised and excised designs. These motifs differ from the fine-incised and are also highly standardized.

Most of our Fine Red examples bear no incised design on the wall (between basal flange and lip), but a number do have a characteristic step motif such as those found in Mound E-III-3. The most common decoration is faceting or scalloping on the lip and flange and horizontal grooves on both wall and lip surfaces.

Verbena White Incised is largely restricted to the Terminal Formative and, like some Black-Brown Fine Incised examples, often utilizes incising and horizontal ridges to separate vessel zones. The most common vessel forms are simple hemispherical, flat-based simple-silhouette and composite silhouette bowls; standardized designs are incised through the thick white slip to expose the brick-red coarse paste beneath.

Coarse incising occurs in two other wares without horizontal zoning. One of these, Osuna Coarse Ware, has only one type, Arenal Coarse Incised. Deep and frequently large bowls with flat bases and flaring walls, and the "flower pot" vase form are the only two forms, although the former is often large enough in diameter to be termed a basin. Both forms bear standardized motifs thickly incised/excised between framing lines, with the vertical patterns repeated in sets of two or four.

The other incised ware is Miraflores Polished Black, present as Verbena Black during Providencia times in completely different forms and usually undecorated. Here, during the latter part of Terminal Formative and continuing well into the Aurora Phase, the type recurs in the form of deep hemispherical bowls and, occasionally, restricted-orifice jars. Designs are heavily incised around the rim and in large half-circles pendant from the rim. The motifs are distinctive and frequently accompany modeled animal faces. Incised designs are usually in sets of two on opposite sides, with the design centers frequently pinched inward. The shape strongly resembles cut gourd dishes common in Guatemala today and presumably common in prehistoric times.

Modeled effigies and appliqués on vessel rims are common during this sub-period, on simple vertical-wall bowls, on jars with necks modeled into faces, and on the shallow Fine Red toad-bowl. The latter represents the finest example of modeled effigy design and execution during the Formative.

The Usulutan decorative mode, which had become standardized in cross-hatching and parallel wavy-line motifs during Providencia times, is broadly applied in the Terminal Formative. It occurs on Verbena Ivory (Miraflores White-Paste Ware) and on three types within Mirador Red Ware. While reaching its highest frequency during the Verbena Phase, Usulutan treatment (in all its forms) continues through the Classic Period. Not a true resist technique, the Usulutan design resulted from removing the surface pigment from the vessel with a multiple-toothed implement before the pigment dried or was absorbed (Wetherington, n.d.).

A final important characteristic of the Verbena Phase is the appearance of tripod and tetrapod vessel supports. At first only solid conical nubbins occur, but hollow mammiform supports with rattles are present before the end of the phase.

## The Classic Period (353)

The Classic Period witnessed major changes in the quality and kinds of ceramic production. The trends towards standardization and mass production accelerated. The resulting reduction in ceramic variety and in wares showing high craftsmanship is particularly evident by the middle of the period, when simple and hurriedly made containers replace the embellished vessels of the Formative.

### Early Classic Period (Aurora Phase) (104)

This initial phase of the Classic is best seen as transitional. During this phase most of the Formative wares and their types are terminated and new, generally coarser, wares and types characteristic of the Classic are introduced. Highly polished vessels are rare and painted decoration remains uncommon. Vessel walls and rims in most cases become thicker, and less attention is paid to surface finish and evenness of firing. On the other hand, paste becomes less friable, coarser yet more cohesive, and the incipient vitrification occasionally seen is a prelude to the highly vitrified pastes to come.

Vessel forms differ little in style and frequency from those that preceded, although there is a tendency for larger scale. Introduced in Aurora and continuing as a major attribute throughout the Classic is the ringstand vessel support. During the Aurora Phase this support is restricted to vessels of the Esmeralda Flesh Color type (Pantaleon Hard Ware), which are also common along the southern piedmont and coastal plain (Parsons, 1967). Although a few vases with outslanting walls occur in this type, most are of four bowl forms, each with ringstand supports: simple hemispherical, basal angle, basal shoulder, and basal flange, the last three with outflaring walls and unmodified rims and lips. The closest predecessors of the last three are the Verbena Fine Red and Fine Red-Orange (both continuing through the Middle Classic) tripod and tetrapod bowls, but these have modeled embellishments and composite silhouettes in the wall-lip break.

Esmeralda Flesh Color has a medium-fine light colored paste and a variable surface treatment, ranging from an unslipped matte or low polished light orange surface with lustrous streaks to a rather sloppy creamy-buff wash. Some examples are clearly predecessors of the Amatle Hard Ware of the Late Classic, both in paste and surface treatment. Some forms are identical, particularly ladle censers, which have hollow handles in the Flesh Color type and solid in the Hard Ware type.

A coarse ware with somewhat problematic occurrence during the Formative begins its growing popularity in Aurora. This is Baul Reddish-Brown Paste Ware. Two highly distinctive forms occur during Aurora. The first of these is a large flat-based sarten with solid conical supports, the rim bearing large hollow human effigy heads. Occasionally of life-size proportions, the heads have circular ear spools and labrets and are often painted in fugitive white, yellow and red pigments. There is some evidence of this form late in the Formative; it continues into the early part of the Middle Classic.

The second form occurs in the type Felicidad White-Washed, also present on the coastal plain. This flat-based unsupported sarten has straight outslanting walls, frequently with abruptly incurving rim. Usually two but sometimes four horizontal triangular handles project outward from the lip and the rim is frequently painted in fugitive white. This type continues well into the Late Classic.

Among the types to continue from the Formative perhaps the most important is Verbena Black-Brown Coarse Incised with its distinctive motifs. A deeply-carved plano-relief variety characterizes Aurora, although it first appears late in the Terminal Formative.

## Middle Classic (Amatle 1 and Esperanza Phases) (66)

The two synchronic phases of the Middle Classic have apparent functional and class distinctions. The latter represents an interregional component bearing vessels manufactured in the Valley of Mexico or local imitations of Teotihuacan wares. Peten polychromes as well as classic wares from closer highland neighbors are also represented. Slab supports, cylinder covers, and painted stuccoed wares comprise part of the distinctive ceramics of this component. Very few examples were recovered from the test pit or mound excavations. Our knowledge of this component comes mainly from prior excavations whose collections were studied in the Guatemalan National Museum. The most thorough and widely known of the previous works are the Classic tombs from mounds A and B (Kidder, Jennings and Shook, 1946). Test pits located within a few hundred meters of the original location of these mounds revealed abundant Middle and Late Classic ceramics, but no Esperanza Phase materials. This and other evidence supports the view that the possessors of Esperanza wares maintained a cultural distinction of their own, whether they comprised an indigenous elite class or were resident authorities from elsewhere.

The Amatle 1 phase is less well represented at Kaminaljuyu than in the sustaining area, where the density of occupational debris indicates a population 40-50 percent above that in Terminal Formative times. All wares initiated in Aurora times continue with no significant change in forms. Two varieties of a new type, Esperanza Mud, are added to the inventory of the coarse paste ware previously discussed. One of these is a crude bowl with basal break whose base was routinely formed in a mold made from a depression dug out of the soil. Occurring in quantity in the Esperanza tombs as well as in our test pits, this type was obviously mass-produced. In one excavation quantities were stacked together on the occupational surface.

Most distinctive of Amatle 1 is Amatle Bichrome, a micaceous purple-on-buff, -cream, or -orange with conventional design motifs. The forms are almost exclusively ringstand bowls duplicating the modes of the still-present Esmeralda Flesh Color.

Amatle 1 continues the trend towards reduction in ceramic variety and increase in undecorated coarse wares. The bichrome, although well-fired and well-finished, was not carefully made. Its thick walls are frequently uneven and vessels seldom show good symmetry. Reduction in ceramic variety was not accompanied by refinement in manufacture. During Amatle 1 even the Verbena Fine Red and Fine Red-Orange degenerate in quality.

*Late Classic (Amatle 2 Phase) (183)*

The Late Classic ceramic innovations accompany an even more significant population increase than earlier, not only in the sustaining area but particularly at Kaminaljuyu. Almost three times as many Amatle 2 components were represented in the test pits as Amatle 1, and over 100 of the 550 test pits showed no earlier ceramic component. A similar, though not quite so abrupt, picture exists in the valley.

New ceramic forms accompany new types during this phase. Amatle Hard Paste, a fine volcanic-ash paste commonly vitrified, occurs in globular tall-necked jars, hemispherical everted rim bowls, and deep bowls and vases with vertical and outslanting walls. Ladle censers are also common. Amatle Polychrome is essentially the Purple-on-Orange Bichrome with white paint added. Rarely, black paint occurs. Further micaceous-slipped types appear, principally in the form of globular jars, and a micaceous paste type, Santa Rita Micaceous, appears. A new type, Amatle Yellow Paste (Pantaleon Hard Ware), is introduced which continues apparently well into historic times. Its highly polished, often deep yellow surfaces frequently appear to be slipped. Predominant forms are globular jars with strap handles bearing serrated fillets.

During this phase, probably near its beginning, Mirador Red Ware along with the several Usulutan types are discontinued, while a white paste type indistinguishable in paste from Verbena Ivory occurs in low frequency.

## Postclassic Period (19)

Two Postclassic ceramic phases have been identified: Amatle 3, as the initial Postclassic, is distinguished by the introduction of San Juan Plumbate; and Chinautla, the Late Postclassic, has a more complex ceramic inventory. Both of these were only sparsely present at Kaminaljuyu. The analysis of the Early Postclassic and what are probably several subsequent phases prior to Chinautla must await more thorough study of the valley collections. Since these are mostly surface manifestations, excavations of selected sites will be necessary to achieve a sequence.

The Last Postclassic assemblage is better represented in the valley and particularly at the site of Chinautla Viejo (Beleh) where excavations by Dr. Lawrence Feldman have provided well-controlled data on ceramic relationships and associations. The ceramic report on this site is forthcoming (Wetherington, in press).

Neither of these two phases is accurately represented by the percentage charts (Figs. 2 and 3), which were constructed on the basis of small samples at Kaminaljuyu prior to our more recent analysis.

## Comments on Further Analysis

The work remaining to be done with the ceramic data is considerable. The sequence of phases described must be further refined. Careful seriation and comparative study of the test pit levels with mixed components should clarify the nature of continuity between phases. Incorporation of ceramic data from the nineteen mounds excavated during the project will enlighten our knowledge of changing sociopolitical and ceremonial organization through time, as will study of the spatial distribution and density of occupation by phase. The latter is now almost complete and reveals shifting patterns of residence from dispersed to concentrated through the Formative-Classic transition.

Separate studies have involved classification of incensarios and figurines, the former complete and the latter in progress. Aside from their contribution to understanding the sequence, these studies will help clarify the ceremonial and social character of Kaminaljuyu society as it developed.

The bulk of remaining work involves the distribution, by phase, of the ceramic wares and types among the six hundred sites in the valley. We already have a reasonably coherent picture of changes in settlement pattern and in ceremonial and political focus. Further analysis should allow better interpretation of the sources and directions of ceramic influence.

Association of non-ceramic artifacts with the temporal sequence and its spatial distribution has already identified periods and locations of obsidian workshops. It is expected that evidence for other occupational specializations will be identified as well as the relationships of such specializations to social stratification and class structure.

The sequencing of phases presented here and their ceramic attributes differ in some important respects from previously published syntheses. These differences lie chiefly in the increments of ceramic change and not in the tempo or overall character of change. One reason for the differences is the restrictive criteria applied to identifying a ceramic phase. The decision to use only stratified test pit collections, only those with identifiably pure components, and to distinguish phases by the magnitude of qualitative as well as quantitative content, tends to compress phases without overall truncation of the sequence. It becomes essentially an exercise in lumping rather than splitting. Variability in sample size also affects this process.

There is another, more philosophical reason for the differences. It is my feeling that taxonomic and developmental categories should be minimized in formal diagnosis. This not only aids comparative study but avoids establishing a local proprietorship based on needless complexity. At the analytical level, descriptive categories can be numerous; at the interpretive level, if interpretation is synthesis, they should not be. One cannot always avoid increasing numbers of categories, and certainly should not if it means ignoring what we deem to be cultural reality. Classifications and sequential categories are necessary but arbitrary. They tend to reflect both a reality which we impose and a reality we do not. Hopefully, the interpretation at Kaminaljuyu and the analyses which underscore it reflect primarily the latter.

## Footnotes

1. The coding and recording of ceramic attributes, done in the laboratory in Guatemala from 1968 through 1971, was supported by NSF grants to the Pennsylvania State University (W. T. Sanders and J. W. Michels, co-principal investigators). Taxonomic analysis and chronological sequencing were accomplished in 1972-73 with support of NSF grant GS-32328 to Southern Methodist University under the author's direction. Gratitude is expressed to the student assistants who helped in the analysis—particularly Susan Guyette, James Baker, Sandra Dawson, Linda Sampson and Judith Wetherington.

## References Cited

Berlin, H.
    1952    Excavations en Kaminaljuyu: Monticulo D-III-13. Antr. Hist. Guat. 4:3-18.

Borhegyi, S. F.
    1965    Archaeological synthesis of the Guatemalan highlands. Item *in:* Handbook of Middle American Indians, edited by G. R. Willey, vol. 2, pt. 1, pp. 3-58.

Coe, M. D.
    1961    La Victoria, an early site on the Pacific coast of Guatemala. Papers Peabody Museum, Harvard University, vol. 53.

Kidder, A. V.
    1945    Excavations at Kaminaljuyu, Guatemala. American Antiquity 11: 65-75.
    1948    Kaminaljuyu, Guatemala: addenda and corrigenda. Carnegie Institute Washington, Notes on Middle American Archaeology & Ethnology, no. 89.

1961   Archaeological investigations at Kaminaljuyu, Guatemala. Proceedings of the American Philosophical Society, 105:559-70.
_____ , J. D. Jennings and E. M. Shook
1946   Excavations at Kaminaljuyu, Guatemala. Carnegie Institute Wash, Pub. 561.
Michels, J. W. and W. T. Sanders
1973   Kaminaljuyu project—1969, 1970 seasons. Part I—mound excavations. Occasional Papers in Anthropology 9, Pennsylvania State University, Dept. of Anthropology.
Parsons, L. A.
1967   Bilbao, Guatemala, vol. 1. Publication in Anthropology 11, Milwaukee Public Museum.
Rands, R. L. and R. E. Smith
1965   Pottery of the Guatemala highlands. Item *in:* Handbook of Middle American Indians, edited by G. R. Willey, vol. 2, pt. 1, pp. 95-145.
Sanders, W. T. and J. W. Michels
1969   Kaminaljuyu project—1968 season. Occasional Papers in Anthropology 2, Pennsylvania State University, Dept. of Anthropology.
Shook, E. M.
1945   Archaeological discovery at Finca Arizona, Guatemala. Carnegie Institute Washington, Notes on Middle American Archaeology Ethnology, no. 57.
1947   Guatemala highlands. Carnegie Institute Washington, Yearbook 46:179-84.
1948   Guatemala highlands. Ibid., Yearbook 47:214-18.
1949   Guatemala highlands. Ibid, Yearbook 48:219-24.
1950   Guatemala. Carnegie Institute Washington, Yearbook 49:197-98.
1951a  The present status of research on the preclassic horizons in Guatemala. Item *in:* The civilizations of ancient America, edited by S. Tax. Chicago: Univ. of Chicago Press, pp. 93-100.
1951b  Guatemala. Carnegie Institute Washington Yearbook 50:240-41.
1952   Lugares arqueologicos del altiplano meridional central de Guatemala. Antropologia e Historia de Guatemala 4:3-40.
_____ and A. V. Kidder
1952   Mound E-III-3, Kaminaljuyu, Guatemala. Carnegie Institute Washington pub. 596, contrib. 53.
_____ and T. Proskouriakoff
1956   Settlement patterns in Meso-America and the sequence in the Guatemalan highlands. Item *in:* Prehistoric Settlement Patterns in the New World, edited by G. R. Willey, Viking Fund Publications in Anthropology 23:93-100.
Warren, B. W.
1961   The archaeological sequence at Chiapa de Corzo. Item *in:* Los

Mayas del sur y sus relaciones con los Nahuas Mendionales, pp. 75-83.

Wetherington, R. K.
  1969  The ceramic program at Kaminaljuyu. Paper read at annual meeting, American Anthropological Association, New Orleans (mimeo).
  n.d.  The ceramics of Kaminaljuyu, Guatemala. Parts I-II. Report to NSF on grant GS-32328.
  in press  A description of post-classic ceramics. Appendix I. Item *in:* L. A. Feldman, Archaeology at Beleh. Occasional Papers in Anthropology, Pennsylvania State University, Dept. of Anthropology.

# THE EDGE-TRIMMED TOOL TRADITION
# OF NORTHWEST SOUTH AMERICA

*Wesley R. Hurt*
Indiana University Museum

Previous classifications of preceramic lithic tool traditions that lack stone projectile points by such writers as Krieger (1964), Lanning and Patterson (1967), MacNeish (1971) and Stothert (n.d.) do not encompass the full range of variation found in representative sites. Therefore, a new stone tool tradition, "The Edge-trimmed Tool Tradition," characteristic of northwest South America, is defined. Diagnostic of this tradition are simple scrapers and spokeshaves which have their working edges retouched by percussion flaking. The efficiency of these tools is evident in their persistence from a time of about 12,500 years ago well into the ceramic periods (after 2000 B.P.). In fact, the historic Chibcha sites are characterized by the same types of flaked stone tools. It is postulated that the tools of this lithic tradition were used primarily for fabricating implements of wood by peoples adjusted to a forest environment. Although the possibility exists that the edge-trimmed tools did not represent the total flaked lithic assemblage of the associated cultural complexes, there is little evidence to support such a conclusion.

Selected as type sites for the Edge-trimed Tool Tradition are the El Abra Rockshelters in the Sabana de Bogotá, even though their preceramic lithic industries have been assigned by other investigators to different taxonomic units. For example, MacNeish assigns the El Abra preceramic assemblages to his "Flake and Bone Tool Tradition" (1971:152). The lack, however, in the El Abra tool kit of diagnostic traits such as biface implements, burins, unifaced stone projectile points, and bone tools warrants a separate classification. Based upon the limited information gathered from a test pit made in El Abra Rockshelter 2 by Correal and van der Hammen in 1967, Willey assigns the preceramic lithic industries to his "Andean Hunting-Collecting Tradition" (1971:59), but more extensive excavations made in 1969 failed to confirm the presence of stone projectile points, a major diagnostic trait in his tradition. Recently Lynch has suggested that the El Abra industries "... would logically be included in Willey's Flake Tradition" (1974:370). This assignment is also questionable in that Willey's Flake Tradition is defined as including only tools made of flakes while the lithic artifacts from El Abra have as raw materials edge-trimmed cores, cobbles, and natural fragments of tabular chert and siltstone. Willey has also included in the Flake Tradition such industries as that of the Chivateros Red Zone Complex of the Chillon Valley, Peru, which have such tools as burins, punches, and bi-pointed "perforators," all absent at El Abra and at other sites of the Edge-trimmed Tool Tradition.

Recently Stothert (n.d.) has defined in an unpublished manuscript a "Northwest South American Tradition" that has the El Abra type of edge-trimmed flake artifacts but she did not mention any artifacts made of cores, cobbles, and naturally fragmented chunks of chert. In personal communication with Stothert, however, she mentioned that the sites she assigned to her tradition did have artifacts made from these other materials. It would appear, therefore, that the Edge-trimmed Tool Tradition and the Northwest South American Tradition are similar if not identical in diagnostic traits, and thus it is not of great importance which label is used.

## The Edge-Trimmed Tool Tradition

The artifacts of the Edge-trimmed Tool Tradition have the following characteristics:

1) *raw materials and blanks:* natural fragments or "chunks" of tabular chert and siltstone, water-worn cobbles of chert and quartzite. Prior to the final edge-trimming some of the raw material was altered by percussion-flaking, forming flakes and cores; other artifacts were made by simply retouching the working edge of the raw material. In flaking, 14 percent of the striking platforms were prepared first by "nibbling," that is by the removal of small flakes. No attempt was made to alter the remaining surface of the artifacts with the sole exception of several plano-convex objects that were probably rejected cores. Thus the term "uniface" is inappropriate if the category is limited to artifacts that are flaked all over one face. 2) *tool types* (Figures 1, 2, and 3): if a tool type is considered to be an artifact with a definite, regular geometric shape and a single function, only a small number can be defined, since the final form of most artifacts departs only a little from the irregular shapes of the raw material. The types described below do have regular shapes, and their possible function has been determined by experimentation, that is, an "end scraper" can

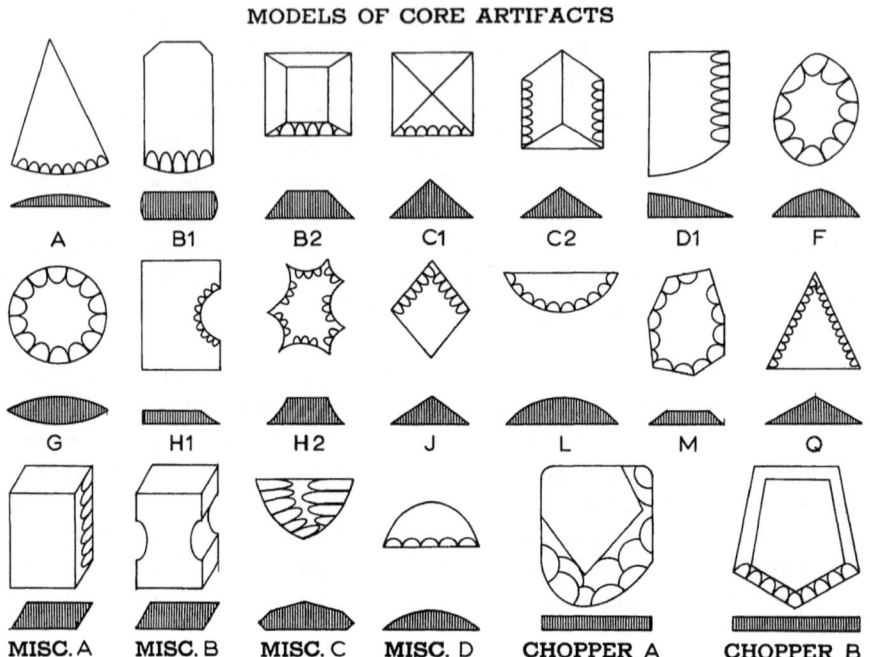

Figure 1. Artifacts from El Abra Rockshelters.

actually be used to scrape both wood and hides. It must be realized, however, that it cannot be proved that a tool type had this function. On this basis the most common tools are the numerous unretouched flakes that can be used for cutting, drilling, engraving, and punching, but it is doubtful that they all were tools; the majority probably were debitage resulting from tool manufacture. The next most common tool consisted of rectanguloid or ovoid chunks and flakes of chert with a single working end or an edge trimmed to an obtuse angle by percussion flaking; such tools can be used to scrape wood and hides. Similar-shaped tools with one side trimmed to an acute angle that can serve as a cutting tool for both wood and hides are also common. Irregular-shaped flakes and chunks with a single or multiple concave working edge, which can function as a spokeshave are also frequent, while ground stone tools such as hammerstones and polishing stones made of quartzite pebbles are rare. The relative proportions of the varieties both of raw materials and tool types for all the sites assigned to the Edge-trimmed Tool Tradition are unknown, while those described later in this report for the El Abra Rockshelters are not necessarily representa-

# The Edge-Trimmed Tool Tradition of Northwest South America

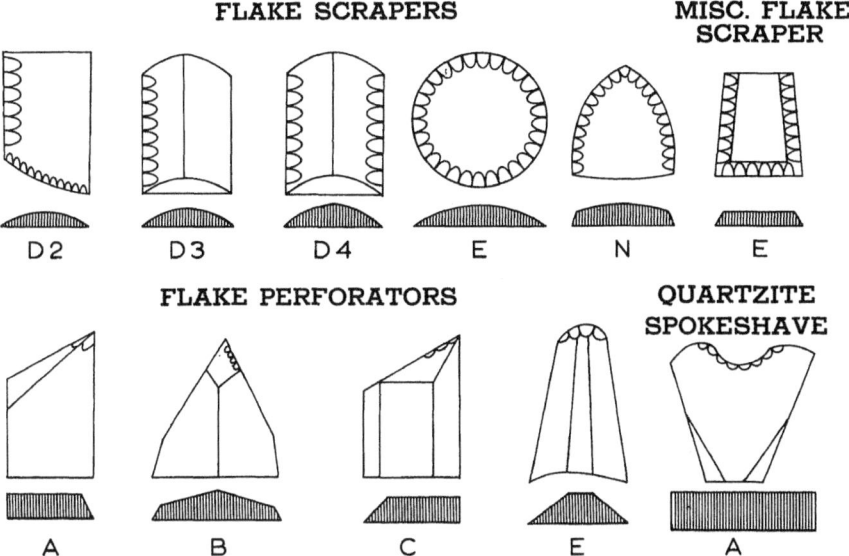

Figure 2. Artifacts from El Abra Rockshelters.

tive of the entire tradition. At El Abra, the flaked stone artifacts are small, almost all being under 5 cm in length, but the dimensions of tools from other sites of this tradition have not been analyzed.

## The El Abra Rockshelters

The El Abra Rockshelters, three of which were partially excavated in 1967-1969 (Correal, van der Hammen, and Lerman, 1969; Hurt, van der Hammen, and Correal, 1972), are located in the Sabana de Bogotá, a high intermontane plain in the Cordillera Oriental. At one time the Sabana formed the basin of a Pleistocene lake that drained by the downcutting of its outlet to the Magdelena Valley about 40,000–30,000 years ago. At present the basin is drained by the Bogotá River and its tributaries, although here and there are relic ponds and swamps, such as the Laguna de Fuquene.

The rockshelters lie in the bases of two sandstone escarpments that frame a narrow corridor in a mountainous mass that projected as a peninsula into Lake Bogotá. The corridor was flooded with water from the lake and therefore its fill corresponds with the general fill of the Sabana. By utilizing radiocarbon dates, pollen, volcanic ash layers, and the physical

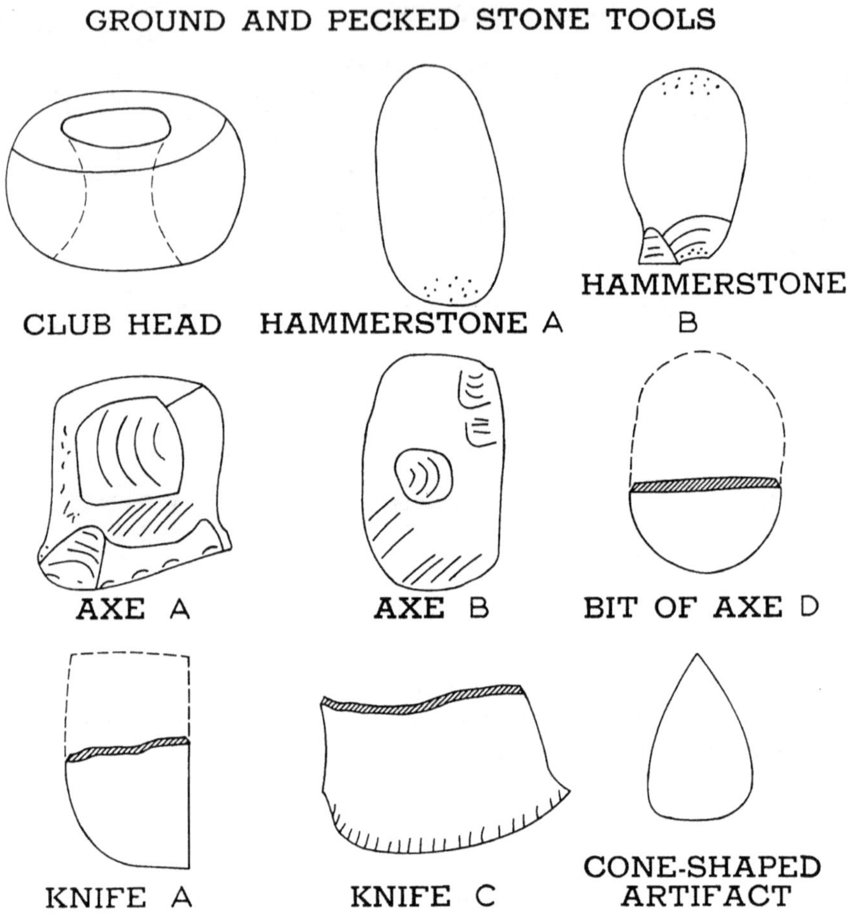

## GROUND AND PECKED STONE TOOLS

Figure 3. Artifacts from El Abra Rockshelters.

characteristics of the sediments it is possible to define a series of widespread depositional units, present not only in the rockshelters but throughout the entire lake basin. Because of the greater thickness and completeness of the deposits in Rockshelter 2, this site is used as a reference in defining the depositional units (Table 1) of all the local rockshelters. In this paper, however, only those units with evidence of human occupation will be discussed. Estimates of dates of these depositional units are based upon radiocarbon dates from the El Abra Rockshelters and upon correlations with estimated dates given by van Geel and van der Hammen for the pollen

## TABLE I

Stratigraphic Units and Climate of the El Abra Rockshelters

| Estimated time B.P. | Depositional unit | | Pollen zone | Climate | North American glacial periods | Local periods | |
|---|---|---|---|---|---|---|---|
| 2000 | E | | | warm | . | | |
|  | | | | cool | | | |
| 4000 | | | | | | | |
|  | | | | warm but cooling | | | |
|  | | D2B | Z-II | | | | |
| 6000 | | | | | | | |
|  | D | | | | | | HOLOCENE |
|  | | | | hot and wet | | | |
| 8000 | | | | | | | |
|  | | D2A | Z-I | warming and moist | | | |
|  | | D1 | | | | | |
| 10,000 | | | | | Cochrane halt | | |
|  | | C4 | Y-II | return of cold and dry | Valders stadial | El Abra interstadial | |
| 11,000 | | | | | Two creeks interstadial | | |
| 12,000 | C | C3 | Y-I | warming moist trend but slightly cooler than today | | Guantiva interstadial | LATE PLEISTOCENE |
| 13,000 | | | | | Woodfordian stadial | | |
|  | | | W-IV | | | | |
| 14,000 | | | | | | | |

zones of the Laguna de Fuquene, obtained in part from radiocarbon dates of organic material and of dated volcanic ash levels at the latter site (1973).

*Sub-Unit C3*

The earliest tools in Rockshelter 2 are found in sub-unit C3 (ca. 13,500–10,800 B.P.), from which a single radiocarbon date of 12,400±160 B.P. (10,450 B.C.) was obtained (Table 2). During the climatic phase (the "Susaca Interstadial" and the "Guantiva Interstadial") associated with this depositional sub-unit, forests gradually invaded the Sabana and the lower slopes of the surrounding mountains. On the slopes oak was the dominant tree, while alder brook forest was present in the flats adjacent to swamps and ponds. The altitude limits of the forest were more or less like those of today, while the temperature was only slightly lower, probably no more than 2°C (van Geel and van der Hammen, 1973: Fig. 8). The increase in moisture resulted in the raising of water levels in the ponds. Such a habitat would be more attractive to man than that of the previous C2 sub-unit which was associated with a cold, dry glacial climate.

In the sub-unit C3 of Rockshelter 2 were found 18 small flakes made of types of stone, such as brown chert, that are not found in the El Abra corridor, and they must have been transported to the site by man (Table 3); a single rectangular scraper made by chipping the edge of a plano-convex flake of black chert (Fig. 2, Misc. Flake Scraper E) was also found. Because of their small numbers and their small size, it seems possible that these artifacts were intrusive from higher levels, although no intrusive feature such as pits or animal burrows were visible on the surface of the excavation profiles. The lack, however, of features such as dense ash layers and firepits in the C3 strata of Rockshelter 2 indicates that there was very little human occupation of the site during the deposition of this sub-unit.

Evidence is inconclusive that Rockshelter 3 was occupied during the deposition of the C3 sub-unit. Here a siltstone, rectanguloid chopper with a percussion-flaked, biface bit was found in what appeared to be a C3 strata below the original base of the test pit made by Correal in 1967. Unfortunately the pit had been backfilled, and it could not be determined with certainty in the re-excavation of 1969 at what depth the underlying undisturbed deposits began. The only other chopper of this type at El Abra was encountered in the backdirt from a pit made by vandals in Rockshelter 4. Thus, it remains in doubt with which lithic assemblage these choppers were associated. In Rockshelter 4, the strata composing the C2, C3, and C4

The Edge-Trimmed Tool Tradition of Northwest South America 275

Table II

Radiocarbon Dates from the El Abra Rockshelters and Bore Holes

| Sample Number | Years Ago | Christian Calendar Date | Rockshelter Number 2 | Rockshelter Number 3 | Rockshelter Number 4 | Bore Hole Number | Depositional Unit | Gross Depths From Surface | Associations |
|---|---|---|---|---|---|---|---|---|---|
| GrN-5942 | >50,000 | | | | | B1 | | 325-350 cm. | Peat |
| GrN-5556 | 12,400±160 | 10,450 B.C. | X | | | | C3 | 150-175 cm. | Charcoal flecks |
| GrN-5941 | 11,210±90 | 9,660 B.C. | | | | B3 | C3? | 185-190 cm. | Humic clay above, sandy loam below |
| B-2134 | 10,720±400 | 8,770 B.C. | X | | | | C4 | 148 cm. | Charcoal accumulation |
| GrN-5746 | 9,325±100 | 7,375 B.C. | X | | | | D1 | 125-155 cm. | Feature 8 |
| GrN-5561 | 9,340±90 | 7,390 B.C. | X | | | | D1 | 100-125 cm. | Feature 8 |
| GrN-5710 | 9,025±90 | 7,075 B.C. | X | | | | D1 | 75-100 cm. | Feature 3 |
| B-2133 | 8,810±430 | 6,850 B.C. | | X | | | C4-D1 | 190-191 cm. | Charcoal lens |
| B-2137 | 8,760±350 | 6,810 B.C. | | X | | | D2A | 100-118.5 cm. | Bone level-floor? |
| B-2135 | 7,250±100 | 6,300 B.C. | | | X | | D2B | Under large fallen rock | Fireplace Feature 16 |
| B-2136 | 340±260 | 1,610 A.D. | | X | | | E2 | 50 cm. | Colonial and Chibcha ceramics |
| I-6362 | 495±104 | 1,455 A.D. | | X | | | E1 | 45 cm. | Child burial No. 2 |
| I-6363 | 9,050±470 | 7,100 B.C. | | | X | | D2A | 94 cm. | Clay-lined fireplace |

## TABLE III
### Distribution of Man-Made Flakes and Flaked Stone Artifacts at El Abra

| | Depositional unit | Estimated age B.P. | Estimated time span years | Rockshelter 2 | | | Rockshelter 3 | | | Rockshelter 4 | | |
|---|---|---|---|---|---|---|---|---|---|---|---|---|
| | | | | flakes total | flakes per year | artifacts total | flakes total | flakes per year | artifacts total | flakes total | flakes per year | artifacts total |
| E | E2 | 1500 | 475 | 1723 | 3.44 | 42 | 2642 | 5.28 | 35 | 2242 | 4.54 | 69 |
| | E1 | 2000 | 1500 | 1564 | 1 | 78 | 3885 | 2.52 | 44 | 2528 | 1.6 | 78 |
| | D2B | 8700 | ? | 2307 | | 41 | 790 | | 15 | 3600 | | 140 |
| D | D2A | 8800 | 100 | 585 | 5.85 | 17 | 222 | 2.22 | 11 | 274 | 2.74 | 31 |
| | D1 | | 700 | 331 | .45 | 15 | 38 | .05 | | 51 | .025 | 19 |
| C4-D1 | 4 | 9500 | 1300 | 31 | .0026 | | 18 | .013 | | | | |
| C | 3 | 10800 | 2200 | 18 | .0008 | 1 | | | 1 | | | |
| | | 13000 | | | | | | | | | | |

layers were so thin and undulating that it proved impossible to segregate the artifacts by depositional sub-units.

*Sub-Unit C4*

The deposition of the overlying sub-unit C4 (the El Abra Stadial) is estimated to have a time span from 10,800–9,500 B.P. Representative of this period is a radiocarbon date from Rockshelter 2, which has an age of 10,720±400 B.P. (8770 B.C.). The climate became drier and colder and the levels of the ponds and swamps fell. The forest limit lowered to about 900 m, so that it lay on the mountain slopes somewhat below that of the Sabana de Bogotá, but some oak forest still remained in the lower protected reaches of valleys in the Sabana, and on the plain itself dwarf groves of Compositea stood. Even though the climate was more disagreeable to man, the open park-like habitat would have accommodated more game animals and thus the population would not necessarily have decreased. However, too few artifacts were found in the El Abra sites during the depositions of the C3 and C4 sub-units to draw any conclusions in respect to relative population figures.

In Rockshelter 2, 31 flakes made of types of silicates other than the locally occurring sandstone were encountered. On the basis of such a small number of flakes, only about twice the number of those in the lower sub-unit C3, it might be asked whether these objects also were not intrusive. The conclusion that they are a valid association is indicated by evidence from the Falls of Tequendama Rockshelter in the Sabana de Bogotá. According to Correal and van der Hammen (van der Hammen, personal communication), who excavated this site, the next oldest strata, which produced radiocarbon dates between 11,000–10,000 B.P., contained artifacts of the El Abra types. It is possible also that the El Abra Rockshelter 4 was occupied at this time since chert flakes were found directly on top of the sterile C2 sub-unit. What prevents a definite conclusion regarding the occupation of Rockshelter 4 at this time is the fact that strata of the C3, C4, and D1 sub-units are so thin and interdigitated that their contents could not be segregated with any degree of precision.

*Sub-Unit D1*

The deposition of sub-unit D1 is estimated to have spanned the time from 9500 to 8800 B.P. Representative radiocarbon dates are 9325±90 (7075 B.C.) from Rockshelter 2, and 8810±430 (6850 B.C.) from Rockshelter 3. A warm moist trend set in during the deposition of sub-unit D1 with the result that the oak forest spread once more into the Sabana de Bototá and the water table rose.

The relatively more favorable climate during the deposition of the D1 sub-unit may have resulted in an increase in local populations, if the relative quantity of artifacts left in the El Abra Rockshelters provide any evidence. Thus in Rockshelter 2, 331 lithic artifacts were found in the D1 sub-unit in contrast to 31 in C4. For the first time there is definite evidence of occupation in Rockshelter 3, where 38 chert flakes were encountered. Strong evidence exists that Rockshelter 4 was occupied at this time, i.e., charcoal from a clay-lined fireplace dated 9050±470 B.P. (7100 B.C.). We also encountered 15 artifacts, other than simple unretouched flakes, in Rockshelter 2 and 9 in Rockshleter 3.

In sub-unit D1, for the first time, there were found sufficient artifacts to obtain an idea of the possible tool functions (Table 4; Figs. 1, 2, 3). In addition to the flakes, which can be used for cutting, punching, and engraving, the main tool types were rectangular and ovoid flakes and cores made from chunks of tabular chert, fragments of water-worn chert nodules, and cores of elongated quartzite pebbles. From this raw material, tools that could be used for scraping both wood and hides were made by trimming the working edges at an end or side by percussion flakes at an obtuse angle. These were followed in numbers by similar artifacts with a working edge formed at an acute angle, a tool useful for cutting both wood and skins. Lesser in number were flakes and cores with a single or multiple concave cutting edge (sometimes called spokeshaves) that were useful for shaving wood shafts and similar objects. Exceedingly rare are hammerstones made of quartzite pebbles. With the exception of two siltstone choppers of unknown provenience, no bifaced tools were found in the D1 sub-unit or in any of the other deposits of the El Abra Rockshelters. Likewise no tools directly related to hunting or food-gathering activities, such as projectile points, were found.

The presence of clay-lined firepits and disc-shaped firehearths, as well as numerous layers of ash and fire-cracked rocks, indicate that the rockshelters were inhabited by man at this time, and the clay-lined firepits in particular suggest that man used the shelters for more than single-night camping places. Nevertheless, the total number of artifacts and debitage is so small that the sites seem never to have been occupied for more than a few days at a time.

*Sub-Unit D2A*

The D2A sub-unit is estimated to have ranged in time from 8800 to

**TABLE IV**

**Distribution of Artifacts from El Abra Rockshelters**

| DEPOSITIONAL SUBUNIT | CORE ARTIFACTS ||||||||||||| FLAKE ARTIFACTS ||||||||||||||||||||| TOTAL |
|---|---|---|---|---|---|---|---|---|---|---|---|---|---|---|---|---|---|---|---|---|---|---|---|---|---|---|---|---|---|---|---|---|---|
| | End-Scrapers ||||| Spoke-Shaves ||| Side-Scrapers | Semi-Lunar Scrapers Choppers || Disc-Shaped Cores ||| Misc. Flaked Cores |||| Plano-convex Cores | Irregular-Shaped Cores | End-Scrapers | Spoke-Shave | Rectangular Scraper ||| Perforators ||| Misc. Scraper || Ovoid Scraper | Retouched Flakes | |
| | A | B1 | B2 | C1 | C2 | J | H1 | H2 | I | Q | L | A | B | G | A | B | C | D | F | M | K | I | D2 | D3 | D4 | A | B | C | E | E | E | N | |
| E2 | 12 | 26 | 5 | 3 | 5 | 4 | 10 | 20 | 7 | 3 | 14 | 1? | 12 | 1? | | | 1 | | 6 | 6 | 1 | 3 | | | | 2 | | | | | 2 | 8 | 151 |
| E1 | 11 | 23 | 2 | 2 | 8 | 5 | 9 | 11 | 14 | 4 | 14 | | 5 | | 1 | | | 1 | 13 | 3 | | 11 | 3 | 1 | 1 | | 1 | | | | 10 | 9 | 157 |
| D2B | 12 | 18 | 9 | 5 | 2 | 6 | 10 | 15 | 21 | 2 | 24 | | | | | 1 | | | 10 | 13 | 4 | 9 | 3 | 2 | 3 | | | 1 | 1 | | 1 | 14 | 185 |
| D2A | | 6 | | 1 | | 1 | 7 | 7 | 7 | 1 | 4 | | 3 | | | | | | 1 | 4 | 11 | | | | 6 | | | | | | | 2 | 63 |
| D1 | 2 | 1 | | 1 | | | 2 | 1 | 1 | 1 | | | 2 | | | | | | 2 | 1 | 1 | 4 | | | | | | | | | | 2 | 17 |
| D1-C4 | | 3 | | | 2 | 1 | 1 | 6 | 2 | 1 | 3 | | | 1? | | | | | | 2 | 1 | 1 | | | | | | | | | | | 24 |
| C4 | | | | | | | | | | | | | | | | | | | | | | | | | | | | | | | | | |
| C3 | | | | | | | | | | | | | | | | | | | | | | | | | | | | | | 1 | | | 1 |
| TOTAL | 37 | 77 | 14 | 16 | 17 | 16 | 39 | 60 | 52 | 10 | 56 | 1? | 22 | 1? | 1? | 1 | 1 | 1 | 32 | 29 | 17 | 25 | 6 | 3 | 10 | 2 | 1 | 1 | 1 | 1 | 13 | 35 | 598 |

8700 B.P. This may be too short a time period considering the standard deviation of the radiocarbon dates. In addition, the sediments are as thick as those of the underlying D1 sub-unit. But before the thickness of the deposits are used to estimate the time range, it would have to be proved that the same number of men through time were depositing their refuse at an even rate. Selected as the lowest boundary between sub-units D1 and D2A was a demarcation in the deposits visible to the naked eye containing charcoal sample from Rockshelter 3, which had an age of 8810±430 B.P. (6850 B.C.). As an upper boundary between D2A and D2B a concave living surface with deer bone in Rockshelter 3, which dated 8760±350 B.P. (6810 B.C.), was selected.

The warm and moist trend, which began during the deposition of the D1 sub-unit, continued, resulting in further spreading of the oak forests in the Sabana and a continued rise in the water levels of ponds and swamps.

If the greater number of artifacts in subunit D2A is any indication, there was an increase in the amount of human habitation of the El Abra Rockshelters. Thus, in Rockshelter 2 was found 585 simple flakes and 17 distinguishable tools, 222 simple flakes and 11 tools in Rockshelter 3, and 274 simple flakes and 31 artifacts in Rockshelter 4. Since on an annual basis an average of only 5.85 flakes was deposited in Rockshelter 2, 2.22 in Rockshelter 3, and 2.74 in Rockshelter 4, the sporadic, short-time occupation evidently continued (Table 2). No major changes occurred in the lithic tools except for the addition of triangular flake scrapers. Because of poor preservation in the lowermost strata, mammal bone was present for the first time in the D2A sub-unit. However, no bone tools were encountered, either in this sub-unit or in the later D2B, E1, and E2 sub-units. The mammal bones indicate that a major source of livelihood was hunting yet no hunting implements, such as projectile points, were encountered in the rockshelters. Possibly these artifacts were made of wood as they were in the historic Amazonian tribes, but because of poor preservation conditions none has persisted to the present day in the fill.

*Sub-Unit D2B*

The beginning date for this sub-unit is estimated to have been about 8700 B.P., while the terminal date is unknown. The only associated radiocarbon date was taken from a charcoal sample in a clay-lined firepit in Rockshelter 4, which had an age of 7250±100 (6350 B.C.). Possibly the deposition continued until the beginning of the ceramic phase (E2) estimated between 2000 and 1500 years ago. The overlying E2 sub-unit rests uncomfortably on top of the D2A sub-unit, and this suggests a time gap;

## The Edge-Trimmed Tool Tradition of Northwest South America

on the other hand, the continuity in artifact types is indicative of continuous occupation.

Based on evidence in other parts of the world, the warm post-glacial trend peaked between 7000 and 4000 years ago, although in the deposits of the El Abra Rockshelters no evidence was found of this terminal maximum. If it did indeed occur in the Sabana there would have been a forest and moisture climax. A cooler and drier period followed (ca. 4000–2000 B.P.), accompanied by a minor maximum of oak forests (van Geel and van der Hammen, 1973:88). Since the time duration of the D2B sub-unit is unknown, it is not possible to state that there was an increase, on a mean annual basis, of artifacts. The total number, however, was greater than that of the underlying D2A sub-unit. In Rockshelter 2, were found 2307 simple flakes and 41 distinguishable tools, in Rockshelter 3, 790 simple flakes and 15 tools, and in Rockshelter 4, 3600 simple flakes and 140 tools.

A major unresolved problem in delineating the lithic assemblage in the D2B sub-unit is the presence of ground stone tools in the upper layer, for it cannot be assumed arbitrarily that they were not intrusions from the overlying E1 sub-unit (associated with the early ceramic complex). That intrusions did occur in this level is evident in the presence of scattered sherds, historic burials, and deep firepits. In addition, only a small number, 5, of ground stone tools were found. In spite of the possible addition of ground stone tools such as basalt celts, notched axes and semilunar knives, the basic simple-flaked chert artifacts persisted.

### Sub-Units E1 and E2

These units were associated with the ceramic cultures of the Sabana de Bogotá. Although many new artifacts were added to the material culture such as sherds, bronze poncho pins, and porcelain (in E2) the basic preceramic lithic industry continued. The introduction of agricultural activities in the region resulted in deforestation, and thus it is possible that the Sabana might still be covered with forests if it were not for the interferrence of man.

### General Observations on the Artifacts from the El Abra Rockshelters

A detailed analysis of the lithic assemblages of the Edge-trimmed Tool Tradition has been made only on artifacts of the El Abra Industries. The most common of the flaked artifacts are unretouched flakes. Although the vast majority of the flakes probably resulted from the manufacture of tools, nevertheless it cannot be stated arbitrarily that some simple flakes were not deliberately fabricated for use as cutting, drilling or engraving tools. In the three El Abra Rockshelters a grand total of 16,849 unretouched flakes were found, while 35 had minute flaking on their edges either from use or from deliberate fabrication. There were also 475 cores which had had their working edge trimmed by percussion flaking, and 77 large flakes with one edge trimmed, probably for use as tools. Classifying the edge-trimmed artifacts, whether made from flakes or cores, was difficult because they were so poorly fabricated that it was not always possible to be sure whether the object was actually a tool or was a reject from tool manufacture. Those considered tools had a definite geometric shape and are tabulated in Table 4 and illustrated in Figures 1 and 2.

## Other Sites of the Edge-Trimmed Tool Tradition in Colombia

Near the Falls of Tequendama, Sabana de Bogotá, Correal and van der Hammen, excavated a rockshelter in 1973 that had in its second level from the bottom a stone industry reported to be similar to the preceramic lithic assemblages from El Abra (van der Hammen, personal communication). The radiocarbon dates from this level range between 11,000 and 10,000 B.P., indicating a rough contemporaneity with the lowest occupational levels of El Abra. Comparing the lithic industries of the Falls of Tequendama Rockshelter with those of El Abra, van der Hammen states:

> The artifacts [from the lowest level] are partly very different from the later ones (bifaces and even a fragment of a nice bifacially-worked point) and partly made material from outside the Sabana de Bogotá, with greater technical skill than the more El Abra-like material from after 10,000. The black chert scraper [Fig. 2, Misc. E] from the 10,000-11,000 B.P. level [from El Abra] would fit excellently in the lower Tequendama level (personal communication).

The writer examined color slides of four artifacts from the lower level at the Falls of Tequendama Rockshelter and reached the following conclusions: 1) two of the tools are bifacially flaked, a manufacturing technique absent at El Abra; 2) one biface is a broad tool with a tapered base that probably was an end-scraper, although the possibility that it was a blunt-tipped projectile point cannot be discounted; another has an ovoid shape, broad, shallow side notches and a blunt tip and it may have been a hafted end-scraper; and 3) the remaining tool is lenticular blade with flaking over all the upper surface.

The nearest preceramic site to the El Abra Rockshelters lies in an eroded bank of the lower terrace of the Sopó River, Sabana de Bogotá. A large number of brown chert flakes and core artifacts similar to the El Abra industry were found on the surface mixed with sherds. A vertical exposure, one meter long and one and one-half meters wide was cut in 1967, exposing the following strata:

*Strata 0 - .36m*, silty humus, light brownish-grey color, relatively uncompacted, contained chert flakes and sherds;

*Strata .36 - .51m*, indurated silty soils mixed with humus, grey-brown color, contained chert flakes but no sherds;

*Strata .51 - .62m*, uncompacted silts with black streaks, contained a brown chert retouched flake that may have served as a scraper;

*Strata .62 - .95m*, indurated grey-brown silts with black flecks resting on top of a soil line; contained no flakes or other man-made objects.

At a greater distance is the Tibitó site, located on an eroded bank of the Bogotá River between the Fleischman Yeast Plant and Zipaquirá. Here on the eroded upper surface and bank of the lowest terrace were found many brown chert flakes and other artifacts of the El Abra type mixed with Chibcha type of sherds and green-glazed Colonial porcelain. No excavations were made at the site other than straightening a profile of the eroded bank.

A further section of the Sabana de Bogotá that may have contained an El Abra-like industry are the gravel terraces east of Mosquera. On the surface of eroded areas and within the gravel deposits occur thousands of water-worn nodules and fragments of tabular chert of the type utilized as raw material at El Abra. In the few areas where recognizable artifacts were found, they were associated with sherds. Since there are outcrops of brown chert much closer to El Abra, it is doubtful if the Mosquera gravels were utilized by people of this site.

Since projectile points are characteristic of sites of the Edge-trimmed Tool Tradition, the extensive collections of artifacts from the Sabana de Bogotá at the University of the Andes and the Instituto Colombiano de Antropología were examined by the writer. No projectile points were seen, and in fact Reichel-Dolmatoff reported that as of 1969 he was aware of only a single stone projectile point, an artifact from a garden a short distance east of Bogotá, having been found in the Sabana.

Reichel-Dolmatoff has described several sites in Colombia which, on the basis of surface collections, lack projectile points and have lithic artifacts similar to those of El Abra (1965:48-50; 1957:123-125). One such site is at San Nicolás on an eroded hilltop overlooking the lower Sinú River, which drains into the Caribbean Sea. This is an important site since it lies near the Isthmus of Panama, a major route of immigration into South America. Another site found by Reichel-Dolmatoff lies on an eroded terrace overlooking the Canal del Dique, a silted arm of the Magdelena River near its mouth. The writer, who visited the site, collected from the surface sherds and ground stone tools, such as celts, mixed with the El Abra types of flaked artifacts.

Reichel-Dolmatoff and the writer made a collection from eroded pathways in the town of Carare, on the lower terrace of the middle Magdelena Valley, which included many chert flakes and other artifacts similar to those from El Abra. A single exception was a well-made rectanguloid scraper with an edge that may have been retouched by pressure flaking. Near Carare, in the sides of a quarry, a series of cobble choppers, unlike any artifacts from El Abra, were collected by the writer in 1967. The tools lay in the upper .50 m stratum of sandy silts that lay directly on top of gravels and cobbles; they had been made by removing by percussion from a single face, large flakes on one edge of ovoid or flattened-ovoid quartzite cobbles. Reichel-Dolmatoff also lists other sites in Colombia that lack projectile points and have a simple lithic technology. These lie in the terraces of rivers emptying into the Pacific Ocean, such as the upper Baudó, Juruvidá, and Chorí (ibid.:49).

Reichel-Dolmatoff makes these general remarks about sites in Colombia that lack stone projectile points:

> All were found on eroded ridges or hill-tops, on old river terraces, or in gravel beds. ... The total tool assemblages consisted mainly of unifacial scrapers and knives, with a few chopping tools, a number of small boring or engraving tools, and no projectile points at all. Crude percussion flaking is predominant, with secondary retouch by controlled percussion or pressure flaking occurring only rarely. The range of tools and the riverine or lagoon environment suggests bands of food gatherers and fisherman, but certainly not groups dependent upon hunting or cultivation. The emphasis upon scraping and cutting edges may well be connected with the daily tasks of scaling and cleaning fish, and with the manufacture of fishing gear or other wooden instruments (ibid.:51).

Although Reichel-Dolmatoff may be correct in assigning a food gathering and fishing economy to the sites he lists, the conclusion is not inevitable. River valleys are also possible sites for hunting groups. That at least some of the cultural complexes of the Edge-trimmed Tool Tradition were based upon hunting is suggested by the deer bone found associated with the El Abra industries and by the presence of mammal bones in the Falls of Tequendama Rockshelter.

## The Northwest South American Tradition

Stothert has defined recently a Northwest South American Tradition characterized by artifacts made from simple flakes and modified only with a minimal retouch (n.d.). Although some industries she cites, such as the Vegas complex, also have ground tools like sandstone pestles or manos and notched axes of green andesite, none has stone projectile points. Sites she assigns to this tradition include the Siches, Hondo and Estero complexes of northern coastal Peru, the Vegas and Achallan complexes of southwestern Ecuador, the San Nicolás and Pomares from Colombia, and the Cerro Mangote from Panama. As previously mentioned, the Northwest South American Tradition appears to be identical with the Edge-trimmed Tool Tradition, the only difference being in the criteria selected for definition. Core tools, although they are also present in the Northwest of South America, are not included by Stothert in the selected criteria. In the Edge-trimmed Tool Tradition, however, core tools are included. In addition, there is no evidence of notched axes, manos, and pestles in the Edge-trimmed Tool Tradition, but neither are they present in all sites of Stothert's tradition. On the basis of radiocarbon dates, Stothert considers the El Abra industries as the prototypes for the sites in the Northwest South American Tradition.

A major site included in Stothert's tradition is the Vegas site in the Santa Elena Peninsula of Ecuador (ca. 6700–5000 B.C. or 8650–6550 B.P.). Lanning, who did the field work, describes the Vegas lithic industry (Lanning and Patterson, 1967:9):

> Vegas artifacts, other than hammerstones, choppers, and pestles, are almost all very small, made on chips or on tiny pyramidal and discoidal cores. By far the most abundant artifacts are denticulates, gravers, and spokeshaves ... other typical Vegas artifacts include chisel-like tools, minute side scrapers, rare snub-nosed, thumbnail and end scrapers, a few plain and retouched blades used as knives, abundant cobble hammerstones ... cobble choppers and pestles now appear in the sequence, but are found only at shell midden sites (Lanning, n.d.:13).

The Vegas complex included two distinct settlement patterns: hunting camps along the river banks inhabited during the summer; and fishing and shellfish gathering sites near the ocean shore inhabited during the winter (Lanning and Patterson, 1967:13). Lanning postulates that the Santa Elena Peninsula, arid and denuded today, has undergone drastic dessication during post-glacial times, a process that became accelerated about 5000 B.C. or after Vegas times (ibid.:27). At one of the Vegas sites (No. 8) Stothert notes that a great variety of resources were exploited from adjacent niches, such as swamps, rivers, littoral areas, hills and wooded valleys (Stothert n.d.:3).

The Achallan complex (ca. 4685 B.P. or 2735±95 B.C.) succeeds in time the Vegas industry on the Santa Elena Peninsula (ibid.:4-7). The majority of the artifacts are made of simple chert flakes showing minimal modification. No grinding or chopping tools were found. The presence of a few sherds indicates that the ceramic period had already begun. Bones of deer, sea mammals, a few small mammals, and fish indicate exploitation of several environmental niches.

Related to the Edge-trimmed Tool Tradition are lithic assemblages from the Siches and El Estero complexes of the Northwest Peruvian coast. The former is estimated by Richardson to date between 6000 and 4000 B.C. (7950–5950 B.P.), contemporary with the Vegas complex (1973). The basic chipped stone industry of Siches is characterized by direct percussion manufacture of uniface artifacts struck from quartzite pebbles and includes single-notched forms (spokeshaves) and multiple-notched forms (denticulates). The total lithic industry, however, is more elaborate than that of El Abra in that it includes cup-shaped mortars, ground stone T-shaped axes, and grooved pebbles.

Apparently the Siches people concentrated more on collecting shellfish than those of the Vegas complex since their refuse consisted mainly of mollusk shells, although two grooved pebbles may have been used as bola stones for hunting sea mammals and birds. The presence of a mangrove type of mollusk indicates that the habitat, now arid, was more humid then, and possibly the river valleys were forested. Incipient agriculture may have begun since a fragment of the bottle gourd, *Lagenaria*, and a few carbonized seeds were found, while the mortars suggest that wild vegetable products were also gathered for food.

The basic flaked stone industry continued in the Estero complex (ca. 4000 B.C. or 5950 B.P.) except for an increase in the numbers of T-shaped axes and the addition of stone bowls and pestles. In the following Hondo assemblage (ca. 3100 B.C. or 5050 B.P.) the same basic chipped stone industry continued, but it was augmented by the addition of two unifacially chipped scrapers and the tip of an obsidian point.

## Relationship of the Edge-Trimmed Tool Tradition to Other Early South American Cultures

In this discussion no detailed summary of all the known non-stone-projectile point cultures in South America will be attempted. Rather, emphasis will be placed upon those which aid in the understanding of the origins and chronological position of the Edge-trimmed Tool Tradition. In addition, discussion will be limited to lithic assemblages from stratified sites.

Even though from a technological point of view the lithic assemblages of the Edge-trimmed Tool Tradition are among the simplest in South America, it can not be concluded that they are necessarily the prototype of this continent. For example, the earliest dates of the tradition, those from El Abra Rockshelters (12,500 B.P.) are only a little more than half as old as those from an Ayacucho cave, Peru (20,000 B.P.) excavated by MacNeish (1971).

At Ayacucho the oldest assemblage is the Paccaicasa complex from Pikamachay Cave (Flea Cave), assigned by MacNeish to his Core Tool Tradition. Here was found a series of crude, percussion-flaked and unifaced chopper-like core tools, large side scrapers, large spokeshaves, heavy denticulates, plus large choppers and sawed bone implements. Although it might be questioned that some of the Paccaicasa "tools" were actually implements since they were formed from the locally occurring volcanic tuff, MacNeish has pointed out that some are made of a green stone that had to be transported to the site by man (personal communication). Such an early date is not out of the question for man in the New World, considering the evidence for human population ca. 20,000 years ago near the central valley of Mexico, in such sites as Valsequillo (Irwin-Williams, 1973) and Tlapacoya (Mirambell, 1967).

Following in time in Flea Cave is the Ayacucho assemblage of the Flake and Bone Tradition, with a radiocarbon date of 14,150±180 B.P. (12,550 B.C.). In addition to the Paccaicasa types of core tool there were unifaced triangular projectile points, polishers, punches, and one ornament. MacNeish states that the unifaced stone projectile points resemble those from Valsequillo (personal communication) but Irwin-Williams points out that at the latter site there are major differences in the artifact, such as tapered and ground bases (personal communication). In spite of these differences in projectile points, it appears that they were in existence in South America long before the oldest lithic assemblages of the Edge-trimmed Tool Tradition.

More controversial are a series of lithic assemblages from the Chillon Valley, Peru, described by Lanning and Patterson (1967). The oldest is the Red Zone complex at the Chivateros site estimated to date from 14,000–12,500 B.P., an age theoretically greater than that of the oldest El Abra industry. The main tool types are little quartzite implements, the working edges of which have been made steeper by direct percussion. Although this is the main technique for the manufacture of artifacts of the Edge-trimmed Tool Tradition, the presence of burins and double-pointed perforators is not characteristic. Even less similar is the Chivateros

I complex, which lies under a wood sample dated ca. 8470 B.C. (10,690 B.P.). This industry has large bifaced implements, among them artifacts that may have been spear points. Because of the bifaces, Lanning and Patterson have assigned them to an Andean Biface Tradition. Fung, Cenzano, and Zavaleta (1972) have questioned Lanning's and Patterson's interpretation of the Chivateros' stratigraphy and also the estimated ages of the cultural complexes, while Lynch has postulated that its lithic assemblages form parts of a single cultural complex (1974:363).

Several lithic industries, lacking in stone projectile points, have estimated ages greater than those of the oldest industries from El Abra. Rouse and Cruxent have established a preceramic cultural sequence from the Rio Pedergal on the basis of the relationship of the sites to a series of terraces, the highest being the oldest (1963). They include, in chronological order, the Camare, Las Lagunas, El Jobo, and Las Casitas complexes. The diagnostic Camare artifact is a large, crude biface chopper made by battering the edges and sides. Associated with these artifacts are large trimmed flakes that may have been scrapers or knives, while the Las Lagunas complex has much thinner biface tools. Willey estimates the Camare complex (assigned to a "Chopper Tradition") spans the time from 16,000 to 13,000 B.P. and the Las Lagunas (assigned to a "Biface Tradition") to range from 13,000 to 11,500 B.P. (Willey, 1971:Fig. 2-3). If these dates are indeed correct the Edge-trimmed Tool Tradition, which lacks bifaces, is more recent than these Venezuelan cultural complexes. Lynch, however, has commented on the dating of the Core Tradition and the Biface Tradition in these words, "Field evidence is very weak for early Biface and Chopper Traditions, but it is not likely to precede the use of stone projectile points" (1974:356). Factors he cites are that most such complexes lie on the surfaces of terraces where mixing can take place, that there is a scarcity of proven association with radiocarbon dates, and that many of the artifacts actually may be quarry "blanks."

The evidence for assigning a definite date to the El Jobo complex, characterized by biface stone projectile points with a lanceolate shape, is somewhat better. El Jobo points were first found at the Mauco site, mixed with bones of extinct Pleistocene megafauna. Because of the possibility of mixing at the site, which is an extinct ascending spring, the association of artifacts with the radiocarbon date of 14,300±500 (Tamers, 1969:407) has been questioned. At the Taima-Taima site, however, El Jobo points, lying in situ beside fragments of mastodon bones, were dated by radiocarbon dates which range from 14,400±435 B.P. to 13,010±280 B.P. This is evidence that cultural complexes with stone projectile points were as old, if not older, than the El Abra industries.

Numerous other early sites with stone projectile points have been described for South America, but, if the date of 12,500 B.P. is correct for the beginnings of the Edge-trimmed Tool Traditions, none of them appear to be older. Such sites include El Inga of Ecuador (ca. 8950–3950 B.P., Bell, 1965), Guitarrero Cave of Peru (ca. 10,500 B.P., Lynch and Kennedy, 1970), Lauricocha Cave of Peru (ca. 9525 B.P., Cardich, 1964), Fells Cave I of Chile (10,710 B.P., Bird, 1965:Fig. 6), and Lagoa Santa, Brazil (ca. 9700 B.P., Hurt and Blasi, 1969).

## Summary and Conclusions

The technologically simplest lithic industries in South America are found in the El Abra Rockshelters, the Pomares site, the Falls of Tequendama Rockshelter, and the Carare village site, all in Colombia. Because of the close relationship with the Vegas and Achallan complexes of Ecuador and the Siches and Estero of Peru all these complexes have been assigned to the Edge-trimmed Tool Tradition. Included in this tradition are percussion-flaked artifacts made from natural raw material, such as chunks and fragments of tabular chert and water-worn chert quartzite pebbles. Some of this raw material has been reduced in size by rough percussion flaking to form flakes and cores. To make tools, the cores and flakes have been generally flaked only on the edges of one face with the remainder retaining the cortex. An even smaller number have been further modified by secondary percussion retouching of the working edge. The vast majority of artifacts are, however, unretouched flakes which could have served for cutting, drilling, and engraving. Defining other tool types is difficult because only a small percentage of artifacts have regular geometric forms. In this group are those with an obtuse-angled working edge, which could have served as end-scrapers and side-scrapers, and those with an acute-angled cutting edge which could have served as cutting and sawing tools. Some tool artifacts have single or multiple concave working edges and could have been shaving implements. All these tools, as shown by experiment, could have been used for wood working, hide working, and as artifacts for making tools of wood or bone.

Other lithic tools are not universally present. At El Abra, quartzite hammerstones and polishing tools were rare. In some cultural complexes, such as Vegas, a few sandstone manos, pestles, and andesite notched axes were encountered. Reichel-Dolmatoff refers to choppers found in some sites in Colombia, assigned by the writer to the Edge-trimmed Tool Tradition. At El Abra, two rectanguloid percussion-flaked siltstone choppers were found but are of unknown provenience since they occurred in what seemed to be backfill from pits made by previous excavators. In none of the sites assigned to the Edge-trimmed Tool Tradition have stone projectile points been found; they are in fact rare in the whole area of Colombia covered by this tradition. For example, Reichel-Dolmatoff stated in 1969 that he knew of only one projectile point having been found in the entire Sabana de Bogotá, while only a few points have been encountered in the Magdelena Valley.

The origin of the Edge-trimmed Tool Tradition and its relationship to other South American preceramic traditions are uncertain. In a summary of "Early Man in the New World," Krieger has postulated a "pre-projectile point" stage followed by a "Paleo-Indian" state characterized by projectile points and knives (1964). He explains the absence of projectile points by concluding that "the fact of percussion does not adequately describe the technology; more important is the inability of the people at this stage to flatten and thin knives of bifaced form" (ibid.:42).

It still remains to be demonstrated that sites lacking stone projectile points are necessarily older than those that have them, and again the lack of stone projectile points does not necessarily indicate that some of them were not made of wood or bone. Certainly the oldest radiocarbon dates (ca. 12,500 B.P.) of the Edge-trimmed Tool Tradition, which has the simplest of lithic technologies, suggest that it is more recent than some cultural complexes such as those from Ayacucho (ca. 14,000 B.P.), which has both stone and bone projectile points. The earliest lithic industries of the Edge-trimmed Tool Tradition appear to be no older than the El Jobo cultural complex that has stone projectile points. It is doubtful then that, even though the Edge-trimmed Tool Tradition has the simplest lithic technology and lacks stone projectile points, it necessarily represents the initial South American cultural complex.

Although no stone projectile points have been found in the sites of the Edge-trimmed Tool Tradition, it cannot be concluded necessarily that projectile points were absent, for they may have been made of some other material. The presence of deer bones in the prehistoric levels at El Abra indicates that hunting was an important economic activity, and, unless some other kind of artifact or artifacts were utilized to kill the game, projectile points probably were so used. At El Abra, it is doubtful that bone was used for projectile points; in spite of numerous mammal bones, no tools of any type were encountered that were made of this material. Possibly wood was used for tipping projectiles in the manner of contemporary Amazonian tribes.

Assuming, then, that the cultural complexes of the Edge-trimmed Tool Tradition indeed chose wood rather than stone for their projectile points, this choice of raw material must be explained. That suitable lithic raw material was available is clear from the fact that scrapers were made of stone. Perhaps the answer lies partially in the fact that there is strong evidence that nearly all if not all the sites of this tradition were located within or lay close to tropical forests abundant in hardwood. In such an environment projectile points made of hardwoods may have been found to be as efficient, if not more efficient, in killing the local game than those made of stone, and thus wood would continue to be used as long as the supply lasted. This does not explain why scrapers and spokeshaves were made of stone, but the answer may lie in the fact that wood would not retain a sharp cutting edge for so long a time as scrapers and spokeshaves made of silicates like chert. Again for hammerstones, manos, and axes, stone appears to be a more efficient raw material.

The place of origin of the lithic technology of the Edge-trimmed Tool Tradition is unknown. On the basis of its simplicity of manufacture, theoretically it should represent one of the earliest, if not the earliest, industry in South America. Yet the fact that the oldest dates, those from the El Abra and Falls of Tequendama rockshelters, are more recent than those from sites already containing projectile points, such as the early complexes of the Ayacucho caves and the Valsequillo sites, cast doubt on such a conclusion. In this report, the hypothesis has been offered that the lack of stone projectile points is not necessarily indicative of a primitive origin but that these artifacts may have been made from hardwood obtained from a tropical forested environment. On the basis of the theory that man migrated into South America from North America, a logical place of origin of the Edge-trimmed Tool Tradition would be the tropical forested region of Central America. As yet, however, no sites that lack stone projectiles points but are definitely as old as the El Abra sites have been described from Central America. For example, the oldest non-stone projectile point industry described from Central America is the Casita de Piedra complex of Panama, estimated to have an age greater than 5850 B.P., but how much greater is uncertain (Sapir and Ranere, 1971:150).

Likewise, there is no clear evidence that the Edge-trimmed Tool Tradition originated at El Abra even though it has produced the oldest dates so far. In fact, because of the isolation of the El Abra sites in a high intermountain valley, it seems less probable as a place of origin than a site like Carare, located in the middle of the Magdelena Valley, a long corridor providing easy movement and communication among prehistoric peoples.

The persistence of the Edge-trimmed Tool Tradition throughout a period of about 12,500 years (from the earliest preceramic to the late historic Chibcha cultural complexes) also needs explaining. It is doubtful that this long continuity can be attributed to lack of knowledge as to how to make stone projectile points or biface tools in general, since it is difficult to believe that there was no contact with surrounding cultures that knew how to make them. As mentioned previously, stone projectile points were made by cultures surrounding the area of the Edge-trimmed Tool Tradition, for example the El Jobo and El Inga industries and the tradition seems to have been adapted efficiently to a tropical forested environment. Since there is no evidence of major changes in the forests of the core area in Colombia, other than the deforestation brought about by agricultural activities of the historic Chibcha, there probably was no overwhelming necessity to change the technology. Even today the Indian tribes in the tropical forests of Colombia still make their projectile points of wood.

The Edge-trimmed Tool Tradition was based upon the exploitation of a wide variety of natural food resources. These include coastal sites and sites located along rivers which were based upon a fishing and shellfish gathering economy, as well as those in mountainous areas that were based on hunting and gathering. In the later sites, because of poor preservation of bone, there is no clear evidence that the earliest complexes hunted extinct Pleistocene megafauna, but the date of 12,500 makes such activity seem probable.

## References Cited

Bell, Robert E.
    1965   Archaeological investigations at the site of El Inga, Ecuador. Casa de la Cultura Ecuatoriana.

Bird, Junius B.
    1965   The concept of a "pre-projectile point" cultural stage in Chile and Peru. American Antiquity 31:262-70.

Cardich, Augusto
    1964   Lauricocha fundamentos para una prehistoria de los Andes centrales. Studia Prehistorica III. Centro Argentino de Estudios Prehistoricos.

Correal, G., T. van der Hammen, and J. C. Lerman
    1969   Artefactos liticos de abrigos rocosos en: El Abra, Colombia. Revista Colombiana de Antropologia 14:9-53. Instituto Colombiana de Antropologia.

Fung Pineda, Rosa, Carlos F. Cenzano Z., and Amaro Zavelta C.
   1972   El taller litico de Chivateros, Valle de Chillon. Revista del Museo Nacional, pp. 62-74.

Hurt, Wesley R. and Oldemar Blasi
   1969   O projecto arquelogico "Lagoa Santa"—Minas Gerais Brazil. Arquivos do Museu Paranaense, Arqueologia, No. 4.

Hurt, Wesley R., Thomas van der Hammen, and Gonzalo Correal Urrego
   1972   Preceramic sequences in the El Abra Rockshelters, Colombia. Science, 175:1106-1108.

Irwin-Williams, Cynthia
   1973   Summary of archaeological evidence from the Valsequillo region, Puebla Mexico. 9th International Congress of Anthropological Sciences.

Krieger, Alex D.
   1964   Early man in the New World. Item *in:* Prehistoric man in the New World, edited by J. D. Jennings and E. Norbeck, pp. 23-81. Univ. of Chicago Press.

Lanning, Edward P.
   n.d.   Archaeological investigations on the Santa Elena Peninsula, Ecuador. Report to the National Science Foundation on Research Carried out under Grant GS-402, 1964-1965.

Lanning, Edward P. and Thomas C. Patterson
   1967   Early man in South America. New World archaeology, readings from Scientific American, 1974:44-50.

Lynch, Thomas F.
   1974   The antiquity of man in South America. Quaternary Research 4: 356-77.

Lynch, Thomas F. and Kenneth A. R. Kennedy
   1970   Early human cultural and skeletal remains from Guitarrero Cave, Northern Peru. Science 169:1307-09.

MacNeish, Richard S.
   1971   Early man in the Andes. New World archaeology, readings from Scientific American, 1974:143-53.

Mirambell, Lorena
   1967   Excavaciones en un sitio pleistocenico de Tlapacoya, Mexico. Instituto Nacional de Antropologia e Historia. Boletin 29:37-41.

Reichel-Dolmatoff, G.
   1965   Colombia. New York: Frederick A. Praeger.

Reichel-Dolmatoff, Gerardo and Alicia
   1957   Reconocimiento arqueologico de la Hoya del Rio Sinu. Revista Colombia de Antropologia 6:261-71.

Richardson III, James B.
   1973   The preceramic sequence and the Pleistocene and post-Pleistocene climate of northwest Peru. Item *in:* Variations in anthropology, pp. 199-211. Illinois Archaeological Survey.

Rouse I., and J. M. Cruxent
   1963   Some recent radiocarbon dates for western Venezuela. American Antiquity 28:537-40.

Sapir, Olga Linares de and Anthony J. Ranere
   1971   Human adaptation to the tropical forests of western Panama. Archaeology 24:346-47.

Stothert, Karen E.
   n.d.   The early prehistory of the Santa Elena Peninsula, Ecuador: continuities between the preceramic and ceramic cultures. Paper presented to the 61st Congress of Americanists, Mexico City, Mexico, Sept. 2-9, 1974.

Tamers, M. A.
   1969   Instituto Venezolano de investigaciones cientificas natural radiocarbon measurements IV. Radiocarbon Supplement 11:396-422.

Van Geel, B., and T. van der Hammen
   1973   Upper quaternary vegetational and climatic sequence of the Fuquene area (eastern Cordillera, Colombia). The Quarternary of Colombia 1:8-92. Amsterdam: Elsevier Scientific Pub. Co.

Willey, Gordon R.
   1971   An introduction to American archaeology, South America, vol. 2. Englewood Cliffs: Prentice-Hall.

# ADAPTATIONS OF THE EARLY NEOLITHIC FARMERS IN CENTRAL EUROPE

*Sarunas Milisauskas*
The State University of New York, Buffalo

The adaptations of the first farming populations in Central Europe during the Early Neolithic from 4600-3800 B.C. based on radiocarbon dates or 5500-4600 B.C. (calibrated dates will be given in parantheses) using tree-ring calibrated dates can be understood by examining their subsistence strategy, settlement system, and trade networks. The resulting analysis will consider their utilization of the natural environment, the possible methods for land exploitation, and their relationship to persisting hunting and gathering groups.

The earliest farming societies in Central Europe are associated with the so-called Linear (*Linienbandkeramik, Bandkeramik*, Linear Pottery or Danubian I) culture, which derives its name from the ceramics decorated with incised straight or curved lines. Linear culture material is found over a vast territory in Europe, from the Maas (Meuse) River Valley in the Low Countries to the Dnestr River in the Soviet Union, and from the Drava (Drau) River in Yugoslavia to the mouth of the Odra (Oder) River in Poland (Fig. 1). The Linear people did not by any means occupy all of this enormous territory; rather they limited their settlements to loess lands or other areas of good soil. Thus the pattern of the Linear settlements in Central Europe has an island-like character, and it is very likely that hunting and gathering societies continued their way of life in other areas. This is clearly illustrated by the distribution of Linear culture sites in Poland (Fig. 2).

The spread of farmers into Central Europe occurred during the Atlantic climatic period. At that time, the dominant vegetation in Central Europe was mixed broad-leaf forests. Elms, lindens, maples, ashes, and especially oaks were the typical trees. In areas of sandy soil and in mountainous regions conifers predominated. A variety of trees and other plants that grew at higher altitudes than they do today suggest that during the Early

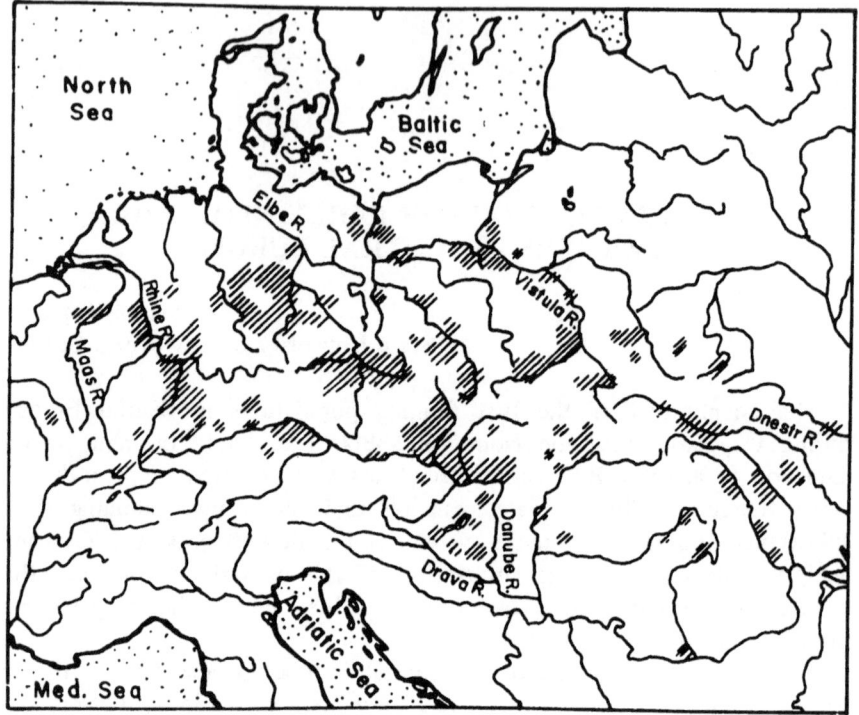

Figure 1. Distribution of Linear Culture sites in Europe.

Neolithic the temperature in Central Europe was warmer by 2°C, at least during the summer (Butzer, 1971). The expansion of the first farmers into Central Europe modified the landscape in some areas. For the first time large areas of forests were cleared and non-local plants and animals were introduced.

The earliest Linear ceramics are found in the Middle Danube area. (Quitta, 1967:264). It is speculated that Linear culture groups expanded from this area north into Central Europe following major water routes such as the Danube, Rhine, Elbe, Morava, Váh, Vltava, Neckar, Vistula, etc. Radiocarbon dates put the earliest Linear sites aound 4600-4500 B.C. (5500-5400 B.C.)

The Linear communities expanded very rapidly over Central Europe, reaching the Netherlands around 4400 B.C. (5300 B.C.) and northern Poland around 4350 B.C. (5250 B.C.) What caused this rapid expansion? It is highly unlikely that there was a single migration, since at the tribal level

# Adaptations of Early Neolithic Farmers in Central Europe

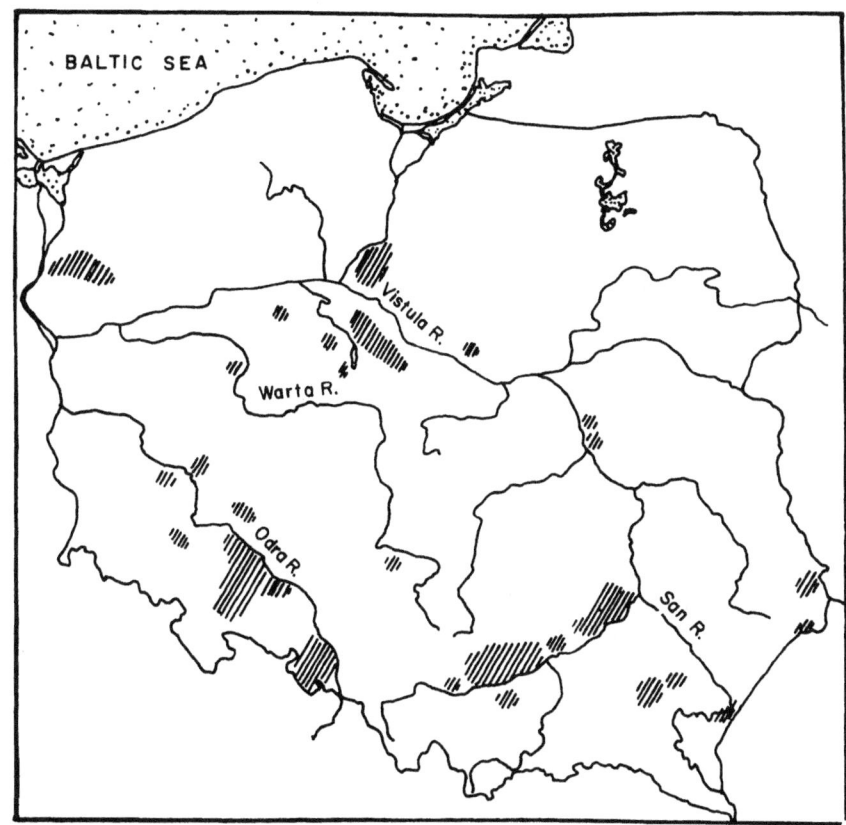

Figure 2. Distribution of Linear Culture sites in Poland.

of development people usually do not migrate long distances; these people had domestic animals such as cattle, pigs, and sheep/goats and it would not be easy to migrate with such animals over long distances. Probably population increases, internal and external conflicts, and preference for certain types of soils led to the segmenting or budding off of daughter villages from parent communities and thus to the duplication of Linear communities over all of Central Europe. The productivity of the horticulture practiced by the Linear people was obviously sufficient for population increase. Internal conflicts in villages may have been settled by one faction's moving away and establishing a new community. War between communities may have driven one group to seek refuge in a new area. It should be noted that the Linear people were basically expanding into open niches and could be very selective about how long they would exploit an area. When yields fell because of soil exhaustion, they could move into new territory.

The expansion of Linear people led to the occupation of some areas or territories of hunters and gatherers. Perhaps there was some fighting between Linear and hunting and gathering people, but since a society organized into large village communities commands great competitive advantages over small migratory bands, the hunters and gatherers were defeated and pushed out from some areas. Others could have been assimilated into Neolithic communities or even willingly have adopted farming. In any case, these events are so ephemeral that archaeologists have difficulty in identifying them.

Archaeologists have emphasized the great homogeneity of the Linear culture, especially of the ceramic material. The early Linear culture ceramics exhibit little stylistic differentiation throughout Central Europe. This probably can be accounted for by the rapid initial expansion of small Linear communities into good soil areas of Central Europe. For example, only seventeen sites in Central Germany belong to the Early phase of Linear ceramics (Fig. 3). During the Middle and Late phases of the Linear ceramics, there is more regional stylistic variability. The regional stylistic zones probably reflect more intense communication and exchange among Linear communities within regional physiographic areas and increased endogamy due to continued population increases and greater population density.

Despite an appearance of homogeneity, there were always some differences among individual early Linear communities. The simple splitting of a village creates a contrast between parent and daughter villages, for one is not usually an exact duplicate of the other. This may affect the physical composition of the population and produce stylistic differences in the material culture. For example, some differences in ceramic ornamentation can occur in the daughter community because it does not represent a random sample of the pottery styles present in a village. Also when a village splits into two parts, there is less communication or interaction between the people of different communities than when they lived in a single community. This leads to greater stylistic differences between the artifacts of the two communities.

The Linear people probably represented the tribal level of sociocultural development. We can assume that the individual villages were politically and economically autonomous. Villages located close together may have been tied to one another by kin relationships or by common membership in non-kinship sodalities or associations, such as warrior or ceremonial

Adaptations of Early Neolithic Farmers in Central Europe

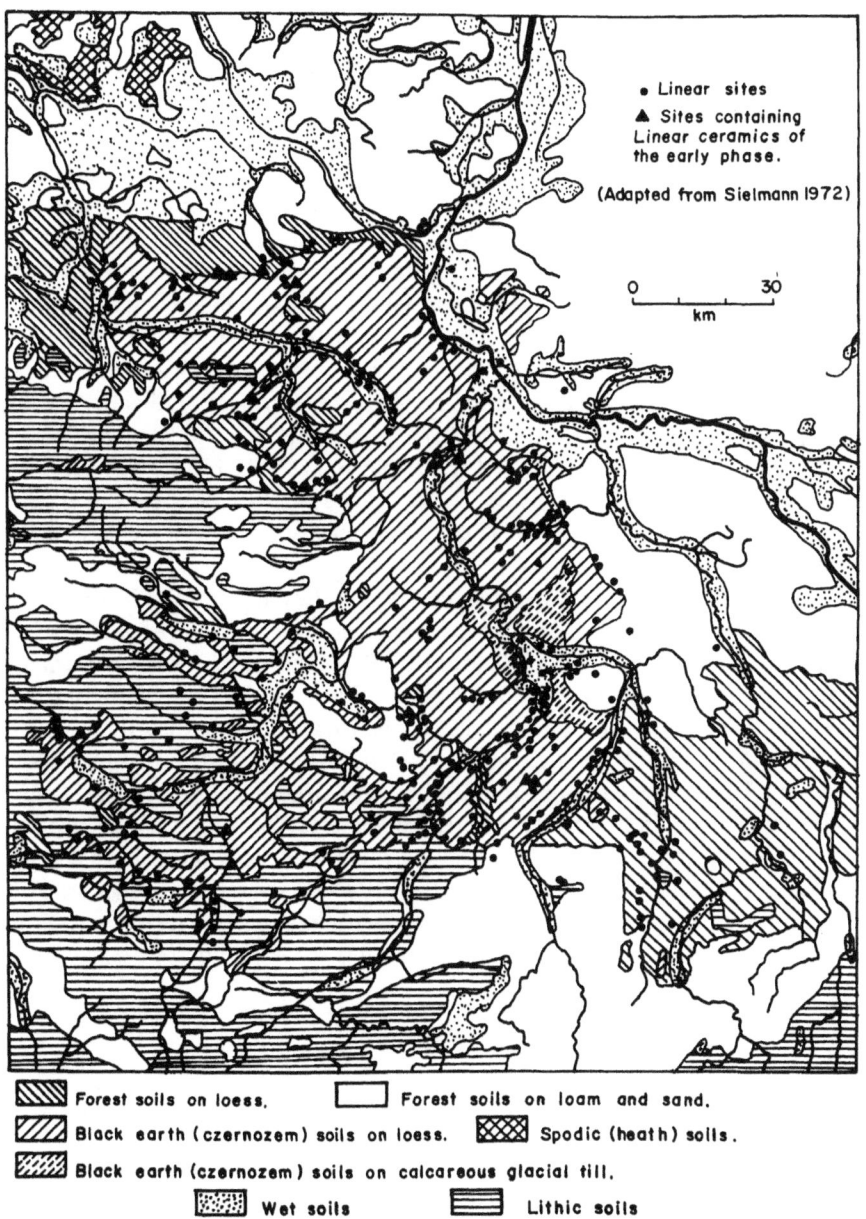

Figure 3. Distribution of Linear Culture sites in Central Germany.

societies. In general, there is little evidence for warfare between Linear communities: only small quantities of projectile points have been found and there are no fortifications except during the late phase at the Köln-Lindenthal site in Germany (Buttler and Haberey, 1936). Thus interaction among Linear communities probably was comparatively peaceful.

The Linear sites are usually located near or on low-lying terraces of rivers or major streams. J. Kruk's (1973) survey in southern Poland indicates that most of the Linear sites are located 2 to 6 meters above the flood plain. However, this location of the sites in low-lying areas left the uplands for hunting, the gathering of wild resources, and grazing or browsing.

Linear sites are usually situated on the edges of the loess or black earth soils areas. It is evident that they exploited prime agricultural land. Settlement studies conducted in various areas of Germany indicate that the majority of the Linear sites, 68 to 97 percent, were located on loess or other good soils (Fig. 3; Table 1 and Sielmann, 1971, 1972). The loess soils are easily worked and are very fertile. However, the loess soils themselves exhibit variability in fertility. Usually the Linear people selected well-drained soils.

Along rivers or major streams, the Linear sites are not evenly distributed but occur in clusters. Such a pattern was observed by Kruk (1973) in southeastern Poland and by Quitta (1970) in the Leipzig area of Germany. Kruk's survey east of Kraków, Poland along the left-bank tributaries of Vistula, i.e., Dłubnia, Szreniawa, and Nidzica, indicate that these clusters include from three to nine sites. The distance between individual sites is usually less than one kilometer (Fig. 4), while the distance between the site clusters ranges from two to several kilometers. The sites vary in size, and the differences to some extent may be functional. It is possible that at one time period the size of Linear settlements was quite homogeneous. Since the differences in the size of the settlements may reflect differences in the number of occupational phases present, sites having numerous occupational

TABLE I

| Sites on loess and various types of *czernozem* | | Sites not on loess |
|---|---|---|
| Central Germany | 246 (72%) | 96 (28%) |
| Lower Main Area | 114 (80%) | 29 (20%) |
| Middle Rhine Area | 62 (87%) | 9 (13%) |
| Southern Upper Rhine Area | 63 (85%) | 11 (15%) |
| Worms Area | 33 (68%) | 15 (32%) |
| Middle Neckar Area | 328 (97%) | 13 (03%) |
| Bavaria | 48 (96%) | 2 (04%) |

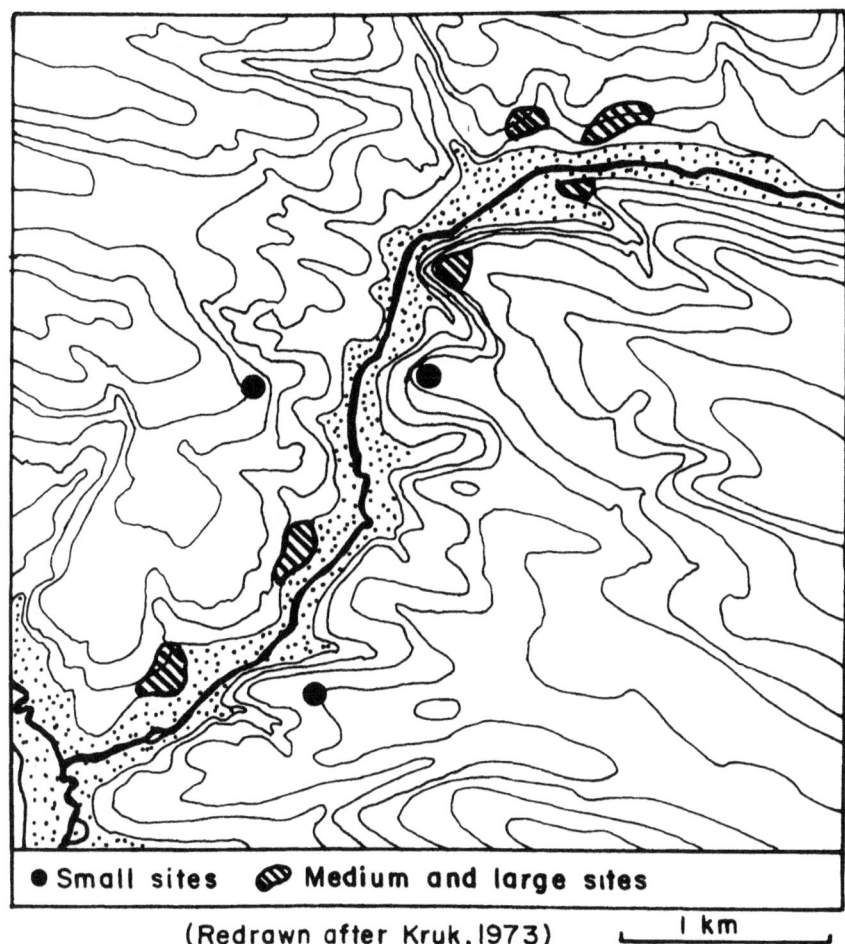

Figure 4. Linear Culture sites along the Szreniawa River near Szczepanowice, Miechów district, Southern Poland.

phases usually cover a larger area than those with a single occupation. Known sites containing multiple occupational phases are very large; for example, Bylany occupies 22 hectares, Olszanica 50 hectares, and Sittard 10 hectares. At any one time, only a portion of these sites were occupied by an actual village.

A Linear culture village consisting of longhouses and various work activity areas occupied 2-3 hectares or 5-7 acres. While longhouses covered most of this area, other parts of the village contained ovens, probably used for drying grain, and borrow pits that had been converted to garbage dumps. The longhouses usually were spaced 15-20 meters apart, and 7-12 or perhaps as many as 15 of them comprised a village at any one time. At Bylany in Czechoslovakia, there are 7-10 houses for each of the 7 occupational phases (Soudský and Pavlů, 1972). At least 8 longhouses formed a village during the so-called "music note" phase at Olszanica in Poland (Milisauskas, 1972, in press). Ninety-five structures were excavated at Elsloo, Netherlands (Modderman, 1968, 1970). Perhaps the Dutch sites had greater numbers of longhouses at one time period. If there are many closely spaced or overlapping longhouses in an area of the site, we can assume that the area was occupied by more than one phase. Elsloo is 10 hectares in size, and approximately one-third of it was excavated. Assuming the same density in the unexcavated area at Elsloo, the entire site may contain over 200 longhouses. Modderman suggests a total of 200 to 250 houses. Based on radiocarbon dates, the settlement lasted for 400±50 years. Depending on the time estimate for the duration of the settlement, one phase could have had 11 to 17 buildings if each occupation lasted for 25 years, or 9 to 14 buildings if each lasted for 20 years.

Linear longhouses are 6-45 meters long and 5-7 meters wide. At Bylany, 48 longhouses are 6-45 meters long (average 17.3 m) (Soudský and Pavlů, 1972). At Olszanica, the 13 longhouses were 7-41.5 meters long (average 17.2 m). The frames of the rectangular houses were built of five rows of wooden posts, two exterior and three interior. Earth from pits along the sides of the longhouses was used for daubing the walls. The longhouses were constructed of deciduous or coniferous trees, e.g., oaks at Bylany and conifers at Olszanica. Because of the rain and snow in Central Europe, they probably had gabled roofs. The longhouses are usually oriented NW-SE or N-S, probably in order to shelter their long sides from the prevailing winds which usually blow from the northwest.

The extremely long longhouses showing structural differences, such as the placement of the larger postmolds, probably were functionally different from other structures. Around these longhouses occur more of certain tool types, e.g., polished stone tools. These longhouses may have served for communal activities, or perhaps they were utilized by tribal associations or sodalities. It is also possible that the most important man of the village inhabited the longest longhouse. The size of the house does not imply that there was ranking of individuals in Linear society, but only that a man or woman might have achieved greater status on the basis of personal skills or personality traits and had the concomitant responsibility to host visitors and villagers alike.

Analyses of archaeological data from Linear cemeteries indicate status differences based on sex and age. For example, at the Nitra cemetery in Slovakia, *Spondylus* shells, polished stone tools and chipped stone artifacts are associated with adult males and especially with old males (Pavúk, 1972). At Sondershausen in Germany, *Spondylus* ornaments are associated with adult males and females (Kahlke, 1954). It is possible that those older males who owned more animals and land were of greater importance in the community and had the resources to participate more in an interregional exchange system. Some of these males may have achieved a status comparable to the so-called "Big Man" in Melanesia (Sahlins, 1963).

The number of people who inhabited a Linear culture village and its individual longhouses is probably overestimated by most archaeologists. In estimating the population of a single longhouse, it is usually assumed that the entire longhouse was occupied by a number of families. However, the density of artifacts, such as pottery, in Linear sites is too low for the various projected population figures. It is more likely that some animals shared a part of the house, with the loft serving as a storage area for fodder during the winter months. The population of a Linear village can be estimated from the total size of its component longhouses: it is assumed that the length of a longhouse reflects the size of the family inhabiting it. For example, using a measure based on the number of hearths and ovens found in Lengyel and Tripolyean houses, Soudský (1964, 1966) concluded that one family was present for every 5 to 6 meters of the house length. However, as previously mentioned an entire longhouse was not necessarily occupied by people only. Using Soudský's method, the population at Olszanica in Poland is estimated to be 16 or 17 families at any one time while 10-19 families per phase can be estimated by Bylany.

Except for the extremely long longhouses, we do not know what the variability in the size of individual Linear houses indicates in terms of socioeconomic organization; they may simply reflect family size differences or relative wealth in animals. Ethnographic studies suggest that longhouses occur frequently in matrilocal societies, and this may be true of the Linear communities. Ember's crosscultural study indicates that societies with houses in which the average roofed-over living area is more than 70 square meters, or 600 square feet, are usually matrilocal (Ember, 1973). There are many large houses in a Linear culture village, but likewise there are many small ones. Furthermore, since the Linear houses were not occupied by people only, a meter to meter comparison is not always valid.

The social organization of Linear people may have been very flexible; kindred may have been just a group of relatives. Corporate groups like clans and lineages are usually associated with landholding. Since the Linear people were not restricted in their choice of land, there may be no need to postulate the presence of corporate landholding groups.

The subsistence strategy of Linear people was based on horticulture, the raising of livestock, gardening, hunting, fishing, and gathering. The food potential from the different resources varied from season to season, and the availability of potential resources probably fluctuated from year to year. Hunting and gathering was more important in the economy than has previously been postulated by archaeologists. Results from the simple agriculture of the Linear people probably fluctuated: good and bad years, and in lean years hunting and gathering could make the difference between survival and starvation. Disease, insects, weather, and activities of animals and humans could all affect the cultivation of crops.

The mixed broad-leaf forests were rich in floral and faunal resources and the Linear people exploited a variety of wild plants and animals (Tables II & III). Also the forests supplied wood for construction and various domestic uses. The various wild resources were available for exploitation only during certain seasons. Berries, honey, fruits, and nuts, and mushrooms could be collected during the summer and fall, and hazelnuts and acorns in late summer and fall to be stored for the winter. Acorns could be eaten both by pigs and by humans. Domestic animals could graze in the forests, feeding especially on the leaves of trees, and leaves of deciduous trees could be collected for animal fodder for the winter. A great variety of wild animals were hunted by the Linear people, but most were wild ungulates. Frequently, the percentage of wild ungulates appears smaller at a site because of various small animals such as rabbits. However, the contribution of ungulates to the diet in terms of the total weight of meat was much greater than that shown by bone percentages. Wild animals constitute 20 to 30 percent of the total faunal array or even more at Linear sites when estimates utilize the minimum number of individuals derived from the bones found. It should be noted that the percentage of wild animals decreases to 10 percent if only the counts of bones at the sites are utilized in the estimates (Müller, 1964). Wild animals not only supplied meat for man, but also raw materials for making tools and clothing. Fishing and exploitation of water fowl are indicated by finds of the remains of carp, sturgeon, wild goose and wild duck (Müller, 1964).

It is unclear what methods or weapons were used for hunting by the Linear people. There are very few flint projectile points found in Linear culture sites in Czechoslovakia or Poland. On the western flank of the Linear culture area, the Netherlands and the Rhineland, more projectile points are found which may indicate the use of bow and arrow. Perhaps traps were used in hunting various animals in Poland and Czechoslovakia.

## TABLE II
### Domesticated and Wild Plants Found at Langweiler, Germany

| Sample Number | | sample #1 L.* 6C | sample #2 L. 6C | sample #3 L. 6C | sample #4 L. 6C | sample #5 L. 6C | sample #6 L. 3 | sample #7 L. 3 | sample #8 L. 3 | sample #9 L. 3 | sample #10 L. 3 |
|---|---|---|---|---|---|---|---|---|---|---|---|
| Sample Size | | 3.5 dm$^3$ *2 | 0.2 dm$^3$ | 7.7 dm$^3$ | 4.0 dm$^3$ | 6.0 dm$^3$ | 6.0 dm$^3$ | 3.7 dm$^3$ | 1.0 dm$^3$ | 0.7 dm$^3$ | 0.5 dm$^3$ |
| Einkorn Wheat (Triticum monococcum) | grain | 1 | | 10 | 2 | ,2 | | 8 | | | |
| | spikelet | | | 4 | 14 | 1 | | 289 | 4 | 1 | |
| | glume | 12 | 1 | 21 | 31 | 3 | | 3142 | | | |
| Emmer Wheat (Triticum dicoccon) | grain | 1 | | 24 | 4 | 1 | | 1 | 2 | 2 | |
| | spikelet | | | 3 | | 1 | | 111 | | | |
| | glume | 5 | | 15 | 6 | | 1 | 294 | 4 | | |
| Einkorn/Emmer | grain | 6 | 3 | 103 | 25 | 12 | 2 | 61 | 1 | | 2 |
| | spikelet | 17 | | 30 | 7 | | | 448 | 10 | | 2 |
| | glume | 1 | | | 3 | | | 138 | 3 | | |
| Rye brome (Bromus secalinus) | | | 1 | 140 | 8 | 5 | 1 | 24 | 1 | | 1 |
| Peas (Pisum sativum) | | | 1 | 2 | | 3 | 1 | 1 | | | |
| Broomcorn millet (Panicum spec.) | | | | | | | | 1 | | | |
| Opium poppy (Papaver setigerum) | | | | 2 | | | | | | | |
| Hazelnut (Corylus avellana) | | 1 | | | | | | 1 | | | |
| Goosefoot (Chenopodium album) | | 15 | | 470 | 2 | 2 | | 292 | 21 | 1 | 3 |
| Goosefoot (Chenopodium spec.) | | | | 47 | | | | | | | |
| Black bindweed (Polygonum convolvulus) | | 2 | | 45 | 1 | 1 | | 11 | 1 | | 1 |
| Timothy grass (cf. Phleum spec.) | | | | 17 | | | | | | | |
| Barren brome (Bromus sterilis) | | | | 2 | 1 | 1 | | 3 | | | |
| Redshank (Polygonum persicaria) | | 1 | | 1 | 1 | | | | | | |
| Sorrel (Rumex tenuifolius) | | 1 | | | | | | | | | |
| Nipplewort (Lapsana communis) | | | | 1 | | | | 1 | | | |
| Cleavers (Galium spurium) | | | | | | | | | | | |

*1 L. = Langweiler   *2 dm = decimeters; 10 decimeters - 1 meter   (After Knörzer 1972)

## TABLE III

Frequency of Animals Based on the Minimum Number of Individuals at Linear Culture Sites

| | Müddersheim, Germany (a) | | Bylany, Czechoslovakia (b) | | Jeleni Louka, Czechoslovakia (c) | | Samborzec, Poland (d) | | Győr Papai, Hungary (e) | | Pomaz-Zdravlyak, Hungary (f) | | Floreshti, U.S.S.R. (g) *1 | | Noviye Ruseshti, U.S.S.R. (h) *2 | | Traian, Romania (i) | | |
|---|---|---|---|---|---|---|---|---|---|---|---|---|---|---|---|---|---|---|---|
| | N | % | N | % | N | % | N | % | N | % | N | % | N | % | N | % | N | % | |
| Cattle | 7 | 27% | 7 | 25% | 8 | 36% | 36 | 36% | 354 | 60% | 30 | 38% | 20 | 28% | 56 | 22% | 9 | 29% | *2 not included: 5 bear, 3 elk, 6 wild dog, 8 fox, 1 marten, 3 lynx, 1 wild cat, 2 beaver, 4 bison bonasus. |
| Sheep/goat | 4 | 15% | 3 | 11% | 11 | 36% | 13 | 13% | 100 | 17% | 17 | 22% | 6 | 8% | 36 | 14% | 3 | 10% | |
| Pig | 3 | 12% | 8 | 29% | 4 | 13% | 24 | 24% | 64 | 11% | 16 | 20% | 12 | 17% | 36 | 14% | 5 | 16% | |
| Dog | 1 | 4% | 1 | 4% | 1 | 3% | | | 5 | 0.8% | 3 | 4% | 4 | 5% | 5 | 2% | | | |
| Aurochs | 4 | 15% | 1 | 4% | 1 | 3% | | | 51 | 7% | 4 | 5% | 8 | 10% | 18 | 7% | | | |
| Wild Horse | 2 | 8% | | | 1 | 3% | 9 | 9% | | | | | | | 17 | 6.5% | 1 | 3% | *3 not included from other sites: 1 or 2 species: hamster, buzzard, rodent, mussel, beaver. |
| Red deer | 1 | 4% | 1 | 4% | 1 | 3% | 7 | 7% | 2 | 0.8% | 2 | 2.5% | 10 | 13% | 12 | 5% | 6 | 19% | |
| Roe deer | 1 | 4% | 1 | 4% | 1 | 3% | 5 | 5% | 5 | | 1 | 1% | 2 | 3% | 14 | 5% | 3 | 10% | |
| Wild pig | 2 | 8% | 1 | 4% | 1 | 3% | 3 | 3% | 8 | 1.2% | 4 | 5% | 10 | 13% | 10 | 4% | 3 | 10% | |
| Other wild animals | 1 | 4% | 5 | 18% | 2 | 6% | 2 | 1% | 1 | 1% | 2 | 1% | 5 | 5% | 56 | 21.5% | 1 | 3% | |
| TOTAL | 26 | | 28 | | 31 | | 99 | | 590 | | 79 | | 76 | | 260 | | 31 | | |

*1 Tsalkin (1970) presents a more complete analysis of the faunal remains from Floreshti, but he groups cattle and aurochs into one group.

a) Stampfli, 1965
b) Clason, 1967
c) Kratochvil, 1972
d) Kulczycka-Leciejewiczowa, 1970
e) Bökönyi, 1959
f) Bökönyi, 1959
g) Passek and Chernysh, 1963
h) David and Markevich, 1967
i) Necrasov and Haimovici, 1962

The Linear people had domestic cattle, pigs, sheep, goats, and dogs. Cattle were the most important in the economy in terms of number and yield of available meat. It is to be noted that some bulls were already castrated (Müller, 1964). Pigs were usually the next most frequently found animal: the deciduous forest environment was ideal for their breeding.

The Linear people cultivated a variety of plants: emmer wheat, einkorn wheat, bread wheat, barley, oats, flax, lentils and peas. At a few sites in Austria and Poland rye has been found, but probably it was only a weed plant accompanying wheat. The cultivated plants differed in yield, vitamin content, disease resistance, climatic and soil needs, and to some extent usage. This variability demanded the cultivation of a variety of plants.

Wheat was the most important cereal in the Linear culture economy and probably the main source of carbohydrates. Emmer wheat was most extensively cultivated. For example, at Bylany in Czechoslovakia, 80 percent of the recovered wheat is emmer, 15 percent einkorn wheat, and 5 percent bread or club wheat (Soudský and Pavlů, 1972). Tempir (1971:1326) analyzed the wheat remains from 14 pits at Opava-Katerinky in Czechoslovakia, and in 12 of the pits emmer wheat made up 62.2 to 78.1 percent of the floral array and einkorn wheat 21.9 to 36.8 percent. However, at the Langweiler site in Rheinland, Germany, einkorn wheat predominates (Knörzer, 1972).

Since emmer wheat is relatively intolerant of variations in soil quality, temperature, and rainfall, it would be risky to rely on it heavily, for a bad harvest could threaten the existence of the entire community. The insurance against bad harvests was provided by other domesticated and wild plants and animals. For example, barley is a hardier cereal than emmer wheat and it may have been a very important plant in years of poor wheat harvests.

It is unclear whether or not opium poppy and goosefoot (*Chenopodium album*) were cultivated. Opium poppy is a drug plant and perhaps was utilized in rituals. Goosefoot is commonly found in emmer fields, although it may have been cultivated separately during the Neolithic. As a food plant it provides two useful products: its leaves, whose protein, mineral, and calcium values are considerably higher than those of spinach (Reynolds, 1974), can be picked from young plants; and its seeds, which can be cooked as a porridge, are collected at maturity (Richard I. Ford, personal communication).

Many archaeologists assume that the Linear people practiced slash and burn agriculture and thus would have been forced to shift their villages periodically because of soil exhaustion. As frequently happens in archaeology, this untested hypothesis is treated as a fact. In recent years one of the more forceful supporters or proponents of shifting cultivation and village movement has been B. Soudský (1962, 1966, 1972). Utilizing data from the Bylany settlement in Czechoslovakia, he estimated the length of occupation of a Linear site to be 14 or 15 years. His technique is to count the number of linings or layers in the pits, where supposedly cereals were stored. Soudský assumes that these storage pits were "annually daubed inside to provide a new basal lining and burned for disinfection" (Soudský, 1962:198). He maintains that after shifting their settlement, the Linear people would not occupy that general area for 30 years in order to allow the soil and the forest to recover (Soudský and Pavlů, 1972).

There are pits at Linear sites showing alternate layering of pit fill and loess, but it is hard to demonstrate their annual daubing. It is doubtful that pits located outside the longhouses were used for storing grain, though they may have served for processing it. Grain stored in pits outside houses would be exposed to the elements, especially rain, and domestic and wild animals would be able to grub up cereals so stored. Here we not only have to consider the small creatures who would dig into a pit, but also take into account the possibility of losing the stored grain to bears, pigs, etc. Pigs were present, and since no special pigpens have been found, the grains hypothetically stored in the pits would have had to be protected from them.

It is possible that the Linear people did not shift their villages every 14 or 15 years. In analyzing this problem, we need to consider soil fertility, size of the needed plots, availability of cultivated land, production techniques, size of the population, and social and economic needs. The soil exploited by the Linear people was very fertile and probably not readily exhausted. A wooden digging stick was probably used for working the cultivated fields, while the cereals were harvested with flint sickles inserted in a wooden handle. Availability of land for cultivation was no problem, since the population of farmers in Central Europe at that time was small. In considering the amount of cereals that would have had to be cultivated every year, we have to remember dietary needs, the quantity needed for the next year's seed, and social and exchange needs. The population estimates for the Linear culture villages vary from 60 to 150 depending on the assumption and the methods used in making the estimate.

If one family could be supported by 1.23 hectares of cultivable land (Soudský and Pavlů, 1972), the estimated population of each Linear culture village would have needed approximately 12.5 to 31 hectares of land if they depended totally on wheat. Generally, several times this area of arable land is available within walking distance of most sites. Thus people could shift fields without moving their villages. If valid, this conclusion supports Modderman (1970) who argues for greater stability and longer occupation of Linear villages.

Inter-community trade is indicated by the presence at Linear sites of non-local raw material or products: obsidian, stone, flint, pottery, and *Spondylus* shells. It does not mean that all these products were exchanged over the entire Linear territory. For example, obsidian was traded only in the eastern zone of the Linear culture.

*Spondylus* shells are usually cited as examples of trade in Linear communities. These shells are found along the Black and Mediterranean Sea coasts and involved Linear communities in trade probably with Vinča A, a Middle Neolithic culture in southern Europe, and other cultures in southeastern Europe. Recently oxygen isotope analyses carried out on *Spondylus* shells from the Balkans indicate that they came from the Aegean (Shackleton and Renfrew, 1970).

To explain the trade in *Spondylus* shells during the Balkan Neolithic, Shackleton and Renfrew have proposed a prestige chain exchange model (1970). This model has four characteristics: 1) exchange of goods takes place between high status individuals on a basis of balanced reciprocity; 2) the prestige goods are passed on in subsequent exchanges; 3) these goods are not utilized in daily activities; 4) these goods are usually found in burials or in other contexts through accidental breakage or loss.

They compare the exchange in *Spondylus* shells to the kula trade of the Trobriand Islanders. In the kula trade some of the exchanged goods have great social significance that transcends the utilitarian value of the gifts.

However, in the kula ring type of exchange model, not only are prestige goods being passed on between individuals, but many subsistence goods are exchanged at the same time. This type of exchange probably did not occur among the Linear people. The Linear communities were self-sufficient in subsistence needs. They occupied good land and the population was small, thus there would be little pressure to exchange foodstuffs. It would be difficult to transport large amounts of foodstuffs for long distances. The goods exchanged among the Linear people such as *Spondylus* shells, probably were meant to reinforce status differences, or they may have been used as a bride price. We have postulated the so-called "Big Man" society organization for the Linear culture, and these exchanged goods would move among the "Big Men."

To illustrate the exchange networks of a Linear community, we will look at Olszanica in Poland. The non-perishable evidence for exchange at Olszanica consists of stone, flint, ceramics, and obsidian (Fig. 5). The

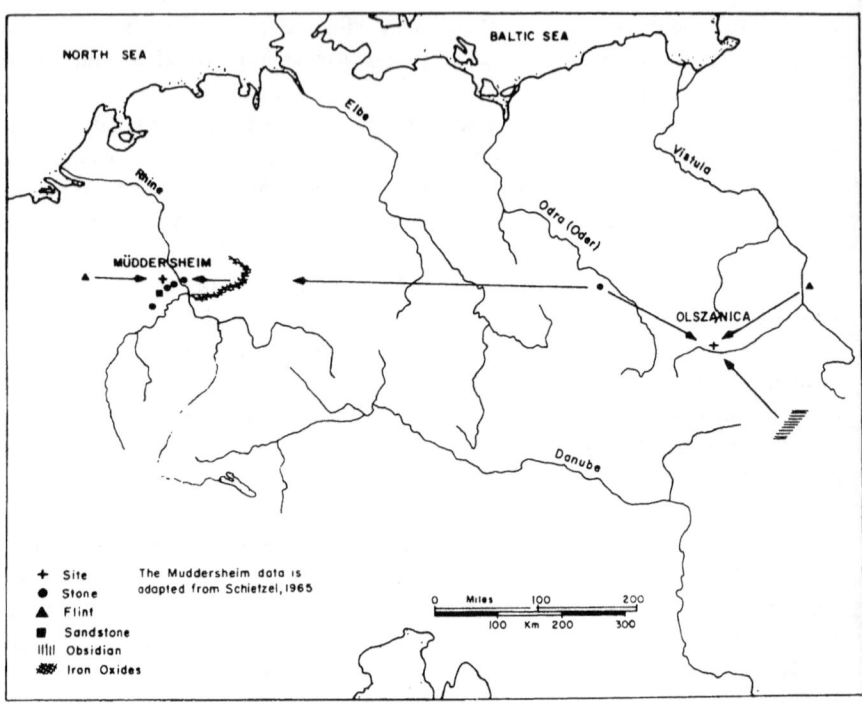

Figure 5. The Evidence for Trade Networks at the Müddersheim and Olszanica Sites.

ceramics and obsidian came from the south of the Carpathians, in Slovakia and Hungary. Most of the axes and adzes were made of stone having actinolite as the main mineral constituent. This stone came to Olszanica from Silesia in Poland. It should be noted that some of the polished stone tools found at Müddersheim in Germany were made of the same material from Silesia (Schietzel, 1965). The few non-local flint pieces at Olszanica came from the Świeciechów area in Poland. All the non-local materials found at Olszanica came from a straight linear distance of at least 150 kilometers or 93 miles; probably the goods had to pass through other communities until they reached Olszanica. Perhaps the stone coming from Silesia had to pass through a territory occupied by hunters and gatherers, for to the west of Olszanica there were no farming communities for approximately 100 kilometers, or 62 miles. It is possible also that the Olszanica people took long trips on the Vistula River to visit Linear communities situated along the Odra (Oder) River, although the ceramic material indicates little interaction between the Odra and Vistula communities. It is unclear with what materials, products, or favors the Olszanica people reciprocated for the obsidian or stone. Jurassic flint occurring around Olszanica could have been used in exchange. There are finds of Jurassic flint during the Early Neolithic in Slovakia (J. K. Kozłowski, 1971).

None of the materials or goods received through exchange by the Olszanica people was critical for daily subsistence activities. Good quality flint and stone is locally available. Over 40,000 flint pieces were found, only a few of them made from non-local raw material. Approximately 200 pieces of obsidian were found in an area of 15,578.75 square meters containing over 20 longhouses (Milisauskas, in press) which belong to at least two occupational phases. The small number of obsidian pieces probably indicates that it was not essential for daily activities and indeed flint artifacts could have been used for the same purposes as obsidian tools. Probably the products obtained through exchange networks were socially important for the Linear people; non-local products may have been used as status markers, for rituals, and for maintenance and expansion of social relations. The value of the exchanged product was not so important as the idea of gift.

The evidence for exchange from Linear settlements and cemeteries indicates that not all families or individuals participated equally in this exchange. For example, the distribution of obsidian at Olszanica shows clustering of it only around some of the longhouses, and some contemporary longhouses have very little of the obsidian. Probably the obsidian exchange occurred between prominent families or individuals. Most of the polished stone tools made of non-local material in Linear cemeteries, such as Nitra in Slovakia, are associated with adult males. Probably only the adult males participated in the exchange involving stone or polished stone tools.

The density of population during the Early Neolithic varied in Central Europe. The areas occupied by farmers had greater population density than those inhabited by hunters and gatherers. The density of Linear culture sites is low if it is expressed in terms of sites per square kilometer, but the density appears greater if we consider it in terms of distance along rivers or streams.

The density of Linear sites in the Middle Neckar area in Germany, approximately 7200 kilometers$^2$, varied greatly during four ceramic phases. The initial expansion of Linear communities in the area reflects a very small population of farmers, one community or village per 1028.5 kilometers.

These estimates, derived from Sielmann's (1972) article, also demonstrate a "filling in" process, which was discussed previously.

| Phase | No. of Sites | 1 site per km$^2$ |
|---|---|---|
| Phase 1 | 7 | 1028.5 km$^2$ |
| Phase 2 | 62 | 116.1 km$^2$ |
| Phase 3 | 122 | 59.0 km$^2$ |
| Phase 4 | 59 | 122.0 km$^2$ |

One of the more interesting problems of the Early Neolithic is the relationship between farmers and hunters and gatherers. Since actual archaeological evidence for any type of interaction is almost non-existent at present, most of my comments will be only speculations. Hopefully some of the hypotheses presented here about this relationship can be tested with archaeological data in the future.

One of the major problems in establishing this relationship is the inability of archaeologists to date more precisely the so-called "Mesolithic" sites of hunters and gatherers. Most of the recovered archaeological material from Mesolithic sites consist of flint artifacts that are impossible to date precisely by present techniques. The dating problem is well illustrated in southern Poland. There are many Mesolithic sites in southeastern Poland in Post-Pleistocene or Post-glacial times, i.e., after the 9th millenium B.C., but typology of flint artifacts permits only very general chronological observations (Fig. 6; and S. Kozlowski, 1972). It is also possible that some of the Mesolithic sites belonged to farmers; that is, that they were hunting camps of agriculturalists. Sites containing flint artifacts without ceramics are always classified as being Mesolithic. The hunting and gathering sites are located both in the uplands and lowlands. Access to streams and rivers were important both for hunters and farmers, for both utilized water for drinking, fishing, and transportation.

A simple model of interaction would have the hunters and gatherers supplying most of the wild animals to the farmers and the farmers supplying grain to the hunters and gatherers. Perhaps the scarcity of projectile points at Linear sites can be explained by this type of interaction. Middle and Late Neolithic farmers have more projectile points; also at this time the number of hunters and gatherers was declining in Europe as farmers expanded into areas occupied by hunting and gathering societies. Alternatively, the increase of projectile points during the Middle Neolithic may point to an increase in warfare or to the appearance of new hunting methods.

After 3900-3800 B.C., based on radiocarbon dates, the Linear ceramics are no longer found in Central Europe. In subsequent periods there is much

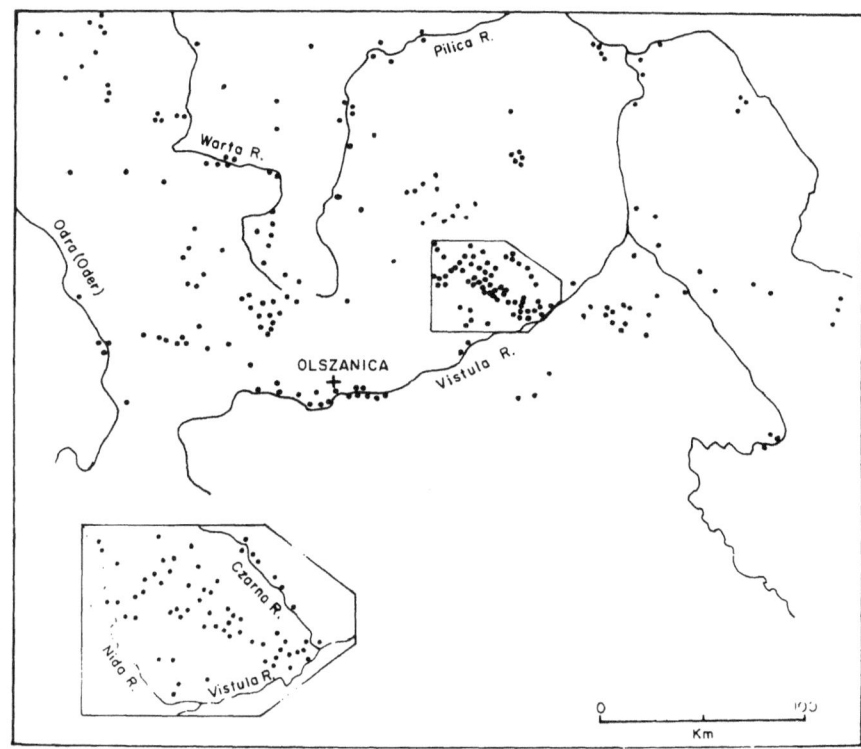

Figure 6. Distribution of Mesolithic Sites in Southeastern Poland.

more sociocultural diversity and complexity. However, the Linear people should be credited with the extensive modification of the Central European landscape for the first time. It is evident that their adaptive strategies were very successful.

## Acknowledgments

I thank Richard I. Ford, Gregory Johnson, Peter Reid, John Speth, and my wife Vita for reading this article and for helpful comments. I am indebted to Charles E. V. Ebert for help with soil terminology. The drawings were made by Gordon Schmahl. I am grateful to the Smithsonian Institution for the financial support (Grant nos. SFG-1-1064 and SF3-00109) of my research on the Linear culture communities in Poland.

## References Cited

Bökönyi, S.
  1959 Die Frühalluviale Wirbeltierfauna Ungarns (vom Neolithikum bis zur La Tène Zeit). Acta Archaeologica 11:39-102.
Buttler, W. and W. Haberery
  1936 Die bandkeramische Ansiedlung bei Köln-Lindenthal. Berlin: Walter de Gruyter and Company.
Butzer, K.
  1971 Environment and archeology: an introduction to Pleistocene geography. Chicago: Aldine.
Chmielewski, W., K. Jaźdźewski, and J. Kostrzewski
  1965 Pradzieje Polski. Ossolineum, Wrocław.
Clason, A. T.
  1967 The animal bones found at the Bandkeramik settlement of Bylany. Archeologické rozhledy 19:90-96.
David, A. I. and V. I. Markevich
  1967 Fauna mlekopitayushchikh poselenia Noviye Ruseshti. I. Izvestia Adademii Nauk Moldavskoi SSR 4:3-26.
Ember, M.
  1973 An archaeological indicator of matrilocal versus patrilocal residence. American Antiquity 38:177-82.
Kahlke, D.
  1954 Die Bestattungssitten des Donauländischen Kulturkreises der jüngeren Steinzeit. Teil I: Linienbandkeramik. Berlin: Rutten and Loening.
Knörzer, K. H.
  1972 Subfossile Pflanzenreste aus der bandkeramischen Siedlung Langweiler 3 und 6, Kreis Jülich, und ein urnenfelderzeitlicher Getreidenfund innerhalb dieser Siedlung. Bonner Jahrbücher 1972: 395-403.
Kozłowski, J. K.
  1971 Uwagi o znaczneniu i metodach badań nad neolitycznymi inventarzami krzemiennymi. Item *in:* Z badań nad krzemieniarstwen neolitycznym i eneolitycznym. Polskie Towarzystwo Archeologiczne Oddział w Nowej Hucie, Muzeum Archeologiczne w Krakowie, Kraków, pp. 139-46.
Kozłowski, S. K.
  1972 Pradzieje ziem Polskich od IX do V tysiąclecia p.n.e. Warszawa.
Kratochvil, Z.
  1972 Knochenüberreste von der neolithischen Siedlung Jeleni Louka bei Mikulov. Přehled Vyzkumů 1971, pp. 24-27.

Kruk, J.
1973   Studia osadnicze nad neolitem wyżyn lessowych. Ossolineum, Wrocław-Warszawa-Kraków-Gdańsk.
Kulczycka-Leciejewiczowa, A.
1970   Kultura ceramiki wstęgowej rytej w Polsce (zarys problematiki). Item in: Z badán nad kulturą ceramiki wstęgowej rytej, edited by J. K. Kozłowski. Polskie Towarzystwo Archeologiczne Oddział w Nowej Hucie, Kraków, pp. 11-28.
Milisauskas, S.
1972   An analysis of Linear culture longhouses at Olszanica B1, Poland. World Archaeology 4:57-74.
in press   Archaeological investigations on the Linear culture village of Oszanica. Ossolineum, Polish Academy of Sciences.
Modderman, P. J. R.
1968   Die Hausbauten und Siedlungen der Linienbandkeramik in ihrem westlichen Bereich. Item in: Die Anfänge des Neolithikums vom Orient bis Nordeuropa, part Va, edited by H. Schwabedissen. Köln: Böhlau, pp. 77-84.
1970   Linearbandkeramik aus Elsloo und Stein. Analecta Praehistorica Leidensia III, Leiden.
Müller, H.-H.
1964   Die Haustiere der Mitteldeustchen Bandkeramiker. Deutsche Akademie der Wissenschaften zu Berlin, Vol. 17, Berlin.
Necrasov, O. and S. Haimovici
1962   Studiul resturilor de faună descoperite in 1959 la Traian. Materiale şi cercetǎri Arheologice 8:261-66.
Passek, T. S. and E. K. Chernysh
1963   Pamyatniki kulturi lineyno-lentochnoy keramiki na territorii SSSR. Akademii Nauk SSSR, Moscow.
Pavúk, J.
1972   Neolithisches Gräberfeld in Nitra. Slovenská Archeóliga 20:5-105.
Quitta, H.
1967   The C14 chronology of the central and SE European Neolithic. Antiquity 41:263-70.
1970   Zur Lage und Verbreitung der bandkeramischen Siedlungen in Leipziger Land. Zeitschrift für Archäologie 4:155-76.
Reynolds, P. J.
1974   Little Butser: bringing home the harvest. The Times, September 28, 1974.
Sahlins, M.
1963   Poor man, rich man, big-man, chief: political types in Melanesia and Polynesia. Comparative Studies in Society and History 5: 285-303.

Schietzel, K.
1965   Müddersheim, eine Ansiedlung der jüngeren Bandkeramik in Rheinland. Köln: Böhlau.
Schackleton, N. and C. Renfrew
1970   Neolithic trade routes re-aligned by oxygen isotope analyses. Nature 228:1062-5.
Sielmann, B.
1971   Der Einfluss der Umwelt auf die neolithische Besiedlung Südwestdeutschlands unter besonderer Berücksichtigung der Verhältnisse am nördlichen Obberhein. Acta Praehistorica et Archaeologica, vol. 2:65-197.
1972   Die frühneolithische Besiedlung Mitteleuropas. Item *in:* Die Anfänges des Neolithikums vom Orient bis Nordeuropa, part Va, edited by H. Schwabedissen, Böhlau, Köln, pp. 1-65.
Soudský, B.
1962   The Neolithic site of Bylany. Antiquity 36:190-200.
1964   Sozialökonomische Geschichte des älteren Neolithikums in Mitteleuropa. Aus der Ur-und Frühgeschichte II, pp. 62-81.
1966   Bylany osada nejstarších zemědělců z mladší doby kammené. Českoclovenska akademie věd, Praha.
Soudský, B. and I. Pavlů
1972   The Linear pottery culture settlement patterns in Central Europe. Item *in:* Man, settlement, and urbanism, edited by P. J. Ucko, R. Tringham, and G. W. Dimbleby. London: Gerald Duckworth, pp. 317-28.
Stampfli, H. R.
1965   Tierreste der Grabung Müddersheim, Kr. Düren. Item *in:* Müddersheim, eine Ansiedlung der jüngeren Bandkeramik in Rheinland, by K. Schietzel. Köln: Böhlau, pp. 115-23.
Tempir, Z.
1971   Einige Ergebnisse der archäoagrobotanischen Untersuchungen des Anbaus von Kulturpflanzen auf dem Gebiet der ČSSR. Actes du VIII$^e$ Congrès International des Sciences Prehistoriques et Protohistoriques, Prague, 1966, vol. 2:1326-29.
Tsalkin, V. I.
1970   Drevneyshie domashnie zhivotnie vostochnoy evropi. Akademia Nauk SSSR, Moscow.

# STYLISTIC BEHAVIOR AND INFORMATION EXCHANGE

*H. Martin Wobst*
University of Massachusetts

Much of what archaeologists commonly label "stylistic" behavior may be viewed as a strategy of information exchange. This interpretation accommodates the traditional archaeological notions of style, but it is more inclusive. It overcomes some of the confining theoretical perspectives of traditional stylistic analysis, and it may stimulate research into the evolution and multiple articulations of stylistic behavior. I will review some of the shortcomings of traditional approaches to this area of artifact variability, draw attention to some of the functions of stylistic behavior, and evaluate these functions against a set of ethnographic materials. Stylistic analysis has become a boring routine which rests on shaky foundations. This paper is an attempt to offer an alternative and to add some perspective to the traditional approaches.

## "Style" and "Stylistic" Analysis

> The meaning of style has so many ramifications that an attempt at a comprehensive definition must either arrive at a vague theoretical statement or become involved in an extensive review of specific usages (Whallon, 1968:224).

This statement defines an archaeological dilemma: although style is integral to most archaeological research, it lacks meaning. Either it is explicitly defined as a negative category (e.g., aspects of artifact variability which cannot be attributed to other agencies such as productive advantage, mechanical factors, or chance), or it is unmanageably multidimensional (e.g., aspects of artifact variability which are congruent with specific areas, time periods, or sets of personnel regardless of the cause for this congruence).

It is a symptom of a more general malaise that most stylistic analysis proceeds without a clear notion of what is being measured and what this may be sensitive to. Style is commonly treated as if it neither articulated with other cultural variables nor bestowed any adaptive advantages on human populations. While archaeologists tend to interpret much formal variability in artifacts as "functional"—in the sense of systemic articulation, in a mathematical sense, or in terms of adaptive value—"stylistic" variability is usually *contrasted* with functional aspects of artifact form (for example, Sackett 1973:321). The "non-functionality" of style is reinforced by other considerations: archaeologists derive style almost exclusively from the communication contexts of enculturation and acculturation, via learning theory. This derivation discourages us from investigating the articulations of style in the production and in the use life of an artifact. For, if style is applied by a Skinnerian automaton and thus given before an artifact is made, nothing is gained by pondering the articulations of style during the use life of artifacts. Style then becomes a strangely self-contained, a-cultural, a-systemic variable within the system that is culture. It relates solely to processes which precede its sociocultural articulations, so much so, that these articulations are irrelevant to the persistence and change of particular stylistic regularities. In this sense, the traditional paradigms of stylistic analysis are self-fulfilling and circular: style is "acquired" before it is applied to artifacts and before these artifacts articulate with other cultural processes; therefore, the articulations of style are irrelevant to the dynamics of stylistic behavior, and style can be treated as if it were a phenomenon without function.

If the styles that individuals or social units perpetrate were acquired quasi-automatically and if style lacked function, it would require rather complex logical constructions to bring stylistic hypotheses within the reach of archaeological test implications. On the other hand, the contexts of enculturation (as, for example, child training and education) are so weakly and remotely reflected in archaeological remains that alternative hypotheses could not be confidently rejected as predictors of a given "stylistic" archaeological form and structure. Thus, stylistic behavior would be virtually inaccessible to archaeological problem solving at the operational level commonly assumed by style analysts (enculturation and learning) and the paradigm would be almost impossible to falsify through archaeological research.

Instead, stylistic behavior is usually investigated at such a broad level of generalization that enculturation and learning are almost immaterial to the truth value of stylistic hypotheses: the maintenance of particular styles through time is delegated to homeostasis in communication processes within a given social unit; uniformity through space is taken to imply high communication density over the area in question. Given this paradigm, changes in particular styles can be accounted for by random errors in enculturation or acculturation; by disturbances in previously existing enculturation equilibria (temporal dimension); and by breaks in communication density (spatial dimension).

This line of reasoning does not require operational information about the enculturative milieu in which a particular style is perpetrated and passed along, if we want to demonstrate the persistence or disturbance of communicative homeostasis. Rather conveniently, the paradigm permits us to measure the degree of communicative equilibrium directly, i.e., by means of the temporo-spatial distribution of stylistic form and structure. So equipped, we can make and support statements about communication density or socio-cultural isolation, and about disturbances in these variables. And we can utilize style to identify temporal and spatial socio-cultural discontinuities, and even socio-cultural units. At this point, the goal of "stylistic" analysis has been achieved, and we can turn our research efforts to more interesting behaviors.

This fairly standardized, though polemically exaggerated, routine leaves little if any room to question the articulations of stylistic form in the use life of an artifact; to elicit the potential advantages that stylistic behavior of different sorts may bestow on its practitioners; to investigate the processes by which stylistic behavior is calibrated and equilibrated among interacting individuals; to determine why there are marked differences in stylistic variability between different classes of material culture even within a given society; and to find out why some artifacts, more than others, are predestined to covary with socio-cultural boundaries. Even the most imaginative *uses* of style in archaeological research designs of the last decade (for example, Deetz, 1965; Hill, 1968; Longacre, 1968; Whallon, 1966) have contributed little to our general knowledge of stylistic dynamics and stylistic behavior. As long as we do not know more about the functions of stylistic behavior, in terms of its systemic articulations, the use of stylistic variability in archaeological research rests on shaky foundations. This knowledge will not be accumulated as a by-product of traditional stylistic analysis. Rather it will be generated only by means of problem directed research in which stylistic behavior is the *explanandum*, and in which style is more realistically integrated into the systemic matrix of which it forms a part.

## Material Culture and Style

Like other populations, human populations maintain themselves by exchanging matter, energy, and information with their environment (i.e., other human populations, and the biological and abiotic world around them) as well as among their members (Flannery, 1972; Rappaport, 1971). For human populations, these life-supporting exchanges are facilitated by the ability to symbol (White, 1959), which considerably enhances the amount, diversity, and dynamism of learned behavior relative to genetically inherited behaviors. Learned behavior and symboling ability greatly increase the capacity of human operators to interact with their environment through the medium of artifacts. This capacity in turn allows human populations to respond more readily to environmental stress; it improves their ability to harness and process energy and matter; and it diversifies their options for information exchange. Material culture thus participates in and enhances exchanges of energy, matter, and information in the human populations that fashion it.

The role of material culture in exchanges of matter and energy, for example in the extraction, processing, use and consumption of raw materials and processed items, has received much attention from archaeologists. Archaeological theory and practice are heavily dependent on the assumption that these areas of artifact articulation contribute in a major way to the formal variability and structure of material culture. That this assumption is reasonable within limits has been demonstrated frequently (for hunter-gatherer archaeology see for example: Binford, 1972; Binford and Binford, 1966; Clark and Haynes, 1970; Feustel, 1973; Semenov, 1964; 1968). Most archaeologists would agree that the articulation of artifacts in exchanges of energy and matter is definable; that we can isolate the aspects of form contributed by this articulation; and that we can generate testable hypotheses either about the systemic context given their formal variability, or about formal variability given their prehistoric systemic context. Equally broadly shared is the assumption that artifacts convey "adaptive advantage" on their users in exchanges of matter or energy. By this I mean that they help to assure survival, they help to satisfy vital needs and indispensable requirements, and they help to provide for, and equilibrate, certain optimal conditions of maintenance in the face of random, cyclical or directional change in the variables people interact with (compare with Rappaport, 1971).

We are leaving the area of archaeological consensus when we consider the role of artifacts in information exchange as, for example, in the symboling of territory or social boundaries, in the context of ritual, in the support of ethnicity, or in maintaining and strengthening mating networks, exchange relationships, and structural poses. No doubt most artifacts articulate with information exchange processes, in addition to energy and matter exchanges, and these processes contribute to artifact form. But there is very little explicit theory to assure archaeologists that the articulation of artifacts in prehistoric information exchange is knowable, and even less is known about specific relationships between the form of artifacts and their roles in information exchange. When it comes to the "adaptive advantage" (as defined here) that artifacts bestow in information exchanges, one encounters an almost complete void in the archaeological literature. It is my contention that this void offers some promising avenues for archaeological research, particularly if we realize that much of the stylistic behavior archaeologists are accustomed to measure and interpret is congruent with information exchange.

## The Distinctive Features of Stylistic Behavior

The working definition I will employ in the remainder of this paper equates style with that part of the formal variability in material culture that can be related to the participation of artifacts in processes of information exchange. This definition does not cover the totality of phenomena presently included under the definition of style in the archaeological literature. Yet it removes a significant proportion of stylistic behavior from its present, customary pedestal of processual isolation and makes it conducive to problem solving research. It avoids the semantic muddle of counterposing "style" and "function" by explicitly acknowledging that much stylistic behavior does have functions, at least in the sense of articulation with other variables in the cultural and ecosystem; it also invites investigations into the adaptive advantages style may convey and into the stresses that act upon it. Since most animals engage in information exchange, this definition allows for a broader ecological perspective on stylistic behavior, and accommodates research on the evolution of this mode of communication among the hominids.

Information exchange includes all those communication events in which a message is emitted or in which a message is received. For any given message emitted there is at least one potential receiver who may intercept the message (including illegitimate receivers; compare with Otte, 1974: 385). While the emission of information of necessity precedes its reception, reception does not actually need to take place (as long as there is a potential receiver), and emission and reception may be separated from each other spatially and temporally. If we restrict ourselves to the intrahuman realm, the modes of reception include at least the senses of vision, hearing, smell, taste, and touch, while the modes of emission range from verbal behavior through a variety of non-verbal behaviors. With their vocabulary of signs, signals, and symbols, message contents satisfy the totality of human communicative needs. Any human behavior involves at least potential information exchange. Thus, the context of message transmission is as diversified as human behavior (see Otte, 1974 for a general review of signalling systems).

Since artifacts contribute heavily to human survival in energy and matter exchanges, and since artifact production and use involve at least potential information exchange, it is not surprising that human populations should avail themselves of the option to transmit messages in the artifact mode, and that artifact form should be utilized to carry a variety of messages. There are important differences, however, between the artifact mode and most other modes of human communication. For example, in the artifact mode, emitters can produce messages in the absence of *any* receivers, and these messages can be received without any emitters physically present. Once produced, these messages change slower than in other modes. Thus they require more of a commitment on the part of the emitter. Conversely, once the message is in artifact form, its maintenance does not require further energy and matter. Both emission (artifact use and production) and reception (access to artifact) require access to energy and matter, besides access to information. This makes it easier to monopolize information exchange in this mode via certain artifacts and to control the emission of messages (if this is defined as originally committing a signal to the artifact mode) by specifying rare matter or costly energy for the signal. Coupled with the relative longevity of artifact signals, it also facilitates standardization of certain types of messages. Finally, messages in artifact mode are received almost exclusively through the sense of vision, if only because all artifacts have at least a visual dimension, and the visual dimension of artifacts is most easily manipulated to take on a message function.

To delineate some of its potential functions within the cultural matrix, it is useful to establish the costs of emission and reception in the stylistic mode, relative to other modes of human information exchange. If emission is defined as the initial production of an artifact that carries a message (usually in addition to energy and matter exchange functions), the cost of message emission is greater than in the non-stylistic modes. Subsequently, however, the artifact takes over the message emission at little further energy and matter cost. This greatly reduces the cost of emission and reception, since the signal has great relative longevity, does not change rapidly, and can be made portable and thus broadcast widely. The more frequent the message event in which a given artifact is utilized, the lower the cost of both reception and emission will be relative to alternative modes of information transfer.

The frequency of the anticipated message events is only one of the variables that delimit the relative costs of stylistic behavior. The complexity and variability of the message are at least as important. If the messages to be conveyed are highly variable, the cost per message event becomes prohibitively expensive in the stylistic mode, since modification of artifact form (the cost intensive aspect of stylistic behavior) would have to accompany each message modification. The more standardized the message, the more the frequency variable reduces the cost per message event. If the message conveyed is very complex (and neither frequent nor standardized), both the initial cost of artifact production and the cost of decoding the message may become prohibitive. Thus, the simpler the message, the lower the relative cost per message event will be.

## Content and Functional Matrix of Stylistic Behavior

These distinctive features suggest a relatively narrow range of information content for stylistic messages. Although potentially any message could be expressed in this mode, only simple invariate and recurrent messages will normally be transmitted stylistically. The following broad types of information appear to satisfy these restrictions particularly well: messages of emotional state, identification (class affinity, social group affiliation, and position along ranked scale), messages of authorship and ownership, messages of pre- and proscription, messages of religious and political objectification, and deictic messages. While these categories are not exhaustive, they do include the most common contents of stylistic messages. Table I counterposes each type of message content with sample messages and with some American artifacts which convey these messages.

It is interesting that the utility of stylistic messaging decreases the closer emitter and potential receivers are acquainted with one another. For, if a nurse or a general were communicating their occupational status to their family in the stylistic mode, the message soon would become redundant. There are few messages which would not be known already, or which could not be communicated at lower cost in other modes of messaging, in the context of the household. Stylistic messages gain in value, if the potential receivership is not partial to the most intimate life experiences and behavioral peculiarities of the message emitter. Regardless of content, stylistic messages gain in utility relative to other modes, if the potential receivers have little opportunity to receive the message otherwise, but nevertheless

TABLE I

Message Content in Stylistic Behavior

| Type of Information Conveyed | Example of Message | Example from American Material Culture Which Shows This Behavior |
|---|---|---|
| 1) Identification | | |
| a) emotional state | I am mourning | black armband, flag at halfmast |
| b) social or economic class affiliation | I am a nurse<br>I am married | nurse's dress<br>wedding band |
| c) position along ranked scale | I am wealthy<br><br>I am a general | display of Rolls Royce, mink coat, or platinum jewelry<br>number of stars on shoulders |
| 2) Ownership | This key is not any key but belongs to the last motel you slept in. | heavy, impractically shaped attachment to motel key |
| | This cow belongs to farmer XYZ | cattle brand |
| 3) Authorship | We the Shakers manufactured this chair | distinctive shape of Shaker furniture |
| | This is brand X by company XYZ | LOVE cosmetics, distinctive packaging |
| 4) Prescription | Walk here | Zebra stripes on road |
| 5) Proscription | Stay away from here<br>Evil spirits, keep out | Skull and crossbones<br>Pennsylvania Dutch hex signs |
| 6) Religious or political objectification | Jesus Christ is watching over you | Crucifix |
| 7) Deictic | Look | Goodyear Blimp. Exaggeration of messages 1 through 6. |

are likely to encounter it and are able to decode it. This circumscribes a potential target of receivers intermediate in social distance to the emitter of the message: not too close—since the message usually would be known already or generally could be more easily transmitted in other communication modes, and not too distant—since decoding or encountering the message could not be assured (Fig. 1). This target group, the personnel that

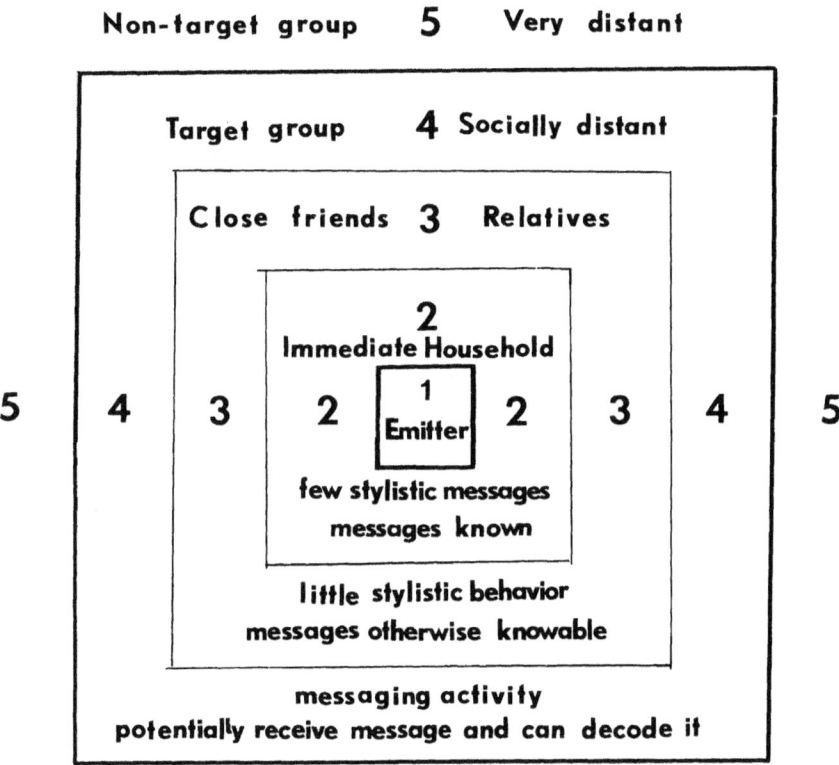

Figure 1. The target groups of stylistic messages.

communicates stylistic messages to it, the artifacts that convey these messages, and the processes and relationships that link these individuals beyond stylistic communication constitute the functional matrix for the majority of stylistic behaviors.

The presence, and if present, the size of this target group should be of immediate relevance to the presence and prevalence of stylistic behavior. Imagine a society in which all members fell into categories 1, 2 and 3 in Fig. 1 and never encountered individuals in category 4. In such a society, most stylistic behavior would represent a dysfunctional waste of energy and matter. If we increased the size of this social network so that more and more people were tied to each other in economic and other relationships, it is particularly category 4 in Fig. 1 which increases. The more members there are in this category, the more efficient stylistic behavior becomes relative to the other communication modes. Thus, in the absence of other factors, the amount of stylistic behavior should positively correlate with the size of the social networks that individuals participate in. Beyond this, given our cost considerations above, it should also positively correlate with the amount of replication in message content: the more individuals in category 4 have to be reached by the same (simple) signal, the more advantageous it becomes to convey the message content stylistically. It is not surprising to find that certain aspects of band society material culture show so little evidence of "stylistic" elaboration. Either category 4 is completely lacking in the societies in question so that the functional matrix for stylistic behavior is only weakly developed, or few messages are sufficiently replicative to justify the energy and matter investment required by stylistic communication. As societies increase in size and complexity, more and more aspects of behavior become intertwined with personnel in category 4, and more and more of these behaviors become repetitious and anticipated. It is in the latter societies that stylistic behavior structures important aspects of artifact form.

The fact that artifacts lend themselves to the transmission of *simple* messages, coupled with the capacity of all artifacts to *potentially* carry messages, raises the specter of misinformation by means of artifacts. Misinformation becomes a problem as soon as a few artifacts in a category of material culture are utilized to transmit messages. For, at this point, all similar artifacts lose their original signalling neutrality: they either *do* or *do not* carry messages, but they have lost their signalling innocence. Those artifacts which have messages affixed to them can contribute relatively little misinformation: given verbal behavior, encoding and decoding can be sufficiently standardized to prevent gross errors in decoding. But it is exceedingly difficult to prevent artifacts without message content from emitting a message, as long as some such artifacts do carry a message. Thus, given a category of material culture, stylistic messaging is either absent altogether or it is all-pervasive. This set of considerations has some interesting implications for the evolution of signalling in the artifact mode. For example, it argues for the sudden appearance of stylistic form in material culture, instead of the gradual incremental evolution often anticipated: a state of no-stylistic-messaging should suddenly be replaced by a state in which stylistic form has pervaded at least one (or more) categories of material culture. In the same vein, as the functional matrix of stylistic behavior becomes more complex, the different categories of material culture should reflect an off-on behavior in regard to stylistic form, with more and more categories switching in a step-like progression from stylistic neutrality (off) to stylistic ubiquity (on).

The more appropriate contents of stylistic messages (Table I) circumscribe some of the potential advantages which stylistic messaging may confer in information exchanges. As stylistic messages should be particularly appropriate in contexts where category 4 is frequent (Fig. 1), the majority of functions of stylistic behavior should relate to processes of social integration and social differentiation. Stylistic messages of identification, ownership, and authorship link efficiently those members of a community who are not in constant verbal contact and who have little opportunity to observe each others' behavior patterns (to make their reciprocal behavior on encounter predictable). Stylistic messages establish the mutual *bona fide*, in visual mode, before any verbal contact has taken place or in the absence of any verbal contact. In this context, stylistic messaging defines mutually expectable behavior patterns and makes subsequent interaction more predictable and less stressful. If such individuals (categories 1 and 4) were solely surrounded by stylistically neutral and messageless material culture, behavior patterns to be expected during initial encounter would either have to be estimated through lengthy prior observation, or they would not be predictable at all. Thus, an important function of stylistic messaging derives from the fact that it makes social intercourse more predictable: it reduces the stress inherent in first or intermittent encounters, and it broadcasts the potential advantages or disadvantages to be realized from a more intimate encounter, before such encounter has taken place.

By summarizing an individual's economic and social situation, stylistic messages may play a more active role in the integration of social groups. Stylistic messages are there for anyone to see: the message content of the material culture that individuals surround themselves with forms a sort of check list. It helps other members of the group to evaluate how closely a given individual is subscribing to the behavioral norms of that group. Without having to observe the details of an individual's behavior, the other members of the group can read the abstracts of these behaviors as they are expressed in the stylistic messages that individuals enter into social contexts. This greatly reduces the cost of measuring, maintaining and enforcing conformity and compliance with behavioral norms and facilitates the recognition of deviance. If, through the messages on his clothing, home, and other artifacts, an individual says: "I am an individual who belongs to social group X," he is also saying that he is in conformity with the other behavioral norms and with the ideology behind these norms. Aside from costly ritual, compliance to norms and conformity in ideology are difficult to observe and even more difficult to demonstrate unambiguously. As artifacts emit their messages continously (even in the absence of any other action on the part of their users), the compliance of individuals is continuously advertised and a continuous control on it can be maintained.

Conversely, stylistic messaging adds support to processes of social differentiation. It allows individuals to summarize and broadcast the uniqueness of their rank or status within a matrix of ranks or statuses, or to express their social and economic group affiliation toward outsiders. Complex differences in ideology, in niche-space, or in other group specific features can be reduced to, and advertised as, simple and unambiguous stylistic messages (cf. Table I, categories 1 a to c). It is particularly advantageous that artifacts will emit their messages even without direct interaction between emitters and receivers, and that messages can be decoded before any direct contact has taken place. This renders superfluous more explicit and costly boundary maintenance and competitive behaviors. Where a number of different socio-economic groups competes for niche-space, stylistic messages furnish predictors for the behavior that may reasonably be expected from individuals of the different groups. Style helps to mark, maintain, and further the differences between these groups at little cost.

## Some Predictions for Stylistic Form

Traditional archaeological practice is heavily dependent on the assumption that stylistic form, to a major extent, is coincident with social or "cultural" boundaries. Based on our discussion above, more realistic and more sensitive predictions for stylistic form can be advanced. If stylistic messages on artifacts are received in the visual mode, the distance at which an artifact becomes visible, the number of people by whom it is potentially seen, the number of contexts it is entered into, and the content of the message itself all tend to argue against an overly simplistic relationship between any single variable and stylistic form.

For example, the less an artifact is visible to members of a given group, the less appropriate it is to carry stylistic messages of any kind. Classes of artifacts which never leave the contexts of individual households and which are not usually visible to members of other households (such as ordinary kitchen utensils, underwear, bedding and mattresses, tools utilized by individuals in solitary task pursuits, etc.) are unlikely to carry messages of social group affiliation. Neither is it likely that this kind of artifact contains messages of any sort that would be expressed in society-specific stylistic form. Even if the members of a given society explicitly utilized such items for broadcasting social group affiliation, it would be unrealistic to expect society-specific stylistic forms on these items: for the number of individuals which potentially could receive this message is so small, and the number of these items that are seen by a given individual through his lifetime is so insignificant, that it would be impossible to achieve a uniform expression of the message throughout the entire group. As a result, whatever the message content, stylistic form on these items would be distributed clinally across the given local group and, very likely, also across its boundaries.

On the other hand, those sets of material culture which potentially are visible to all members of a given social group are much more likely to show a society specific expression of stylistic form, if they carry stylistic messages. Unfortunately, material culture does not contain many items that are broadly visible and that enter a multitude of social contexts. Examples of more common items in this category include, for example, the outer layers of clothing and the outer surfaces of living structures. Any stylistic messages affixed to artifacts in this category are exposed continuously to the critical eyes of a large number of members of the given social group. Any systematic deviations in the expression of a given stylistic message, among different sets of group members, would disrupt communication and give rise to dysfunctional misinformation within the social group. At the same time, the fact that potentially any or all members may be exposed to the stylistic message makes it much easier to fine-tune the stylistic signals so that they will either be uniformly expressed thoroughout the entire group in question or show only random deviations around a norm.

There is still no guarantee under these conditions that a given stylistic signal would differ from those in surrounding social groups. This assumption becomes more realistic only if an item carries a signal which explicitly broadcasts social group affiliation and if this item is entered into processes of boundary maintenance. We would expect to find social-group-specificity of stylistic signals particularly in those instances where all members of a social group potentially encounter a given stylistic message (and thus its expression would be standardized among all the members of the group), *and* where this message enters into contexts of boundary maintenance (so that it will be maintained *in contrast* to similar signals of surrounding social groups). It is not surprising that only a relatively small number of items in a material culture inventory shows group-specific distribution of stylistic form, since only a subset of the items potentially seen by any member of a social group is regularly entered into boundary maintaining contexts.

To recapitulate our expectations of stylistic behavior briefly, the following relationships should hold: 1) those artifacts are more appropriate for stylistic messages (regardless of other articulations) which are more visible, which enter more information exchanges, and which are potentially encountered by more individuals; 2) those specific stylistic forms will have the widest distribution that are affixed to artifacts which are the most visible and the most accessible to other individuals; 3) specific stylistic forms will be clinally distributed within and between social units if they are seen only by a relatively small number of individuals; 4) social-group-specific stylistic form should occur only among those messages that are most widely broadcast, that broadcast group affiliation, and that enter into processes of boundary maintenance.

## An Evaluation of the Expectations

I decided to evaluate these predictions in southeastern Europe, specifically in Yugoslavia with which I am most familiar in terms of the ethnographic literature and personal observations. Yugoslavia is particulary appropriate for this evaluation since folk material culture has been studied there at least since the period of romanticism. Many local societies have recorded it faithfully. But, especially after the first World War, folklore study, human and cultural geography and ethnohistory have documented the traditional material culture that was rapidly disappearing.

Yugoslavia also forms an appropriate testing ground for my hypotheses because it has been, and continues to be, an extremely segmented social mosaic of almost Near Eastern complexity. Within present borders of the country there are three major religions (Orthodox and Catholic Christians, and Moslems), four major nationalities (Serbs, Croats, Slovenes, Macedonians), and three major languages (Serbo-Croatian, Slovenian, Macedonian), as well as a multitude of large (Albanian, Hungarian) and small (Bulgarians, Czechs, Germans, gypsies, Jews, Italians, Romanians, Slovaks, Turks) ethnic groups. Thanks to a lack of clear natural boundaries and due to a turbulent history, there are only very few small regions today that are made up of homogeneous populations who have resided in situ for more than a few generations. Throughout history, people became Islamized or baptized as Orthodox and Catholic Christians, often depending on the given administration. Depending on the general state of lawlessness, people would be either peasants or transhumant pastoralists. People became albanized, serbianized, or affiliated with whatever group was the most opportune. Patricularly in the mountainous parts of the country, the basic geographic unit is usually a small area of level land surrounded on all sides by mountains; such units are usually not self-sufficient beyond basic subsistence, necessitating strong local specialization and heavy dependence on markets. Thus, the functional matrix for stylistic messaging should be strongly developed, heavily involving people of our category 1 in Fig. 1 with those in category 4.

The test required a category of material culture which would play a part in information exchange in as many different contexts as possible —from the confines of a household to encounters between different ethnic or social groups. Folkdress is the only category that satisfies these restrictions. At the same time it is well recorded in the literature. Folkdress is worn inside the household, it is worn during work within the settlement, and it is worn at the market and in all other contexts that articulate members of the same or different social groups. I limited myself, at least initially, to male dress, since Yugoslavia is a strongly patriarchal society and the role of women in public is severely limited.

The following literature was utilized in this analysis of stylistic form in folkdress: for Albanians: Çabej, 1966, Degrand, 1901; Durham, 1909; Grothe, 1913; Hecquard, n.d.; Kuhač, 1892; Lane, 1924; Louis, 1927; Lutovac, 1935; Smiljanić, 1900; Trifunoski, 1953/4; Uroševič, 1953/4, 1965; for Croats: Čulić, 1957, 1959; Gavazzi, 1936; Karger, 1963; Krauss, 1885; Kuš-Nikolajev, 1958; Marković, 1954; Tomasić, 1942; West, 1964; for Hercegovinian Croats or Serbs: Milojević, 1937; Vlahović, 1953; for Montenegrin Serbs: Durham, 1928; Grothe, 1913; Karger, 1931; Lutovac, 1933, 1935; Milojević, 1937; Smiljanić and Lutovac, 1932; for Hungarians: Kresz, 1956; Michaelis, 1940; for Romanians: Dunăre et al., 1963; Ionescu, 1955; Irimie, 1964, 1965; Lutovac, 1960; Michaelis, 1940; for Serbs: Arandjelović, 1966; Bjeladinović, 1966/7, Čulić, 1957, 1959; Djordjević, 1923; Draškić and Pantelić, 1965/6; Djordjević, 1958; Goff and Fawcett, 1921; Halpern, 1958; Krauss, 1885; Lutovac, 1933; 1935; 1953; 1960; Marković, 1952; 1954; Mijatović, 1911; Niković, 1953/4; Petrović, 1953/4; Tomasić, 1948; for Slovenians: Brejčeva, 1933; Novak, 1952; Orel, 1953; for Vlachs and other herder populations: Aranjelović, 1966; Atlas..., 1949; 1954; Capidan, 1942; Dunăre, et al. 1963; Goff and Fawcett, 1955; Kopozyńska, 1961; Marnow, 1961; Simonjenko, 1961; Vladuţiu, 1961; Wace and Thompson, 1914. These sources are supplemented by personal observation in Yugoslavia and eastern Europe in 1959, 1962, 1967, 1968, 1970, 1971, 1974 and 1975.

In terms of our predictions from the last chapter, male dress items worn in the area can be classified by a simple, sensitive and objective criterion, namely, in terms of the distance at which they become visible to an observer. Items that are worn on the outside of several layers of clothing show up first, and the higher an item is located on the body, the earlier it becomes visible. This led me to define three broad categories of male dress: category 1 consists of items visible over long distances, such as from one mountain side to another, or over some distance along the road. Only headdress and coat fit this description. In the second category I placed those items that can be differentiated at intermediate distances, as, for example, in a market crowd or from one side of the road to the other. This definition circumscribes the gross features of skirts, shirts, jackets, and pants. Category 3 comprises any item of dress that becomes visible only at short range; inside the house or at a social gathering. Here we deal with socks and shoes, belts, and decorative items worn in addition to dress or on other dress items. Finally there is a residual category of items never seen by members outside the immediate household, such as underwear, or jewelry that may be worn underneath the other dress items. This last category will not be considered further since I lack personal information about these items and they are not covered in the ethnographic literature.

Given this classification scheme, we can make our predictions somewhat more specific. All dress items in our 3 categories are eminently visible; thus they all should be appropriate for the expression of stylistic messages. Yet, the distribution of specific stylistic form should positively correlate with the degree of visibility of the different categories, with the potential distances between the message receiver and the artifact-cum-message which differ among the categories, and with the number and kinds of people who are exposed to the different categories.

Let us begin with category 1, the headdress and coat. Being visible over the greatest distance, they are the only parts of dress which allow one to decipher a stylistic message before one gets into the gun range of one's enemy. They allow one to decide whether contact and interaction with an unknown person would be advantageous or not, before one gets uncomfortably close to the individual. We can exclude the coat because its use depends upon temperature and humidity and thus, if it does contain messages, it would not emit them as continuously as the headdress. Headdress, on the other hand, can be worn in winter for warmth, in summer for insulation against the heat, and at all times of the year against the humidity.

In an environment of intense competition between a multitude of different social groups, a premium is placed on processes of social integration, differentiation between interacting (and competing) groups, and boundary maintenance among the competitors. Headdress, under these circumstances, is singularly appropriate to take on messages of social group affiliation, because it is potentially visible to any member of a given social group and it enters into most boundary maintaining interactions. Thus, not only should stylistic form in headdress be uniformly or modally distributed within social groups, but it should also be social-group-specific and contrasting between interacting groups. Further, since headdress is potentially encountered by any or all members of the *largest, most inclusive* social group to which an individual claims affiliation, the major stylistic messages on headdress should signal an individual's affiliation to that entity.

Around 1939, the largest social groups to which individuals claimed affiliation in Yugoslavia were either language groups (Albanian, Hungarian, Slovene, German); groups united by language and a common way of life (Romanians in the far east, as peasants, vs. the Vlachs as herders); or those groups which, although they spoke the same or very similar languages, were separated through their history, such as the Serbs, the Montenegrin Serbs, the Hercegovinian Croats or Serbs, and the Croats. All these mentioned groups were wearing group-specific and different headdress in 1939, particularly in those areas where they lived interspersed among one another. All these headdresses are equivalent in terms of guarding against the elements. None of the shapes is predetermined by the raw material, and all groups were familiar with the same techniques of hat manufacture as the other groups.

It is interesting to note that Muslim Slavs do not fit this correlation between hat style and the largest unit of an individual's group affiliation. Their prior association with the Turks had ceased to be opportune in 1918, so that, in 1939 and at present, they are a people in search of group affiliation.

In areas of strong inter-group competition one would expect a higher proportion of people wearing hats that signal group affiliation than in areas with relatively stable homogeneous populations. This is well borne out by the ethnographic data. For example in 1959, both Peć and Prizren in the Albanian autonomous region had a thriving hatmaker trade. This area is characterized by strong competition between Serbs, Montenegrin Serbs, and Albanians. Cetinje, a town of comparable size and not too far away, but settled with a homogeneous population of Montenegrin Serbs, did not support a single hatmaker establishment. Similarly, the Bazaar of Sarajevo sports a large section of hatmakers in residence. The city is known for the intense competition among its Serbian, Croatian, and Muslim inhabitants. The capitals of Croatia and Slovenia, with relatively homogeneous and stable populations, had no hatmaker craft in evidence.

Since style in headdress seems to signal the most inclusive social entity to which an individual has allegiance, we would expect changes in stylistic form as this group changes. This again is well illustrated by data from Yugoslavia. Before the state had established its monopoly on force in the Montenegrin mountains, each of the mountain tribes in this region was characterized by a different type of headdress. Another means of signalling social affiliation had been the *struka* (a kind of cloak), differing by tribe in color or combination of colors. Only after the central state had acquired superior fire power and vendetta and raiding had consequently ceased in the mountains (depending on the area, between 1900 and 1945), we find the mountain tribes aligning by ethnic group. This is reflected in folkdress by the disappearance of the struka and the area wide adoption of Albanian, Serbian, or Montenegrin headdress. After 1945, the largest unit of social affiliation became the partisan-derived Communist administration. Thus, if young people wear a distinct headdress at all today, it is the World War II partisan cap. Another case in point is the headdress of the Romanian speaking herding populations in southeastern Europe. Recently, these groups, from southern Yugoslavia to southern Poland, have given up their sheep-skin kalpak headdress and adopted the hat of Romanian peasants. This is accounted for by their official recognition as Romanian speaking minorities and their subsequent identification with the Romanian nation state.

To summarize, headdress—as an artifact that is extremely well visible and exposed to the largest number of contexts of information exchange (including those involving boundary maintenance)—carries stylistic messages specific in terms of the largest group that an individual affiliates with. The message content of stylistic form in headdress is the affiliation with this group.

Categories 2 and 3 of our classification scheme include those items visible only over intermediate and small distances. Concomitant with this decrease in visibility, they are not as predictably visible. For example, the use of a coat will prevent any artifacts worn underneath it from emitting the stylistic messages they may carry. Also, as they can transmit messages only over shorter distances, the number of individuals who are potentially exposed to them is smaller, and the number of information exchange contexts into which these items may enter is more narrowly circumscribed. Therefore, we would expect specific stylistic form in these items to have a more constricted distribution, and the stylistic messages emitted by these artifacts to have a different content from those in category 1. We can be more explicit in these predictions. If, for example, artifacts in category 2 or 3 contain messages of group identification, they should refer to smaller groups than in category 1. Specific stylistic form, whatever the message content, would not necessarily coincide with the most inclusive groups of individual allegiance, and, unless the message specifically were to express group affiliation and be broadcast in boundary situations among different groups, the stylistic form should vary clinally, within and between the subunits of major social groups.

I was able to evaluate these expectations against Albanian, Hungarian, Serbian, and Romanian ethnographic materials. The results were parallel to each other; and the Albanian and Romanian data are summarized in detail in Tables II and III. I want to list here only the conclusions. The further the distance from which a specific stylistic message can be deciphered, the wider its geographic distribution; and the more predictably an item is worn or visible, the wider the distribution of specific stylistic form carried by the item. Referring specifically to messages of group affiliation, stylistic messages that are more visible symbolize more inclusive groups, and, at close distance visibility, the message content shifts from identifying social groups to defining an individual's position along a ranked scale, such as wealth, status, or age. One additional observation relates to stylistic messaging in female dress in the area. Female dress items in all three categories either carry messages which summarize the individual's affiliation with intermediate social units, or define her position along a ranked scale. The distribution of specific stylistic messages in female dress most closely approximates the distribution of male dress style of category 3. This is to be expected in a strongly patriarchal society where males determine most kin affiliations, where most public activities are in the hands of males, and where the movement of women is restricted to the context of the local group.

## Conclusion

In my paper I have attempted to demonstrate that style is a pleasantly multidimensional and surprisingly dynamic phenomenon. It reacts with great sensitivity to changes in other cultural variables and, of itself, actively supports other cultural processes, such as cultural integration and differentiation, boundary maintenance, compliance with norms and enforcing conformity. I have interpreted stylistic behavior as that aspect of artifact form and structure which can be related to processes of information exchange. Specific stylistic form is seen to emit messages which are broadcast throughout the use life of artifacts. Depending on message content, message

## TABLE II
### Message Distributions in Albanian Folkdress Exclusive of Headdress

| Message Content | Stylistic Form and Sample Messages |
| --- | --- |
| general area | coat color: black wool coat (south Albania) vs. white or grey coat (north and central Albania); these areas are divided through history, custom, religion and ideology and the boundary in message expression is sharp. |
| subregion | pants or jacket style: Turkish pants are worn in Central Albania, for example, while tight pants are characteristic for northern Albania; this message divides the people in the region by religion (Moslem vs. Christian) and a sharp boundary is maintained in stylistic form of pants between these two groups |
| valley or village | gross ornamentative features of shirts, pants, and sometimes coats; this does not circumscribe closed populations which maintain sharp boundaries between each other; the distribution of specific stylistic form appears to be clinal, paralleling communication patterns. |
| position of individuals along ranked scale | small decorative features: amount of silver or gold on belt; make of gun; etc. |

## TABLE III
### Romanian Folkdress—Message Contents and stylistic forms

| Message Content | Stylistic Form and Sample Messages |
| --- | --- |
| Area of residence | Shirt cut or color: Dacian shirt, Fustanella, long embroidered shirt; these messages have clinal distributions already. |
| Village of residence | Color of motifs and combination of motifs; these items do not have sharply defined distribution patterns, but change clinally through space. |
| Status, occupation, family | Quality and quantity of decoration, ornamentation and elaboration on other dress items; for example, the amount of gold thread reflects wealth. |

visibility, and social contexts to which artifacts are exposed, as well as on the cultural matrix in which this stylistic communication takes place, different artifacts carry different kinds of messages and stylistic form has different meanings, although some general relationships between the distribution of stylistic form and the functional matrix of stylistic behavior can be deduced. Some of these general relationships have been developed here, and a few of them have been evaluated against a set of ethnographic materials from southeastern Europe. Only a few artifacts are appropriate for carrying messages which identify the most inclusive social group that individuals affiliate with (I used headdress as an example) and even fewer of these artifacts will be preserved archaeologically. Certainly the assumption of specificity in stylistic form by major social groups in warranted only in the fewest cases, and a priori not very likely for most of the artifacts that archaeologists commonly work with, such as household utensils.

While my discussion of style does not cover all phenomena currently subsumed under this term, it removes a number of them from their pedestal of processual isolation and integrates them into the cultural system of which they form a part. I hope that my paper will stimulate further research into stylistic dynamics and into the evolution of style, so that the present guiding principles of stylistic analysis can be repaired or, if necessary, replaced.

## Acknowledgments

I would like to dedicate this paper to James B. Griffin. His constant support allowed me, as a bungling foreigner, to obtain a first-rate education in anthropological archaeology at The University of Michigan. I hope that the ethnographic material in this paper will bring back to Jimmy pleasant memories of the field season we shared in 1970 at Visoko Brdo in Bosnia, somewhere deep in Yugoslavia.

This paper recieved its initial impetus from a seminar on Style in Archaeology and Ethnology at the Museum of Anthropology of the University of Michigan in the spring semester of 1969, with two students (Gregory Johnson and myself) and two professors (Robert Whallon and Richard Beardsley). I am happy to acknowledge the devil's advocacy of Robert W. Paynter of the University of Massachusetts in the formative stage of this paper as well as financial support from the Wenner-Gren Foundation, which supported me for two months in the field in eastern Europe in 1970.

# References Cited

Arandjelović, J.
    1966    Narodna nošnja u Resavi. Beograd. Etnografski Muzej. Glasnik 28-9:125-51.
Atlas polskich strojow Ludowych.
    1949    Część 5, Małopolska. Zeszyt 18. Stróje Górale Szczawnickich. Lublin.
    1954    Część 5. Małopolska. Zeszyt 15. Strój Spiski. Lublin.
Binford, L. R.
    1972    Model building, paradigms and the current state of Paleolithic archaeology. Item *in:* An archaeological perspective, by L. R. Binford. New York: Seminar Press, pp. 245-94.
Binford, L. R. and S. R. Binford
    1966    A preliminary analysis of functional variability in the Mousterian of Levallois facies. Item *in:* Recent studies in paleoanthropology, edited by J. D. Clark and F. C. Howell, American Anthropologist 68 (pt. 2):238-95.
Bjeladinović, J.
    1966    Narodna nošnja u Radjevini. Beograd. Etnografski Muzej. Glasnik 28/9:257-71.
Brejčeva, M.
    1933    Slovenske noše na Koroškem. Etnolog (Ljubljana) 5/6:1-30.
Çabej, E.
    1966    Albanische Volkskunde. Südost-Forschungen 25:333-87.
Capidan, Th.
    1942    Darstellung der ethnologischen Lage am Balkan mit besonderer Berücksichtigung der Mazedorumänen (Aromunen). Südost-Forschungen 7:497-545.
Clark, J. D. and C. V. Haynes Jr.
    1970    An elephant butchery site at Mwanganda's Village, Karonga, Malawi, and its relevance for Paleolithic archaeology. World Archaeology 1:390-411.
Čulić, Z.
    1957    Narodna nošnja u Posavini, II. Sarajevo. Zemaljski Muzej. Glasnik 12:5-16.
    1959    Narodna nošnja u Posavini, III, Sarajevo. Zemaljski Muzej. Glasnik 14:5-23.
Cvijič, J.
    1918    La peninsule Balkanique. Geographie humaine. Paris.
Deetz, J. D. F.
    1965    The dynamics of stylistic change in Arikara ceramics. Illinois Studies in Anthropology 4. Urbana.

Degrand, A.
 1901 Souvenirs de la Haute Albanie. Paris.
Djordjević, D. M.
 1958 Život i običaji narodni u leskovackoj Moravi.
Djordjević, T. R.
 1923 Naš narodni život. Beograd.
Dunăre, N., et al.
 1963 Arta populară din Valea Jiului. Cluj.
Durham, E.
 1909 High Albania. London.
 1928 Some tribal origins, laws, and customs of the Balkans. London.
Feustel, R.
 1973 Technik der Steinzeit. Böhlau, Leipzig.
Filipović, M. S.
 1949- Narodna nošnja u Rami. Sarajevo. Zemaljski Muzej. Glasnik 4/5:
 1950 121-33.
Flannery, K. V.
 1972 The cultural evolution of civilizations. Annual Review of Ecology and Systematics 3: 399-426.
Gavazzi, M.
 1936 Der Aufbau der kroatischen Volkskultur. Baessler Archiv 20: 138-67.
Goff, A. and H. A. Fawcett
 1921 Macedonia. London.
Grothe, H.
 1913 Durch Albanien und Montenegro. München.
Halpern, J. M.
 1958 A Serbian village. New York.
Hecquard, H.
 n.d. Histoire et description de la Haute Albanie. Paris.
Hill, J. N.
 1968 Broken K pueblo: patterns of form and function. Item *in:* New perspectives in archaeology, edited by S. R. and L. R. Binford. Chicago: Aldine, pp. 103-42.
Ionescu, E.
 1965 Tomanian folk art. Antiquity and Survival 1:155-68.
Irimie, C.
 1964 Arta populară in Muzeul Brukenthal. Bukarest.
 1965 Das Hirtenwesen der Rumänen. Südosteuropa-Studien 7.
Karger, A.
 1963 Die Entwicklung der Siedlungen im westlichen Slawonien. Kölner Geographische Arbeiten 15. Wiesbaden.
Kayser, K.
 1931 Westmontenegro. Eine kulturgeographische Darstellung. Stuttgart.

Kopczyńska, B.
1961 Das Hirtenwesen in den polnischen Karpathen. Item *in:* Viehzucht und Hirtenwesen in Ostmitteleuropa, edited by L. Földes. Budapest, pp. 389-438.

Krauss, F. S.
1885 Sitten und Bräuche der Südslawen. Wien.

Kresz, M.
1956 Magyar parasztviselet. Budapest.

Kuhać, F. B.
1892 Albanesen in Slawonien. Ethnographische Mitteilungen aus Ungarn 2:25-32, 169-75.

Kuš-Nikolajev, M.
1958 Biološki kvalitet u morfogenezi Hrvatske seljačke nošnje. Slovenski Etnograf 11:155-65.

Lane, R. W.
1924 The peaks of Shala. London.

Longacre, W. A.
1968 Some aspects of prehistoric society in east-central Arizona. Item *in:* New perspectives in archaeology, edited by S. R. and L. R. Binford. Chicago: Aldine, pp. 89-102.

Louis, H.
1927 Albanien. Eine Landeskunde. Stuttgart.

Lutovac, H. V.
1933 La vie pastorale dans le Prokletije Nord-Orientales. Beograd.

Lutovac, M.
1935 Metohija. Etude de géographie humaine. Paris.
1953 Zanati u Prizrenu. Beogard. Etnografski Muzej. Zbornik 1901-1951:58-63.
1960 Etnički sastav i etnički procesi u Timočkoj krajini. Rad kongresa folklorista Jugoslavije u Zaječaru i Negotinu 1958:13-19. Beograd.

Marinow, W.
1961 Die Schafzucht der nomadisierenden Karakatschanen in Bulgarien. Item *in:* Viehzucht und Hirtenwesen in Ostmit-teleuropa, edited by L. Földes. Budapest, pp. 147-96.

Marković, R.
1952 Stara srpska narodna nošnja u Severnom Banatu. Srpska Akademija Nauka. Etnografski Institut. Glasnik 1:457-67.

Marković, Z.
1954 Narodna nošnja u okolini Travnika. Sarajevo, Zemaljski Muzej. Glasnik 9:115-26.
Narodna nošnja na Kupresu. Sarajevo, Zemaljski Muzej. Glasnik 9:95-110.

Michaelis, H. H.
1940 Beiträge zur Kulturgeographie des Südbanats und Nordserbiens. Berliner Geographische Arbeiten 19.

Mijatović, C.
  1911    Servia of the Servians. London.
Milojević, B.
  1937    La vie humaine dans la montagne de Durmitor. Revue de Géographie Humaine 25:509-20.
Niković, V.
  1953-   Narodna nošnja u Sumadiška Kolubari. Beograd Etnografski
  1954    Muzej. Glasnik 2/3:463-510.
Novak, V.
  1952    Der Aufbau der slowenischen Volkskultur. Zeitschrift für Ethnologie 77:227-37.
Orel, B.
  1953    Slovenska ljudska noša v zbirki Nikole Arsenoviće. Beograd. Etnografski Muzej. Zbornik 1901-1951:179-87.
Otte, D.
  1974    Effects and functions in the evolution of signalling systems. Annual Review of Ecology and Systematics 5:285-418.
Petrović, P. Z.
  1953-   Raška. Antropogeografska i etnološka monografija varošice. Srpska
  1954    Akademija Nauka. Etnografski Institut. Glasnik 2/3:213-56.
Rappaport, R. A.
  1971    The sacred in human evolution. Annual Review of Ecology and Systematics 2:23-44.
Sackett, J. R.
  1973    Style, function and artifact variability in palaeolithic assemblages. Item in: The explanation of culture change, edited by C. Renfrew. Duckworth: The Old Piano Factory, pp. 317-28.
Semenov, S. A.
  1964    Prehistoric technology. Bath: Adams & Dart.
  1968    Razvitie texniki v kamennom veke. Moscow: Nauka.
Simonjenko, I.
  1961    Almenwirtschaftliche Schafzucht der Ukrainischen Bevölkerung. in Viehzucht und Hirtenwesen in Ostmitteleuropa, edited by L. Földes. Budapest, pp. 363-88.
Smiljanić, M. V.
  1900    Beiträge zur Siedlungskunde Südserbiens. Abhandlungen der Geographischen Gesellschaft Wiens 2(2).
Smiljanić, T. and M. Lutovac
  1932    Contributions à la connaissance de la vie pastorale sur les hautes montagnes en Yougoslavie. Beograd.
Tomasić, D.
  1948    Personality and culture in eastern European politics.
Trifunoski, J. F.
  1950    Debar. Antropogeografska ispitivanja. Srpska Akademija Nauka. Etnografski institut. Glasnik 2/3:257-75.

Urošević, A.
1953- Kosovska Mitrovica. Srpska Akademja Nauka. Ethnografski in-
1954 stitut. Glasnit 2/3:187-211.
Urošević, A.
1965 Kosovo. Beograd.
Vlăduţiu, I.
1961 Almenwirtschaftliche Viehhaltung und Transhumanz im Brangebiet (Südostkarpathen, Rumänien). Item *in:* Viehzucht und Hirtenwesen in Ostmitteleuropa, edited by L. Földes. Budapest, pp. 196-241.
Vlahović, M. S.
1953 O najstarijoj kapi kod jugoslovena s obzirom na zbirku kapa etnografskog muzeja u Beogradu Beograd. Etnografski Muzej. Zbornik 1901-1951:144-63.
Wace, A. J. B. and M. S. Thompson
1914 The nomads of the Balkans, London.
West, R.
1964 Black lamb and grey falcon. New York.
Whallon, R. Jr.
1966 The Owasco period: a reanalysis. Unpublished Ph.D. dissertation, University of Chicago.
1968 Investigations of late prehistoric social organization in New York. Item *in:* New perspectives in archaeology, edited by S. R. and L. R. Binford. Chicago: Aldine, pp. 223-44.
White, L. A.
1959 The evolution of culture. New York: McGraw Hill.

# PART IV

Published works of
James Bennett Griffin

# PUBLISHED WORKS OF JAMES BENNETT GRIFFIN

*Compiled by Richard I. Ford and Volney H. Jones*

### 1930

Mortuary customs in the western half of the northeast Woodland Area. Master's thesis, University of Chicago.

### 1931

The Athens excavations. Society for Pennsylvania Archaeology, Bulletin 2:3.

### 1934

Archaeological remains in Adams County, Illinois. Illinois State Academy of Science, 2:97-99.

### 1935

Aboriginal methods of pottery manufacture in the eastern United States. Pennsylvania Archaeologist 5:19-24.
An analysis of the Fort Ancient culture. Repository for the eastern United States, Notes 1. Ann Arbor, Mich.
An experimental study of the technique of Indian pottery making (with C. W. Angell). Papers of the Michigan Academy of Science, Arts, and Letters 20:1-6.
Report on pottery sherds from near Abilene, Texas. Texas Archaeological Paleontological Society Bulletin 7:57-70.
Review of A. T. Jackson. Types of east Texas pottery. American Antiquity 1:169-170.
Review of Emerson F. Greenman. Excavation of the Reeve Village site. Lake County and Seven prehistoric sites in northern Ohio. Ibid.:73-74.

## 1936

The cultural significance of the ceramic remains from the Norris Basin. Doctoral dissertation, University of Michigan.

General comments on the classification of the Fort Ancient Aspect and its ethnological affiliations. Item *in:* The Indianapolis Archaeological Conference, Indianapolis Indiana, December 6, 7 and 8, 1935, edited by Carl E. Guthe, pp. 48-58 with the ensuing discussion.

Pottery from the Nowlin Mound. Item *in:* Excavation of the Nowlin Mound, edited by Glenn A. Black. Indiana Historical Bulletin 13:385-87.

Report on pottery sherds from Safe Harbor, Lancaster County, Pennsylvania. Item *in:* Donald A. Cadzow, Archaeological studies of the Susquehannock Indians of Pennsylvania, Pennsylvania Historical and Museum Commission 3:139-47, 188-90.

## 1937

The archaeological remains of the Chiwere Sioux. American Antiquity 2:180-81.

The chronological position and ethnological relationships of the Fort Ancient Aspect. Ibid.: 273-76.

Culture identity of the Ozark "top layer." Ibid.: 296-97.

Review of D. A. Cadzow. Archaeological studies of the Susquehannock Indians of Pennsylvania. American Antiquity 3:96-99.

## 1938

The ceramic remains from Norris Basin, Tennessee. Item *in:* An archaeological survey of the Norris Basin in eastern Tennessee, edited by W. S. Webb. Bureau of American Ethnology, Bulletin 118:253-358.

Report of the conference on southeastern pottery typology (with James A. Ford). Ann Arbor: Proceedings of the First Southeastern Archaeological Conference. Mimeographed.

Review of Earl H. Bell. Chapters in Nebraska archaeology. (Nos. 1-4). American Anthropologist 40:148-49.

## 1939

Report on the ceramics of Wheeler Basin. Item *in:* W. S. Webb, An archaeological survey of Wheeler Basin on the Tennessee River in northern Alabama. Bureau of American Ethnology, Bulletin 122:127-65.

A note of correction. American Antiquity 5:150.

## 1940

Review of W. D. Funkhouser and W. S. Webb. The Chilton site. American Antiquity 6:185-86.

Review (with Georg K. Neumann) of W. S. Webb and W. G. Haag. The Chiggerville site. Ibid.: 186-88.

## 1941

Additional Hopewell material from Illinois. Indiana Historical Society Prehistory Research Series 11 (3):165-223.

Contributions to the archaeology of the Illinois River Valley (with F. C. Baker, R. G. Morgan, G. K. Neumann, and J. L. B. Taylor). Transactions of the American Philosophical Society 32, Pt. 1:1-208.

A preliminary synthesis of eastern United States archaeology, abstract in Society for American Archaeology Notebook 2 (2):33-34.

Reel-shaped gorgets. American Antiquity 6:265.

Report on pottery from the St. Louis area. The Missouri Archaeologist 7:1-18.

Review of Paul and Henriette Van De Velde. The black pottery of Coyotepec. American Antiquity 7: 193-94.

Notes and News—Northern Mississippi area. Ibid.: 76-78, 179-182.

## 1942

Adena pottery. American Antiquity 7:344-58.

An interpretation of Siouan prehistory, abstract in Society for American Archaeology Notebook 2 (4):65.

On the historic location of the Tutelo and the Mohetan in the Ohio Valley. American Anthropologist 44:275-80.

Review of David I. Bushnell, Jr. Virginia before Jamestown. American Antiquity 7:328-29.

Review of F. M. Setzler. Archaeological perspectives in the northern Mississippi Valley. Ibid.:329-31.

Review of M. W. Stirling. The historic method as applied to southeastern archaeology. Ibid. 12:328.

Review of Waldo R. Wedel. Cultural sequence in the central Great Plains. Ibid. 7:331-32.

Review of Wm. Duncan Strong. From history to prehistory in the northern Great Plains. Ibid.:332-33.

Notes and News—Northern Mississippi area. Ibid.: 411-412.

## 1943

Adena village site pottery from Fayette County, Kentucky. University of Kentucky. Reports in Anthropology and Archaeology 5:666-71.

An analysis and interpretation of the ceramic remains from two sites near Beaufort, South Carolina. Bureau American Ethnology Bulletin 133: 155-68.

The Fort Ancient Aspect: its cultural and chronological position in Mississippi Valley archaeology. Ann Arbor: University of Michigan Press.

## 1944

Archaeological horizons in the Southeast and their connections with the Mexican area. Item *in:* El Norte de Mexico y el Sur de Estados Unidos 3. Mexico, D. F.: Societe Mexico de Anthropologia.

The De Luna expedition and the "buzzard cult" in the Southeast. Journal of the Washington Academy Sciences 34:299-303.

The Iroquois in American prehistory. Papers of the Michigan Academy of Science, Arts, and Letters 29:357-75.

The Keyser farm site (with Carl Manson and Howard A. MacCord). Ibid.:375-418.

## 1945

The Box Elder Mound, Lasalle County, Illinois. American Antiquity 11:47-48.

The ceramic affiliations of the Ohio Valley Adena culture. University of Kentucky Reports in Anthropology and Archaeology 6:220-46.

Ceramic collections from two South Carolina sites. Papers of the Michigan Academy of Science, Arts and Letters 30:465-78.

An interpretation of Siouan archaeology in the Piedmont of North Carolina and Virginia. American Antiquity 10:321-30.

The Museum of Anthropology. Item *in:* The president's report for 1944-45. University of Michigan Official Publication 47:227-29.

Painted pottery figurines from Illinois (with W. C. McKern and P. T. Titterington). American Antiquity 10:295-302.

Review of William A. Ritchie. The Pre-Iroquoian occupations of New York state. Ibid.:401-7.

The significance of the fiber tempered pottery of the St. Johns area in Florida. Journal of the Washington Academy Sciences 35:218-23.

An unusual Oneota vessel from Minnesota. American Antiquity 11:120-21.
Notes and news—Northern Mississippi area. Ibid.: 135-6.

## 1946

Cultural change and continuity in eastern United States archaeology. Item *in:* Man in Northeastern North America, edited by Frederick Johnson. Robert S. Peabody Foundation for Archaeology Paper No. 3:37-95.

Review of Maurice Robbins. The Faulkner Spring site. American Antiquity 12:58-59.

## 1947

La Alfareria correspondiente al ultimo periodo de ocupación Nahua del Valle de Mexico: I (with Antonieta Espejo). Item *in:* Tlatelolco a traves de los tiempos 9:10-26, Reprinted from: Memorias de la Academia de la Historia.

The archaeological zone of Buena Vista, Huaxcama, San Luis Potosi (with Wilfrido du Solier and Alex D. Krieger). American Antiquity 13:15-33.

The Museum of Anthropology. Item *in:* The president's report for 1945-1946. University of Mighigan Official Publication 49:289-91.

Notes on some ceramic techniques and intrusions in central Mexico (with Alex D. Krieger). American Antiquity 12:156-68.

Review of John L. Champe. Ash Hollow cave: A study of stratigraphic sequence in the central Great Plains. Nebraska Historical Magazine 28:144-46.

Review of W. C. McKern. Preliminary report of the Upper Mississippi phase in Wisconsin. American Antiquity 13:189-91.

The Spruce Run earthworks: A forgotten Adena site in Delaware County, Ohio. Ohio State Archaeological and Historical Quarterly 56:188-200.

## 1948

An interpretation of the Glacial Kame culture. Item *in:* Wilbur M. Cunningham. A study of the Glacial Kame culture in Michigan, Ohio, and Indiana. Occasional Contributions, Museum of Anthropology, University of Michigan 12:46-51.

The Museum of Anthropology. Item *in:* The president's report for 1946-1947. University of Michigan Official Publication 49:328-31.

Review of Richard G. Morgan and James H. Rodabaugh. Bibliography of Ohio archaeology. Ohio State Archaeological and Historical Quarterly 57:205-6.
Review of Tatiana Proskouriakoff. An album of Maya architecture. American Antiquity 13:263-64.

1949

The Cahokia ceramic complexes. Proceedings of the Fifth Plains Conference of Archaeology, University of Nebraska: 44-58.
Meso-America and the Southeast: A commentary. Item *in:* The Florida Indian and his neighbor, edited by John W. Griffin. Florida: Rollins College, pp. 77-99.
The Museum of Anthropology. Item *in:* The president's report for 1947-1948. University of Michigan Official Publication 41:305-9.
Notes and news. American Antiquity 15:80.

1950

La Alfareriá correspondiente al ultimo periodo de ocupación Nahua del Valle de Mexico II (with Antonieta Espejo). Item *in:* Tlatelolco a través de los tiempos, Memorias de la Academia Mexicana de la Historia 11:15-66.
The Museum of Anthropology. Item *in:* The president's report for 1948-1949. University of Michigan Official Publication 51:287-91.
Prehistoric pottery of the eastern United States (with William H. Sears). Museum of Anthropology, University of Michigan.
Review of H. Perry Newell and Alex D. Krieger. The George C. Davis site, Cherokee County, Texas. Memoirs of the Society for American Archaeology No. 5. American Anthropologist 52:413-15.
Review of Kenneth Macgowan. Early man in the New World. Archaeology 3:187.
The Viking Fund seminar on the excavation, preservation, and identification of archaeological data. American Antiquity 16:85-88.
Review of William R. Adams. Archaeological notes on Posey County, Indiana. Ibid. 15:351-52.

1951

Archaeological survey in the lower Mississippi Alluvial Valley, 1940-1947 (with Philip Phillips and James A. Ford). Papers of the Peabody Museum of American Archaeology and Ethnology No. 25.

The central Mississippi Valley archaeological survey, season 1950: A preliminary report (with A. C. Spaulding). Journal of Illinois State Archaeological Society, New Series 1:74-82. (Also in Prehistoric Pottery of the Eastern United States 2-52:1-7.)
Essays on archaeological methods. University of Michigan Museum of Anthropology, Anthropological Papers No. 8 (editor).
The Museum of Anthropology. Item *in:* The president's report for 1949-1950. University of Michigan Official Publication 53:317-18.
A preliminary statement on the collection from the Grassy Lake site (Ms 4), Madison County, Illinois. The Greater St. Louis Archaeological Society Bulletin 6:35-44.
The radiocarbon laboratory at The University of Michigan. American Antiquity 17:174.
Some Adena and Hopewell radiocarbon dates. Item *in:* Radiocarbon dating, edited by Frederick Johnson. Society for American Archaeology, Memoir 8:26-29.

1952

Archeology of eastern United States. Chicago: Univ. Chicago Press (editor and contributor).
The late prehistoric cultures of the Ohio Valley. Ohio State Archaeological and Historical Quarterly 61:186-95.
The Museum of Anthropology. Item *in:* The president's report for 1950-1951. University of Michigan Official Publication 54:313-15.
Preface *and* An interpretation of the place of Spiro in southeastern archaeology. Item *in:* Henry W. Hamilton, The Spiro Mound. Missouri Archaeologist 14:13-16, 89-106.
A preview of the ceramic relationships of the Snyders site, Calhoun County, Illinois. Mimeographed. The Greater St. Louis Archaeological Society, pp. 14-17.
Review of Fay-Cooper Cole and others. Kincaid: a prehistoric Illinois metropolis. Ohio State Archaeological and Historical Quarterly 61:449-52.
Review of William S. Webb and Charles G. Wilder. An archaeological survey of Guntersville Basin on the Tennessee River in northern Alabama. American Antiquity 18:74-75.
Some Early and Middle Woodland pottery types in Illinois. Item *in:* Hopewellian communities in Illinois, edited by Thorne Deuel. Illinois State Museum Scientific Papers 5:93-129.

Some highly specific Middle Mississippi ceramic types. Indian tribes of aboriginal America, Selected Papers 29th International Congress of Americanists. Chicago: Univ. Chicago Press, pp. 136-38.

### 1953

Comments on the cultural position of the Bintz site, Campbell County, Kentucky. American Antiquity 18:362.
Erratum. Ibid.:303.
The Museum of Anthropology. Item *in*: The president's report for 1951-1952. University of Michigan Official Publication 55:328-33.
Prehistoric chronology estimates in the eastern United States and central Mexico, 1940-1950. Revista Mexicana de Estudios Anthropologicos 13 (2) and (3):485-96.
A preliminary statement on the pottery from Cape Denbigh, Alaska. Item *in:* Asia and North America: transpacific contacts. The Society for American Archaeology, Memoir 9:40-42.
United States and Canada: Indigenous Period. Program of the history of America I, 3. Mexico: Panamerican Institute of Geography and History, pp. 1-104.

### 1954

The Museum of Anthropology. Item *in:* The president's report for 1952-1953. University of Michigan Official Publication 56:338-44.
Review of A. Hyatt Verrill and Ruth Verrill. America's ancient civilizations. Scientific Monthly 2:123.
Review of A. L. Kroeber. Anthropology today. American Antiquity 19:301-2.

### 1955

Chronology and dating processes. Item *in:* Yearbook of Anthropology-1955, edited by William L. Thomas, Jr. New York: Wenner-Gren Foundation for Anthropological Research, Inc., pp. 133-47.
The Museum of Anthropology. Item *in:* The president's report for 1953-1954. University of Michigan Official Publication 57:324-26.
Observations on the grooved axe in North America. Pennsylvania Archaeologist 25:32-44.
Review of J. L. Giddings, Jr. The Arctic Woodland culture of the Kobuk River. American Antiquity 29:53-54.

Review of Mortimer Wheeler. Archaeology from the earth. Scientific Monthly 80:324.
Review of O. G. S. Crawford. Archaeology in the field. Scientific Monthly 80 (5):324-25.
Review of Walum Olum or Red Score. The migration legend of the Lenni Lenape or Delaware Indians: A new translation, interpreted by linguistic, historical, archaeological, and physical anthropological studies. Indiana Magazine of History 51:59-65.

1956

The American southwest: A problem in cultural isolation (with others in Seminars in Archaeology). The Society for American Archaeology, Memoir 11:59-127.
Chronology and dating processes. Item *in:* Current anthropology: A supplement to anthropology today, edited by W. L. Thomas Jr. Chicago: Univ. of Chicago Press, pp. 133-147.
The Museum of Anthropology. Item *in:* The president's report for 1954-1955. University of Michigan Official Publication 58:327-32.
The Museum of Anthropology. Item *in:* The University of Michigan, an encyclopedic survey, 8, edited by W. A. Donnelly. Ann Arbor: Univ. of Mich. Press, pp. 1479-81.
Prehistoric settlement patterns in the northern Mississippi Valley and the Upper Great Lakes. Item *in:* Prehistoric settlement patterns in the New World, edited by G. R. Willey. Viking Fund Publications in Anthropology 23:63-71.
The reliability of radiocarbon dates for late glacial and recent times in central and eastern North America. Papers of the Third Great Basin Archaeological Conference. The University of Utah Anthropological Papers 26: 10-34.
Review of Geoffrey Bibby. The testimony of the spade. Saturday Review of Literature, April 1956.
Review of Max Loehr. Chinese Bronze Age weapons. Michigan Alumnus Quarterly Review 63:87-89.
Review of Stuart Piggott. The Neolithic cultures of the British Isles: A study of the stone-using agricultural communities of Britain in the second millenium B.C. American Antiquity 21:316-17.
Review of William A. Ritchie. Recent discoveries suggesting an Early Woodland burial cult in the northeast. American Anthropologist 58: 196-97.

The study of early cultures. Item *in:* Man, culture, and society, edited by H. L. Shapiro. Oxford Univ. Press, pp. 22-48.

The University Museums. Item *in:* The president's report for 1954-1955. University of Michigan Official Publication 58:343-49.

## 1957

The Exhibit Museum. Item *in:* The president's report for 1955-1956. University of Michigan Official Publication 58:306-12 (with Irving G. Reimann).

The Museum of Anthropology. Item *in:* The president's report for 1956-1957. University of Michigan Official Publication 58:327-32.

Review of Dorothy Cross. Archaeology of New Jersey, Vol. 2, The Abbott Farm. American Journal of Archaeology 62:135-36.

Review of Melvin L. Fowler and Howard Winters. Modoc rock shelter. A preliminary report. Report of Investigations No. 4, Illinois State Museum, Springfield. American Antiquity 2:197.

Review of Richard F. Flint. Glacial and Pleistocene geology. American Anthropologist 60:621-23.

## 1958

The chronological position of the Hopewellian culture in the eastern United States. University of Michigan, The Museum of Anthropology, Anthropological Papers No. 12.

Improving the use of existing facilities. Item *in:* The identification of non-artifactual archaeological materials, edited by W. W. Taylor. National Academy of Sciences Pub. 565:59-60.

The Museum of Anthropology. Item *in:* The president's report for 1956-1957. University of Michigan Official Publication 59:219-23.

Pre-Columbian art. Item *in:* Mexican art: Pre-Columbian to modern times. Ann Arbor: Univ. of Michigan Press, pp. 9-19.

Radiocarbon dates for the Crable site. Central States Archaeological Journal 5:19.

Review of Gordon R. Willey and Philip Phillips. Method and theory in American archaeology. Inter-American Review of Bibliography 8:387-89.

Review of Gordon R. Willey and Philip Phillips. Method and theory in American archaeology. Ohio Historical Quarterly, 67:283-84.

University of Michigan radiocarbon dates II (with H. R. Crane). Radiocarbon Supplement 127:1098-1105.

University of Michigan radiocarbon dates III (with H. R. Crane). Radiocarbon Supplement 128:1117-23.

## 1959

The pursuit of archeology in the United States. American Anthropologist 61:379-89.
Review of Erik Wahlgren. The Kensington Stone. Archaeology 12:220.
Review of J. R. Caldwell. Trend and tradition in the prehistory of the eastern United States. American Journal of Archaeology 63:414-16.
Review of Jack L. Hough. Geology of the Great Lakes. Archaeology 12:294-95.
Review of R. N. C. Bowen. The exploration of time. Archaeology 12:220.
Review of T. M. N. Lewis and Madeline Kneberg. Tribes that slumber: Indian times in the Tennessee region. American Anthropologist 61:1142.
Review of William S. Webb and Raymond S. Baby. The Adena People. Wisconsin Magazine of History 43:144.
University of Michigan radiocarbon dates IV (with H. R. Crane). Radiocarbon Supplement 1:173-98.

## 1960

Climatic change: A contributory cause of the growth and decline of northern Hopewellian culture. The Wisconsin Archaeologist 41:21-33.
A hypothesis for the prehistory of the Winnebago. Item *in:* Culture in history, essays in honor of Paul Radin, edited by Stanley Diamond. New York: Columbia University Press, pp. 809-65.
Some prehistoric connections between Siberia and America. Science 131: 801-12.
University of Michigan radiocarbon dates V (with H. R. Crane). Radiocarbon Supplement 2:31-48.
Review of Robert Heizer, editor. The archaeologist at work. American Antiquity 25:611.

## 1961

Commentary on "Neolithic diffusion rates." Current Anthropology 2:92-93.
An interpretation of Asiatic contributions to the prehistoric Woodland culture of eastern North America. V International Congress für Vor und Fruhgeschichte, 347.

Lake Superior copper and the Indians. University of Michigan, Museum of Anthropology, Anthropological Papers 17 (editor and contributor).

North America: Prehistory and archaeology. Encyclopaedia Brittanica 16: 506-13.

Post-glacial ecology and culture changes in the Great Lakes area of North America. Proceedings of the 4th Conference of Great Lakes Research. Great Lakes Research Division Publ. 7:147-55.

Relationships between the Caddoan area and the Mississippi Valley. Texas Archeological Society Bulletin 31:27-51.

Some correlations of climatic and cultural change in eastern North America prehistory. New York Academy of Science, Annals 95:710-17.

University of Michigan radiocarbon dates VI (with H. R. Crane). Radiocarbon 3:105-125.

Review of William A. Ritchie and Don W. Dragoo. The eastern dispersal of Adena. American Antiquity 26:572-3.

1962

A discussion of prehistoric similarities and connections between the arctic and temperate zones of North America. Arctic Institute of North America Tech. Paper No. 11:154-63.

University of Michigan Radiocarbon Dates VII (with H. R. Crane). Radiocarbon 4:183-203.

1963

Archaeological materials from the Chukchi Peninsula, by N. N. Dikov. American Antiquity 28:529-36 (edited with Chester S. Chard).

A new radiocarbon date on corn from the Davis site, Cherokee County, Texas (with Richard A. Yarnell). American Antiquity 28:396-97.

Proceedings of the conference on the climate of the eleventh and sixteenth centuries, National Center for Atmospheric Research Technical Notes 63-1:12-13, 75-76.

A radiocarbon date on prehistoric beans from Williams Island, Hamilton County, Tennessee. Tennessee Archaeologist 19:43-46.

Review of R. J. Braidwood and G. R. Willey, eds. Courses toward urban life. Archaeology 16:216-17.

University of Michigan radiocarbon dates VII (with H. R. Crane). Radiocarbon 5:228-53.

## 1964

The ceramic complexes at Iyatayet (with R. H. Wilmeth). Item *in:* The archaeology of Cape Denbigh, by J. L. Giddings. Brown University Press, pp. 271-303.

The short-nosed god from the Emmons site, Illinois. American Antiquity 26:560-563.

The Northeast Woodlands area. Item *in:* Prehistoric man in the New World, edited by J. D. Jennings and Edward Norbeck. Chicago: Univ. of Chicago Press, pp. 223-58.

Post-glacial ecology and culture changes in the Great Lakes area of North America. Report of the Sixth International Congress on Quaternary, Vol. IV, Archaeological and Anthropological Section, Lódź, Poland, pp. 291-99.

Review of Charles Green. Sutton Hoo: The excavation of a royal ship burial. American Anthropologist 66:1443-44.

Review of H. C. Shetrone. The mound builders. Ethnohistory 11:289-91.

Review of J. D. Jennings and E. Norbeck, (eds.). Prehistoric man in the New World. Michigan Archaeologist 10:66.

Review of W. C. McKern. The Clam River focus. The Wisconsin Archaeologist 45:104-11.

University of Michigan radiocarbon dates IX (with H. R. Crane). Radiocarbon 6:1-36.

## 1965

Ceramic complexity and cultural development—the eastern United States as a case study. Item *in:* Ceramics and man, edited by F. R. Matson. Viking Fund Publications in Anthropology 41:104-13.

Hopewell and the dark black glass. Michigan Archaeologist 11 (3-4):115-155.

Late Quaternary prehistory in the Northeastern Woodlands. Item *in:* The quaternary of the United States, edited by H. E. Wright, Jr., and David G. Frey. Princeton: Princeton University Press, pp. 655-69.

The Museum of Anthropology in research and scholarship: A survey. Research News 16, (1-2): 39-40. Office of Research Administration, Ann Arbor: University of Michigan.

Prehistoric pottery from southeastern Alberta. Item *in:* An introduction to the archaeology of Alberta, Canada, by H. M. Wormington and Richard G. Forbis. Proceedings No. 11, Denver Museum of Natural History, pp. 209-48.

Review of Frank Hole and Robert F. Heizer. An introduction to prehistoric archaeology. Science 150:874-75.
Review of J. Hawkes, (ed.). The world of the past. American Antiquity 30:356.
Review of Joseph R. Caldwell and Robert L. Hall, (eds.). Hopewellian studies. American Anthropologist 67:1061-63; also in Ohio History 74:136-37.
Review of M. McKusick. Men of ancient Iowa: As revealed by archaeological discoveries. The Wisconsin Archaeologist 46:157-65.
University of Michigan radiocarbon dates X (with H. R. Crane). Radiocarbon 7:123-52.

1966

The Fort Ancient Aspect, University of Michigan Museum of Anthropology, Anthropological Papers No. 28 (Reissue of 1943 edition).
The Calumet ancient pit. The Michigan Archaeologist 12:130-33.
A Non-Neolithic copper industry in North America. 36th Congreso Internacional de Americanistas, Seville 1:281-85.
The origins of prehistoric North American pottery: Atti Del VI Congresso Internationale delle Scienze Prehistoriche e Protohistoriche III Communicazioni Sezioni 5-8:266-71. Union Internationale des Sciences Prehistoriques et Protohistoriques. Rome: DeLuca Editore.
Radiocarbon dating and the cultural sequence in the eastern United States. Proceedings of the Sixth International Conference, Radiocarbon and Tritium Dating, National Bureau of Standards, Springfield, Va. pp. 117-30.
Review of Creighton Gable (ed.) Man before history. American Antiquity 31:763.
Review of William A. Ritchie. The archaeology of New York State. The American Midland Naturalist 75:251-52.
University of Michigan radiocarbon dates XI (with H. R. Crane). Radiocarbon 8:256-85.

1967

Climatic change in American prehistory. Item *in:* The Encyclopedia of Atmospheric Sciences and Astrogeology. Encyclopedia of Early Sciences Series, II, edited by Rhodes W. Fairbridge. New York: Reinhold Publishing Corp., pp. 169-71.
A copper point from Presque Isle County, Michigan (with Norman Grigg). The Michigan Archaeologist 13:135-37.

Eastern North American archaeology: A summary. Science 156:175-91.
Mesoamerica and the eastern United States in prehistoric times. Item *in:* Handbook of Middle American Indians, Vol. 4, Archaeological Frontiers and External Connections. Austin: Univ. of Texas Press, pp. 111-31.

1968

Neutron activation analyses of obsidian: An example of its relevance to northwestern plains archaeology (with George C. Frison, Gary A. Wright, and Adon A. Gordus). Plains Anthropologist, Journal of the Plains Conference 13:209-17.
Observation on Illinois prehistory in late Pleistocene and early recent times. The Quaternary of Illinois. University of Illinois College of Agriculture Special Publication No. 14. Urbana: Illinois, pp. 123-137.
Obsidian sources characterized by neutron activation analysis (with A. A. Gordus and G. A. Wright). Science 161:382-84.
The origin and dispersion of American Indians in North America. "Biomedical challenges presented by the American Indian." Scientific Pub. No. 165. Pan American Health Organization, Washington, D.C., pp. 1-10.
Review of Glenn A. Black, Gayle Thornbrough and James H. Kellar. Angel site: An archaeological, historical and ethnological study. Indianapolis Indiana Historical Society. American Anthropologist 70:1021-22.
University of Michigan radiocarbon dates XII (with H. R. Crane). Radiocarbon 10:61-114.

1969

Archaeology: New World. Item *in:* Science year. The World Book science annual. Chicago: Field Enterprises, Ed. Corp., pp. 256-57.
Identification of the sources of Hopewellian obsidian in the Middle West (with A. A. Gordus and G. A. Wright). American Antiquity 34:1-14.
Obsidian samples from archaeological sites in northwestern Alaska: A preliminary report (with Gary A. Wright and A. A. Gordus). Arctic 22:152-55.
Preliminary report on obsidian samples from Veratic Rockshelter, Idaho (with Gary A. Wright and A. A. Gordus). Tebiwa, The Journal of the Idaho State University Museum 12:27-30.
Richard G. Morgan, 1903-1968. American Antiquity 34:467-70.

## 1970

Archaeology: New World. Item *in:* Science year. The World Book science annual. Chicago: Field Enterprises Ed. Corp., pp. 259-60.

The burial complexes of the Knight and Norton Mounds in Illinois and Michigan (with Richard E. Flanders and Paul F. Titterington). University of Michigan, Museum of Anthropology, Memoirs 2.

Foreward to Hiwasse Island: An archaeological account of four Tennessee Indian peoples, by Thomas M. N. Lewis and Madeline Kneberg. Knoxville: Univ. of Tennessee Press, pp. v-vii.

Northeast Asian and northwestern American ceramics. Proceedings of Eighth International Congress of Anthropological and Ethnological Sciences III:327-30. Tokyo and Kyoto, Science Council of Japan.

A preliminary study of the source of Hopewellian obsidian in the United States (with A. A. Gordus). Actes du $VIII^e$ Congre International des Sciences Prehistoriques et Protohistoriques. Academie-Institut d'Archaeologie de l'Academie Tchecoslovaque des Sciences a 'Prague, pp. 57-63.

## 1971

Activation analysis identification of the geologic origins of prehistoric obsidian artifacts (with Adon A. Gordus and Gary A. Wright). Item *in:* Science and archaeology, edited by Robert H. Brill. Cambridge: MIT Press, pp. 222-34.

Archaeology: New World. Item *in:* Science year. The World Book science annual. Chicago: Field Enterprises Ed. Corp., pp. 261-62.

A commentary on an unusual research program in American anthropology. Dedication Program, Glenn A. Black Laboratory of Archaeology. Bloomington: Indiana Univ. Publications, pp. 9-26.

Review of archaeological investigations in the Grand Rapids, Manitoba Reservoir 1961-62, by William J. Mayer-Oakes. Arctic 24:309-310.

Review of Ohio's prehistoric peoples, by Martha A. Potter. American Anthropologist 73:419.

The study of early cultures. Item *in:* Man, culture, and society, (rev. ed.), edited by Harry L. Shapiro. Oxford: Oxford University Press, pp. 22-46.

## 1972

Archaeology: New World Item *in:* Science year. The World Book science annual. Chicago: Field Enterprises Ed. Corp., pp. 262-64.

An Old Copper point from Chippewa County, Michigan. The Michigan Archaeologist 18:30-36.
Review of the first American: A story of North American archaeology, by C. W. Ceram, trans. by Richard and Clara Winston. Indiana Magazine of History 68:96-97.
University of Michigan radiocarbon dates XIV (with H. Richard Crane), Radiocarbon 14:155-94.
University of Michigan radiocarbon dates XV (with H. Richard Crane), Radiocarbon 14:195-22.

1973

Archaeology: New World. Item *in:* Science year. The World Book science annual, 1974. Chicago: Field Enterprises Ed. Corp., pp. 251-53.
Introduction. Item *in:* Ancient monuments of the Mississippi Valley comprising the results of extensive original surveys and explorations, by E. G. Squier and E. H. Davis. New York: AMS Press, Inc., for Peabody Museum of Archaeology and Ethnology, Harvard University, Cambridge, Massachusetts, pp. vii-ix.
Review of archaeological survey in the Lower Yazoo Basin, Mississippi, 1949-1955. Philip Phillips. American Antiquity 38:374-80.

1974

Archaeology: New World. Item *in:* Science year. The World Book science annual. Chicago: Field Enterprises Ed. Corp., pp. 244-45.
The ceramic affiliations of the Ohio Valley Adena culture. Item *in:* The Adena People (new ed.), by W. S. Webb and C. E. Snow. Knoxville: Univ. of Tennessee Press, pp. 220-46.
Emerson F. Greenman, 1895-1973. American Antiquity 39:271-73.
Foreword. Item *in:* The Adena People (new ed.) by W. S. Webb and C. E. Snow. Knoxville: Univ. of Tennessee Press, pp. v-xix.

1975

Archaeology: New World. Item *in:* Science year. The World book science annual, 1976. Chicago: Field Enterprises Ed. Corp., pp. 233-35.
Notes on the early history of anthropology at The University of Michigan. Michigan Discussions in Anthropology 1:133-37.

Review of B. K. Swartz, Jr. (ed.). Adena: The seeking of an identity. American Antiquity 40:377-78.

Review of Elden Johnson (ed.) Aspects of Upper Great Lakes anthropology: Papers in Honor of Lloyd A. Wilford. Minnesota History 44:192-93.

Review of Donald W. Lathrap and Jody Douglas (eds.). Variation in anthropology: essays in honor of John C. McGregor. American Anthropologist 77:142-43.

1976

The ancient midwest—twelve thousand years. Art of the first Americans. Cincinnati: Cincinnati Art Museum, pp. 23-39.

Carl Eugen Guthe 1893-1974. American Antiquity 41:168-73. Bibliography compiled by V. H. Jones, pp. 173-77.

A commentary on some archaeological activities in the mid-continent 1925-1975. Mid-Continental Journal of Archaeology, 1:5-38.

Some suggested alterations of certain portions of "An archaeological perspective." American Antiquity 41:114-19.

An appreciation of Ben Rouse. Item *in:* Essays for Benjamin Irving Rouse, edited by R. D. Dunnell and E. S. Hall. (In press.)

Archaeology: New World. Item *in:* Science year. The World Book science annual. Chicago: Field Enterprises Ed. Corp. (In press.)

A chronological alignment of prehistoric eastern United States culture complexes. Item *in:* Chronologies in New World archaeology, edited by R. E. Taylor and C. W. Meighan. (In press.)

A commentary on certain opinions about Mississippian cultural complexes. Item *in:* Studies of the development of Mississippian culture, edited by S. Williams. Santa Fe: New Mexico. (In press.)

A commentary on early man studies in the northeast. Item *in:* Amerinds and their paleoenvironments in northeastern North America. New York Academy of Sciences. (In press.)

Late prehistory of the Ohio Valley. Item *in:* Handbook of North American Indians, Vol. XII. The Northeast Woodland Area. W. C. Sturtevant and B. G. Trigger (eds.). Smithsonian Institution. (In press.)

The Middle West and Northeast. Item *in:* Ancient Native Americans, edited by J. D. Jennings. (In press.)

Some early men I have known. Journal of Alabama Archaeology. (In press.)

(Compiled to August 1976)